Advance Praise for
The Story About the Story

"Czeslaw Milosz cooly dismisses Robert Frost, and Cynthia Ozick crushes Truman Capote, but mainly there is the deep appreciation of one writer for another, often an equal, sometimes thrilling in perception and prose. Poets on other poets they admire, D. H. Lawrence describing that singular masterpiece *Moby Dick*. You may never have heard, even remotely, of an effete English writer named Ronald Firbank, but when you read about Evelyn Waugh's brief 1929 essay on him, you'll want—curious about his influence—to immediately pick up Waugh's *Vile Bodies*, not when it arrives in a few days from Amazon or when you can get to the library, but this minute, now!

That's the problem with this book: too many irresistible things."

—JAMES SALTER, author of *A Sport and a Pastime*

"Fiction, yes. Film, yes. But when have you ever been sorry for a book of essays to end? I was with this book. Each of these essays investigates good writing by writing well about it. They are all formally elegant and smart, smart, smart. And a delight to read."

—MARY JO BANG, author of *Elegy: Poems*

The Story

About the Story
Great Writers Explore Great Literature

Edited by J. C. Hallman

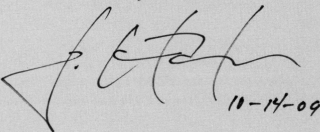

11-14-09

Tin House Books

Published by Tin House Books, Portland, Oregon, and
New York, New York

Distributed to the trade by Publishers Group West, 1700 Fourth St., Berkeley, CA 94710, www.pgw.com

Library of Congress Cataloging-in-Publication Data

The story about the story : great writers explore great literature / edited by J. C. Hallman. -- 1st U.S. ed.

    p. cm.

ISBN 978-0-9802436-9-7

1. Literature--History and criticism. 2. Authors--Books and reading. I. Hallman, J. C.

PN45.S857 2009
809--dc22

                         2009015717

First U.S. edition 2009
Interior design by Janet Parker
Printed in Canada
www.tinhouse.com

Table of Contents

Introduction

Toward a Fusion

by J. C. Hallman

THESE DAYS, THE DEBATE OVER HOW TO WRITE ABOUT READING IS A COLD affair: a de-militarized zone. I avoid the terms *literature* and *criticism* here, and perhaps even *debate* is too hifalutin a word to describe what has amounted to a decades-long pissing match between creative writers and critics. The current steely silence is evidence only of empty bladders; the combatants have become preoccupied with internal skirmishes.

Not long ago, Cynthia Ozick, weighing in on a writers' spat between Jonathan Franzen and Ben Marcus in *Harper's*, announced that there was no good literary criticism happening despite the ongoing deluge from academic presses. Franzen and Marcus, arguing over how far fiction should bend toward publishing's fickle sun, weren't good models, either, Ozick said, and her proclamation was as much plea as elegy.

Yet Ozick herself (*Art & Ardor*, *Fame & Folly*, etc.) is a pioneer of a wholly different kind of writing about reading, work that reads the self as closely as it reads the examined text and that is every bit as creative as it is critical. Writers are often *reviewers*—John Updike produced a smooth-flowing river of work, and Joyce Carol Oates's hurried affairs appear often enough—but there is as well a kind of personal literary analysis, criticism that contemplates rather than argues, and while it's never amounted to a formal trend or school, a consistent trickle of this kind of response to literature has flowed like an underground stream all the while the piss battles poisoned the surface.

My assertion is this: a writer's model for how to write about reading is now in ascension, and it's largely the upshot of a debate conducted on the other side of the aisle.

I'm not a scholar and I don't claim to be able to cite all the battles in the history of literary criticism, but there have been a few important moments. In 1910, the critic J. E. Springarn fired off "The New Criticism," an essay that used an offhand remark from Goethe to argue that criticism should limit its concerns to what a writer has attempted to express and how he has attempted to express it. T. S. Eliot lashed out at Spingarn, claiming that his treatment of dogmatic criticism was dogma itself and that "new criticism" was a misnomer precisely because it followed in the footsteps of all those Spingarn had cited: Benedetto Croce, Carlyle, Arnold, and Goethe. H. L. Mencken weighed in as well with "Criticism of Criticism of Criticism," in which he agreed with Spingarn and dubbed him "Major Springarn," true to the martial character of the debate.

It wasn't until decades later that people began to bat around the term "reader response" to describe what Spingarn ultimately called "creative criticism." But this flew far beneath the radar of theory-based criticism, which ruled the day until criticism sank into a period of soul-searching. Susan Sontag's clarion call "Against Interpretation" (1963) had asked what criticism would look like if it set out to "serve the work of art, not usurp its place," and almost twenty years later Steven Knapp and Walter Benn Michaels offered the blunt-force trauma "Against Theory" (1982), in which they questioned assumptions about meaning and text that had come about in the post–World War II years and eventually suggested that the "theoretical enterprise should therefore come to an end." A year later, Terry Eagleton attempted to rechampion theory in *Literary Theory* (1983), but recanted in *After Theory* (2004). James Wood's *The Broken Estate* (1999) honed in on what was wrong. He noted the tendency of critics to regard themselves as sleuths and texts as criminals: "Having been caught out, the poem is triumphantly led off in golden chains; the detective writes up his report in hideous prose, making sure to flatter himself a bit, and then goes home to a well-deserved drink."

But Wood had even more to say. In 2005, in an essay in *n+1*, he gave voice to what writers had understood all along: the no-man's-land between creative writing and criticism is fertile ground:

> Writers also properly remind us that a great deal of criticism is not in fact especially analytical but a kind of persuasive redescription. Sometimes to hear a poet or a fine critic read a poem aloud is to have been party to a critical act; there is a good reason after all, why writers have always been very interested in actors and acting—there is a sense in which the actor is the purest, the first critic. The written equivalent of the reading of a poem or a play aloud is the retelling of the literature one is talking about; the good critic has an awareness that criticism means, in part, telling a good story about the story you are criticizing.
>
> How to achieve that retelling? There is a kind of writing through books rather than about them that we recognize in the greatest writer-critics. This writing-through is often achieved by using the language of metaphor and simile that art itself uses.

The essays collected here are evidence of the power of the writing-through that Wood describes. Out of the carnage of the critics' battle a new fusion has emerged. Or reemerged. Whichever. Currently, there are a few consistent venues for innovative essays about literature. *Tin House*'s regular Lost and Found feature attempts to rescue out-of-print books from the critical dustbin; the *New Republic* and *Harper's* offer space to criticism that celebrates subjectivity instead of repressing it; and the minuteman armies of literary magazines and online lit bloggers have more and more become a venue for inventive critical work. There are innovators among critics, as well. Fred Setterberg's blend of travel writing and criticism, *The Roads Taken*, won the AWP award for creative nonfiction in 1993, and Sven Birkerts has long been something of a critic dropped behind enemy lines—he hides in the jungle, makes his own crossbows, survives on wild boar, and has established his own private utopia where the close read and the personal essay live together in bliss.

Indeed, it's probably someone like Birkerts or Wood who ought to be introducing an anthology like this one. Which is not to say that I come to the project empty-handed. My own relationship with criticism began a long time ago with a study of Henry James's *The Turn of the Screw*, the history of which, I think, captures many of the salient points of the critic-writer debate.

The Turn of the Screw caught my attention because even as a naïve young reader I sensed that something was not right with the simple read of the governess-narrator as a repressed spinster—the poster child of hysteria dangled carrotlike before the horse of psychoanalytic criticism. There was more there, I knew it. I began my research and discovered that *The Turn of the Screw*, pound for pound, might just be the most discussed text in the English language. (This is evidenced by Robin P. Hoople's *Distinguished Discord*, a treatment not of the book, but of its "critical tradition"—it's a two-hundred-fifty-page *catalog* of papers about what James thought to be a short story.) I eventually came to the conclusion that one hundred years of "tradition" had completely missed what James was writing about.

The debate over *The Turn of the Screw* is echoed in the essays included in this volume. James *loathed* critics. He claimed that critics heaped meanings onto his work to wriggle themselves out of their own "queer predicaments" (Geoff Dyer's rant against criticism in the excerpt from *Out of Sheer Rage* printed here owes its fervor to James), and he called the prefaces to the New York Edition of his novels a "plea for criticism on other than infantile lines" (a sentiment Vladamir Nabokov repeats in his treatment of Franz Kafka in "The Metamorphosis"; Nabokov *loathed* Freud). James's complaint in "The Art of Fiction" that critics of literature have "little interest for [its] producer" anticipates later debates over meaning and authorial intent (interest in the "producer" is precisely what compels Birkerts's extremely close read in "On a Stanza by John Keats"), and the tendency of James scholars to ignore his own comments on *The Turn of the Screw* stirs up questions of authorship and the extratextual (Salman Rushdie's tongue-in-cheek look at *The*

Wizard of Oz, "Out of Kansas," explores what he calls "the bugbear of modern criticism: the authorless text"). And so on and so forth, until I too came to the conclusion that maybe the whole business of criticism ought to be chucked.

Or maybe not.

Early in 2004, I wandered into the offices of the Critical Writing Program at the University of Pennsylvania, looking for adjunct work. I had one published book and was working on another, but I was living month to month. I was lucky that the head of the program, Val Ross, had once been an editor at *Esquire.* She wasn't a knee-jerk academic. I was woefully unprepared for the meeting. I had hoped they might have some entry-level composition classes I could teach. They didn't. It was a program designed to get students writing about whatever they actually cared about—imagine!—and as soon as I plopped into the leather seat across from Val's desk, she prompted me to devise an entire course on the fly.

I didn't have enough time to think of a lie.

I mumbled something about having once written a personal essay on *The Turn of the Screw*—maybe something designed around a kind of "creative criticism" was possible? At that point, I'd never even heard of J. E. Spingarn.

"Sounds like a class!" Val said.

So I set out on a quest for creative criticism. I canvassed writers, readers, bookstore owners. Many had a favorite piece—some essay that had helped cement the idea of literature for them. I spent hours in libraries paging through the collected essays of notable authors: often there was one unique piece in which a writer approached literature from some kind of personal angle (Charles D'Ambrosio's look at J. D. Salinger through the lens of his own suicide-afflicted family in "Salinger and Sobs") or, as with my work on James, attempted to resuscitate a text critics had left on the autopsy table (Wallace Stegner's retelling of a John Steinbeck short story in "On Steinbeck's Story 'Flight'"). There were older book-length treatments (most prominent among them D. H. Lawrence's unclassifiable *Studies in Classic American Literature*) and newer book-length treatments (Alain De Botton's equally difficult to categorize *How Proust Can Change Your Life*). Almost invariably, the work touched on subjects that would have been verboten in a critical context: Walter Kirn stabbed a stern finger at his high school English teacher's rotten take on Salinger ("Good-bye, Holden Caulfield. I Mean It. Go! Good-bye!"); E. B. White, despite *The Elements of Style*, acknowledged that in Thoreau the "quality of the ramble" is more important than grammar ("A Slight Sound at Evening"); and Seamus Heaney admitted that, for him, the sound of Eliot is more important than the content ("Learning from Eliot"). Writers, I noticed, often stressed the tactile sensation of books. They rejected the "literary pilgrimage" (some even as they executed one), and they were perfectly comfortable saying that they simply liked a book—or disliked it. While critics tend to use literature to expose writers' biographies, writers use biography to shed additional light onto the work. They are also comfortable with inconvenient realities, like the fact that we forget stories, or that a book *means* something different if you read it at eighteen and again at fifty. Writers set out to celebrate the work rather than exhaust it, and all the essays I found, in keeping with Wood, amounted to a story about a story. It was impossible to identify a common thread among them, but it was clear that they were all part of a movement—not a movement based on some critic's theory, but one that emerged organically out of a common love and creative insight.

I see no way to examine the essays in *The Story About the Story*— kin on a broad spectrum—and find in them anything like a common denominator. You cannot tell me that Lawrence's stream-of-consciousness ("Herman Melville's *Moby Dick*") has any direct connection with Robert Hass's far more sober consideration ("Lowell's Graveyard"). But you would be even harder pressed to link either to the dry, tenure-desperate prose of critics, who already have far too much say over how literature is perceived in the world. A better criticism has come around. And if this temporal splatter of essays does indeed indicate the emergence of a trend, then Spingarn's advice "to have sensations in the presence of a work of art and express them" was a prophetic art in and of itself.

Salinger and Sobs

CHARLES D'AMBROSIO

In the days immediately after my brother killed himself I'd go into the backyard and lie on our picnic table and watch the November wind bend the branches of a tall fir tree across the street. Really hard gusts would shake loose a raucous band of black crows and send them wheeling into the sky. They'd caw and cackle and circle and resettle and rise again, crowing, I guess, a noisy mocking counterpart to the flock of strangers in funerary black who'd shown up to bury my brother. About a week after Danny'd put a gun to his head and pulled the trigger and a couple days after his lame orthodox funeral at our childhood church, I went for a walk along a street of patched potholes that runs around Lake Union (near where, a year or so into the future, a future I was sure had ended tragically the night Danny shot himself, my other brother Mike would pull a similar stunt, jumping off the Aurora Bridge and living to tell about it, thus revealing to me the comic, the vaudevillian underside of suicide), and saw a scavenging crow jabbing its beak into the breast of an injured robin. The robin had probably first been hit by a car. It was flipped on its back and badly maimed, but it wasn't carrion quite yet. One wing was pinned to its breast and the other flapped furiously in a useless struggle for flight and thus the bird, still fiercely instinctive, only managed to spin around in circles like the arrow you flick with your finger in a game of chance. The robin was fully alive, but it was caught in a futile hope, and I knew this, and the crow knew this, and while the crow taunted the bird, hopping down from its perch on a nearby fence, pecking at the robin, returning to his roost, waiting, dropping down and attacking again, I stood off to the side of the road and watched.

I'll tell you the ultimate outcome of this lopsided contest a little later, but for now I bring it up only because, some years ahead, fully inhabiting my aborted future, I often ask myself a koanlike question re. my brother that goes something like this: if I could intervene and change my own particular history would I alter past events in such a way that I'd bring Danny back to life? Would I return the single rimfire bullet to its quiet chamber in the gun and let the night of November 26, 19__, pass away in sleep and dreams or drink or television or whatever the anonymous bulk of history holds for most people? Would I uncurl the fingers from the grip, would I take away the pain, would I unwrite the note and slip the blank sheet back in the ream and return the ream to pulp and etc., would I exchange my own monstrous father for some kindly sap out of the sitcom tradition, would I do any of this, would I? And where would I be? Would I be there, in the room? Would my role be heroic? And where exactly would I begin digging into the past, making corrections, amending it? How far back do I have to go to undo the whole dark kit and caboodle? I mean from where I sit now I can imagine a vast sordid history finally reaching its penultimate unraveled state in the Garden, under the shade of the tree of knowledge, begging the question of whether or not I'd halt the innocent hand, leaving the apple alone, unbitten.

I'm a little wary of prelapsarian schemes in much the same way I'm leery of conspiracy theories, both of which only seem to describe the limitations, like Hamlet's nutshell, of the holder's mind. You don't really want to crash down the whole universe just to satisfy your situational unease or your incapacity to see the whole picture, do you? You don't want a life based on your failure to understand life, right? If I were able to undo Danny's death would that mean, too, that Mike's suicide attempt would never occur, or would it simply mean that he'd find an alternate, more surefire lethality than leaping over the rail of Seattle's most famous suicide spot, a spot that's worked just hunky-dory for hundreds of others? Or would my remaining brother drown or die of internal injuries instead of, as it turned out, smacking the water, breaking his pelvis, destroying his bladder, dislocating his shoulder and yet, that screwed up (plus I forgot to mention his chronic schizophrenia), still having the presence of mind to kick off his boots, swim for shore, pull a quarter out of his pants, and call an ambulance for himself, easy as a man catching a cab? Would that little miracle not happen in this revamped history of mine? Would I just be trading one brother for another? Would I even be writing this, or would a lovely silence reign over my uneventful life, leaving me free to consider other, happier fortunes?

I'd never read J. D. Salinger or John Knowles, both staples of the high-school curriculum, because somehow out of the always ripening ambient culture I'd picked up a whiff of the East Coast, of the uppercrust and hoity-toity and, ipso facto, at least for me, a kind of irrelevance, irrelevance tinged with a defensive countersnobbery that's so characteristic of the West. I couldn't identify with the prep-school scene. I thought it was socially atavistic, some stupid idea invented in England. So instead of the boarding-school experiences of Salinger or Knowles I read Joyce's *Portrait of the Artist as a Young Man* strictly for its creepy Jesuit milieu and the way Stephen Dedalus used difference and snobbery to escape. The reading of *Portrait* was itself a Dedalean act of snobbery on my part, a pose I hoped would piss off the jocks at my Jesuit boys' school. Why? Because I *was* a jock, but had recently quit all sports in order to take up managing my misery full-time. At that age, at sixteen, seventeen, I read fiction because I needed advice on how to live, and I needed it to be totally free of judgment. I wanted to see how other people did life. I had exiled myself from the kind of order found on the athletic field, and the alternatives that presented themselves most obviously at my school were to become a dope fiend or a scholar. I tried both and bookishness stuck. By reading I hoped to get as far as I could from Catholic homiletics, and quickly discovered that the best place for moral-free advice was really good fiction. Immediately I saw that stories looked squarely and bravely at lives without criticizing or condemning them. Admittedly, wanting practical advice is a pretty primitive idea of what a book should do, but that's the sort of literary sense I had, treating novels and stories like the self-help manuals that cycle through the decades, reinventing relevance. I didn't know any better, and probably still don't. Anyway, I came late to *The Catcher in the Rye*, as an adult, and thought I'd be somewhat cold to its charms.

I wasn't. Right from the beginning my reading of Salinger's work was lopsided, eccentric, obsessed with the reclusive writer's legendary silence and the theme of suicide that seems to stitch a quilt out of the extant work. As is always, perhaps inevitably, the case, the unbalanced weight my own life brought to the material gave the work this off-center, wobbly orbit, and even now I can't seem to read the stuff any differently. It's all about Suicide and Silence. Suicide is first mentioned when Holden, standing on a hill above the football field, says the game with Saxon Hall "was the last game of the year, and you were supposed to commit suicide or something if old Pencey didn't win." Other direct mentions of suicide or thinly veiled threats run through the story. The very word has a casual suggestive presence in Holden's vocabulary. He volunteers to ride on top of the next atomic bomb. And then there's the story he tells of James Castle, the boy who leaps from the window, killing himself, while wearing a black turtleneck he'd borrowed from Holden. It's now generally a given in the literature of suicidology that every attempt is ambivalent, that some degree of chance is worked into each plan, a savior chosen, an opportunity for rescue extended, a tortured hope hidden near the heart of the suicide's rapidly constricting universe. For instance, suicides tend to move *toward* society—and possible intervention—the closer they come to making and carrying out concrete plans. And of course *The Catcher in the Rye* takes its title from precisely this sort of ambivalence, and the story itself, in some ways an extended riff on saving and being saved, is otherwise full of specific strategies for rescue—with Holden nervously alternating point of view, vacillating between rescuer and rescued.

The passage below gives the book its name and is obviously as much about Holden's hope for himself as it is about the fantasy of saving others:

> I keep picturing all these little kids playing some game in this big field of rye and all. Thousands of little kids, and nobody's around—nobody big, I mean—except me. And I'm standing on the edge of some crazy cliff. What I have to do, I have to catch everybody if they start to go over the cliff—I mean if they're running and they don't look where they're going I have to come out from somewhere and catch them. That's all I'd do all day. I'd just be the catcher in the rye . . .

I generally don't read biographical gossip about writers, and don't know a thing, not one scrap, about Salinger's life (other than the silence), but the theme of suicide feels authentic to me, and so does his recurrent big family thing, two elements I share with—who? Salinger, or his various narrators, or both? I don't know. Like the Glasses (let's say), we too had seven kids, and one thing that seems to happen in large families more often than in small is that nicknames flourish, partly because there's always some little kid around who can't pronounce the real names of his older siblings. Little kids forming their first syllables corrupt those names, and the corruptions stick because they're cute or funny or whatever. Salinger's Glass family seems to be all nicknames except for Seymour. As the oldest child, I too was somewhat exempt— more namer than named—but a good example of the process from our family would be my sister Patricia, who quickly migrated from Tricia to Trish and then skipped sideways to Didya before finally arriving at Did. And Did's sisters were Mugs, Gith, and Bean, and Did called my brother Danny Mr. Sobs, or plain Sobs, because when they played house he was always the baby. These goofed-up, singsong names recall Franny, Zooey, Boo Boo, etc. And too, in large families, children form their own fairly populous society, separate from the parents, and the nicknames become a kind of argot, a secret language, whereas in small families, I imagine, there's more of an emphasis on vertical and direct contact with the adults. Anyway, Salinger's use of nicknames, the proliferation of them, and the fact that the oldest, Seymour, doesn't have one, has always been for me an important detail in understanding the work.

In Salinger's work, there is an ongoing failure of the various narrators that occupy center stage, a failure to find a separate and distinct identity outside the corporate idea of family. Holden is a little bit D.B. and Allie and Phoebe, and Buddy is Seymour and Zooey, etc., etc. People from big families tend to have this intense group identity. I don't know why, even though, for instance, I fall easily into the first-person plural when asked about my past. My gut instinct, looking back, is to use "we." Is it size alone that accounts for the blurring of identity in a big family? The fact that you grow up crowded into the same bathroom, brushing your teeth in front of a mirror that has three or four other foamy white grins reflecting back at you, is that it? Or the way you end up wearing some other kid's clothes, or finding a favorite outfit, years after you last wore it, in your brother's drawer, as if he were just another, later edition of you—is that it? Possibly. Privacy, too, is a problem. You rarely get time alone. And with so many competing parties, a constantly negotiated peace accord is necessary if you hope to get along; and for the simplest things, for using a car on Friday night or choosing a channel on the television, you end up working closely, and in concert, with the other kids. In our house, taking this closeness a step further, we institutional-ized the buddy system, a permanent arrangement in which every older kid was assigned a younger, and you were strictly accountable for that child's safety at crosswalks as well as his mischief in the aisles of super-markets and his happiness during the long wait to buy new play-shoes at Penny's. As the oldest, my assigned buddy was my brother Danny, the youngest and rowdiest.

For Salinger's narrators, there's never sufficient separation from the family, at least that sense of family defined horizontally by siblings. Holden really only loves D.B., his dead brother Allie, and his sister Phoebe, mistrusting everyone else. Nobody outside the circle of family seems to make any sense to him, or at least they aren't given the same ample room for oddity he grants his brothers and sisters. Other people simply aren't real to Holden, not in the solid, reassuring way family is. My point here, in discussing identity and family, isn't to draw near a psychological reading of the work. In fact, it seems to me that the decade of the fifties, which saw the first flush of a mass psychological processing of life, right away meets in Holden Caulfield its staunchest resistance. (In *Seymour—An Introduction*, Salinger writes of the psychiatric profession: "They're a peerage of tin ears. With such faulty equipment, with those ears, how can anyone possibly trace the pain, by sound and quality alone, back to its source? With such wretched hearing equipment, the best, I think, that can be detected, and perhaps verified, is a few stray, thin overtones—hardly even counterpoint—coming from a troubled childhood or a disordered libido.") There doesn't *seem* to be anything really wrong with Holden, and yet everything is messed up. The conceit of the novel is that Holden's telling the story from inside an institution, and you can imagine, you can *hear* in the loud nervous prose, that he's making a direct appeal to the reader, going over the heads of doctors and nurses and various experts who don't get it.

The subject of big families might seem fringy but it brings me to the organizing idea of authenticity. It's a central question in all the work. What is real? What is trustworthy? Holden, of course, is famously on guard against phonies, watchful for insincere people or hypocrites, anyone giving a false impression, the pretentious, impostors and perverts. In "Bananafish" the trite phone conversation—the false narrative—between the wife and her mother is brutally wrong about Seymour. It's untrue, it says nothing real or accurate about the world. And Buddy Glass, the narrator in *Seymour—An Introduction*, says, "I can usually tell whether a poet or prose writer is drawing from the first-, second-, or tenth-hand experience or is foisting off on us what he'd like to think is pure invention." It's not so much the content of this statement but the very issue of authenticity that piques my interest. The ability to detect authenticity is a critical faculty, something all of us develop, more or less. You can fail on either side, you can be gullible, easily duped, or you can be too skeptical, believing nothing. And with Holden, for example, it's quite clear that something else, a voracious doubt, is driving him to question even the simplest interactions with people. *Nothing* is authentic for Holden, and his problem is not so much a superficial sorting of the true from the false—he can't figure out how we come to know anything at all. That's the noise, the frightening disturbance in the story, and it will only stop when Holden finds the authentic thing, the real (what?), or when he's too exhausted to continue.

What can Holden rely on, what does he trust, what's real for him? Holden's response to life is like a body in shock, to withdraw into the core of identity, in his case the family, in order to keep the self functioning and alive. There's a love and warmth and security to the way Salinger writes about family, a kind of bulwarked intimacy most readers respond to, that sits in contrast to the false, unfriendly, wolfish world huffing and puffing right outside the door. What I feel reading Salinger is an emotional power that comes from the writer's ingrained *assumption* of the value and integrity of family, in particular the idea of family defined by siblings. Family is worthy of trust. The siblings in Salinger are fiercely loyal and extremely close to one another. So there's that clear separation of family from everyone else, but something in-between is missing, some understanding—for the writer, and for Holden. Holden can't negotiate the boundaries between himself and others—Antolini's touch freaks him out—and can only imagine returning to his family as a refuge. But it's my suspicion that that refuge isn't really a haven the way Holden imagines it—nor is it safe for Salinger, who seems to defang his work by taking the parents out of almost every story. You wonder, where are the adults in this world that's populated almost solely by precocious children?

This is guesswork, this is supposition: the real stress in Holden's life comes from having no safe place, with his family offering him the least security of all. This remains unstated *on purpose*. In the injunctive first paragraph of *The Catcher in the Rye*, Holden says his parents would have "about two hemorrhages apiece" if he "told anything pretty personal about them. They're quite touchy about anything like that, especially my father. They're *nice* and all—I'm not saying that—but they're also touchy as hell." It's that "touch," rather than Antolini's, that's really got Holden running. It should be obvious by now that I don't see *The Catcher in the Rye* as a coming-of-age story, especially not in the dismissive or pejorative sense; to me it's no more about the anxious life of an average teenager than *Huckleberry Finn* is. The feelings Salinger's trying to pinpoint don't really have much to do with the fluctuating moods of a representative teen; adolescence isn't the source of Holden's outsized feelings. Possibly because I came to the book as an adult, for me it's never been about the typical, but rather the exceptional; it's not meant to illustrate a phase of life we all pass through and share but instead to explore a disturbing and extreme loss of identity that leaves this one boy absolutely alone. And the depth of that loss comes from the fact that it's not directly his, but his family's. My guess is that in high school students learn that Holden doesn't go home right away because he knows he's going to be in big trouble. He's been kicked out of school again. He's failed and disappointed his parents once more, and his odyssey through New York is fueled by guilt and contrition. In my reading he doesn't go home after leaving Pencey because home is the problem. His real expulsion is from the family, not school, and his sojourn through New York renders that loss in literal terms: we see the resulting anomie, the thoroughness of his horror. Two very different engines drive the respective readings. In one, he's ultimately headed home, in the other he has nowhere to go, and never will.

Here's the assumption behind my guesswork. Suicide is a kind of death that makes you doubt what you know about the deceased or what you can ever know about anybody. It strikes clear to the core of identity, reaching down into the heart of your life. Since my brother died I haven't slept a single night alone with the lights off; I wake up afraid, and I have to know where I am, I need to see right away. And when I go out, I always leave a radio on, just so that when I come home I'll hear voices or, more precisely, I won't hear the silence and get all spooky imagining the surprises waiting for me. By a curious mechanism my brother's death has extended the vivid fears of my childhood into my adult life. I find that I'm alert in ways that adults don't need to be, and I'm ignorant of things grownups care most about. When a suicide happens within a family, that organism takes on the taint just as much as any individual. But that taint doesn't necessarily mean the dissolution of the family; it might have an opposite effect, banding the family together even tighter than before. (I felt like shameful secrets had been aired publicly, and I was first of all defensive, protective.) In reality, I think both things happen: you're pulled together, and that intense proximity exposes lines of cleavage that had begun cracking years earlier. The suicide is just a piece finally falling out. And from then on the family story can't be the same. Its identity must include death, a death shared in the blood. The old narrative breaks at precisely the moment you need it to speak for you. This death, this suicide, is shattering to what, at that exact moment, is your deepest need—family, security, identity.

———◆———

Rereading Buddy's statement about his ability to detect authenticity, I find a harmonic floating just above the fundamental tone, and I think it can be heard distinctly in isolation here:

> For the terrible and undiscountable fact has just reached me, between paragraphs, that I yearn to talk, to be queried, to be interrogated, about this particular dead man. *It's just got through to me, that apart from my many other—and, I hope to God, less ignoble—motives, I'm stuck with the usual survivor's conceit that he's the only soul alive who knew the deceased intimately.* [my italics]

This is the overtone you hear in Salinger's work, the knowingness, the high proud insistent certainty; and what accounts for the sound— the instrument, so to speak—is the faculty of mind that's meant to sift through supposed facts and separate the truth from what's false; and the tone is this, the *belief* that he alone holds the key, the final authentic word on the deceased (or any other matter). The emphasis here is on the belief, not the particular key, whatever it may be. (And I want to make clear that for me this is a musical sound as much as a matter of content. It's what makes *Raise High the Roof Beam, Carpenters* nearly unreadable for me—too much snotty all-knowing prep-school smugness in the prose, a vague assumption of values, a social vulgarity found in the rich and privileged that's just as revolting, and similar to, the arrogant know-nothingism of the various middle classes, upper to lower. Open the story to almost any page and you can hear the sound in the overpunctuated prose. It's as if the pissy aggrieved prose itself were defending Seymour. You can even hear a trace of the problem in the quote above, in the word "undiscountable"—the leftover locution of a kid putting on adult airs, afraid that someone will realize he doesn't know what he's talking about.) And so, if there really is a single truth, and you alone possess it, there is also, by definition, a lot of falseness out there—the bulk of life, in fact. And this construction, this arrangement or priority, pitting the defense of your holy truth against the entire world's falseness, is suicide refused, refused at least temporarily.

And it's silence refused, too.

Here's what I mean. A longstanding and widely accepted formulation is that suicide is redirected homicide. Edwin Shneidman, the father of the modern study of suicide, coined the phrase: "Suicide is murder in the 180th degree." There are variations on this, of course. Suicide's not always—probably never—an act of pure hostility. There's a fairly old article by Ives Hendrick of the Harvard Medical School that argues the case for suicide as a form of identification with the lost love object, a fantasy of reunion rather than murder, and while this thinking doesn't occupy a place in the fat mainstream of suicidology, it is accepted, a tributary that helps explain some cases. I'm throwing these ideas out scattershot, hoping to indicate a central theme within the wide range of psychodynamic meanings attributed to suicide: that it's always accompanied by some shift away from life's normal priority, where it's perfectly natural and expected that you'd defend yourself from danger, to a condition where you give up, defenseless, or even join in on the attack. In Freud's still-fascinating "Mourning and Melancholia," he begins by openly admitting to being flummoxed by suicide and the self's attack on itself. He says the ego is usually fierce and robust in the protection of itself, rallying the troops when under siege, so how or why does ego-functioning break down and become defenseless in the suicide? In short, the self can only hate the self to the point of suicide when a lost internalized object—an object, moreover, of love—turns against the self. In other words, it's your inner daddy—protected by your love of him—messing with your defenseless inner child—or whatever, some variation of that. Later (1933), Karl Menninger develops his triadic theory of suicide—the wish to die, the wish to kill, the wish to be killed—to which, years afterward, he speculated on the need to add a fourth condition, the wish to be loved—and he talks about a mechanism by which the suicide's "hostile component, since it would otherwise have to be directed against the whole world, is turned inward upon the self." I'm really oversimplifying here, reducing complex theories into these candied bits, and I'm skipping the work of so many, of Maltsberger, Hendin, Leenars, Jamison, etc., but I'm trying to get at something, this general tendency in suicide, that will bring us back to Salinger.

In suicide, then, a couple of the main poles of life flip, and the desire to talk or communicate turns into a longing for a colossal silence (most suicides don't write a note), and the fierce defense of the self becomes an equally fierce and final defeat. It's like the mind, exhausted by the enormous work of defending itself, turns around out of some need for efficiency or economy, and begins hating itself, doubting or attacking its reality. Being suicidal *is* really tiring. A lot of suicides are so lethargic and lacking in affect they aren't able to kill themselves until their mood improves—spring, for that reason, has the highest rate of what people in the business call "completed" suicides. The ego first tries to protect itself and then can't, in part because to do so would be to attack a forbidden love object. (Buddy Glass says he can't *finish* writing a description of Seymour, "even a bad description, even one where my ego, my perpetual lust to share top billing with him, is all over the place"—making a sideways admission of jealousy, and also expressing resentment for the sainted brother he can no longer defeat and no longer even describe without desecration.) What's salient in *The Catcher in the Rye* is that Holden achieves a fragile truce between hating himself and hating the world. Holden Caulfield is probably identified in the minds of most readers as a boy whose anger at and suspicion of the world is fragilely offset by his inviolate love for Allie and Phoebe. As long as he keeps that love immaculate, as long as he defends and protects it and maintains its purity, he's alive, and that's what I mean by suicide refused. Holden without his holy love is a goner, and the unalloyed quality of that love is really the register of his isolation. He's cornered, and you can see the gargantuan project he's set for himself, that vast defense. In the novel he ends up in an institution which isn't really a lasting solution to his problem but instead a sort of DMZ between himself and the world.

Similarly, Buddy Glass, a writer (in two other institutions, the military and the academy—and all these institutions, these supporting structures, stand in for a neutral family), asserts his identity by claiming close inner knowledge of his dead brother, Seymour. His relation to Seymour is sacerdotal and similar to the Holden Antolini says he can imagine dying nobly for an unworthy cause. But even in the passage quoted and italicized above, in the middle of his assertion, Buddy's already begun to undermine it, calling it a "conceit," an instance of cleverness that, but for the writer's vigilance, would have hardened into a fixed posture, would have become false, phony. And I would argue that only a little farther down this line of thinking we come to the idea that all writing, fixed on the page, claiming truth, is false. It's imaginable that a writer, in the wake of a suicide, might find all coherent narratives suspect, all postures false, and, looking at life up-close under a new magnifying hypervigilance, finally come to question and mistrust the integrity of his own inventions as well. The word "conceit" cancels Buddy's claim to know Seymour, dismissing it and sending it on its way toward silence. And silence—a kind of reunion with Seymour, or a way to equal or defeat him, head to head, silence for silence—is one possible response to this powerful but confused idea of falsity. If *The Catcher in the Rye* is noisy in its search for authenticity, then the rest of Salinger's work looks for the real by stilling the very engine that drives Holden's vast doubt—words. And this silence is related to and yet something beyond the interest in Zen quietude that crops up in Salinger's later work.

<hr/>

Holden's isolation in an institution as he tells his story points to a formal problem Salinger himself seems to have resolved through withdrawal and writerly silence. At least it's tempting to see it that way. I've poked around in all the work for prodromal clues somehow indicating Salinger's plunge into silence was symptomatic of something. What is the silence about? In some people (usually willful or grandiose or highly defended types) there's only a very small difference between talking incessantly and saying nothing. I vaguely remember a quote from Roland Barthes, who claimed his rhetorical needs alternated between a little haiku that expressed everything and a great flood of banalities that said nothing. And in *Seymour—An Introduction*, Buddy Glass says of his brother, "Vocally, he was either as brief as a gatekeeper at a Trappist monastery—sometimes for days, weeks at a stretch—or he was a non-stop talker." Interestingly, *The Catcher in the Rye*, Salinger's most *voluble* book, begins and ends with specific comments concerning what will *not* be written.

Holden starts his story with a refusal:

> If you really want to hear about it, the first thing you'll probably want to know is where I was born, and what my lousy childhood was like, and how my parents were occupied and all before they had me, and all that David Copperfield kind of crap, but I don't feel like going into it, if you want to know the truth.

And he ends the novel with this hardened commandment:

> "Don't ever tell anybody anything. If you do, you start missing everybody."

The quotes above bracket the book, suggesting prohibitions of both point of view and content. Holden will not look at the life of his parents or take the tack of examining his past or childhood—this is no remembrance—and by the end of the novel his instinct, in a sense, proves him right, proves that the process of writing only creates further problems. He's not newly wise like Nick Carraway. He has no new perspective or understanding. The only thing Holden seems to learn from telling even this restricted story is that, confirming his first hunch, it would have been better to say nothing.

Silence is already there, waiting in the wings of Salinger's most clamorous and fluent book.

Is silence for a writer tantamount to suicide? In some ways it is, I believe, but the question for me is why—why does the writer choose silence? The deliberate decision to quit clawing at the keyboard is too mechanical to be an answer. Stopping isn't the real matter, but rather the result of some other prior disturbance that can't be named. Silence in this sense isn't the equivalent of suicide or death, but of secrecy. That's what it's about—what is *not* said. Taking Salinger's oeuvre as a unified field, I find a couple elements that don't square with either my experience or my avocational reading in the literature of suicide—elements where a silence rules. He never really looks at the role of parents in family life, and never examines, in particular, their position re. Seymour's suicide. It's a substantial omission, and perhaps not an omission at all but instead a protective silence. I don't know, and on this point I don't care to speculate beyond the observation that, in general, people from good, functioning families rarely kill themselves. And in crappy, broken-down families a child's attention is often focused on nothing but the parents. Suffice it to say there's something big missing in Salinger's account. And the other thing not present in Salinger's work is outright anger toward Seymour or a sense of doubt about him. As Buddy describes him, Seymour really has no flaws at all, and to me this absence of flaws and of anger and doubt is a texture that's conspicuously absent. Why? I can't say, although I feel the effects. In *Seymour—An Introduction* Buddy never lets the reader forget that he, Buddy, is sitting alone at his desk, writing. It's all just writing, he wants us to know, the lumber of it, the cut and stacked phrases, the punctuation nailed to the paper, the parentheses put up to frame different doubts, etc.—as if to say this project, this monument under construction, will always fall short of honoring the actual character. Where Holden insists on Phoebe's innocence and pretty easily posits an idea of her essence, Buddy sees past his brother into the conceits and constructions that create him on the page. And because of this, perhaps, Seymour never feels real, never seems to emerge from the workbench of the writer, to live and walk among men.

The writer won't or can't let him die:

> What I am, I think, is a thesaurus of undetached prefatory
> remarks about him. I believe I essentially remain what I've
> almost always been—a narrator, but one with extremely
> pressing personal needs. I want to introduce, I want to describe,
> I want to distribute momentos, amulets, I want to break out my
> wallet and pass around snapshots, I want to follow my nose.

Here again you get a kind of intense identification with Seymour, one that blocks Buddy's way—he's "undetached," he has "pressing personal needs," and because of this he can only make "prefatory" remarks. The isolated *I am* is telling; with the comma where it is, the weight of the sentence remains stuck to the subject, rather than shifting forward via the verb to its object. The *I am* seems open-ended, perpetual. (Is time taken out of the sentence because the writer won't let history happen, won't let his character die? It's curious that in a life that's ended, that's so emphatically finished, the writer can't begin, can't offer anything more than an introduction. Would finishing Seymour mean outliving him? Or the converse: does failing to finish Seymour leave him alive?) The identity thing here is ruthless, close, smothering, endless. Consider that quote and the problem when set beside this:

> . . . I privately say to you, old friend (unto you, really, I'm afraid), please accept from me this unpretentious bouquet of very early-blooming parentheses: (((( )))). I suppose, most unflorally. I truly mean them to be taken, first off, as bow-legged—buckle-legged—omens of my state of mind and body at this writing.

There's that cowardly, obfuscating "un-" construction—*unpretentious, unflorally*—cropping up again (which nearly always works as a mask, sneaky and meaning the very opposite of what it states; meaning, in this case, pretentious, floral), but the point now is to draw attention to the parentheses. (Although in working through various drafts of this essay I realized my second paragraph was full of precisely this construction. It appears five times, and occupies the privileged key position as the last word in the paragraph. It crossed my mind to correct the problem by burying it in some low geological stratum of the piece, but I haven't. There's that desire in writing, as in life, to rewind everything after a suicide, to return to some pristine moment, and so in this, too, Salinger's *mon frere, ma semblable*.) The parentheses sit like Kevlar jackets all through the writing, protecting Buddy's identity from attack, keeping the sentences safe. *Seymour—An Introduction* is like a story in hiding, its prose on the lam, its characters putting on disguises, its ideas concealed. The whole thing is preambular, it's all excursus, and it's a bad sign that for me the best or most accurate language for describing the story comes from classical rhetoric and oratory. The sentences spin eloquently over an absence—it's as if progress has stopped, and the last few words are draining out. Earlier I said that Holden is making a loud shouted appeal directly to the audience, over the heads of those who don't understand. The whole story is directed at you, the reader. In *Seymour* Buddy Glass speaks directly to the reader too, but now he resorts to the aside, the isolated whispered phrase, safely enclosed in parentheses, addressing the *audience* in a low voice supposedly *inaudible* to others nearby.

Who is nearby?

I know: his brother.

<hr/>

Salinger isn't primarily a funny writer, and humor, except sporadically in *The Catcher in the Rye*, is largely absent from his work. His primary thing is empathy, the yearning for it, the hope and the need, both as giver and receiver. Buddy's desire for empathic union with his brother is single-minded and loyal and makes for an interesting case, but Seymour never finally comes to life. The book is one long stutter and a fascinating failure. Buddy can't write Seymour because, when he tries, Seymour fragments and falls apart—you get the parts, you get the eyes, the nose, the voice, etc. He wants his brother so bad, it's a sad thing to watch, to see Seymour breaking to pieces in Buddy's hands. The Salinger I've been discussing seems at times to feel he's got a corner on The Truth, this unwieldy lump he keeps hidden like the kid with the secret goldfish in D.B.'s story, who won't show it to anybody because he bought it with his own money. Perhaps this Truth is centrally important because the suicide takes his secret with him, and it's easy to get caught up in a monomaniacal search for The Answer, pinning your painfully vast hope to a single Idea. Up to a point, you believe the person who killed himself took the ultimate truth, and life afterward often feels like a sorrowful search for that last, unknown key to the life, which will explain everything. The paradox is that this hope or need for certainty seems to make the world less stable. The belief in a single Truth leads to doubt about everything. The need for empathic union makes the actual separation just terribly, terribly huge.

When we shift the relationship away from Buddy-Seymour to Salinger-Holden, then, as an act of writing, Salinger's empathy for

Holden Caulfield makes *The Catcher in the Rye* something special, an intense and fierce and intimate look at a character who arouses in readers—in me, let's say—a level of sympathetic identification nearly equal to the one felt for Fitzgerald's Gatsby.

After my brother's death I felt I had too much feeling to be myself. I felt attacked by my emotions, under siege, and the sensation, day after day, was like life had stuck to me. Like it was pinned to my back. This whatever, this stab of feeling, probably influenced the fate of the doomed robin. I could have stood by until the crow killed it, or sat still until somebody a little more altruistic came down the street and stepped in to save it, rushing the bird off to a Humane Society shelter; or someone else could have come down the street, this time in a car, and run it over. Lots of things could have happened. But instead, I scooped the bird up in my Filson cap, folding the hat like a taco shell so it couldn't escape, and carried it to a vacant lot with a weedy path that led down to the lake. For some reason I thought the crow might follow us, but crows are comical birds and that one's interest had already moved on to something new. I walked into the murky water of Lake Union, my mind blank, and, bending down, dunked the hat under. The bird was still trying to fly, brushing its one good wing against the fabric, and when that stopped I pulled my hat away. The robin floated to the surface, lifelessly riding the tiny waves, and I smacked the hat against my leg, knocking beads of water off the waxed cotton. I picked a few gray feathers from the inner brim and put the hat on, looking west across the water to the Aurora Bridge. And while now the bridge reminds me of my brother Mike, comically pratfalling through an indifferent universe, back then it made me think of Danny, tragically dead at twenty-one after shooting himself in my bedroom.

With Danny, years have passed and I still feel a deathly guilt. I never did anything but love my brother and that wasn't enough. And now every breath I take is a betrayal, a refusal of his choice. It's not sentimental indulgence, it's not so much that I ask myself what happened to the hand I held in crosswalks, but rather that I cross all those streets again. I stay with him now, I'm *always* nearby. I am always ten and he is always three, and I sit in the kitchen spooning canned peas into his mouth, swallowing most of them myself, and he gets a bowl of spumoni for being a good boy and eating his vegetables. I'm with him and I never feel like I belong entirely to present-day life. I've never really held a serious job or applied myself to anything worthwhile, I'm an unreliable, shitty friend, and I've never loved anyone deeply or satisfactorily. Killing the robin was an early experiment in grieving and acceptance that didn't work too well. I knew the bird had no life ahead of it, and I wanted to anticipate that doom rather than stand off at a safe distance. I didn't want to be uncertain. But where before I had too much feeling, after drowning the bird I felt nothing, I was indifferent, I was remorseless. I thought I could rejoin the universe by being cruel and unfeeling, but obviously I was having trouble with focal distance and zeroing in on the exact right place where most of life was happening.

Here is a quote from Dietrich Bonhoeffer that I treasure for capturing one side of how I feel. It gets me closer to acceptance and understanding than anything else. It's from his *Letters & Papers from Prison*, and written, I think, at a time when he knew he would die in the concentration camp, so he speaks from inside the heart of his death:

> Nothing can make up for the absence of someone whom we love, and it would be wrong to try to find a substitute; we must simply hold out and see it through. That sounds very hard at first, but at the same time it is a great consolation, for the gap, as long as it remains unfulfilled, preserves the bonds between us. It is nonsense to say that God fills the gap. God doesn't fill it, but on the contrary, keeps it empty and so helps us to keep alive our former communion with each other, even at the cost of pain.

From the get-go, my brother Mike's suicide attempt struck me as a piece of comedy. Maybe that's because it came to me like the comedian's idea of the topper, the rule that says you follow up a good joke with a second, even better joke. Keep them laughing! Maybe it's because I always picture Mike tumbling haplessly through space, and falls are a staple of comedy and clowning, as is anything that turns the body into an object. Maybe it's because when he jumped over the rail he was being chased by the devil and then he was aware, halfway down, that the devil was gone and he was all alone, falling like a rock. Or maybe, as in *King Lear*, it's just too much, and the wise man sees life like the fool and laughs, either that or he cracks. Mike was really wrecked-up, his body broken, and when I saw him at the VA hospital he had nuts and bolts and this kind of light-gauge medical rebar rising like a scaffolding from his smashed pelvis. His right shoulder was immobilized, so that, in combination with the broken pelvis, and his ruined bladder, which was being drained by a catheter, he seemed like just another malfunctioning contraption or a Rube Goldberg contrivance. At home we always had old jalopy equipment like black and white televisions with no horizontal hold and our cars were ancient and unreliable and broken-down—in one of our cars the transmission would overheat and the carpet in the backseat would catch fire and smolder on any drive longer than ten miles, so we did the obvious thing, we kept a jug of water in the car. In the hospital Mike looked to me just like another one of our crappy busted things, where the attempt at repair was funny in a way that the initial problem was not. Whereas I remember helping Danny eat his peas, I remember laughing at Mike as he tried to get a hamburger to his mouth. I sat in a chair and watched. He couldn't do it—you can't sit up straight with a broken pelvis—and his mouth and the hamburger just hung there, apart from each other, it seemed, for all time.

And so over here, Henri Bergson's essay on the comic suggests another side, a possible path for me in my ongoing attempt to understand life by reading books:

> . . . I would point out . . . the absence of feeling which
> usually accompanies laughter. . . . Indifference is its natural
> environment, for laughter has no greater foe than emotion.
> . . . In a society composed of pure intelligences there would
> probably be no more tears, though perhaps there would still
> be laughter; whereas highly emotional souls, in tune and
> unison with life, in whom every event would be sentimentally
> prolonged and re-echoed, would neither know nor understand
> laughter.

Put in a slightly different way, it was Charlie Chaplin, I think, who said that life up-close is a tragedy, but from a distance it's a comedy. Somebody slipping on a banana peel is still funny, unless it's you. And the genius of Salinger is that, speaking through Holden Caulfield, highly emotional, in tune and unison with life, with events re-echoing still, he told us exactly what it feels like to feel too much.

An Essay in Criticism

VIRGINIA WOOLF

Human credulity is indeed wonderful. There may be good reasons for believing in a King or a Judge or a Lord Mayor. When we see them go sweeping by in their robes and their wigs, with their heralds and their outriders, our knees begin to shake and our looks to falter. But what reason there is for believing in critics it is impossible to say. They have neither wigs nor outriders. They differ in no way from other people if one sees them in the flesh. Yet these insignificant fellow creatures have only to shut themselves up in a room, dip a pen in the ink, and call themselves 'we', for the rest of us to believe that they are somehow exalted, inspired, infallible. Wigs grow on their heads. Robes cover their limbs. No greater miracle was ever performed by the power of human credulity. And, like most miracles, this one, too, has had a weakening effect upon the mind of the believer. He begins to think that critics, because they call themselves so, must be right. He begins to suppose that something actually happens to a book when it has been praised or denounced in print. He begins to doubt and conceal his own sensitive, hesitating apprehensions when they conflict with the critics' decrees.

And yet, barring the learned (and learning is chiefly useful in judging the work of the dead), the critic is rather more fallible than the rest of us. He has to give us his opinion of a book that has been published two days, perhaps, with the shell still sticking to its head. He has to get outside that cloud of fertile, but unrealized, sensation which hangs about a reader, to solidify it, to sum it up. The chances are that he does this before the time is ripe; he does it too rapidly and too definitely. He says that it is a great book or a bad book. Yet, as he knows, when he is content to read only, it is neither. He is driven by force of circumstances and some human vanity to hide those hesitations which beset him as he reads, to smooth out all traces of that crab-like and crooked path by which he has reached what he chooses to call 'a conclusion'. So the crude trumpet blasts of critical opinion blow loud and shrill, and we, humble readers that we are, bow our submissive heads.

But let us see whether we can do away with these pretences for a season and pull down the imposing curtain which hides the critical process until it is complete. Let us give the mind a new book, as one drops a lump of fish into a cage of fringed and eager sea anemones, and watch it pausing, pondering, considering its attack. Let us see what prejudices affect it; what influences tell upon it. And if the conclusion becomes in the process a little less conclusive, it may, for that very reason, approach nearer to the truth. The first thing that the mind desires is some foothold of fact upon which it can lodge before it takes flight upon its speculative career. Vague rumours attach themselves to people's names. Of Mr. Hemingway, we know that he is an American living in France, an 'advanced' writer, we suspect, connected with what is called a movement, though which of the many we own that we do not know. It will be well to make a little more certain of these matters by reading first Mr. Hemingway's earlier book, *The Sun Also Rises*, and it soon becomes clear from this that, if Mr. Hemingway is 'advanced', it is not in the way that is to us most interesting. A prejudice of which the reader would do well to take account is here exposed; the critic is a modernist. Yes, the excuse would be because the moderns make us aware of what we feel subconsciously; they are truer to our own experience; they even anticipate it, and this gives us a particular excitement. But nothing new is revealed about any of the characters in *The Sun Also Rises*. They come before us shaped, proportioned, weighed, exactly as the characters of Maupassant are shaped and proportioned. They are seen from the old angle; the old reticences, the old relations between author and character are observed.

But the critic has the grace to reflect that this demand for new aspects and new perspectives may well be overdone. It may become whimsical. It may become foolish. For why should not art be traditional as well as original? Are we not attaching too much importance to an excitement which, though agreeable, may not be valuable in itself, so that we are led to make the fatal mistake of overriding the writer's gift?

At any rate, Mr. Hemingway is not modern in the sense given; and it would appear from his first novel that this rumour of modernity must have sprung from his subject matter and from his treatment of it rather than from any fundamental novelty in his conception of the art of fiction. It is a bare, abrupt, outspoken book. Life as people live it in Paris in 1927 or even in 1928 is described as we of this age do describe life (it is here that we steal a march upon the Victorians) openly, frankly, without prudery, but also without surprise. The immoralities and moralities of Paris are described as we are apt to hear them spoken of in private life. Such candour is modern and it is admirable. Then, for qualities grow together in art as in life, we find attached to this admirable frankness an equal bareness of style. Nobody speaks for more than a line or two. Half a line is mostly sufficient. If a hill or a town is described (and there is always some reason for its description) there it is, exactly and literally built up of little facts, literal enough, but chosen, as the final sharpness of the outline proves, with the utmost care. Therefore, a few words like these: 'The grain was just beginning to ripen and the fields were full of poppies. The pasture land was green and there were fine trees, and sometimes big rivers and chateaux off in the trees'—which have a curious force. Each word pulls its weight in the sentence. And the prevailing atmosphere is fine and sharp, like that of winter days when the boughs are bare against the sky. (But if we had to choose one sentence with which to describe what Mr. Hemingway attempts and sometimes achieves, we should quote a passage from a description of a bullfight: 'Romero never made any contortions, always it was straight and pure and natural in line. The others twisted themselves like corkscrews, their elbows raised and leaned against the flanks of the bull after his horns had passed, to give a faked look of danger. Afterwards, all that was faked turned bad and gave an unpleasant feeling. Romero's bullfighting gave real emotion, because he kept the absolute purity of line in his movements and always quietly and calmly let the horns pass him close each time.') Mr. Hemingway's writing, one might paraphrase, gives us now and then a real emotion, because he keeps absolute purity of line in his movements and lets the horns (which are truth, fact, reality) pass him close each time. But there is something faked, too, which turns bad and gives an unpleasant feeling—that also we must face in course of time.

And here, indeed, we may conveniently pause and sum up what point we have reached in our critical progress. Mr. Hemingway is not an advanced writer in the sense that he is looking at life from a new angle. What he sees is a tolerably familiar sight. Common objects like beer bottles and journalists figure largely in the foreground. But he is a skilled and conscientious writer. He has an aim and makes for it without fear or circumlocution. We have, therefore, to take his measure against somebody of substance, and not merely line him, for form's sake, beside the indistinct bulk of some ephemeral shape largely stuffed with straw. Reluctantly we reach this decision, for this process of measurement is one of the most difficult of a critic's tasks. He has to decide which are the most salient points of the book he has just read; to distinguish accurately to what kind they belong, and then, holding them against whatever model is chosen for comparison, to bring out their deficiency or their adequacy.

Recalling *The Sun Also Rises*, certain scenes rise in memory: the bullfight, the character of the Englishman, Harris; here a little landscape which seems to grow behind the people naturally; here a long, lean phrase which goes curling round a situation like the lash of a whip. Now and again this phrase evokes a character brilliantly, more often a scene. Of character, there is little that remains firmly and solidly elucidated. Something indeed seems wrong with the people. If we place them (the comparison is bad) against Tchekov's people, they are flat as cardboard. If we place them (the comparison is better) against Maupassant's people they are crude as a photograph. If we place them (the comparison may be illegitimate) against real people, the people we liken them to are of an unreal type. They are people one may have seen showing off at some café; talking a rapid, high-pitched slang, because slang is the speech of the herd, seemingly much at their ease, and yet if we look at them a little from the shadow not at their ease at all, and, indeed, terribly afraid of being themselves, or they would say things simply in their natural voices. So it would seem that the thing that is faked is character; Mr. Hemingway leans against the flanks of that particular bull after the horns have passed.

After this preliminary study of Mr. Hemingway's first book, we come to the new book, *Men Without Women*, possessed of certain views or prejudices. His talent plainly may develop along different lines. It may broaden and fill out; it may take a little more time and go into things—human beings in particular—rather more deeply. And even if this meant the sacrifice of some energy and point, the exchange would be to our private liking. On the other hand, his is a talent which may contract and harden still further, it may come to depend more and more upon the emphatic moment; make more and more use of dialogue, and cast narrative and description overboard as an encumbrance.

The fact that *Men Without Women* consists of short stories makes it probable that Mr. Hemingway has taken the second line. But, before we explore the new book, a word should be said which is generally left unsaid, about the implications of the title. As the publisher puts it . . . 'the softening feminine influence is absent—either through training, discipline, death, or situation'. Whether we are to understand by this that women are incapable of training, discipline, death, or situation, we do not know. But it is undoubtedly true, if we are going to persevere in our attempt to reveal the processes of the critic's mind, that any emphasis laid upon sex is dangerous. Tell a man that this is a woman's book, or a woman that this is a man's, and you have brought into play sympathies and antipathies which have nothing to do with art. The greatest writers lay no stress upon sex one way or the other. The critic is not reminded as he reads them that he belongs to the masculine or the feminine gender. But in our time, thanks to our sexual perturbations, sex consciousness is strong, and shows itself in literature by an exaggeration, a protest of sexual characteristics which in either case is disagreeable. Thus Mr. Lawrence, Mr. Douglas, and Mr. Joyce partly spoil their books for women readers by their display of self-conscious virility; and Mr. Hemingway, but much less violently, follows suit. All we can do, whether we are men or women, is to admit the influence, look the fact in the face, and so hope to stare it out of countenance.

To proceed then—*Men Without Women* consists of short stories in the French rather than in the Russian manner. The great French masters, Mérimée and Maupassant, made their stories as self-conscious and compact as possible. There is never a thread left hanging; indeed, so contracted are they that when the last sentence of the last page flares up, as it so often does, we see by its light the whole circumference and significance of the story revealed. The Tchekov method is, of course, the very opposite of this. Everything is cloudy and vague, loosely trailing rather than tightly furled. The stories move slowly out of sight like clouds in the summer air, leaving a wake of meaning in our minds which gradually fades away. Of the two methods, who shall say which is the better? At any rate, Mr. Hemingway, enlisting under the French masters, carries out their teaching up to a point with considerable success.

There are in *Men Without Women* many stories which, if life were longer, one would wish to read again. Most of them indeed are so competent, so efficient, and so bare of superfluity that one wonders why they do not make a deeper dent in the mind than they do. Take the pathetic story of the Major whose wife died—'In Another Country'; or the sardonic story of a conversation in a railway carriage—'A Canary for One'; or stories like 'The Undefeated' and 'Fifty Grand' which are full of the sordidness and heroism of bull-fighting and boxing—all of these are good trenchant stories, quick, terse, and strong. If one had not summoned the ghosts of Tchekov, Mérimée, and Maupassant, no doubt one would be enthusiastic. As it is, one looks about for something, fails to find something, and so is brought again to the old familiar business of ringing impressions on the counter, and asking what is wrong?

For some reason the book of short stories does not seem to us to go as deep or to promise as much as the novel. Perhaps it is the excessive use of dialogue, for Mr. Hemingway's use of it is surely excessive. A writer will always be chary of dialogue because dialogue puts the most violent pressure upon the reader's attention. He has to hear, to see, to supply the right tone, and to fill in the background from what the characters say without any help from the author. Therefore, when fictitious people are allowed to speak it must be because they have something so important to say that it stimulates the reader to do rather more than his share of the work of creation. But, although Mr. Hemingway keeps us under the fire of dialogue constantly, his people, half the time, are saying what the author could say much more economically for them. At last we are inclined to cry out with the little girl in 'Hills Like White Elephants': 'Would you please please please please please please stop talking?'

And probably it is this superfluity of dialogue which leads to that other fault which is always lying in wait for the writer of short stories: the lack of proportion. A paragraph in excess will make these little craft lopsided and will bring about that blurred effect which, when one is out for clarity and point, so baffles the reader. And both these faults, the tendency to flood the page with unnecessary dialogue and the lack of sharp, unmistakable points by which we can take hold of the story, come from the more fundamental fact that, though Mr. Hemingway is brilliantly and enormously skilful, he lets his dexterity, like the bull-fighter's cloak, get between him and the fact. For in truth story-writing has much in common with bullfighting. One may twist one's self like a corkscrew and go through every sort of contortion so that the public thinks one is running every risk and displaying superb gallantry. But the true writer stands close up to the bull and lets the horns—call them life, truth, reality, whatever you like—pass him close each time.

Mr. Hemingway, then, is courageous; he is candid; he is highly skilled; he plants words precisely where he wishes; he has moments of bare and nervous beauty; he is modern in manner but not in vision; he is self-consciously virile; his talent has contracted rather than expanded; compared with his novel his stories are a little dry and sterile. So we sum him up. So we reveal some of the prejudices, the instincts and the fallacies out of which what it pleases us to call criticism is made.

On a Stanza by John Keats

SVEN BIRKERTS

Season of mists and mellow fruitfulness,
    Close bosom-friend of the maturing sun;
Conspiring with him how to load and bless
    With fruit the vines that round the thatch-eves run;
To bend with apples the moss'd cottage-trees,
    And fill all fruit with ripeness to the core;
        To swell the gourd, and plump the hazel shells
    With a sweet kernel; to set budding more,
And still more, later flowers for the bees
Until they think warm days will never cease,
    For Summer has o'er-brim'd their clammy cells.
—*from "To Autumn"*

Somehow a stubble plain looks warm—in the same way that
some pictures look warm—this struck me so much in my
Sunday's walk that I composed upon it.
—*Keats, letter to J. H. Reynolds*

"**D**istance is the soul of beauty," wrote Simone Weil. Although it is by no means the only gnomic aphorism on the subject (Dostoevsky: "Beauty will save the world." André Breton: Beauty will be convulsive or it will not be at all." Keats: "Beauty is truth, truth beauty"), it remains for me the most tantalizing. The first time I encountered it, I felt instinctively that it was true; that is, it gave shape to a feeling that had long been inchoate in me. At the same time, however, I could not unravel it into any kind of explanation. The formulation seemed to retain a distance of its own, a subtle paradox at the core. For I find that whatever strikes me as beautiful manifests not distance but nearness, a quality of transparent immediacy; I feel that I am confronting something that I have always known. How can that "nearness" be squared with "distance"?

So long as I persisted in regarding Weil's words in the abstract, I remained baffled. It was only recently, when I tried to discover for myself why a certain poem was beautiful, that I began to understand. What Weil was addressing was the paradox at the heart of the aesthetic encounter. When we are stirred by beauty in a particular work of art, what we experience is the inward abolition of distance. It is only when we try to put our finger on the source of the sensation, when we try to *explain* the beauty, that the horizons are reversed. At that moment the near becomes the far, much as it does when we try to fathom our own reflection in the mirror: The more intently we look, the stranger becomes the object of our scrutiny.

———❖———

I set myself what seemed at first a simple task: to say why Keats's "To Autumn" was beautiful. The poem has always been one of my personal touchstones. Whenever I feel the occupational contamination of "words, words, words . . ." I look to its three stanzas for the rightness that restores faith. Nor am I alone. Generations of readers have singled out this last ode for special praise. I have seen it cited many times as the most perfect poem in the language. A more suitable test case for beauty, it seems, would be hard to find.

Before starting in on my own, I took a quick tour through the writings of certain estimable critics and scholars. I wanted to get a taste for the kinds of approaches that had been adopted in the past, and also to make sure that I did not belabor anything that was old hat. In a few sittings I learned more than a mortal should know about Keats's strategies of "stationing," his deployment of harvest imagery, his secularism, his debt to Milton and Shakespeare, and so on. I found much that was fussy, and just as much that was fascinating. But in all of the pages I read, I found nothing that helped me to understand why the immediate encounter with the words on the page is so thrilling, why the melody of the thing lives on in the mind, or how it is that the sensations are carried from line to line with an almost supernatural rightness. The beauty of the poem was in every case assumed; no one tried to account for it. I had to wonder: Is beauty that has been made out of words impervious to other words? Or is there an etiquette that I remain ignorant of—that one does not bring up certain matters? I left the library with a heady feeling of exploratory license.

Osip Mandelstam once wrote: "Where there is amenability to paraphrase, there the sheets have never been rumpled, there poetry, so to speak, has never spent the night." I let these words guide my first steps. For anyone can see at a glance that "To Autumn" resists summary. It rests on no clearly delineated narrative and carries no capsule message. And while there *is* sense in the poem, it is not the primary source of our response. But neither is that response, as with some poems, a matter of startling, unexpected imagery or metaphoric enlargement/reversal. We do not see the world as we have never seen it before. Rather, we are presented with an array of familiar, if heightened, sensations. Clearly, then, the magic must have to do with the interactions of sense and verbal music, with the rhythmic orchestrations and the intensifications that result.

I am convinced that the beauty of the ode is to be sought with the fine crosshairs of sound and sense, that it inheres in the subtlest details and is sustained from breath to breath—that generalizations will serve for nothing. We experience such a rapid succession of perfectly managed sensory magnifications that we are, in a strange way, brought face to face with the evolutionary mystery of language. The absolute rightness of the sound combinations forces us to a powerful unconscious recognition: Sound is the primal clay out of which all meaning has been sculpted.

I intend here to give a fanatically (and phonetically) close reading of the first stanza of "To Autumn." To work through any more than a stanza with as highly ground a lens would be tiresome to the reader and to some extent redundant. Certain readers may object to the procedure, claiming that the effects I find are too fantastic, that I am amplifying phonic detail out of all proportion, and that my findings are not part of the intended experience of the poem. Let me defend myself (briefly) in advance.

First of all, I believe that when we read a poem we absorb and process a great deal more than we are consciously aware of, and that it is precisely those cues that we pick up at the threshold—that we hear and feel but do not overtly take note of—that combine to give us the aesthetic surge. A passage strikes us as a perfect expression, but we cannot quite say why. Indeed, I wonder if this might not account for some of the mystery of beauty: that we confront an order or pattern that is opaque to the conscious monitors but perfectly transparent to the preconscious, or unconscious. Maybe Weil's "distance" is really referring to a gap between parts of the psyche. In which case, perhaps the feeling of beauty depends on a tension—or charge—born of an opposition within one's own psyche.

My second defense is so rudimentary that it could easily be overlooked. That is, given Keats's poetic endowment—the evidence of which is, of course, the poetry itself—what we might perceive as a hairsplitting discrimination was perfectly conspicuous to him. Let's not forget that we read poetry in the odd hour, as amateurs; Keats pressed his lines into place with the full intensity of his being. When a poet is composing, the value of every sound is magnified a thousandfold. His radar is attuned to frequencies that we are not even aware of. (Yeats characterized this rapt state beautifully: "Like a long-legged fly upon the stream / His mind moves upon silence.") I would argue, therefore, that not only (A) if you find it, it's probably there, but also (B) however much you find, there is sure to be more. Poetry will not disclose its secrets so long as we impose a ceiling on its resonance and reference. The poet does not use language as we do when we write a letter or a report. It is present to him when he composes as a totality of possibilities—the slightest pressure at any point sends waves through the entire system. To limit the associational field is to hobble the response.

> Season of mists and mellow fruitfulness,
>> Close bosom-friend of the maturing sun;
> Conspiring with him how to load and bless
>> With fruit the vines that round the thatch-eves run;

The governing sensation of the full stanza, which is most tellingly enacted in its last four lines, is of active ripening—of nature swelling all living things with her ichor—and overflow. Keats's description is as straightforward as could be, and the lines are crowded with nouns and active, richly suggestive verbs. The presentation proceeds from the unbounded vista of the invocation through a series of increasingly particular close-ups, to culminate in the minute cells of the honeycombs. We do not have to dig past the surface to get at the delights of the sound—they are there to be scooped right off the page. And just as we can enjoy the play of colors in one of Claude Monet's haystacks—with no deeper understanding of his struggle to balance off the objective interactions of light and matter on the retina with the limitations of intermittent perception—so we may respond to the sonorities and the abundance of carefully arranged detail while remaining oblivious, at least consciously, of the underlying intricacies.

Literature is full of picturesque renderings of the natural world. But with "To Autumn" we are well beyond the picturesque. In these lines the words do not merely designate or connote—they take on a gestural life so explicit that they temporarily displace the world to which they refer. They do so by replacing it with a self-sufficient language world, where things are not only named and arranged, but into which are incorporated deep suggestions about the working of physical process. The mystery of it—that language should be capable of so much—defies explanation and analysis. At best, we can note some of the more conspicuous instances of this functioning.

"Season of mists . . ." Mists, as we know from our science primers, result from the condensation and evaporation of ground moisture, the very same moisture that is taken up by the capillary roots of trees and plants and that eventually fleshes out the cells of the fruits. The sun, which from our Ptolemaic perspective rises up as if out of the earth itself, creates the mist by hastening evaporation and subsequently "burns" it away. This process, recalled for us in the poem by the nouns "mist" and "sun," is fully enacted on a phonetic level. Here we get our first evidence of the ode's deeper linguistic rightness.

Observe, first, what the mouth must do to vocalize the line: "Season of mists and mel-low fruit-ful-ness." The lips widen and stretch to make the initial *ee* sound in "Season," contract the same position to pronounce "mists," and contract it yet again, just slightly, to form the syllable "mel-." If we think of these contractions as representing diminishing circumferences—as, say, cross sections of a funnel—then with the small *o* of "-low" and the *oo* of "fruit-" (which cannot be made without a pouting protrusion of the lips and an even smaller aperture) we have come to the narrowed apex. This would not necessarily be significant in itself, but when we consider the unstated physical process—the moisture being siphoned out of the soil and into the fruit through the myriad fine roots, the push against gravity—then these lip movements become instrumental.

But this is not all. There is also a simultaneous *lingual* event. For in order to enunciate cleanly the words "mel-low fruit-ful-ness," the tip of the tongue must sketch out the shape of a fruit. Try the sounds slowly and expressively. Notice how the tongue ticks off points along a circumference. Isn't there a distant impression of rondure? The event is further complicated, and its resonance deepened, by the fact that the sounds we are making signify so directly: "mel" (the Latin root for "honey"), "fruit," and "ful(l)ness." We have spoken only one line, but we have already abetted the ripening process and have tasted the contours of a small, sweet fruit.

One of the first things we notice about the opening lines of the stanza are the many sibilants. These function in several ways. First, their purposeful positioning virtually forces us to create what might be called an associational field. We screen them differently than we would in other contexts. When we hear on the newscast, for example, that there are "early morning mists in low-lying areas," we do not feel free to conjure with the sounds; we know that they are being used in a strictly denotational mode. The situation is obviously different when it is Keats writing: "Season of mists and mellow fruitfulness." And there is more involved than just placement and rhythmic emphasis. We assume an intentional pressure: The sounds were mobilized because they were the best possible equivalents for the desired sensation.

The proximity of the *s* sounds in the first three words—there are four—encourages us to associate the sibilance with mist. This is not that unnatural, in any event: The *s* holds latent suggestions of moisture (if only because rain makes a hissing sound), which a context like this would immediately activate. But there is also a very subtle and effective sensory crossing that takes place once we know the poem. For just as the sense of the first two lines allows us to make a link between the *s* sounds and the mists, so in the fourth and fifth lines the battery of *t*'s ("thatch-eves" and "cottage-trees") invites us to connect the *t* sound with the hard opacity of the actual trees. Pictographically, of course, the shape of the letters encourages such a leap—the sinuosity of the *s* corresponding with the undulant movement of the vapors, and the *t* resembling a branched tree. Once this association has been subliminally registered, we can find in the word "mists" both a phonic and a visual representation of cloudy exhalations swirling about the branches of an orchard tree. And once we make such an association, needless to say, we are drawn into the poem in a profound way.

> Close bosom-friend of the maturing sun;
> Conspiring

The deliberate profusion of sibilants also creates an unmistakable hiss in the opening lines. This gathers momentum through the first two lines and is not released until we encounter the perfectly situated participle "conspiring." The word works on us both etymologically and through the sound itself. To "conspire" means, literally, to breathe together. We get a sense of complicity, of mutual exhalation, of dampness of exhalation (mist represents nothing so much as breath vapor), and, as I will discuss later, sexual activity. At the same time, the word discharges completely the hiss that has gathered in the preceding lines. The vertical thrust of "spire"—which suggests with a single stroke that the sun has moved up in the sky—compresses an otherwise gradual event: The mist is burned off in the space of a syllable. We might observe, too, that "close," "bosom," and "conspiring" all keep the solar emblem *o* near the mist-suggesting *s*—with the pitched *i* of "spire" that connection is sundered.

A series of slight syllables follows the break: "-ing," "with," "him," "how," and "to." We can almost imagine that Keats is drawing out a slender vine or branch, tapering it to slightness before attaching the round and dense-feeling "load." The line is a beautiful illustration of the relative gravity of word sounds. The weighted—but distinctly lighter—sound of the monosyllable "bless," positioned as it is after "load," figures in the ear the supple movement of a laden vine and gives us the aural equivalent of a diminishing bob.

load and bless
With fruit the vines that round the thatch-eves run;

The enjambment of "bless / With" further accentuates the down and up motion, and the appreciably lighter *oo* of "fruit" continues the upward arc, even as the placement of the noun in a passive construction finally connects it to the vine. The syntactical inversion of the rest of the line echoes the preceding "load and bless / With fruit." Both phrases require an extension of the breath and thereby render more palpable our sense of elongated curling vines.

This fourth line is pivotal. With "vines" and "thatch-eves," we cross for the first time from the all-inclusive apostrophe of autumn into a particular kind of landscape. Helen Vendler has worked out the full topography of the poem in *The Odes of John Keats*—I can add nothing to her discoveries. But I would underscore the importance of the transition. Just as the stanza narrows down from a vast environment to the "cells" of the honeycombs, so too does it move us from a diffuse seasonal mistiness into a realm of highly tactile particulars: "thatch-eves," "moss'd cottage-trees," and "hazel shells":

> To bend with apples the moss'd cottage-trees,
>   And fill all fruit with ripeness to the core;
>   To swell the gourd, and plump the hazel shells
>   With a sweet kernel;

The central lines of the stanza are dominated by sensuous detail. I have already proposed that the clustered *t*'s call to mind the actual density of an orchard. The impression is further solidified by the incidence of strong stresses at the end of the line: "*moss*'d *cot*tage-*trees*." And the numerous vowel and consonant doublings add to the effect—*pp*, *ss*, *tt*, *ee*, and *ll* twice in a mere eleven words—as if nature's prodigality extended to the alphabet itself. Nor is their impact strictly visual. An alerted ear—and what ear can fail to be quickened by a poem like this?—finds the subliminal stutter in words like "apples" and "cottage." Again, it is the associational field that imparts significance to these normally incidental combinations.

> And fill all fruit with ripeness to the core;

Here, at last, the iambic pentameter resolves. And with wonderful effect. The harmonic regularity of nature is at last disclosed. The very filling of the fruit conforms to the eternal paradigm. The line both denotes and enacts measure. Nor is it accidental, I think, that the first evenly cadenced line should sit at the very center of the stanza, at its "core," as it were. For as I observed at the outset, the dominant action in these eleven lines is one of gradual overflow. This line, then, as the midpoint, marks the perfect peak of ripeness. The liquid has filled its container to the limit; the next five lines will send it brimming over.

> To swell the gourd, and plump the hazel shells
>   With a sweet kernel;

If *s*'s can be said to invoke mists, and *t*'s trees, then what are we to make of the loading of *l*'s in these central lines—"fill," "all," "swell," "plump," "hazel," and "shells"? Pronouncing the sixth and seventh lines with exaggerated care, we quickly discover how intricately mingled are the *l*'s and the other consonants, especially the *r*'s. It is the consonantal weave that keeps the tongue dancing without rest along the roof of the mouth, an activity that, when wedded to the sense, gives us the suggestion of a great many fruits burgeoning simultaneously. Especially effective is the placement of the exquisitely plosive "plump"—we feel as though things are bursting on every side of us.

It is worth noting here, too, the subtle reversal that Keats has devised. Where "fill all fruit with ripeness to the core" describes an inward movement, as though ripening were a process beginning at the surface and continuing toward the center, the remaining actions of the stanza are all outward: swelling, plumping, and o'erbrimming. Again, this underscores the importance of the sixth line. We can view it, if we choose, as the node of a chiasmus (X) figure, Lines 1–5 *in*-still the fruit with moisture; lines 7–11 move out from the center and culminate in a *dis*-tilling activity.

One curious element in the middle part of this stanza is Keats's repetition of the word "fruit." This is in addition to his use of "fruitfulness" in the first line. In both instances, the general term is followed by cited particulars, either "apples" or "the gourd" and "the hazel shells." The oscillation between the general and the specific (the whole ode, it seems, proposes a landscape that is neither entirely typified nor altogether singular) allows the universality of cyclic return to play against concretely sensuous detail. The repetition of "fruit" prevents us from immersing ourselves in an unequivocally particular setting. What's more, the word sends us back to the original denominations and commands of Genesis ("Let the earth bring forth grass, the herb yielding seed, and the fruit tree yielding fruit after his kind . . ."; "Be fruitful, and multiply . . ."; and so on). I would not like to stress this connection too strongly, however, for the order apostrophized in "To Autumn" is secular, not Edenic. The biblical echo points back to timeless harmonies, but it does not invite us to consider "Man's first disobedience."

Before turning to the final lines of the stanza, we might remark one more interesting subtlety. Keats has, in the sixth line, disassembled the signal word "fruitfulness," scattering its components: "And *fill* all *fruit* with rip*eness* . . ." We pick this up subliminally, unaware that part of our pleasure in the line comes from this all-but-imperceptible echo.

The weft is tightened; the evenly cadenced core of the stanza touches us with what feels like perfect inevitability.

> to set budding more,
> And still more, later flowers for the bees,
> Until they think warm days will never cease,
> For Summer has o'er-brimm'd their clammy cells.

The most remarkable event in the stanza as a whole is Keats's flawlessly executed enactment of the physical sensation of overflow. The cluster of strong accents—"And *still more, la*ter"—instigates a rising tension. The near regularity of the penultimate line cannot quite appease the ear. It inspires, instead, a precarious suggestion of arrest; we feel the tense convexity with which liquid holds shape just before spilling over. And then comes the midline impact of "o'er-brimm'd," a word that both describes and encodes the action. The three unaccented syllables preceding "-brim-" ensure that the emphasis will fall on the instant at which convexity yields.

A number of critics have connected the feeling of surfeit generated by the stanza with Keats's decision to adopt an eleven-line (instead of ten-line) stanza. The added quantity has obvious effects on the reader, and Keats has made the most of these. By giving the penultimate line acceleration and rising pitch—"cease" pitches forward like the crest of a wave—he has made it all but impossible for us to take our natural pause. We are driven on to complete the stanza, to extend our exhalation past the normal limit. We feel the expenditure with our whole pneumatic apparatus, even as we murmur the three sets of doubled *m*'s—"Summer," "o'er-brimm'd," and "clammy"—mimicking the languorous vibration of satiated bees.

The sexual suggestion of these last lines cannot be passed over. If we listen to the whole stanza and follow its rhythmic progression, we cannot but register the climactic moment that comes with "cease" (who was it who called the orgasm "a little death"?), and the echoing contraction of "-brimm'd." Although Keats may not have orchestrated his lines with such an end in mind—consciously, at least—a reader has to be wearing earplugs to be unaware of it. Nor is it just a question of rhythmic emphasis. The honey hoarded by the bees (never named, but conjured up early on by the "mel-" of "mellow") is substantially akin to the "honey of generation" in Yeats's "Among School Children." For that matter, doesn't the entire stanza combine its images of swelling fruits and rising liquids under the aspect of its opening conceit—that the "conspiring" earth and sun are the intimate begetters of all that lives (in which case "Close bosom-friend" is something more than platonic in its suggestion)? Nor should we forget that the thrice-named "fruit" is itself seed. Not just fecundity, but procreative fervor underlies the imagery and sensation of this stanza.

⬧

As I said at the outset, I'm not going to work my way dutifully through the complete ode. My purpose is not to advocate any new interpretation. Neither am I under the illusion that this stitch-by-stitch approach will tell us anything about the "meaning" of the work. As far as I'm concerned, there is in this case no meaning extrinsic to the obvious sense of the words on the page. I do hope, however, that the close reading of a single stanza will emphasize that its aesthetic effect—our perception of beauty, if you will—derives largely from a complex series of sound and sense interactions, many of which are apt to elude us as we read. And that, further, our experience of beauty may well have something to do with the gap, or *distance*, between what we are aware of perceiving and what we pick up subliminally.

Two questions remain. First, let us suppose that we have uncovered a great many of these inconspicuous interactions. Have we then, by eliminating much of the distance between conscious and unconscious perception, somehow slackened the mainspring of beauty? Can we, in other words, pick a poem apart so completely that understanding supplants astonishment? I would say not, for the simple reason that our psyches are not structured in such a way that we can both read in a participatory manner and at the same time reflect on the ways in which that involvement has been achieved. The very workings that we uncover through an operation of willed dissociation—like the ones that I have just pointed out—function, when we read, to keep us fixed inside the language circuit. And if we do, through one of those unaccountable psychic switches, find ourselves staring at the cause of a particular poetic effect, our response might very well be enhanced. For what we recognize at such a moment is the preternatural fitness of language for the transmission of subtleties of perception.

The second question is complex and cannot be fully dealt with here. Namely, to what extent was the poet aware of, and responsible for, the felicities that I have been extracting from his work? Or, to put it another way, can we legitimately locate effects that the poet was not in some way aware of and intending? As I said earlier, we must always keep in mind that the poet's aural endowment is probably greater than ours— though *how much* greater is impossible to gauge. How we answer the question of intention, however, will depend on what we believe about the process of poetic composition. If we believe that it is consciously governed, willed, dependent on the taking of infinite pains—a non-sensical view, in my opinion—then the poet's own awareness matters greatly. If he did not intend x, then x does not exist.

As soon as we allow the unconscious a role in creativity, on the other hand, the reader is given a great deal of license. For then it is not a case of the poet's inventing lines, but rather of his finding sounds and rhythms in accordance with the promptings of the deeper psyche. The poet does not rest with a line until he has released a specific inner pressure. Or, to put it another way, the pressure looks to the language for its release. It magnetizes and attracts certain elements from the phonic spectrum and sets them into combinations. The poet presides over this process—in a sense he is *its* instrument—working toward the feeling of "rightness" that is his ultimate standard. Needless to say, he very often might not know why he brings two sounds together. When we turn up the most uncanny effects in his lines, therefore, we have every reason to believe that his deeper "Muse" put them there, even if *he* did not.

In Terms of the Toenail: Fiction and the Figures of Life

WILLIAM H. GASS

How easy it is to enter. An open book, an open eye, and the first page lifts like fragrance toward us so we read, "Two mountain chains traverse the republic...." Later we say to a friend, "I have begun Malcolm Lowry's novel *Under the Volcano*." A sentence read, a sentence spoken, both imparting information, one accurate as to Mexico, the other to our actions. The town is well south of the Tropic of Cancer, but we are buying groceries in Bayonne or teaching at Vassar. Our eye blinks, our mind wanders, the doorbell buzzes, and time between the two ranges ceases, or rather it waits, hushed, held like a lungful of air; for our hero, the Consul, will always be there, sitting in some bar or other, *perfectamente borracho*, drunk on guilt, and drinking mescal. How easy to enter. How difficult to remain. It reads like a guide, the beginning of this book. The walls of the town are high, the streets and lanes twist, the roads wind. There are four hundred swimming pools—four hundred—and many fine hotels. It's a resort city with the unpronounceable Indian name—Quauhnauhuac—like the groan of a duck. The day is the Day of the Dead, the first of November, 1939. But we are in '50 or '85 and our eyes ache. Still it's like a report on ourselves, despite the differences, an account of Oil City, Pa.: dates, places, persons, conversations, parties, politicking, lies. Or it is history which hasn't happened yet but may begin to any day; and as we read we find ourselves companions to a landscape or a dog, a shattered marriage, broken street, a doctor, brother, drunkard, deep ravine—each familiar (Oil City has its own steep slopes)—and in that sense our meeting with the text can seem quite seamless, the book and cigarette we hold no different fundamentally from the glass which imprisons Geoffrey Firmin. Life here, life there—then much the same. Words here, words there—then similar as well; the sentences hauling their communications from station to station like heavily freighted trains. The Consul has a beard, fair hair, few friends . . . and two mountain chains traverse the republic.

But is *Under the Volcano* really a biography, a one-day history of a man, and is its advantage in being imaginary that it can with confidence report details biographers can rarely have? Novels are made of such details, no doubt of that. But what biographer would want them?—the Consul observing that it is only eight-thirty and taking off his glasses; the Consul tracing with the toe of one dress shoe a pattern in the porch tiles; the Consul hanging up the telephone receiver the wrong way; the Consul sweating profusely and hunting a cantina, or thinking suddenly of Don Quixote, or sucking a lemon, reading a menu, being shaved. Facts by the thousands here, in Henry James, throughout the pages of *War and Peace* or *Ulysses*—all trivialities, items which could never find their way into any serious history. And Geoffrey Firmin is no George Washington or General Lee, even by allegation; he shapes nothing, affects few; and his body slides down a ravine. This novelist, indeed, has a passion for the unimportant: bus and railroad schedules, for example, theater marquees, boxing posters, an old volume of Elizabethan plays; but this passion is in no way extraordinary—Jane Austen liked hats and hair ribbons. What, too, of our own feelings for these obscure, superfluous, nonexistent people, and their queer creators, obscure, superfluous, and nearly nonexistent themselves, who, throughout their lives, do nothing—the man Malcolm Lowry, a drunkard too, who rounded the world as a sailor, wrote a few strange stories, was twice married, and, *perfectamente borracho,* choked to death on his own vomit?

We shall never verify this history. It rests nowhere in our world. Our world, in the first place, lacks significance; it lacks connection. If I swallow now—what of it? if I pass a cola sign—no matter; if I pet a striped cat, or tell a tiny lie, put down the tenth page of the *Times* to train my puppy—nothing's changed. And the real mountains of Mexico, those two chains which traverse the republic, exist despite us and all our feelings. But the Popocatepetl of the novel is yet another mountain, and when, in the first chapter, we are taken on a tour of the town, the facts we are given have quite a different function. Lowry is constructing a place, not describing one; he is making a Mexico for the mind where, strictly speaking, there are no menacing volcanoes, only menacing phrases, where complex chains of concepts traverse our consciousness, and where, unlike history, events take place in the moment that we read them—over and over as it may be, irregularly even, at widely separated times—whenever we restore these notes to music. Each of us, too, must encounter and enter the book alone, bring our lifetime to it, since truly it is a dark wood, this Mexico, a southern hell we're being guided through, and although simply begun, it is difficult to remain, to continue so terrible a journey. In this conceptual country there are no mere details, nothing is a simple happenstance, everything has meaning, is part of a net of essential relations. Sheer coincidence is impossible and those critics who have complained of this quality in Lowry have misunderstood the nature of the novel. They would not complain of the refrain of a song that its constant reappearance was coincidence. So the Ferris wheel of the festival—for this is the Day of the Dead, after all—will turn in our eyes as it turns in the Consul's, the burning wheel of Buddhist law, "its steel twigs caught in the emerald pathos of the trees," appearing just as often as design demands.

Nothing like history, then, *the Volcano* ties time in knots, is utterly subjective, completely contrived, as planned and patterned as a magical rug where the figure becomes the carpet. Nothing like a country or a town— no Oil City—*the Volcano* is made of a series of names which immediately become symbolic, and reverberate when struck like a hundred gongs. Even drunkenness has a different function, for the Consul does not drink so we may better understand drunkenness, and though he is ridden with guilt, his guilt is as fictional as he is. The Consul's drinking frees the language of the book, allows it to stagger and leap like verse, gives Lowry the freedom to construct freely. The Consul's stupors are the stupors of poetry, as madness was for Lear and his fool, and chivalry for Cervantes.

The Volcano is a mountain. We must climb. And it is difficult to maintain a foothold at first. Yet soon we begin to feel the warmth at its core, and few books will finally flow over us so fully, embed us in them as the citizens of Pompeii were bedded by their mountain, the postures of their ordinary days at once their monuments, their coffins, and their graves. Of novels, few are so little like life, few are so formal and arranged; there are few whose significance is so total and internal. Nonetheless, there are scarcely any which reflect the personal concerns of their author more clearly, or incline us as steeply to a wonder and a terror of the world until we fear for our own life as the Consul feared for his, and under such pressures yield to the temptation to say what seems false and pedestrian: that this book is about each of us—in Saint Cloud, Oil City, or Bayonne, N.J.—that it is about drunkenness and Mexico, or even that it is about that poor wretch Malcolm Lowry.

A scene: the Consul and his friend, M. Laruelle, in conversation. M. Laruelle is advising the Consul to go home to bed, for God's sake. His wife has returned to him, and hasn't he been howling for just that? yet here he is drinking, carrying on in the same disagreeable manner which drove her away in the first place. But tequila, the Consul claims, is healthful—not like mescal—and clarifies, marvelously, one's thoughts and perceptions. Perhaps, sometimes, when you have calculated the amount exactly, M. Laruelle admits, you do see more clearly:

> But certainly not the things so important to us despised sober people, on which the balance of any human situation depends. It's precisely your inability to see them, Geoffrey, that turns them into the instruments of the disaster you have created yourself. Your Ben Jonson, for instance, or perhaps it was Christopher Marlowe, your Faust man, saw the Carthaginians fighting on his big toe-nail. That's like the kind of clear seeing you indulge in. Everything seems perfectly clear, because indeed it is perfectly clear, in terms of the toe-nail.

Fiction is life in terms of the toenail, or in terms of the Ferris wheel, in terms of tequila; it is incurably figurative, and the world the novelist makes is always a metaphorical model of our own. It will be my concern, in what follows, to suggest something of the way in which metaphors function, and how such fictional models are made. But let's begin with something simpler—small enough to close our mouths and minds on, something from one of those nail-gazing Elizabethans.

2

Hamlet, Horatio, and Marcellus walk upon the castle platform awaiting midnight and Hamlet's father's ghost. Hamlet says, "The air bites shrewdly; it is very cold," and Horatio answers, "It is a nipping and an eager air." Hamlet and Horatio do not think of it as cold, simply. The dog of air's around them, shrewd and eager, running at heels. The behavior of this dog is wittily precise in their minds. It nags—shrewishly, wifelike. The air is acidulous, too, like sour wine.[1] Hamlet and Horatio, furthermore, are aware of the physical quality of their words. Horatio not only develops Hamlet's implicit figure, he concludes the exchange with the word that began it, and with sonorous sounds. The nature of the weather is conveyed to us with marvelous exactitude and ease, in remarks made by the way, far from the center of action; so that we find ourselves with knowledge of it in just the offhand way we would if, bent on meeting a king's ghost, we too went through the sharp wind. Yet Hamlet's second clause is useless. "The air bites shrewdly" is the clause that tells us everything. It is cold. The wind is out. The wind is alive, malevolent with wise jaws. The two clauses have a very clear relation. The first is metaphorical, the second literal. Both are about the weather, but one is art, the other not.

If we knew the temperature was ten degrees and the wind force five, we might imagine rather well how cold the wind would feel on the cheek, how persistently it might lift the flaps of jackets and enter sleeves, and we might give expression straight away to the fact of our feeling: the wind is cold. The inference we should draw, as familiar as it is, lies dark in its own empowering, for the relation of the pure and empty structure that is mathematics to the scientifically expressed observation, and both of these again to the cold wind of experience, are not yet understood relations. Perhaps one can say that the scientist works always through a quantitatively abstract system, and that his purpose seems to be to find ways to represent the vague and informal qualitative content of experience within a rationally well-ordered formal scheme. But Hamlet's and Horatio's words rely in no obvious way upon the mathematical or scientific, and we are forced, in what is really a very complicated and very peculiar manner, to infer the same phenomenon we reached from ten degrees and force five from logical absurdities, strange comparisons, and silly riddles. The speed with which we make our inferences should not deceive us of the fact we make them. The air bites, therefore the air is alive. The air bites shrewdly, therefore the air is wise. It is eager, so it feels. These deductions, upon the information that it nips, and the immediate conclusion that it nips as dogs nip, give us the dog of the air itself. To communicate the nature of the weather, Shakespeare has introduced an altogether novel set of concepts; novel, that is, with respect to the idea of weather as such; and it is through these concepts that we understand the kind of wind and cold we're in, just as, through the mathematical, the scientist tries to understand the experienced weather too. And I think it will be obvious to anyone who fairly examines the meaning of Shakespeare's language that it renders the weather with a precision quite equal to the precision of the scientific, although the scientific precision is of a different kind.

To resort to a commonplace example: if we represent the strength and direction of any force by the length and position of an arrowed straight line, we can readily examine and resolve, by the construction of parallelograms, any forces collected about a point and expressing themselves from there. Our inferences in these cases are made possible only by the rules of representation we have permitted ourselves to make, for it is these rules which place the physical forces in the maw of Euclid's reasoning machine. In a sense yet to be fully discovered, the technique of the artist is like that of the scientist. He invariably views the transactions of life through a lens of concept: through the shrew, the wife; through the wife, the dog; and through the dog, the cold and persistent wind.

From "the day is without warmth," from "the water is frozen in the well," from "it is ten below," from "it is a nipping and an eager air"—from each of these we can infer the cold; first analytically, from the definition of the state; second, from the effect, reasoning to the cause; third, by construction, from the manner of our representing temperature within a formal system; and fourth, from the characteristic maneuvers of art and metaphor. Metaphor is a manner of inferring; a manner of setting down as directly and briefly and simply as possible whatever is necessary for the inference desired, although the conclusion may require premises that are neither brief nor plain and do not seem direct, since direction, in both art and metaphor, is often indirection elsewhere; for it is as much a matter of concern there to seek the severe straight way as it is in science and mathematics to seek the same. But metaphor is more than a process of inference; it is also a form of presentation or display.

The distinction involved is familiar enough. There are at least two ways of finding out about frogs. You can read about frogs or you can raise frogs and watch them. The Count can be described to you or introduced. Annie can say she is weary or fall all of a heap. A description can serve as a premise from which certain conclusions can be reached and this is the way ordinary argument proceeds. The connective tissues of such an argument, moreover, are linguistic. They fasten words, they do not stretch between things; and the rules that permit the movement that is the essence of every inference are rules about the uses of our language or the uses of some language; they are not laws of nature that experiment discovers. Insofar as metaphor is argumentative and inferential it can be made out to be systematic and formal—bound purely in every part by its own rules, just as art as a whole is, and concerned only with its faithfulness to them. When I say that the Count is fair and tall and frogs are jumpy and green I name their habits and their properties, but when Annie sinks wordlessly to the carpet, nothing is actively inferred; the act does not automatically fall into an abstract system.

Yet Annie has argued her weakness. She has done so directly, her material a rich and inexhaustible context that language can only peevishly pick over. The roll of her eyes, the pallor in her face, the sag of her flesh, the shadow of her bones: they testify together and by no means alone to the correctness of our conclusion. This conclusion is neither described by the event nor reached by logically ordered propositions, although logically ordered propositions could be imagined that would imitate it. It is not displayed as the sag and the pallor of the faint are, nor is it symbolically present. We are not compelled to see in her swoon a moral fall and evidence of a moral frailty, though when the Consul collapses in a steep street while guiltily hunting a cantina, we must. Still, quite apart from these things, Annie's weakness has been shown.

The word "show" is equivocal in a useful way, for it means both display and demonstration. Showing argues and showing produces acquaintance. It presents to the mind one thing in order that the mind may seem to have possession of another. The length of the Count's trousers shows his height to his tailor. The most interminable stream of words can never equal, in its production of detail, the incredible number in Annie's proof, or, in its unity, the complete simplicity of her faint. No curve comes easily of straight lines. Yet metaphor must somehow create the illusion of that context, make with its abstractions some display if it is going to possess the qualities we know it has. Metaphors argue. They endeavor also to produce acquaintance: the frog who jumps, the Count who is tall. "It is a nipping and an eager air" has qualities of both proof and meeting. It describes one very strange thing in order that we may infer and in some equally strange way feel another. It seems to present us with the cold rather than name it, and it seems to argue the cold rather than be it.

It is far from customary to think of metaphor as a kind of model making—in terms of system, presentation, and inference—or of fiction as life in terms of the toenail (more metaphors—curse their constant intrusion); it is, in fact, tactless to suggest any similarities with science, for isn't it the cold destroyer of the qualitative world, an enemy of feeling, concubine to the computer? More metaphors—and surely false ones. The scientist, after a time, finds himself with a store of observations of the natural world on the one hand, and a system of pure mathematical connections on the other. Within the mathematical system he can make inferences with great speed and accuracy. Unfortunately the system is empty; it has no content; it tells him nothing about the world.

His observations tell him nothing either, for logical connections cannot be perceived; his data remain disorganized; there are no paths through it for the mind. But if he decides to represent a body by a point and motion by a line, then the system becomes concrete, at once trapping a vast number of physical things in a web of logical relations. In this way the scientist makes his model. The model is not to be confused with the world of ordinary experience, and the connections it establishes, made possible entirely by the rules of representation the scientist adopts, are not connections in any sense inherent in things. The model can be used to make predictions which mere observation is helpless to do, and in that manner its utility can be estimated. Thus the shadow made by a tree can be carried past the rather qualitative understanding of the eye into the dominion of number by representing the passage of light as a straight line. The light, the shadow, and the tree now form the sides of an Euclidean triangle, and upon that triangle all kinds of useful operations can be performed. The system is a lens through which the world is seen . . . or rather, it furnishes a scheme through which the world is thought.

Metaphors rarely have a thoroughly formal and abstract lens, but when they do the resemblance to the scientific case is striking. If one lover says sadly to the other: "We shall always be as far apart as we are now; we meet only in illusion," the figure is drawn from geometry and the rule is: let lives travel in straight lines; while the conclusion is: since our lives are parallel, we shall never meet. And it is a commonplace that such lines seem to converge at the horizon. Donne's famous compass comparison is of the same sort.

Metaphors are used with varying degrees of figurative commitment. If Clifford is truly and completely seen as a mouse, then the character of his skin, the size and color of his eyes, the quality of his movements, the strength of his moral fiber, as well as countless other things, are known at once, and the whole system of meanings gathered under "mouse" is brought to bear upon poor Clifford—not serially, a step at a time, as in a proof, but wholly, totally, and at once. We need to know, too, how long we are to retain this commitment. Is Clifford a mouse just for the moment, in this line or paragraph, or are we to carry the mouse in our pocket through the entire book? The

Consul, momentarily overcome by something more than mescal, has begun to make love to his wife, yet he is certain of failure already, he thinks of the bar he will flee to. Then:

> This image faded also: he was where he was, sweating now, glancing once—but never ceasing to play the prelude, the little one-fingered introduction to the unclassifiable composition that might still just follow. . . .

The commitment of this image is complete; these, indeed, are opening bars, and as it is morning, soon in peace and silence, the cantinas themselves will open, the Consul will enter one—they are named for their music as much as their mescal—to fashion a song from the rhythms of alcohol.

Metaphors which are deeply committed, which really mean what they say, are systematic—the whole net of relationships matters. But the moment the mind moves through the system establishing certain points of comparison and denying others, then the system is replaced by its interpretation. Each time we refer to someone as a mouse we beat the same path through the concept until at last this path is broad and movement is easy and immediate. The sense of traveling through strange lands is lost, and when we no longer have to hunt for the point of the comparison, we begin, quite justly, to wonder why Clifford wasn't called shy and frightened in the first place; for, of course, Clifford could have been a mouse for every reason, his whole life seen through that system; but this particular metaphor has slid even beyond proportion to comparison—where the metaphor says, in effect, Clifford is like a mouse because both are afraid—until it is nearly a case of catachresis, which has little or no figurative commitment, the word "mouse" being wrongly used to mean someone shy and easily frightened.

We are inclined to think that in metaphors only one term is figurative—"mouse," not "Clifford"—but this inclination should be resisted; it is frequently mistaken. When the Consul plays upon the body of his wife, it's not merely love that's seen as music making (he the performer, his wife the instrument); our understanding of music is also altered,

conceived through love (in this case of an inadequate kind). The terms
are inspecting one another—they interact—the figure is drawn both
ways. Sometimes the metaphor's stress is heavier on one side than
another (as I think it is here), but often the emphasis is nearly equal,
as if we were seeing mice through Clifford. This can be determined
only in context, and of course it would take quite a context to Clifford
a mouse.

I should now like to suggest that the form and method of metaphor
are very much like the form and method of the novel. If metaphor is a
sign of genius, as Aristotle argued, it is because, by means of metaphor,
the artist is able to organize whole areas of human thought and feeling, and to organize them concretely, giving to his model the quality of
sensuous display. But I do not wish to suggest, by the comparisons with
science that I have made, that the value of metaphor lies in its truth, or
in its power to produce those brilliant flashes of dogmatic light which
I believe are called 'insights" among the critics who pursue literature
because they prefer philosophy but will not submit to the rigorous discipline of systematic thought.

If the metaphors in a few lines of poetry can be complex—and they
can intoxicate us as easily as mescal can—consider, for instance, the
rather difficult question Lady Macbeth puts to her husband: "Was the
hope drunk wherein you dressed yourself? Hath it slept since? And
wakes it now, to look so green and pale at what it did so freely?" (try
dressing yourself in drunken clothing—it isn't easy), or the great cry
of Antony: "The hearts that spanieled me at heels, to whom I gave
their wishes, do discandy, melt their sweets on blossoming Caesar; and
this pine is barked that overtopped them all" (where he seems to envy
Caesar's being presently pissed on because pissed on so sweetly)—then
imagine the Oriental deviousness, the rich rearrangements, the endless complications of the novel conceived as I suggest it should be, as
a monumental metaphor, a metaphor we move at length through, the
construction of a mountain with its view, a different, figured history to
stretch beside our own, a brand-new ordering both of the world and our
understanding; for most of us do live under our lives like creatures covered by a sea or shadowed by a mountain, a volcano, its edges deepened
further by ravines.

3

In Mexico, Malcolm Lowry was drunk more than once. Perhaps he tipped himself over in the air as the Consul does at the dying edges of the fair when, pursued by begging children who recognize his condition, he cages himself in the loop-o-plane and turns his dizziness topsy-turvy. The Consul has wobbled away from his conversation with M. Laruelle—a conversation, we learn, which was very likely imaginary—to confront menacing images at every step; and let us pretend that Lowry did so too, that at some festival on the Day of the Dead in Mexico he had himself been held upside down, pipe, pennies, passport falling from his pockets; still, however he might have felt about it, it was not himself, not his soul's debris which now showered from him like a cloud, the cage that contained him was not a confessional, and pipe, pennies, passport were all that fell; he was not, even momentarily, absolved; yet the Consul, so suspended, has this experience, rains more than coins upon the kids below, and his overturning moment, composed with extraordinary vividness and power, takes on a brilliant glow, for by putting a piece of possibly personal experience in such language, Lowry has made a marvelous model for us, concrete in its depiction, abstract in its use, and universal in its significance.

In short, even the apparently literal language of the novel has a figurative function, but in saying so I don't mean to suggest that the riderless horses, the mountains, garden, clouds, and cantinas of *Under the Volcano* are metaphors for mountains, horses, gardens, barrancas, or cantinas in our world, in our Oil Cities or Saint Clouds; for, although details are used, they are escaped—pierced through—and when the Consul falls over in the road, the concreteness of the scene presented should keep us to the concreteness of our own, each immediate and personal yet as shared as breathing, so we don't dare make a mean abstraction of it, crying out as though we were critics: ah, look, the fall of man! oh, feel again the foolish frailties of flesh! or, dear me, how hard life is to mount, how slow to summit! (all such shouts are vulgar and may rouse the Consul from his swoon before the proper words do); rather we see our own life in the same fashion Lowry has envisioned Firmin's; what we take away and keep is the novel's figurative form; we reconceive our own acts in his manner; hear, in our own ears, similar symbolic tones; and finally everything becomes clear—clear, that is, in terms of one quite bent and dirty toenail, since on another toe there might not be Carthaginians in combat, but Buicks broken down, or disgraced angels falling into Indiana. The object of that mousy metaphor was Clifford; the object of every novel is its reader. And when the metaphor is meant, we look for Clifford's tail; and when the metaphor is apt, we find it. The novel does the same thing to us; there is no point it does not touch. Certainly details are different. Clifford hasn't a real tail either. Nor does Hamlet's wind bark. What would make the metaphor if they were just the same?

Yes, our lives are safely different. Why is it then that a novel like *the Volcano* is so easy to enter yet so difficult to endure? No, it is not an image of the human condition. That's far too easy. It does not first address, then mail itself to some abstraction. It does not say the wind is cold, that life is hard, that Clifford is timorous and beastie. Beckett's books do not assert that life's absurd. Does that news pain me? I'm sick already if it does. The novel does not say, it shows; it shows me my life in a figure: it compels me to stare at my toes. I live in a suburb of Cincinnati, yet the Consul's bottled Mexican journey is so skillfully constructed that its image fits me—not just a piece of it with which I may identify, such sympathies rend the fabric, but the whole fantastic dangerous country, the tale in its totality.

How does it feel to be the fore end of a metaphor, especially one so fierce and unrelenting? And how does it work, exactly—this book which takes us into hell? The philosophical explanation is complex. Here I can only suggest it. But you remember how Kant ingeniously solved his problem. Our own minds and our sensory equipment organize our world; it is we who establish these *a priori* connections which we later discover and sometimes describe, mistakenly, as natural laws. We are inveterate model makers, imposing on the pure data of sense a rigorously abstract system. The novelist makes a system for us too, although his is composed of a host of particulars, arranged to comply with esthetic conditions, and it both flatters and dismays us when we look at our own life through it because our life appears holy and beautiful always, even when tragic and ruthlessly fated. Still for us it is only "as if." Small comfort for Clifford, the metaphorical mouse.

I mentioned earlier that the terms of some metaphors interact. If a rose bleeds its petals, as much strange is happening to blood as to rose, and if the weight of Lowry's novel at one end of the seesaw lifts me, I, with my weight at the other, will in a moment lift *it*. Thus when Geoffrey Firmin, who lives upside down—standing in Mexico as though it were China—is swung right side up by the loop-o-plane; when his possessions spill from him, cleansing his pockets; when he thinks with fierce delight: let it go! let everything go!—as all these details, these whirling meanings interpret us, put into our world unique new relations (a hunchbacked Chinese sold the Consul *his* ticket), our right side upness is seen suddenly as drunken and wrong; as we are tipped like him and our cars fall from us, our house in the suburbs, our plastic wives or the hubbies whom we are indentured to; as we are put by Lowry's art beneath the volcano, in the cage of the spin plane, in a dangerous cantina; we, from our side, from our point of view, fulfill Geoffrey Firmin, round him in a way no novel by itself could ever do, and there is a perfect metaphorical interaction between us—just as blood becomes petal-like in my little example; indeed, a triple transformation has occurred, for Malcolm Lowry, desperately drunk once and trapped in Cuernavaca (renamed in the novel for that duck's loud groan), more than once threatened with death by tequila, by mescal many times in a soft dark bar, has created an image for his life too, and conceived it as shaded by a shining volcano.

The novelist may fling his language from him as that First Bang blew the stars, pretend to a distance and blacken each relation; he may claim no acquaintance with garbage cans, say he has never ridden a bicycle, assert he's not once crawled through mud, companion to a gunnysack, and not once waited with a cardboard tree and empty road for anyone, let alone Godot (we should accede to this; he *may* be honest); yet we can be confident that sometime it has been "as if"; that he has placed himself only at a metaphorical distance from his creation, has hidden his face while exposing his privates. On the other hand a novelist like Malcolm Lowry may wear his words next to his skin, keep them as close as underclothing, cry out loudly: this is real, true, honest—this happened to me; yet it will no longer matter, his words will never directly describe him, neither terrors nor torso, love affairs or other follies; for they shall have run away to poetry, free of their father and certain to sin. Only a figurative resemblance can be painted on a toenail.

Although *Under the Volcano* has many flaws, it is strong where most recent novels are weak: it has no fear of feeling. Even our finest contemporary work—that of Beckett and Borges and Barth, for instance—as conscious of metaphoric form as it is, with every part internally and wonderfully related; subtle sometimes as Lowry seldom is; scrupulous to maintain a figurative distance between author, work, and reader, and resisting every effort at literal interpretation; insisting, indeed, upon the artifices of the author; has achieved many morose, acid, and comic effects. Certainly the work of these writers is as challenging as any which fiction affords (I don't mean merely puzzling, but profound); yet they've been led too far toward fancy, as Coleridge called it, neglecting, somewhat, in the forming of their figures, the full responsive reach of their readers, that object (as I take it) of their labors.[2] Their books act on us. We are Clifford, and Clifford is a mouse. Unhappy man. But we are too much a passive term in this relation. Listening to the voice that makes up Beckett's *How It Is* saying,

> take the cord from the sack there's another object tie the neck
> of the sack hang it from my neck knowing I'll need both hands
> or else instinct it's one or the other and away right leg right
> arm push pull ten yards fifteen yards halt

or reading the list of Pierre Menard's visible works with which Borges intends to delight us,

> a) A Symbolist sonnet which appeared twice (with variants) in
> the review *La conque* (issues of March and October 1899).
> b) A monograph on the possibility of constructing a poetic
> vocabulary of concepts which would not be synonyms or
> periphrases of those which make up our everyday language,
> "but rather ideal objects created according to convention and
> essentially designed to satisfy poetic needs" (Nîmes, 1901).
> c) A monograph on "certain connections or affinities" between the
> thought of Descartes, Leibniz and John Wilkins (Nîmes, 1903),

and so on through

s) A manuscript list of verses which owe their efficacy to their punctuation,

we find first our physical condition, and then our mental and creative life (have we missed those heavy allusions to Paul Valéry? not we!) rendered in a figure; yet how difficult it is for us to return that favor, to use our lives, as various as they may appear to be, to enfigure *them*. We stay those whiskered Cliffords mice have seen. Still, perhaps not entirely. Often these things are matters of a little more or a little less. We may be writers or academics with bibliographies of our own; we are certainly acquainted with lists, both shopping and laundry, lists of things to do crossed out as they are done, and it is possible to look at the works of Pierre Menard in the light of our own, reverse our positions. Still, not easy. We've been sent no invitation. In Faulkner, Lowry, and Lawrence, however, or in Bellow and Elkin, this reversal is commanded, and carefully controlled.

When I peer at the web of a spider, I can choose to see there geometry; I can discover sine curves on shells or in love affairs angles of ninety degrees. On the other hand, I can also find shell shapes in my sine curves, sexual sinuosities, my geometry can seem haunted and covered with webbery. Similarly, then, do we intermeet Geoffrey Firmin; not merely on our toenail do we perceive Carthaginians fighting; among the tangles of their arms we notice the toes, feet, limbs, and eyeshines which both watch and reflect them; by means of this metaphorical mutuality, our mountains cross Mexico, our addictions become the former British Consul's.

Models, however, aren't real. And metaphorical models are even less so. Light does not travel in straight lines, we only represent it that way. Nor are all the features of our mathematics features of our data. Twice 25 is 50, but 50 Fahrenheit is not twice warmer than its half. With metaphorical models the discrepancies are even greater. Although the scientific model yields testable results (triangulation does give us the height of the steeple), our fictional conclusions, the inferences we draw there, remain forever in the expanding spaces of the novel. Clifford's eyes are bloodshot and tiny, his face pointed, he has a nose twitch, he continually scurries, then attentively stops. We know what his house looks like; we know how he eats, works, and worries; our attitudes are precisely defined. Have we reduced the image? Is he now a list of such facts? Not at all, for Clifford does not scurry like a man, he scurries like a mouse. And if one says, examining Clifford, you see, he hasn't a nose twitch, your figure is false, the proper reply should be: whoever claimed he had? he simply behaves *as if* he had one. In a metaphor that's meant, the descent to the literal can never be made. And as I've pointed out, when the terms interact, we should begin to see Clifford-like qualities among our friends who are mice.

How comparatively easy it is to capture Clifford, whistle up a sour wind, intoxicate the hopes of the Thane of Cawdor—after all, they're only imaginary, these winds, Thanes, and Cliffords; another matter if we must, with the same metaphor, render Chuck, Frank and Harry, Martha and Lou; fashion a lens to look at these lifetimes, both as lived now and as they may be lived later, in Saint Cloud, Sioux City, or Cincinnati; and achieve, when we can, the reader's ardent whole participation in what has to be a purely conceptual relation, a poetic involvement with language. No wonder the novel is long. No wonder, either, that at the edge of *the Volcano*, the danger is real though its source is a fiction, an image perceived on a drunkard's toenail, for such a book says to each of its readers more than that two mountain chains traverse the republic; it says what Rilke wrote of another work of art, the torso of an archaic Apollo:

> There is no place
> that does not see you. You must change your life.

NOTES

[1] This is very likely the primary meaning of "eager."

[2] It seems to me that this is also true, in the same relative and variable way, of the work of John Hawkes, Donald Barthelme ("The Leading Edge of the Trash Phenomenon"), Robert Coover ("Pricksongs & Descants"), and, of course, Vladimir Nabokov ("Mirror, Mirror").

The Border Trilogy by Cormac McCarthy

DAGOBERTO GILB

My mom, a lively, attractive Mexican woman, married two times (and I'm not numbering the almosts) after she and my father—a marine sergeant in World War II—separated and divorced. With lots of suitors, my mom chose them. She was their trophy and they were proud, which she knew and used to her advantage. She didn't have to work anymore, and she made life a party. They gave us a good place to live, furnished—I remember both times I got a new mattress. They were hardworking men, consumed by their jobs, male-only professions. One time, during a move, she decided to show me a photo. It was the love of her life, a handsome guy, probably Mexican or Mexican-American (she called him Spanish, the euphemism of the time), young, at most twenty-one. Black pants, a white shirt, and holding a guitar. I'm sure they were polished black shoes. He was smiling, and he looked happy. He was as poor as me, she said, as if that explained why he wasn't a husband before my dad.

I mention this because I've thought of Cormac McCarthy as I would a stepfather—or, rather, the men of his novels. They're the fully realized versions of the men my mom might choose, the kind I've had to pay attention to as well. They smoke cigarettes, Camels and boxed Marlboros, they drink but not to get drunk—or only in an understandable crisis. They work dirty and stinky when they work. Being unfaithful is as far away as a college degree. They're believers in these personal religions that we all really know deep down. Laconic or nonverbal, you know they mean it, mean nothing but manly good, that they want what they do to stand for what they say. In other words, they're like John Wayne in his Old West movies—*Rio Bravo*, *She Wore a Yellow Ribbon*, *Fort Apache*, all still high on my favorites list. I even wanted to believe in *The Alamo* because the Duke was in it. When I thought of how I was supposed to be as a man, of course I adopted John Wayne as the model. Likewise, now, when I think of how writers are supposed to be, I think of Cormac McCarthy: don't say anything, don't be flattered by praise or disrupted by criticism, don't read anything they write about you, just do your work, because that's the thing. Which is just about everything I can't seem to do and wish I could.

I have mixed-up feelings about my stepfathers and almosts. They were men who needed an exotic, sensuous, wild, south-of-the-border experience, and the love or loving of a beautiful Mexican woman was wish fulfillment, the envied romance for I'm-a-man status, the gold medal of conquest machismo. It's the going-to-Tahiti story of the rugged West—a beautiful Mexican woman stood as real romantic adventure for them, a story that all the other guys would listen to and think about. They were very proud to speak a little of that Spanish language.

I read McCarthy's Gothic *The Orchard Keeper* when it was given to me many years ago by an El Paso bookstore owner who wanted me to know the writer who'd moved to town. I tried, unsuccessfully, to read *Outer Dark*. I liked the more playful *Suttree*. But *Blood Meridian*, my God, that was a book to study a couple of pages a day. It felt translated from something, maybe Greek: Homeric in both historical scope and literary convention, it was an aorta slash of prose, finely elegiac and gaudily ornate, sumptuous, its blood-and-viscera subject chapping the southwestern-desert frontier, riding hard, surviving implausibly from one end of the West to the other. It's a Comanche massacre of a book, oddly inspiring in the beauty and bounty of its gore, impossible not to compare to great tomes. I can't claim to divine an understanding of its bitter meaning, of the metaphorical human truths those characters, the Kid and the Judge, stood for, but, my mouth open in awe as I read, I didn't really care.

All the Pretty Horses, the first volume in McCarthy's Border Trilogy, did not shift the swath of territory of *Blood Meridian* but did its tone, with a sweet, sad story line: John Grady Cole, the sixteen-year-old boy who loves horses, raised bilingual because of the maid Luisa and Abuela (her grandmother), disappointed that his mother won't give or sell him the family ranch in San Angelo, rides his horse south, toward the border, with his friend Lacey Rawlins. They stop for good old ham and beans and biscuits on their way across the floodplain and along fence lines and through pasturelands, shooting and gutting rabbits and building campfires and drinking coffee black. They pick up a younger boy, Jimmy Blevins, who's more trouble than they can account for as they hit the river—crossing the Rio Grande, that baptismal breach, on the other side of which, in sultry and violent Mexico, lay all initiation rites unto manhood for these brave boys, milk- and cow-fattened with the lore of the American West. John Grady falls in love with a girl— and she with him—too rich: a doomed love, one that never could be, was never meant to be.

I had to stop reading when it hit that beautiful Mexican girl riding an Arabian. Put the book away for a long time. I think I told you about my mother. One of the things that one stepfather really liked, decades before it became as popular and well known as ketchup, was that Mexican salsa she could make. In fact, my mom bought it at a store in a can. I saw her pouring it into a bowl once. We both cracked up. At the time, my mom didn't know how to cook so well. That was the marriage that didn't last long.

The Crossing, the story of Billy Parham and his brother, Boyd, is the second installment in the Border Trilogy and a compendium of mythic Westernalia, descriptions of which might be the best ever written: wolves and Indians, bullets, urine for setting traps, squalls of coyotes. Billy feels remorse for crippling one lone wolf ("from another world entire"), her leg maimed in a sprung trap, so he ropes and walks her to Mexico to set her free, encountering all sorts of brutal carnivalesque characters, dogfights, rifles out of scabbards (something about that makes those my favorite words—"rifle out of scabbard"—don't you feel and hear the hollow scrape, the steel against leather? Gives me boyhood goose bumps!), until he has to shoot his now pet wolf to save her. Tasting her blood, which tastes like his, he buries her high in the mountains. Going north, he passes more Indians in wickiups and caves, and bad and good Mexicans, and once crossed back, he finds his childhood home abandoned; he and his brother are orphans, their parents viciously slaughtered by an Indian they befriended, so they become "outlaws" on a dangerous hunt across the wild border to steal their own horses. Billy's brother is killed in the adventure, and he feels a responsibility to take the body home. Sharing black coffee at a campsite, in the darkness, a wise and articulate Yaqui Indian with hardened decency, Quijada, talking of a Mexican *corrido* (ballad) about a *güerito*, explains its meaning—sounding to me a little bit like a definition of McCarthy's literary romanticism:

> The corrido tells all and it tells nothing. . . . It tells what it wishes to tell. It tells what makes the story run. . . . It does not owe its allegiance to the truths of history but to the truths of men. It tells the tale of that solitary man who is all men.

Quijada, musing philosophically, still believes that the brother should be left behind: "I think the dead have no nationality." Billy, almost following the marine credo, will not abandon him there in Mexico. "But their kin do," he tells Quijada. Alone in life now, Billy has grown up, and he is going home with his well-earned maturity and masculinity— taking, no doubt, that souvenir *corrido* with him.

Cities of the Plain, McCarthy's final volume in the trilogy, puts John Grady Cole and Billy Parham together, three years older, working a cattle ranch north of El Paso and south of Alamogordo. They're stomping mud from their boots and shaking off a little monsoon rain and hanging hats on wood pegs. They go whorehousing in Juárez and do some whiskey shooting (which should be one word, too), backing that up with some cold beer. In the morning, in the bunkhouse, after they down some coffee, black, after they eat the ranch cook Socorro's eggs with *pico de gallo*, after they "pass the salsa yonder," they mount their horses and round up stray calves, crossing paths with coyotes. ("What do you reckon he's doin out here in the middle of the day?" "He probably wonders the same about you.") They're in and out of the tack room (which is so very cool). They see deer and talk jackrabbits and owls and mountain lions and rope wild dogs, saving the pups of one of them. They break horses. John Grady, the lead in this volume, is especially stubborn about one that's thrown him. She's a fine horse. He knows horses as he knows himself as we know metaphors.

> I think you can train a rooster to do what you want. But you
> wont have him. There's a way to train a horse where when
> you get done you've got the horse. On his own ground. A good
> horse will figure things out on his own. You can see what's in
> his heart. He wont do one thing while you're watchin him and
> another when you aint. He's all of a piece. When you've got a
> horse to that place you cant hardly get him to do somethin he
> knows is wrong. He'll fight you over it. And if you mistreat him
> it just about kills him. A good horse has justice in his heart.

John Grady Cole has fallen in love with a Juárez whore who works at the White Lake. She's sweet and she's beautiful. Innocent. She's young, seventeen or even younger, stolen away from her home in Chiapas. She has grand mal epileptic seizures. And her name is Magdalena. (Since I never have nor will in the future, please let me write that again: And her name is Magdalena.) John Grady wants and intends to marry her. To visit her and propose, he gets an advance from his boss, Mac. To buy her freedom, he sells that horse. He restores an old shack at the other end of the ranch to make their marital home. But Eduardo, her boss, her pimp, loves her, too, and he is not very interested in selling her or letting her get away. A doomed love. John Grady has a knife scar across his cheek from his days in prison back in *All the Pretty Horses*, when he fought a *pachuco cuchillero* (one of the many badass words I loved saying out loud, imaging any setting I'd be in: See that dude over there? A *cuchillero*. Imagine it better: a *zacateco cuchillero*). (McCarthy's use—a lot, too—of untranslated Spanish is always good. It has never been considered equally exotic or decorative or literary for Chicano writers to do anything similar, but, ironically, only irritating. I think that's because of the English-only fear, which is not a worry in the work of McCarthy, whose main characters drawl.) John Grady and Eduardo meet for a life-and-death fight, exquisitely rendered. The final chapter of the trilogy closes, philosophically, in El Paso.

I was drawn into this book, and not only because so much of it was set in El Paso and the region around her, in cities and streets I know well. Years ago, the White Lake was one of my favorite bars to take out-of-town visitors, not because its prostitutes were beautiful but because they weren't in the slightest—think of a cook in a hair net at an elementary school cafeteria, who's been there many years, extra pounds per year, assembling Wednesday's enchiladas with rice and beans. I was drawn to the trilogy not only because it is so much fun to imagine, through literature, every boyhood nature and gun and knife and whiskey and woman cowboy fantasy ever lived or subliminally conceived. I was drawn not only because I love John Wayne movies, this trilogy being the best John Wayne western ever written. It's the prose. Does anybody know how to do this better? At once complex and simple, erudite and common, inverted and invented, a prose that is Cormac McCarthy:

> They set off across the open tableland with their ropes popping and loud cries, leaning low in the saddle, riding neck and neck. In a mile they'd halved the dogs' lead. The dogs kept to the mesa and the mesa widened before them. If they'd kept to the rim they might have found a place to go down again where the horses could not follow but they seemed to think they could outrun anything that cared to follow and run they did, two of them side by side and the third behind, their long dogshadows beside them in the sun racing brokenly over the sparse taupe grass of the tableland.

It is this archprose that vaults his work so far above the genre western and its popular writers, the late Louis L'Amour and the San Angelo writer touted to be his inheritor, Elmer Kelton, Texas's favorite.

It's also Mexico, that subterranean appeal it makes on the American psyche, coming from a source who knows of it well but is not of it.

It's crossing the frontera into that unknowable land and encountering its inscrutable people, where life is lived and not settled on—or so the mythology would have it.

> "Dont you think if there's anything left of this life it's down there?" "Maybe." "You like it too." "Yeah? I dont even know what this life is. I damn sure dont know what Mexico is. I think it's in your head. Mexico. I rode a lot of ground down there. The first ranchera you hear sung you understand the whole country. By the time you've heard a hundred you dont know nothin. You never will."

Mexico, with its mysteries of violence and love. Where an American boy becomes an American man and, once through, after his passage, rocking on his front-porch chair where few if any Mexicans or descendants live, has some stories to tell.

I remember the first time the awareness of a uniquely literary delusion caught me. I'd been rereading Tolstoy. I'd loved Tolstoy, and, just as I was supposed to, I identified with his main characters, took these trips from one part of Russia to another, maybe Kiev to Moscow, Germany to France and back, considered these journeys we all traveled if we pursued art and intelligence and wisdom. But on the reread, in my thirties, I realized I did not take these trips, and that the characters actually did, because they were rich, that if I'd been around these people, I'd be hanging back at one of those summer or winter homes, picking their cherries. I'd be a minor character, mentioned for the same purpose as a piano. My metaphorical story would be about staying and working and would be the length of a poem, not as exciting as that of the people who lived in the big house, who came and went, riding, too, in horse-drawn carriages. Before I picked up McCarthy, I had just reread Gabriel Garcia Márquez's *One Hundred Years of Solitude*, a story situated farther south of the Mexican border but with bizarre and exotic happenings, love and birth and death and sex. I didn't flinch or sigh once. But it's not a western, and westerns are supposed to have gunfights and knife fights and tack rooms and such, and I got over it. I do love John Wayne movies. Did you know that he married a Mexican woman?

"The Metamorphosis"

VLADIMIR NABOKOV

Of course, no matter how keenly, how admirably, a story, a piece of music, a picture is discussed and analyzed, there will be minds that remain blank and spines that remain unkindled. "To take upon us the mystery of things"—what King Lear so wistfully says for himself and for Cordelia—this is also my suggestion for everyone who takes art seriously. A poor man is robbed of his overcoat (Gogol's "The Greatcoat," or more correctly "The Carrick"); another poor fellow is turned into a beetle (Kafka's "The Metamorphosis")—so what? There is no rational answer to "so what." We can take the story apart, we can find out how the bits fit, how one part of the pattern responds to the other; but you have to have in you some cell, some gene, some germ that will vibrate in answer to sensations that you can neither define, nor dismiss. *Beauty plus pity*—that is the closest we can get to a definition of art. Where there is beauty there is pity for the simple reason that beauty must die: beauty always dies, the manner dies with the matter, the world dies with the individual. If Kafka's "The Metamorphosis" strikes anyone as something more than an entomological fantasy, then I congratulate him on having joined the ranks of good and great readers.

I want to discuss fantasy and reality, and their mutual relationship. If we consider the "Dr. Jekyll and Mr. Hyde" story as an allegory—the struggle between Good and Evil within every man—then this allegory is tasteless and childish. To the type of mind that would see an allegory here, its shadow play would also postulate physical happenings which common sense knows to be impossible; but actually in the setting of the story, as viewed by a commonsensical mind, nothing at first sight seems to run counter to general human experience. I want to suggest, however, that a second look shows that the setting of the story does run counter to general human experience, and that Utterson and the other men around Jekyll are, in a sense, as fantastic as Mr. Hyde. Unless we see them in a fantastic light, there is no enchantment. And if the enchanter leaves and the storyteller and the teacher remain alone together, they make poor company.

The story of Jekyll and Hyde is beautifully constructed, but it is an old one. Its moral is preposterous since neither good nor evil is actually depicted: on the whole, they are taken for granted, and the struggle goes on between two empty outlines. The enchantment lies in the art of Stevenson's fancywork; but I want to suggest that since art and thought, manner and matter, are inseparable, there must be something of the same kind about the structure of the story, too. Let us be cautious, however. I still think that there is a flaw in the artistic realization of the story—if we consider form and content separately—a flaw which is missing in Gogol's "The Carrick" and in Kafka's "The Metamorphosis." The fantastic side of the setting—Utterson, Enfield, Poole, Lanyon, and their London—is not of the same quality as the fantastic side of Jekyll's hydization. There is a crack in the picture, a lack of unity.

"The Carrick," "Dr. Jekyll and Mr. Hyde," and "The Metamorphosis": all three are commonly called fantasies. From my point of view, any outstanding work of art is a fantasy insofar as it reflects the unique world of a unique individual. But when people call these three stories fantasies, they merely imply that the stories depart in their subject matter from what is commonly called reality. Let us therefore examine what *reality* is, in order to discover in what manner and to what extent so-called fantasies depart from so-called reality.

Let us take three types of men walking through the same landscape. Number One is a city man on a well-deserved vacation. Number Two is a professional botanist. Number Three is a local farmer. Number One, the city man, is what is called a realistic, commonsensical, matter-of-fact type: he sees trees as *trees* and knows from his map that the road he is following is a nice new road leading to Newton, where there is a nice eating place recommended to him by a friend in his office. The botanist looks around and sees his environment in the very exact terms of plant life, precise biological and classified units such as specific trees and grasses, flowers and ferns, and for him *this* is reality; to him the world of the stolid tourist (who cannot distinguish an oak from an elm) seems a fantastic, vague, dreamy, never-never world. Finally, the world of the local farmer differs from the two others in that his world is intensely emotional and personal since he has been born and bred there, and knows every trail and individual tree, and every shadow from every tree across every trail, all in warm connection with his everyday work, and his childhood, and a thousand small things and patterns which the other two—the humdrum tourist and the botanical taxonomist—simply cannot know in the given place at the given time. Our farmer will not know the relation of the surrounding vegetation to a botanical conception of the world, and the botanist will know nothing of any importance to him about that barn or that old field or that old house under its cottonwoods, which are afloat, as it were, in a medium of personal memories for one who was born there.

So here we have three different worlds—three men, ordinary men who have different *realities*—and, of course, we could bring in a number of other beings: a blind man with a dog, a hunter with a dog, a dog with his man, a painter cruising in quest of a sunset, a girl out of gas—— In every case it would be a world completely different from the rest since the most objective words *tree, road, flower, sky, barn, thumb, rain* have, in each, totally different subjective connotations. Indeed, this subjective life is so strong that it makes an empty and broken shell of the so-called objective existence. The only way back to objective reality is the following one: we can take these several individual worlds, mix them thoroughly together, scoop up a drop of that mixture, and call it *objective reality*. We may taste in it a particle of madness if a lunatic passed through that locality, or a particle of complete and beautiful nonsense if a man has been looking at a lovely field and imagining upon it a lovely factory producing buttons or bombs; but on the whole these mad particles would be diluted in the drop of objective reality that we hold up to the light in our test tube. Moreover, this *objective reality* will contain something that transcends optical illusions and laboratory tests. It will have elements of poetry, of lofty emotion, of energy and endeavor (and even here the button king may find his rightful place), of pity, pride, passion—and the craving for a thick steak at the recommended roadside eating place.

So when we say *reality*, we are really thinking of all this—in one drop—an average sample of a mixture of a million individual realities. And it is in this sense (of human reality) that I use the term *reality* when placing it against a backdrop, such as the worlds of "The Carrick," "Dr. Jekyll and Mr. Hyde," and "The Metamorphosis," which are specific fantasies.

In "The Carrick" and in "The Metamorphosis" there is a central figure endowed with a certain amount of human pathos among grotesque, heartless characters, figures of fun or figures of horror, asses parading as zebras, or hybrids between rabbits and rats. In "The Carrick" the human quality of the central figure is of a different type from Gregor in Kafka's story, but this human pathetic quality is present in both. In "Dr. Jekyll and Mr. Hyde" there is no such human pathos, no throb in the throat of the story, none of that intonation of "'I cannot get out, I cannot get out,' said the starling" (so heartrending in Sterne's fantasy *A Sentimental Journey*). True, Stevenson devotes many pages to the horror of Jekyll's plight, but the thing, after all, is only a superb Punch-and-Judy show. The beauty of Kafka's and Gogol's private nightmares is that their central human characters belong to the same private fantastic world as the inhuman characters around them, but the central one tries to get out of that world, to cast off the mask, to transcend the cloak or the carapace. But in Stevenson's story there is none of that unity and none of that contrast. The Uttersons, and Pooles, and Enfields are meant to be commonplace everyday characters; actually they are characters derived from Dickens, and thus they constitute phantasms that do not quite belong to Stevenson's own artistic reality, just as Stevenson's fog comes from a

Dickensian studio to envelop a conventional London. I suggest, in fact, that Jekyll's magic drug is more real than Utterson's life. The fantastic Jekyll-and-Hyde theme, on the other hand, is supposed to be in contrast to this conventional London, but it is really the difference between a Gothic medieval theme and a Dickensian one. It is not the same kind of difference as that between an absurd world and pathetically absurd Bashmachkin, or between an absurd world and tragically absurd Gregor.

The Jekyll-and-Hyde theme does not quite form a unity with its setting because its fantasy is of a different type from the fantasy of the setting. There is really nothing especially pathetic or tragic about Jekyll. We enjoy every detail of the marvellous juggling, of the beautiful trick, but there is no artistic emotional throb involved, and whether it is Jekyll or Hyde who gets the upper hand remains of supreme indifference to the good reader. I am speaking of rather nice distinctions, and it is difficult to put them in simple form. When a certain clear-thinking but somewhat superficial French philosopher asked the profound but obscure German philosopher Hegel to state his views in a concise form, Hegel answered him harshly, "These things can be discussed neither concisely nor in French." We shall ignore the question whether Hegel was right or not, and still try to put into a nutshell the difference between the Gogol-Kafka kind of story and Stevenson's kind.

In Gogol and Kafka the absurd central character belongs to the absurd world around him but, pathetically and tragically, attempts to struggle out of it into the world of humans—and dies in despair. In Stevenson the unreal central character belongs to a brand of unreality different from that of the world around him. He is a Gothic character in a Dickensian setting, and when he struggles and then dies, his fate possesses only conventional pathos. I do not at all mean that Stevenson's story is a failure. No, it is a minor masterpiece in its own conventional terms, but it has only two dimensions, whereas the Gogol-Kafka stories have five or six.

—————◆————

Born in 1883, Franz Kafka came from a German-speaking Jewish family in Prague, Czechoslovakia. He is the greatest German writer of our time. Such poets as Rilke or such novelists as Thomas Mann are dwarfs or plaster saints in comparison to him. He read for law at the German university in Prague and from 1908 on he worked as a petty clerk, a small employee, in a very Gogolian office for an insurance company. Hardly any of his now famous works, such as his novels *The Trial* (1925) and *The Castle* (1926), were published in his lifetime. His greatest short story "The Metamorphosis," in German "Die Verwandlung," was written in the fall of 1912 and published in Leipzig in October 1915. In 1917 he coughed blood, and the rest of his life, a period of seven years, was punctuated by sojourns in Central European sanatoriums. In those last years of his short life (he died at the age of forty-one), he had a happy love affair and lived with his mistress in Berlin, in 1923, not far from me. In the spring of 1924 he went to a sanatorium near Vienna where he died on 3 June, of tuberculosis of the larynx. He was buried in the Jewish cemetery in Prague. He asked his friend Max Brod to burn everything he had written, even published material. Fortunately Brod did not comply with his friend's wish.

Before starting to talk of "The Metamorphosis," I want to dismiss two points of view. I want to dismiss completely Max Brod's opinion that the category of sainthood, not that of literature, is the only one that can be applied to the understanding of Kafka's writings. Kafka was first of all an artist, and although it may be maintained that every artist is a manner of saint (I feel that very clearly myself), I do not think that any religious implications can be read into Kafka's genius. The other matter that I want to dismiss is the Freudian point of view. His Freudian biographers, like Neider in *The Frozen Sea* (1948), contend, for example, that "The Metamorphosis" has a basis in Kafka's complex relationship with his father and his lifelong sense of guilt; they contend further that in mythical symbolism children are represented by vermin—which I doubt—and then go on to say that Kafka uses the symbol of the bug to represent the son according to these Freudian postulates. The bug, they say, aptly characterizes his sense of worthlessness before his father. I am interested here in bugs, not in humbugs, and I reject this nonsense. Kafka himself was extremely critical of Freudian ideas. He considered psychoanalysis (I quote) "a helpless error," and he regarded Freud's theories as very approximate, very rough pictures, which did not do justice to details or, what is more, to the essence of the matter. This is another reason why I should like to dismiss the Freudian approach and concentrate, instead, upon the artistic moment.

The greatest literary influence upon Kafka was Flaubert's. Flaubert who loathed pretty-pretty prose would have applauded Kafka's attitude towards his tool. Kafka liked to draw his terms from the language of law and science, giving them a kind of ironic precision, with no intrusion of the author's private sentiments; this was exactly Flaubert's method through which he achieved a singular poetic effect.

The hero of "The Metamorphosis" is Gregor Samsa (pronounced *Zamza*), who is the son of middle-class parents in Prague, Flaubertian philistines, people interested only in the material side of life and vulgarians in their tastes. Some five years before, old Samsa lost most of his money, whereupon his son Gregor took a job with one of his father's creditors and became a traveling salesman in cloth. His father then stopped working altogether, his sister Grete was too young to work, his mother was ill with asthma; thus young Gregor not only supported the whole family but also found for them the apartment they are now living in. This apartment, a flat in an apartment house, in Charlotte Street to be exact, is divided into segments as he will be divided himself. We are in Prague, central Europe, in the year 1912; servants are cheap so that the Samsas can afford a servant maid, Anna, aged sixteen (one year younger than Grete), and a cook. Gregor is mostly away traveling, but when the story starts he is spending a night at home between two business trips, and it is then that the dreadful thing happened. "As Gregor Samsa awoke one morning from a troubled dream he found himself transformed in his bed into a monstrous insect. He was lying on his hard, as it were armor-plated, back and when he lifted his head a little he could see his dome-like brown belly divided into corrugated segments on top of which the bed quilt could hardly keep in position and was about to slide off completely. His numerous legs, which were pitifully thin compared to the rest of his bulk, flimmered [*flicker + shimmer*] helplessly before his eyes.

"What has happened to me? he thought. It was no dream. . . .

Nabokov's sketch of the layout of the Samsa flat

"Gregor's eyes turned next to the window—one could hear rain drops beating on the tin of the windowsill's outer edge and the dull weather made him quite melancholy. What about sleeping a little longer and forgetting all this nonsense, he thought, but it could not be done, for he was accustomed to sleep on his right side and in his present condition he could not turn himself over. However violently he tried to

hurl himself on his right side he always swung back to the supine position. He tried it at least a hundred times, shutting his eyes to keep from
seeing his wriggly legs, and only desisted when he began to feel in his
side a faint dull ache he had never experienced before.

"Ach Gott, he thought, what an exhausting job I've picked on!
Traveling about day in, day out. Many more anxieties on the road than
in the office, the plague of worrying about train connections, the bad
and irregular meals, casual acquaintances never to be seen again, never
to become intimate friends. The hell with it all! He felt a slight itching on the skin of his belly; slowly pushed himself on his back nearer
the top of the bed so that he could lift his head more easily; identified
the itching place which was covered with small white dots the nature
of which he could not understand and tried to touch it with a leg, but
drew the leg back immediately, for the contact made a cold shiver run
through him."

Now what exactly is the "vermin" into which poor Gregor, the seedy
commercial traveler, is so suddenly transformed? It obviously belongs
to the branch of "jointed leggers" (*Arthropoda*), to which insects, and
spiders, and centipedes, and crustaceans belong. If the "numerous little legs" mentioned in the beginning mean more than six legs, then
Gregor would not be an insect from a zoological point of view. But I
suggest that a man awakening on his back and finding he has as many
as six legs vibrating in the air might feel that six was sufficient to be
called numerous. We shall therefore assume that Gregor has six legs,
that he is an insect.

Next question: what insect? Commentators say *cockroach*, which of
course does not make sense. A cockroach is an insect that is flat in shape
with large legs, and Gregor is anything but flat: he is convex on both
sides, belly and back, and his legs are small. He approaches a cockroach
in only one respect: his coloration is brown. That is all. Apart from this
he has a tremendous convex belly divided into segments and a hard
rounded back suggestive of wing cases. In beetles these cases conceal
flimsy little wings that can be expanded and then may carry the beetle
for miles and miles in a blundering flight. Curiously enough, Gregor
the beetle never found out that he had wings under the hard covering
of his back. (This is a very nice observation on my part to be treasured

all your lives. Some Gregors, some Joes and Janes, do not know that they have wings.) Further, he has strong mandibles. He uses these organs to turn the key in a lock while standing erect on his hind legs, on his third pair of legs (a strong little pair), and this gives us the length of his body, which is about three feet long. In the course of the story he gets gradually accustomed to using his new appendages—his feet, his feelers. This brown, convex, dog-sized beetle is very broad. I should imagine him to look like this:

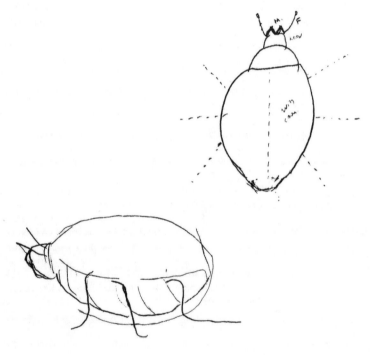

In the original German text the old charwoman calls him *Mistkafer*, a "dung beetle." It is obvious that the good woman is adding the epithet only to be friendly. He is not, technically, a dung beetle. He is merely a big beetle. (I must add that neither Gregor nor Kafka saw that beetle any too clearly.)

Let us look closer at the transformation. The change, though shocking and striking, is not quite so odd as might be assumed at first glance.

A commonsensical commentator (Paul L. Landsberg in *The Kafka Problem* [1946], ed. Angel Flores) notes that "When we go to bed in unfamiliar surroundings, we are apt to have a moment of bewilderment upon awakening, a sudden sense of unreality, and this experience must occur over and over again in the life of a commercial traveller, a manner of living that renders impossible any sense of continuity." The sense of reality depends upon continuity, upon duration. After all, awakening as an insect is not much different from awakening as Napoleon or George Washington. (I knew a man who awoke as the Emperor of Brazil.) On the other hand, the isolation, and the strangeness, of so-called reality— this is, after all, something which constantly characterizes the artist, the genius, the discoverer. The Samsa family around the fantastic insect is nothing else than mediocrity surrounding genius.

PART ONE

I am now going to speak of structure. Part one of the story can be divided into seven scenes or segments:

Scene I: Gregor wakes up. He is alone. He has already been changed into a beetle, but his human impressions still mingle with his new insect instincts. The scene ends with the introduction of the still human time element.

"He looked at the alarm clock ticking on the chest. Good Lord! he thought. It was half-past six and the hands were quietly moving on, it was even past the half-hour, it was getting on toward a quarter to seven. Had the alarm clock not gone off? . . . The next train went at seven o'clock; to catch that he would need to hurry like mad and his samples weren't even packed up, and he himself wasn't feeling particularly fresh and active. And even if he did catch the train he wouldn't avoid a row with the boss, since the firm's messenger would have been waiting for the five o'clock train and would have long since reported his failure to turn up." He thinks of reporting that he is sick, but concludes that the insurance doctor would certify him as perfectly healthy. "And would he be so far wrong on this occasion? Gregor really felt quite well, apart from a drowsiness that was utterly superfluous after such a long sleep, and he was even unusually hungry."

Scene II: The three members of the family knock on his doors and talk to him from, respectively, the hallway, the living room, and his sister's room. Gregor's family are his parasites, exploiting him, eating him out from the inside. This is his beetle itch in human terms. The pathetic urge to find some protection from betrayal, cruelty, and filth is the factor that went to form his carapace, his beetle shell, which at first seems hard and secure but eventually is seen to be as vulnerable as his sick human flesh and spirit had been. Who of the three parasites—father, mother, sister—is the most cruel? At first it would seem to be the father. But he is not the worst: it is the sister, whom Gregor loves most but who betrays him beginning with the furniture scene in the middle of the story. In the second scene the door theme begins: "there came a cautious tap at the door behind the head of his bed. 'Gregor,' said a voice—it was his mother's—'it's a quarter to seven. Hadn't you a train to catch?' That gentle voice! Gregor had a shock as he heard his own voice answering hers, unmistakably his own voice, it was true, but with a persistent pitiful squeaky undertone. . . . 'Yes, yes, thank you, Mother, I'm getting up now.' The wooden door between them must have kept the change in his voice from being noticeable outside. . . . Yet this brief exchange of words had made the other members of the family aware that Gregor was still in the house, as they had nor expected, and at one of the side doors his father was already knocking gently, yet with his fist. 'Gregor, Gregor,' he called, 'what's the matter with you?' And after a while he called again in a deeper voice: 'Gregor! Gregor!' At the other side door his sister was saying in a low, plaintive tone: 'Gregor? Aren't you well? Do you need anything?' He answered them both at once: 'I'm just ready,' and did his best to make his voice sound as normal as possible by enunciating the words very clearly and leaving long pauses between them. So his father went back to his breakfast, but his sister whispered: 'Gregor, open the door, do.' However, he was not thinking of opening the door, and felt thankful for the prudent habit he had acquired in traveling of locking all doors during the night, even at home."

Scene III: The getting out of bed ordeal in which man plans but beetle acts. Gregor still thinks of his body in human terms, but now a human's lower part is a beetle's hind part, a human's upper part is a beetle's fore part. A man on all fours seems to him to correspond to a beetle on all sixes. He does not quite yet understand this and will persistently try to stand up on his third pair of legs. "He thought that he might get out of bed with the lower part of his body first, but this lower part, which he had not yet seen and of which he could form no clear conception, proved too difficult to move; it was all so slow; and when at last almost savagely he gathered his forces together and thrust out recklessly, he had miscalculated the direction and bumped heavily against the lower end of the bed, and the burning pain he felt taught him that it was the lower part of his body that probably for the time being was the most sensitive. . . . But then he said to himself: 'Before it strikes a quarter past seven I must be quite out of this bed, without fail. Anyhow, by that time someone will have come from the office to ask what is the matter with me, since it opens before seven.' And he set himself to rocking his whole body at once in a regular series of jolts, with the idea of swinging it out of the bed. If he tipped himself out in that way he could keep his head from injury by lifting it at an acute angle when he fell. His back seemed to be hard and was not likely to suffer from a fall on the carpet. His biggest worry was the loud crash he would not be able to help making, which would probably cause anxiety, if not terror, behind all the doors. Still, he must take the risk. . . . Well, ignoring the fact that the doors were all locked, ought he really to call for help? In spite of his misery he could not suppress a smile at the very idea of it."

Scene IV: He is still struggling when the family theme, or the theme of the many doors, takes over again, and in the course of this scene he falls out of bed at last, with a dull thud. The conversation is a little on the lines of a Greek chorus. From Gregor's office the head clerk has been sent to see why he has not yet turned up at the station. This grim speed in checking a remiss employee has all the qualities of a bad dream. The speaking through doors, as in the second scene, is now repeated. Note the sequence: the chief clerk talks to Gregor from the living room on the left; Gregor's sister, Grete, talks to her brother from the room on the right; the mother and father join the chief clerk in the living room. Gregor can still speak, but his voice becomes more and more indistinct, and soon his speech cannot be understood. (In *Finnegans Wake*, written twenty years later by James Joyce, two washerwomen talking across a river are gradually changed into a stout elm and a stone.) Gregor does not understand why his sister in the right-hand room did not join the others. "She was probably newly out of bed and hadn't even begun to put on her clothes yet. Well, why was she crying? Because he wouldn't get up and let the chief clerk in, because he was in danger of losing his job, and because the boss would begin dunning his parents again for the old debts?" Poor Gregor is so accustomed to be just an instrument to be used by his family that the question of pity does not arise: he does not even hope that Grete might be sorry for him. Mother and sister call to each other from the doors across Gregor's room. The sister and servant are dispatched for a doctor and a locksmith. "But Gregor was now much calmer. The words he uttered were no longer understandable, apparently, although they seemed clear enough to him, even clearer than before, perhaps because his ear had grown accustomed to the sound of them. Yet at any rate people now believed that something was wrong with him, and were ready to help him. The positive certainty with which these first measures had been taken comforted him. He felt himself drawn once more into the human circle and hoped for great and remarkable results from both the doctor and the locksmith, without really distinguishing precisely between them."

Scene V: Gregor opens the door. "Slowly Gregor pushed the chair towards the door, then let go of it, caught hold of the door for support—the soles at the end of his little legs were somewhat sticky—and rested against it for a moment after his efforts. Then he set himself to turning the key in the lock with his mouth. It seemed, unhappily, that he hadn't really any teeth—what could he grip the key with?—but on the other hand his jaws were certainly very strong; with their help he did manage to set the key in motion, heedless of the fact that he was undoubtedly damaging them somewhere, since a brown fluid issued from his mouth, flowed over the key and dripped on the floor. . . . Since he had to pull the door towards him, he was still invisible when it was really wide open. He had to edge himself slowly round the near half of the double door, and to do it very carefully if he was not to fall plump upon his back just on the threshold. He was still carrying out this difficult manoeuvre, with no time to observe anything else, when he heard the chief clerk utter a loud 'Oh!'—it sounded like a gust of wind—and now he could see the man, standing as he was nearest to the door, clapping one hand before his open mouth and slowly backing away as if driven by some invisible steady pressure. His mother—in spite of the chief clerk's being there her hair was still undone and sticking up in all directions—first clasped her hands and looked at his father, then took two steps towards Gregor and fell on the floor among her outspread skirts, her face quite hidden on her breast. His father knotted his fist with a fierce expression on his face as if he meant to knock Gregor back into his room, then looked uncertainly round the living room, covered his eyes with his hands and wept till his great chest heaved."

Scene VI: Gregor tries to calm the chief clerk so that he will not be discharged. "'Well,' said Gregor, knowing perfectly that he was the only one who had retained any composure, 'I'll put my clothes on at once, pack up my samples and start off. Will you only let me go? You see, sir, I'm not obstinate, and I'm willing to work; traveling is a hard life, but I couldn't live without it. Where are you going, sir? To the office? Yes? Will you give a true account of all this? One can be temporarily incapacitated, but that's just the moment for remembering former services and bearing in mind that later on, when the incapacity has been got over, one will certainly work with all the more industry and concentration." But the chief clerk in horror and as if in a trance is stumbling towards the staircase to escape. Gregor starts to walk towards him—a wonderful bit here—on the hind pair of his three pairs of legs, "but immediately, as he was feeling for a support, he fell down with a little cry upon his many little legs. Hardly was he down when he experienced for the first time this morning a sense of physical comfort; his legs had firm ground under them; they were completely obedient, as he noted with joy; they even strove to carry him forward in whatever direction he chose; and he was inclined to believe that a final relief from all his sufferings was at hand." His mother springs up, and in backing away from him she upsets the coffeepot on the breakfast table so that it pours over the rug. "'Mother, Mother,' said Gregor in a low voice, and looked up at her. The chief clerk, for the moment, had quite slipped from his mind; instead, he could not resist snapping his jaws together at the sight of the streaming coffee. That made his mother scream again." Gregor, looking now for the chief clerk, "made a spring, to be as sure as possible of overtaking him; the chief clerk must have divined his intention, for he leaped down several steps and vanished; he was still yelling 'Ugh!' and it echoed through the whole staircase."

Scene VII: The father brutally drives Gregor back into his room, stamping his feet and flourishing a stick in one hand and a newspaper in the other. Gregor has difficulty getting through the partly opened door, but forced by his father he tries until he gets stuck. "One side of his body rose up, he was tilted at an angle in the doorway, his flank was quite bruised, horrid blotches stained the white door, soon he was stuck fast and, left to himself, could not have moved at all, his legs on one side fluttered trembling in the air, those on the other were crushed painfully to the floor—when from behind his father gave him a strong push which was literally a deliverance and he flew far into the room, bleeding freely. The father caught at the handle of the door with the stick and slammed it behind him, and then at last there was silence."

PART TWO

Scene I: The first attempt is made to feed coleopteron Gregor. Under the impression that his condition is some kind of foul but not hopeless illness that may pass with time, he is placed at first on the diet of a sick human being and he finds that a human meal of milk has been offered to him. We are always aware of those doors, doors opening and closing stealthily in the dusk. From the kitchen, across the hallway, to the hallway door of Gregor's room light footsteps had come, his sister's, awakening him from sleep, and he discovers that a basin with milk has been placed within his room. One of his little legs has been damaged in the collision with his father; it will grow better, but in this scene he limps and trails it uselessly behind him. He is a big beetle as beetles go, but he is smaller and more brittle than a human being. Gregor makes for the milk. Alas, while his still human mind eagerly accepts the notion of that sweetish sop, with soft white bread in the milk, his beetle stomach and beetle taste buds refuse a mammal's meal. Although he is very hungry the milk is repulsive to him and he crawls back to the middle of the room.

Scene II: The door theme continues and the duration theme settles in. We shall begin to witness Gregor's usual day and dusk during this fantastic winter of 1912, and his discovery of the security of the couch. But let us look and listen with Gregor through the crack of the parlor door on the left. His father used to read aloud the newspapers to his wife and daughter. True, this has now been interrupted and the flat is silent though not empty of occupants, but on the whole the family is getting used to the situation. Here is the son and brother plunged into a monstrous change that should have sent them scuttling out into the streets for help with shrieks and tears, in wild compassion—but here they are, the three philistines, cosily taking it in their stride.

I don't know if you read a couple of years ago in the papers about that teenage girl and boy who murdered the girl's mother. It starts with a very Kafkaesque scene: the girl's mother has come home and found her daughter and the boy in the bedroom, and the boy has hit the mother with a hammer—several times—and dragged her away. But the woman is still thrashing and groaning in the kitchen, and the boy says to his sweetheart, "Gimme that hammer. I think I'll have to knock her again." But the girl gives her mate a knife instead and he stabs the girl's mother many, many times, to death—under the impression, probably, that this all is a comic strip: you hit a person, the person sees lots of stars and exclamation marks but revives by and by, in the next installment. Physical life however has no next installment, and soon boy and girl have to do something with dead mother. "Oh, plaster of paris, it will dissolve her completely!" Of course, it will—marvelous idea—place body in bathtub, cover with plaster, and that's all. Meanwhile, with mother under the plaster (which does not work—wrong plaster, perhaps) boy and girl throw several beer parties. What fun! Lovely canned music, and lovely canned beer. "But you can't go, fellas, to the bathroom. The bathroom is a mess."

I'm trying to show you that in so-called real life we find sometimes a great resemblance to the situation in Kafka's fantastic story. Mark the curious mentality of the morons in Kafka who enjoy their evening paper despite the fantastic horror in the middle of their apartment. "'What a quiet life our family has been leading,' said Gregor to himself, and as he sat there motionless staring into the darkness he felt great pride in the fact that he had been able to provide such a life for his parents and sister in such a fine flat." The room is lofty and empty and the beetle begins to dominate the man. The high room "in which he had to lie flat on the floor filled him with an apprehension he could not account for, since it had been his very own room for the past five years—and with a half-unconscious action, not without a slight feeling of shame, he scuttled under the couch, where he felt comfortable at once, although his back was a little cramped and he could not lift his head up, and his only regret was that his body was too broad to get the whole of it under the couch."

Scene III: Gregor's sister brings a selection of foods. She removes the basin of milk, not by means of her bare hands but with a cloth, for it has been touched by the disgusting monster. However, she is a clever little creature, that sister, and brings a whole selection—rotten vegetables, old cheese, bones glazed with dead white sauce—and Gregor whizzed towards this feast. "One after another and with tears of satisfaction in his eyes he quickly devoured the cheese, the vegetables and the sauce; the fresh food, on the other hand, had no charms for him, he could not even stand the smell of it and actually dragged away to some little distance the things he could eat." The sister turns the key in the lock slowly as a warning that he should retreat, and she comes and cleans up while Gregor, full of food, tries to hide under the couch.

Scene IV: Grete, the sister, takes on a new importance. It is she who feeds the beetle; she alone enters the beetle's lair, sighing and with an occasional appeal to the saints—it is such a Christian family. In a wonderful passage the cook goes down on her knees to Mrs. Samsa and begs to leave. With tears in her eyes she thanks the Samsas for allowing her to go—as if she were a liberated slave—and without any prompting she swears a solemn oath that she will never say a single word to anyone about what is happening in the Samsa household. "Gregor was fed, once in the early morning while his parents and the servant girl were still asleep, and a second time after they had all had their midday dinner, for then his parents took a short nap and the servant girl could be sent out on some errand or other by his sister. Not that they would have wanted him to starve, of course, but perhaps they could not have borne to know more about his feeding than from hearsay, perhaps too his sister wanted to spare them such little anxieties wherever possible, since they had quite enough to bear as it was."

Scene V: This is a very distressing scene. It transpires that in his human past Gregor has been deceived by his family. Gregor had taken that dreadful job with that nightmare firm because he wished to help his father who five years ago had gone bankrupt. "They had simply got used to it, both the family and Gregor; the money was gratefully accepted and gladly given, but there was no special uprush of warm feeling. With his sister alone had he remained intimate, and it was a secret plan of his that she, who loved music, unlike himself, and could play movingly on the violin, should be sent next year to study at the School of Music, despite the great expense that would entail, which must be made up in some other way. During his brief visits home the School of Music was often mentioned in the talks he had with his sister, but always merely as a beautiful dream which could never come true, and his parents discouraged even these innocent references to it; yet Gregor had made up his mind firmly about it and meant to announce the fact with due solemnity on Christmas Day." Gregor now overhears his father explaining "that a certain amount of investments, a very small amount it was true, had survived the wreck of their fortunes and had even increased a little because the dividends had not been touched meanwhile. And besides that, the money Gregor brought home every month—he had kept only a few dollars for himself—had never been quite used up and now amounted to a small capital sum. Behind the door Gregor nodded his head eagerly, rejoiced at his evidence of unexpected thrift and foresight. True, he could really have paid off some more of his father's debts to the boss with this extra money, and so brought much nearer the day on which he could quit his job, but doubtless it was better the way his father had arranged it." The family believes this sum should be kept untouched for a rainy day, but in the meantime how are the living expenses to be met? The father has not worked for five years and could not be expected to do much. And Gregor's mother's asthma would keep her from working. "And was his sister to earn her bread, she who was still a child of seventeen and whose life hitherto had been so pleasant, consisting as it did in dressing herself nicely, sleeping long, helping in the housekeeping, going out to a few modest entertainments and above all playing the violin? At first whenever the need for earning money was mentioned Gregor let go his hold on the door and threw himself down on the cool leather sofa beside it, he felt so hot with shame and grief."

Scene VI: A new relationship begins between brother and sister, this time having to do with a window instead of a door. Gregor "nerved himself to the great effort of pushing an armchair to the window, then crawled up over the window sill and, braced against the chair, leaned against the windowpanes, obviously in some recollection of the sense of freedom that looking out of a window always used to give him." Gregor, or Kafka, seems to think that Gregor's urge to approach the window was a recollection of human experience. Actually, it is a typical insect reaction to light: one finds all sorts of dusty bugs near windowpanes, a moth on its back, a lame daddy longlegs, poor insects cobwebbed in a corner, a buzzing fly still trying to conquer the glass pane. Gregor's human sight is growing dimmer so that he cannot see clearly even across the street. The human detail is dominated by the insect general idea. (But let us not ourselves be insects. Let us first of all study every detail in this story; the general idea will come of itself later when we have all the data we need.) His sister does not understand that Gregor has retained a human heart, human sensitivity, a human sense of decorum, of shame, of humility and pathetic pride. She disturbs him horribly by the noise and haste with which she opens the window to breathe some fresh air, and she does not bother to conceal her disgust at the awful smell in his den. Neither does she conceal her feelings when she actually sees him. One day, about a month after Gregor's metamorphosis, "when there was surely no reason for her to be still startled at his appearance, she came a little earlier than usual and found him gazing out of the window, quite motionless, and thus well placed to look like a bogey. . . . She jumped back as if in alarm and banged the door shut; a stranger might well have thought that he had been lying in wait for her there meaning to bite her. Of course he hid himself under the couch at once, but he had to wait until midday before she came again, and she seemed more ill at ease than usual." These things hurt, and nobody understood how they hurt. In an exquisite display of feeling, in order to spare her the repulsive sight of him, Gregor one day "carried a sheet on his back to the couch—it cost him four hours' labor—and arranged it there in such a way as to hide him completely, so that even if she were to bend down she could not see him. . . . Gregor even fancied that he caught a thankful glance from her eye when he lifted the sheet carefully a very little with his head to see how she was taking the new arrangement."

It should be noted how kind, how good our poor little monster is. His beetlehood, while distorting and degrading his body, seems to bring out in him all his human sweetness. His utter unselfishness, his constant preoccupation with the needs of others—this, against the backdrop of his hideous plight comes out in strong relief. Kafka's art consists in accumulating on the one hand, Gregor's insect features, all the sad detail of his insect disguise, and on the other hand, in keeping vivid and limpid before the reader's eyes Gregor's sweet and subtle human nature.

Scene VII: Here occurs the furniture-moving scene. Two months have passed. Up to now only his sister has been visiting him; but, Gregor says to himself, my sister is only a child; she has taken on herself the job of caring for me merely out of childish thoughtlessness. My mother should understand the situation better. So here in the seventh scene the mother, asthmatic, feeble, and muddleheaded, will enter his room for the first time. Kafka prepares the scene carefully. For recreation Gregor had formed the habit of walking on the walls and ceiling. He is at the height of the meagre bliss his beetlehood can produce. "His sister at once remarked the new distraction Gregor had found for himself—he left traces behind him of the sticky stuff on his soles wherever he crawled—and she got the idea in her head of giving him as wide a field as possible to crawl in and of removing the pieces of furniture that hindered him, above all the chest of drawers and the writing desk." Thus the mother is brought in to help move the furniture. She comes to his door with exclamations of joyful eagerness to see her son, an incongruous and automatic reaction that is replaced by a certain hush when she enters the mysterious chamber. "Gregor's sister, of course, went in first, to see that everything was in order before letting his mother enter. In great haste Gregor pulled the sheet lower and rucked it more in folds so that it really looked as if it had been thrown accidentally over the couch. And this time he did not peer out from under it; he renounced the pleasure of seeing his mother on this occasion and was only glad that she had come at all. 'Come in, he's out of sight,' said his sister, obviously leading her mother in by the hand."

The women struggle to move the heavy furniture until his mother voices a certain human thought, naive but kind, feeble but not devoid of feeling, when she says: "doesn't it look as if we were showing him, by taking away his furniture, that we have given up hope of his ever getting better and are just leaving him coldly to himself? I think it would be best to keep his room exactly as it has always been, so that when he comes back to us he will find everything unchanged and be able all the more easily to forget what has happened in between." Gregor is torn between two emotions. His beetlehood suggests that an empty room with bare walls would be more convenient for crawling about—all he needed would be some chink to hide in, his indispensable couch—but otherwise he would not need all those human conveniences and adornments. But his mother's voice reminds him of his human background. Unfortunately, his sister has developed a queer self-assurance and has grown accustomed to consider herself an expert in Gregor's affairs as against her parents. "Another factor might have been also the enthusiastic temperament of an adolescent girl, which seeks to indulge itself on every opportunity and which now tempted Grete to exaggerate the horror of her brother's circumstances in order that she might do all the more for him." This is a curious note: the domineering sister, the strong sister of the fairy tales, the handsome busybody lording it over the fool of the family, the proud sisters of Cinderella, the cruel emblem of health, youth, and blossoming beauty in the house of disaster and dust. So they decide to move the things out after all but have a real struggle with the chest of drawers. Gregor is in an awful state of panic. He kept his fretsaw in that chest, with which he used to make things when he was free at home, his sole hobby.

Scene VIII: Gregor tries to save at least the picture in the frame he had made with his cherished fretsaw. Kafka varies his effects in that every time the beetle is seen by his family he is shown in a new position, some new spot. Here Gregor rushes from his hiding place, unseen by the two women now struggling with his writing desk, and climbs the wall to press himself over the picture, his hot, dry belly against the soothing cool glass. The mother is not much help in this furniture-moving business and has to be supported by Grete. Grete always remains strong and hale whereas not only her brother but both parents are going to be soon (after the apple-pitching scene) on the brink of sinking into some dull dream, into a state of torpid and decrepit oblivion; but Grete with the hard health of her ruddy adolescence keeps propping them up.

Scene IX: Despite Grete's efforts, the mother catches sight of Gregor, a "huge brown mass on the flowered wallpaper, and before she was really conscious that what she saw was Gregor screamed in a loud, hoarse voice: 'Oh God, oh God!' fell with outspread arms over the couch as if giving up and did not move. 'Gregor!' cried his sister, shaking her fist and glaring at him. This was the first time she had directly addressed him since his metamorphosis." She runs into the living room for something to rouse her mother from the fainting fit. "Gregor wanted to help too—there was still time to rescue the picture—but he was stuck fast to the glass and had to tear himself loose; he then ran after his sister into the next room as if he could advise her, as he used to do; but then had to stand helplessly behind her; she meanwhile searched among various small bottles and when she turned round started in alarm at the sight of him; one bottle fell on the floor and broke; a splinter of glass cut Gregor's face and some kind of corrosive medicine splashed him; without pausing a moment longer Grete gathered up all the bottles she could carry and ran to her mother with them; she banged the door shut with her foot. Gregor was now cut off from his mother, who was perhaps nearly dying because of him; he dared not open the door for fear of frightening away his sister, who had to stay with her mother; there was nothing he could do but wait; and harassed by self-reproach and worry he began now to crawl to and fro, over everything, walls, furniture and ceiling, and finally in his despair, when the whole room seemed to be reeling around him, fell down on to the middle of the big table." There is a change in the respective position of the various members of the family. Mother (on the couch) and sister are in the middle room; Gregor is in the corner in the left room. And presently his father comes home and enters the living room. "And so [Gregor] fled to the door of his own room and crouched against it, to let his father see as soon as he came in from the hall that his son had the good intention of getting back into his own room immediately and that it was not necessary to drive him there, but that if only the door were opened he would disappear at once."

Scene X: The apple-pelting scene comes now. Gregor's father has changed and is now at the summit of his power. Instead of the man who used to lie wearily sunk in bed and could scarcely wave an arm in greeting, and when he went out shuffled along laboriously with a crook-handled stick, "Now he was standing there in fine shape; dressed in a smart blue uniform with gold buttons, such as bank messengers wear; his strong double chin bulged over the stiff high collar of his jacket; from under his bushy eyebrows his black eyes darted fresh and penetrating glances; his onetime tangled white hair had been combed flat on either side of a shining and carefully exact parting. He pitched his cap, which bore a gold monogram, probably the badge of some bank, in a wide sweep across the whole room on to a sofa and with the tail-ends of his jacket thrown back, his hands in his trouser pockets, advanced with a grim visage towards Gregor. Likely enough he did not himself know what he meant to do; at any rate he lifted his feet uncommonly high and Gregor was dumbfounded at the enormous size of his shoe soles."

As usual, Gregor is tremendously interested in the movement of human legs, big thick human feet, so different from his own flimmering appendages. We have a repetition of the slow motion theme. (The chief clerk, backing and shuffling, had retreated in slow motion.)

Now father and son slowly circle the room: indeed, the whole operation hardly looked like pursuit it was carried out so slowly. And then
his father starts to bombard Gregor with the only missiles that the
living-dining room could provide—apples, small red apples—and
Gregor is driven back into the middle room, back to the heart of his
beetlehood. "An apple thrown without much force grazed Gregor's
back and glanced off harmlessly. But another following immediately
landed right on his back and sank in; Gregor wanted to drag himself
forward, as if this startling, incredible pain could be left behind him;
but he felt as if nailed to the spot and flattened himself out in a complete derangement of all his senses. With his last conscious look he
saw the door of his room being torn open and his mother rushing out
ahead of his screaming sister, in her underbodice, for her daughter
had loosened her clothing to let her breathe more freely and recover
from her swoon; he saw his mother rushing towards his father, leaving one after another behind her on the floor her loosened petticoats,
stumbling over her petticoats straight to his father and embracing
him, in complete union with him—but here Gregor's sight began to
fail—with her hands clasped round his father's neck as she begged for
her son's life."

This is the end of part two. Let us sum up the situation. The sister
has become frankly antagonistic to her brother. She may have loved him
once, but now she regards him with disgust and anger. In Mrs. Samsa
asthma and emotion struggle. She is a rather mechanical mother, with
some mechanical mother love for her son, but we shall soon see that
she, too, is ready to give him up. The father, as already remarked, has
reached a certain summit of impressive strength and brutality. From
the very first he had been eager to hurt physically his helpless son, and
now the apple he has thrown has become embedded in poor Gregor's
beetle flesh.

PART THREE

Scene I: "The serious injury done to Gregor, which disabled him for
more than a month—the apple went on sticking in his body as a visible
reminder, since no one ventured to remove it—seemed to have made even

his father recollect that Gregor was a member of the family, despite his present unfortunate and repulsive shape, and ought not to be treated as an enemy, that, on the contrary, family duty required the suppression of disgust and the exercise of patience, nothing but patience." The door theme is taken up again since now, in the evening, the door leading from Gregor's darkened room to the lighted living room is left open. This is a subtle situation. In the previous scene father and mother had reached their highest point of energy, he in his resplendent uniform pitching those little red bombs, emblems of fruitfulness and manliness; and she, the mother, actually moving furniture despite her frail breathing tubes. But after that peak there is a fall, a weakening. It would almost seem that the father himself is on the point of disintegrating and becoming a feeble beetle. Through the opened door a curious current seems to pass. Gregor's beetle illness is catching, his father seems to have caught it, the weakness, the drabness, the dirt. "Soon after supper his father would fall asleep in his armchair; his mother and sister would admonish each other to be silent; his mother, bending low over the lamp, stitched at fine sewing for an underwear firm; his sister, who had taken a job as a salesgirl, was learning shorthand and French in the evenings on the chance of bettering herself. Sometimes his father woke up, and as if quite unaware that he had been sleeping said to the mother: 'What a lot of sewing you're doing today!' and at once fell asleep again, while the two women exchanged a tired smile.

"With a kind of mulishness his father persisted in keeping his uniform on even in the house; his dressing gown hung uselessly on its peg and he slept fully dressed where he sat, as if he were ready for service at any moment and even here only at the beck and call of his superior. As a result, his uniform, which was not brand new to start with, began to look dirty, despite all the loving care of the mother and sister to keep it clean, and Gregor often spent whole evenings gazing at the many greasy spots on the garment, gleaming with gold buttons always in a high state of polish, in which the old man sat sleeping in extreme discomfort and yet quite peacefully." The father always refused to go to bed when the time had arrived, despite every inducement offered by the mother and sister, until finally the two women would hoist him up by his armpits from the chair, "And leaning on the two of them he would heave himself up, with difficulty, as if he were a great burden to himself, suffer them to lead him as far as the door and then wave them off and go on alone, while the mother abandoned her needlework and the sister her pen in order to run after him and help him farther." The father's uniform comes close to resembling that of a big but somewhat tarnished scarab. His tired overworked family must get him from one room to another and to bed.

Scene II: The disintegration of the Samsa family continues. They dismiss the servant girl and engage a still cheaper charwoman, a gigantic bony creature who comes in to do the rough work. You must remember that in Prague, 1912, it was much more difficult to clean and cook than in Ithaca, 1954. They have to sell various family ornaments. "But what they lamented most was the fact that they could not leave the flat which was much too big for their present circumstances, because they could not think of any way to shift Gregor. Yet Gregor saw well enough that consideration for him was not the main difficulty preventing the removal, for they could have easily shifted him in some suitable box with a few air holes in it; what really kept them from moving into another flat was rather their own complete hopelessness and the belief that they had been singled out for a misfortune such as had never happened to any of their relations or acquaintances." The family is completely egotistic and has no more strength left after fulfilling its daily obligations.

Scene III: A last flash of human recollections comes to Gregor's mind, prompted by the still living urge in him to help his family. He even remembers vague sweethearts, "but instead of helping him and his family they were one and all unapproachable and he was glad when they vanished." This scene is mainly devoted to Grete, who is now clearly the villain of the piece. "His sister no longer took thought to bring him what might especially please him, but in the morning and at noon before she went to business hurriedly pushed into his room with her foot any food that was available, and in the evening cleared it out again with one sweep of the broom, heedless of whether it had been merely tasted, or—as most frequently happened—left untouched. The cleaning of his room, which she now did always in the evenings, could not have been more hastily done. Streaks of dirt stretched along the walls, here and there lay balls of dust and filth. At first Gregor used to station himself in some particularly filthy corner when his sister arrived, in order to reproach her with it, so to speak. But he could have sat there for weeks without getting her to make any improvement; she could see the dirt as well as he did, but she had simply made up her mind to leave it alone. And yet, with a touchiness that was new to her, which seemed anyhow to have infected the whole family, she jealously guarded her claim to be the sole caretaker of Gregor's room." Once when his mother had given the room a thorough cleaning with several buckets of water—the dampness upset Gregor—a grotesque family row ensues. The sister bursts into a storm of weeping while her parents look on in helpless amazement; "then they too began to go into action; the father reproached the mother on his right for not having left the cleaning of Gregor's room to his sister; shrieked at the sister on his left that never again was she to be allowed to clean Gregor's room; while the mother tried to pull the father into his bedroom, since he was beyond himself with agitation; the sister, shaken with sobs, then beat upon the table with her small fists; and Gregor hissed loudly with rage because not one of them thought of shutting the door to spare him such a spectacle and so much noise."

Scene IV: A curious relationship is established between Gregor and the bony charwoman who is rather amused by him, not frightened at all, and in fact she rather likes him. "Come along, then, you old dung beetle," she says. And it is raining outside, the first sign of spring perhaps.

Scene V: The lodgers arrive, the three bearded boarders, with a passion for order. These are mechanical beings; their beards are masks of respectability but actually they are shoddy scoundrels, these serious-looking gentlemen. In this scene a great change comes over the apartment. The boarders take the parents' bedroom on the far left of the flat, beyond the living room. The parents move across to the sister's room on the right of Gregor's room, and Grete has to sleep in the living room but has now no room of her own since the lodgers take their meals in the living room and spend their evenings there. Moreover, the three bearded boarders have brought into this furnished flat some furniture of their own. They have a fiendish love for superficial tidiness, and all the odds and ends which they do not need go into Gregor's room. This is exactly the opposite to what had been happening in the furniture scene of part two, scene 7, where there had been an attempt to move everything out of Gregor's room. Then we had the ebb of the furniture, now the return flow, the jetsam washed back, all kinds of junk pouring in; and curiously enough Gregor, though a very sick beetle—the apple wound is festering, and he is starving—finds some beetle pleasure in crawling among all that dusty rubbish. In this fifth scene of part three where all the changes come, the alteration in the family meals is depicted. The mechanical movement of the bearded automatons is matched by the automatic reaction of the Samsas. The lodgers "set themselves at the top end of the table where formerly Gregor and his father and mother had eaten their meals, unfolded their napkins and took knife and fork in hand. At once his mother appeared in the other doorway with a dish of meat and close behind her his sister with a dish of potatoes piled high. The food steamed with a thick vapor. The lodgers bent over the food set before them as if to scrutinize it before eating, in fact the man in the middle, who seemed to pass for an authority with the other two, cut a piece of meat as it lay on the dish, obviously to discover if it were tender or should be sent back to the kitchen. He showed satisfaction, and Gregor's mother and sister, who had been watching anxiously, breathed freely and began to smile." Gregor's keen envious interest in large feet will be recalled; now toothless Gregor is also interested in teeth. "It seemed remarkable to Gregor that among the various noises coming from the table he could always distinguish the sound of their masticating teeth, as if this were a sign to Gregor that one needed teeth in order to eat, and that with toothless jaws even of the finest make one could do nothing. 'I'm hungry enough,' said Gregor sadly to himself, 'but not for that kind of food. How these lodgers are stuffing themselves, and here am I dying of starvation!'"

Scene VI: In this great music scene the lodgers have heard Grete playing the violin in the kitchen, and in automatic reaction to the entertainment value of music they suggest that she play for them. The three roomers and the three Samsas gather in the living room.

Without wishing to antagonize lovers of music, I do wish to point out that taken in a general sense music, as perceived by its consumers, belongs to a more primitive, more animal form in the scale of arts than literature or painting. I am taking music as a whole, not in terms of individual creation, imagination, and composition, all of which of course rival the art of literature and painting, but in terms of the impact music has on the average listener. A great composer, a great writer, a great painter are brothers. But I think that the impact music in a generalized and primitive form has on the listener is of a more lowly quality than the impact of an average book or an average picture. What I especially have in mind is the soothing, lulling, dulling influence of music on some people, such as of the radio or records.

In Kafka's tale it is merely a girl pitifully scraping on a fiddle, and this corresponds in the piece to the canned music or plugged-in music of today. What Kafka felt about music in general is what I have just described: its stupefying, numbing, animallike quality. This attitude must be kept in mind in interpreting an important sentence that has been misunderstood by some translators. Literally, it reads "Was Gregor an animal to be so affected by music?" That is, in his human form he had cared little for it, but in this scene, in his beetlehood, he succumbs: "He felt as if the way were opening before him to the unknown nourishment he craved." The scene goes as follows. Gregor's sister begins to play for the lodgers. Gregor is attracted by the playing and actually puts his head into the living room. "He felt hardly any surprise at his growing lack of consideration for the others; there had been a time when he prided himself on being considerate. And yet just on this occasion he had more reason than ever to hide himself, since owing to the amount of dust which lay thick in his room and rose into the air at the slightest movement, he too was covered with dust; fluff and hair and remnants of food trailed with him, caught on his back and along his sides; his indifference to everything was much too great for him to turn on his back and scrape himself clean on the carpet, as once he had done several times a day. And in spite of his condition, no shame deterred him from advancing a little over the spotless floor of the living room."

At first no one was aware of him. The lodgers, disappointed in their expectation of hearing good violin playing, were clustered near the window, whispering among themselves and waiting only for the music to stop. And yet, to Gregor, his sister was playing beautifully. He "crawled a little farther forward and lowered his head to the ground so that it might be possible for his eyes to meet hers. Was he an animal, that music had such an effect upon him? He felt as if the way were opening before him to the unknown nourishment he craved. He was determined to push forward till he reached his sister, to pull at her skirt and so let her know that she was to come into his room with her violin, for no one here appreciated her playing as he would appreciate it. He would never let her out of his room, at least, not so long as he lived; his frightful appearance would become, for the first time, useful to him; he would watch all the doors of his room at once and spit at intruders; but his sister should need no constraint, she should stay with him of her own free will; she should sit beside him on the couch, bend down her ear to him and hear him confide that he had had the firm intention of sending her to the School of Music, and that, but for his mishap, last Christmas—surely Christmas was long past?—he would have announced it to everybody without allowing a single objection. After this confession his sister would be so touched that she would burst into tears, and Gregor would then raise himself to her shoulder and kiss her on the neck, which, now that she went to business, she kept free of any ribbon or collar."

Suddenly the middle lodger sees Gregor, but instead of driving Gregor out the father tries to soothe the lodgers and (in a reversal of his actions) "spreading out his arms, tried to urge them back into their own room and at the same time to block their view of Gregor. They now began to be really a little angry, one could not tell whether because of the old man's behavior or because it had just dawned on them that all unwittingly they had such a neighbor as Gregor next door. They demanded explanations of his father, they waved their arms like him, tugged uneasily at their beards, and only with reluctance backed towards their room." The sister rushes into the lodgers' room and quickly makes up their beds, but "The old man seemed once more to be so possessed by his mulish self-assertiveness that he was forgetting all the respect he should show to his lodgers. He kept driving them on and driving them on until in the very door of the bedroom the middle lodger stamped his foot loudly on the floor and so brought him to a halt. 'I beg to announce,' said the lodger, lifting one hand and looking also at Gregor's mother and sister, 'that because of the disgusting conditions prevailing in this household and family'—here he spat on the floor with emphatic brevity—'I give you notice on the spot. Naturally I won't pay you a penny for the days I have lived here; on the contrary I shall consider bringing an action for damages against you, based on claims— believe me—that will be easily susceptible of proof.' He ceased and stared straight in front of him, as if he expected something. In fact his two friends at once rushed into the breach with these words: 'And we too give notice on the spot.' On that he seized the door-handle and shut the door with a slam."

Scene VII: The sister is completely unmasked; her betrayal is absolute and fatal to Gregor. "'I won't utter my brother's name in the presence of this creature, and so all I say is: we must try to get rid of it. . . .

"'We must try to get rid of it,' his sister now said explicitly to her father, since her mother was coughing too much to hear a word. 'It will be the death of both of you, I can see that coming. When one has to work as hard as we do, all of us, one can't stand this continual torment at home on top of it. At least I can't stand it any longer.' And she burst into such a passion of sobbing that her tears dropped on her mother's face, where she wiped them off mechanically." Both the father and sister agree that Gregor cannot understand them and hence no agreement with him is possible.

"'He must go,' cried Gregor's sister, 'that's the only solution, Father. You must just try to get rid of the idea that this is Gregor. The fact that we've believed it for so long is the root of all our trouble. But how can it be Gregor? If this were Gregor, he would have realized long ago that human beings can't live with such a creature, and he'd have gone away on his own accord. Then we wouldn't have any brother, but we'd be able to go on living and keep his memory in honor. As it is, this creature persecutes us, drives away our lodgers, obviously wants the whole apartment to himself and would have us all sleep in the gutter.'"

That he has disappeared as a human brother and should now disappear as a beetle deals Gregor the last blow. Painfully, because he is so weak and maimed, he crawls back to his own room. At the doorway he turns and his last glance falls on his mother, who was, in fact, almost asleep. "Hardly was he well inside his room when the door was hastily pushed shut, bolted and locked. The sudden noise in his rear startled him so much that his little legs gave beneath him. It was his sister who had shown such haste. She had been standing ready waiting and had made a light spring forward. Gregor had not even heard her coming, and she cried 'At last!' to her parents as she turned the key in the lock." In his darkened room Gregor discovers that he cannot move and though he is in pain it seems to be passing away. "The rotting apple in his back and the inflamed area around it, all covered with soft dust, already hardly troubled him. He thought of his family with tenderness and love. The decision that he must disappear was one that he held to even more strongly than his sister, if that were possible. In this state of vacant and peaceful meditation he remained until the tower clock struck three in the morning. The first broadening of light in the world outside the window entered his consciousness once more. Then his head sank to the floor of its own accord and from his nostrils came the last faint flicker of his breath."

Scene VIII: Gregor's dead, dry body is discovered the next morning by the charwoman and a great warm sense of relief permeates the insect world of his despicable family. Here is a point to be observed with care and love. Gregor is a human being in an insect's disguise; his family are insects disguised as people. With Gregor's death their insect souls are suddenly aware that they are free to enjoy themselves. "'Come in beside us, Grete, for a little while,' said Mrs. Samsa with a tremulous smile, and Grete, not without looking back at the corpse, followed her parents into their bedroom." The charwoman opens the window wide and the air has a certain warmth: it is the end of March when insects come out of hibernation.

Scene IX: We get a wonderful glimpse of the lodgers as they sullenly ask for their breakfast but instead are shown Gregor's corpse. "So they entered and stood around it, with their hands in the pockets of their shabby coats, in the middle of the room already bright with sunlight." What is the key word here? *Shabby* in the sun. As in a fairy tale, in the happy end of a fairy tale, the evil charm is dissipated with the magician's death. The lodgers are seen to be seedy, they are no longer dangerous, whereas on the other hand the Samsa family ascends again, gains in power and lush vitality. The scene ends with a repetition of the staircase theme, just as the chief clerk had retreated in slow motion, clasping the banisters. At the orders of Mr. Samsa that they must leave the lodgers are quelled. "In the hall they all three took their hats from the rack, their sticks from the umbrella stand, bowed in silence and quitted the apartment." Down they go now, three bearded boarders, automatons, clockwork puppets, while the Samsa family leans over the banisters to watch them descend. The staircase as it winds down through the apartment house imitates, as it were, an insect's jointed legs; and the lodgers now disappear, now come to view again, as they descend lower and lower, from landing to landing, from articulation to articulation. At one point they are met by an ascending butcher boy with his basket who is first seen rising towards them, then above them, in proud deportment with his basket full of red steaks and luscious innards—red raw meat, the breeding place of fat shiny flies.

Scene X: The last scene is superb in its ironic simplicity. The spring sunshine is with the Samsa family as they write their three letters—articulation, jointed legs, happy legs, three insects writing three letters—of excuse to their employers. "They decided to spend this day in resting and going for a stroll; they had not only deserved such a respite from work, but absolutely needed it." As the charwoman leaves after her morning's work, she giggles amiably as she informs the family: "'you don't need to bother about how to get rid of the thing next door. It's been seen to already.' Mrs. Samsa and Grete bent over their letters again, as if preoccupied; Mr. Samsa, who perceived that she was eager to begin describing it all in detail, stopped her with a decisive hand. . . .

"'She'll be given notice tonight,' said Mr. Samsa, but neither from his wife nor his daughter did he get any answer, for the charwoman seemed to have shattered again the composure they had barely achieved. They rose, went to the window and stayed there, clasping each other tight. Mr. Samsa turned in his chair to look at them and quietly observed them for a little. Then he called out: 'Come along, now, do. Let bygones be bygones. And you might have some consideration for me.' The two of them complied at once, hastened to him, caressed him and quickly finished their letters.

"Then they all three left the apartment together, which was more than they had done for months, and went by trolley into the open country outside the town. The trolley, in which they were the only passengers, was filled with warm sunshine. Leaning comfortably back in their seats they canvassed their prospects for the future, and it appeared on closer inspection that these were not at all bad, for the jobs they had got, which so far they had never really discussed with each other, were all three admirable and likely to lead to better things later on. The greatest immediate improvement in their condition would of course arise from moving to another house; they wanted to take a smaller and cheaper but also better situated and more easily run apartment than the one they had, which Gregor had selected. While they were thus conversing, it struck both Mr. and Mrs. Samsa, almost at the same moment, as they became aware of their daughter's increasing vivacity, that in spite of all the sorrow of recent times, which had made her cheeks pale, she had bloomed into a buxom girl. They grew quieter and half unconsciously exchanged glances of complete agreement, having come to the conclusion that it would soon be time to find a good husband for her. And it was like a confirmation of their new dreams and excellent intentions that at the end of their journey their daughter sprang to her feet first and stretched her young body."

<hr />

Let me sum up various of the main themes of the story.

1. The number *three* plays a considerable role in the story. The story is divided into three parts. There are three doors to Gregor's room. His family consists of three people. Three servants appear in the course of the story. Three lodgers have three beards. Three Samsas write three letters. I am very careful not to overwork the significance of symbols, for once you detach a symbol from the artistic core of the book, you lose all sense of enjoyment. The reason is that there are artistic symbols and there are trite, artificial, or even imbecile symbols. You will find a number of such inept symbols in the psychoanalytic and mythological approach to Kafka's work, in the fashionable mixture of sex and myth that is so appealing to mediocre minds. In other words, symbols may be original, and symbols may be stupid and trite. And the abstract symbolic value of an artistic achievement should never prevail over its beautiful burning life.

So, the only emblematic or heraldic rather than symbolic meaning is the stress which is laid upon *three* in "The Metamorphosis." It has really a technical meaning. The trinity, the triplet, the triad, the triptych are obvious art forms such as, say, three pictures of youth, ripe years, and old age, or any other threefold triplex subject. Triptych means a picture or carving in three compartments side by side, and this is exactly the effect that Kafka achieves, for instance, with his three rooms in the beginning of the story—living room, Gregor's bedroom, and sister's room, with Gregor in the central one. Moreover, a threefold pattern suggests the three acts of a play. And finally it must be observed that Kafka's fantasy is emphatically logical; what can be more characteristic of logic than the triad of thesis, antithesis, and synthesis. We shall, thus, limit the Kafka symbol of three to its aesthetic and logical significance and completely disregard whatever myths the sexual mythologists read into it under the direction of the Viennese witch doctor.

2. Another thematic line is the theme of the doors, of the opening and closing of doors that runs through the whole story.

3. A third thematic line concerns the ups and downs in the well-being of the Samsa family, the subtle state of balance between their flourishing condition and Gregor's desperate and pathetic condition.

There are a few other subthemes but the above are the only ones essential for an understanding of the story.

You will mark Kafka's style. Its clarity, its precise and formal intonation in such striking contrast to the nightmare matter of his tale. No poetical metaphors ornament his stark black-and-white story. The limpidity of his style stresses the dark richness of his fantasy. Contrast and unity, style and matter, manner and plot are most perfectly integrated.

"How to Express Your Emotions": An Excerpt from *How Proust Can Change Your Life*

ALAIN DE BOTTON

There may be significant things to learn about people by looking at what annoys them most. Proust got very annoyed by the way some people expressed themselves. Lucien Daudet tells us that Proust had a friend who thought it chic to use English expressions when he was speaking French, and would therefore say "Good-bye" or, more casually, "Bye, bye" whenever he left a room. "It made Proust positively unhappy," reports Daudet. "He would make the kind of pained, irritated grimace which follows when a stick of chalk has been scraped across a blackboard. 'It really hurts your teeth, that kind of thing!' he would exclaim plaintively." Proust displayed similar frustration with people who referred to the Mediterranean as "the Big Blue," to England as "Albion," and to the French army as "our boys." He was pained by people whose sole response to heavy rain was, "*Il pleut des cordes,*" to cold weather, "*Il fait un froid de canard,*" and to another's deafness, "*Il est sourd comme un panier.*"

Why did these phrases affect Proust so much? Though the way people talk has altered somewhat since his day, it is not difficult to see that here were examples of rather poor expression, though if Proust was wincing, his complaint was more a psychological than a grammatical one ("No one knows less syntax than me," he boasted). Peppering French with bits of English, talking of Albion instead of England and the Big Blue instead of the Mediterranean were signs of wishing to seem smart and in-the-know around 1900, and relying on essentially insincere, overelaborate stock phrases to do so. There was no reason to say "Bye, bye" when taking one's leave, other than a need to impress by recourse to a contemporary fad for all things British. And though phrases like "*Il pleut des cordes*" had none of the ostentation of a "Bye, bye," they were examples of the most exhausted constructions, whose use implied little concern for evoking the specifics of a situation. Insofar as Proust made pained, irritated grimaces, it was in defense of a more honest and accurate approach to expression.

Lucien Daudet tells us how he first got a taste of it:

> One day when we were coming out of a concert where we
> had heard Beethoven's Choral Symphony, I was humming
> some vague notes which I thought expressed the emotion
> I had just experienced, and I exclaimed, with an emphasis
> which I only later understood to be ridiculous: "That's a
> wonderful bit!" Proust started to laugh and said, "But, my dear
> Lucien, it's not your *poum, poum, poum* that's going to convey
> this wonderfulness! It would be better to try and explain it!"
> At the time, I wasn't very happy, but I had just received an
> unforgettable lesson.

It was a lesson in trying to find the right words for things. The process can be counted upon to go badly awry. We feel something and reach out for the nearest phrase or hum with which to communicate, but which fails to do justice to what has induced us to do so. We hear Beethoven's Ninth and hum *poum, poum, poum*; we see the pyramids at Giza and go, "That's nice." These sounds are asked to account for an experience, but their poverty prevents either ourselves or our interlocutors from really understanding what we have lived through. We stay on the outside of our impressions, as if staring at them through a frosted window, superficially related to them, yet estranged from whatever has eluded casual definition.

Proust had a friend called Gabriel de La Rochefoucauld. He was an aristocratic young man, whose ancestor had written a famous short book in the seventeenth century, and who liked to spend time in glamorous Paris nightspots, so much time that he had been labeled by some of his more sarcastic contemporaries "le La Rochefoucauld de chez Maxim's." But in 1904 Gabriel forsook the nightlife in order to try his hand at literature. The result was a novel, *The Lover and the Doctor*, which Gabriel sent to Proust in manuscript form as soon as it was finished, with a request for comments and advice.

"Bear in mind that you have written a fine and powerful novel, a superb, tragic work of complex and consummate craftsmanship," Proust reported back to his friend, who might have formed a slightly different impression after reading the lengthy letter which had preceded this eulogy. It seems that the superb and tragic work had a few problems, not least because it was filled with clichés: "There are some fine big landscapes in your novel," explained Proust, treading delicately, "but at times one would like them to be painted with more originality. It's quite true that the sky is on fire at sunset, but it's been said too often, and the moon that shines discreetly is a trifle dull."

We may ask why Proust objected to phrases that had been used too often. After all, doesn't the moon shine discreetly? Don't sunsets look as if they were on fire? Aren't clichés just good ideas that have proved rightly popular?

The problem with clichés is not that they contain false ideas, but rather that they are superficial articulations of very good ones. The sun is often on fire at sunset and the moon discreet, but if we keep saying this every time we encounter a sun or a moon, we will end up believing that this is the last rather than the first word to be said on the subject. Clichés are detrimental insofar as they inspire us to believe that they adequately describe a situation while merely grazing its surface. And if this matters, it is because the way we speak is ultimately linked to the way we feel, because how we *describe* the world must at some level reflect how we first *experience* it.

The moon Gabriel mentioned might of course have been discreet, but it is liable to have been a lot more besides. When the first volume of Proust's novel was published eight years after *The Lover and the Doctor*, perhaps Gabriel (if he wasn't back ordering Dom Perignon at Maxim's) took time to notice that Proust had also included a moon, but that he had skirted two thousand years of ready-made moon talk and uncovered an unusual metaphor better to capture the reality of the lunar experience:

> Sometimes in the afternoon sky, a white moon would creep up like a little cloud, furtive, without display, suggesting an actress who does not have to "come on" for a while, and so goes "in front" in her ordinary clothes to watch the rest of the company for a moment, but keeps in the background, not wishing to attract attention to herself.

Even if we recognize the virtues of Proust's metaphor, it is not necessarily one we could easily come up with by ourselves. It may lie closer to a genuine impression of the moon, but if we observe the moon and are asked to say something about it, we are more likely to hit upon a tired rather than an inspired image. We may be well aware that our description of a moon is not up to the task, without knowing how to better it. To take license with his response, this would perhaps have bothered Proust less than an unapologetic use of clichés by people who believed that it was always right to follow verbal conventions ("golden orb," "heavenly body"), and felt that a priority when talking was not to be original but to sound like someone else.

Wanting to sound like other people has its temptations. There are inherited habits of speech guaranteed to make us sound authoritative, intelligent, worldly, appropriately grateful, or deeply moved. As of a certain age, Albertine decides that she too would like to speak like someone else—like a bourgeois young woman. She begins to use a range of expressions common among such women, which she has picked up from her aunt, Madame Bontemps, in the slavish way, Proust suggests, that a baby goldfinch learns how to act like a grown-up by imitating the behavior of its parent goldfinches. She acquires a habit of repeating whatever one says to her, so as to appear interested and in the process of forming an opinion of her own. If you tell her that an artist's work is good, or his house nice, she will say, "Oh, his painting's good, is it?" "Oh, his house is nice, is it?" Furthermore, when she meets someone unusual, she now says, "He's a character"; when you suggest a game of cards to her, she will say, "I don't have money to burn"; when one of her friends reproaches her unjustly, she will exclaim, "You really are the limit!"—all these expressions having been dictated to her by what Proust calls a "bourgeois tradition almost as old as the *Magnificat* itself," a tradition laying down speech codes that the respectable bourgeois girl must learn, "just as she has learned to say her prayers and to curtsey."

This mockery of Albertine's verbal habits explains Proust's particular frustration with Louis Ganderax.

Louis Ganderax was a leading early-twentieth-century man of letters and the literary editor of *La Revue de Paris*. In 1906 he was asked to edit the correspondence of Georges Bizet, and to write a preface for the collection. It was a great honor, and a great responsibility. Bizet, who had died some thirty years earlier, was a composer of worldwide significance, whose place in posterity was assured by his opera *Carmen* and his Symphony in C Major. There was understandable pressure on Ganderax to produce a preface worthy of standing at the head of a genius's correspondence.

Georges Bizet

Unfortunately, Ganderax was something of a goldfinch, and in an attempt to sound grand—far grander than he must have thought himself naturally to be—he ended up writing a preface of enormous, almost comic pretension.

Louis Ganderax

Lying in bed reading the newspaper in the autumn of 1908, Proust came upon an extract of Ganderax's preface, whose prose style annoyed him so much that he exorcised his feelings by writing a letter to Georges Bizet's widow, his good friend Madame Straus. "Why, when he can write so well, does he write as he does?" wondered Proust. "Why, when one says '1871', add 'that most abominable of all years.' Why is Paris immediately dubbed 'the great city' and Delaunay 'the master painter'? Why must emotion inevitably be 'discreet' and goodnaturedness 'smiling' and bereavements 'cruel', and countless other fine phrases that I can't remember?"

These phrases were of course anything but fine, they were a caricature of fineness. They were phrases that might once have been impressive in the hands of classical writers, but were pompous ornamentation when stolen by an author of a later age concerned only to suggest literary grandeur.

If Ganderax had worried about the sincerity of what he was saying, he might have resisted capping the thought that 1871 was a bad year with the melodramatic claim that it was in fact "that most abominable of all years." Paris might have been under siege by the Prussian army at the beginning of 1871, the starving populace might have been driven to eat elephants from the Jardin des Plantes, the Prussians might have marched down the Champs-Élysées and the Commune imposed tyrannical rule, but did these experiences really stand a chance of being conveyed in an overblown, thunderous phrase like this?

But Ganderax hadn't written nonsensical fine phrases by mistake. It was the natural outcome of his ideas on how people should express themselves. For Ganderax, the priority of good writing was to follow precedent, to follow examples of the most distinguished authors in history, while bad writing began with the arrogant belief that one could avoid paying homage to great minds and write according to one's fancy. It was fitting that Ganderax had elsewhere awarded himself the title of "Defender of the French Language." The language needed to be protected against the assaults of decadents who refused to follow the rules of expression dictated by tradition, leading Ganderax to complain publicly if he spotted a past participle in the wrong place or a word falsely applied in a published text.

Proust couldn't have disagreed more with such a view of tradition, and let Madame Straus know it:

> Every writer is obliged to create his own language, as every violinist is obliged to create his own "tone". . . . I don't mean to say that I like original writers who write badly. I prefer— and perhaps it's a weakness—those who write well. But they begin to write well only on condition that they're original, that they create their own language. Correctness, perfection of style do exist, but on the other side of originality, after having gone through all the faults, not this side. Correctness this side—"discreet emotion," "smiling good nature," "most abominable of all years"—doesn't exist. The only way to defend language is to attack it, yes, yes, Madame Straus!

Ganderax had overlooked the way that every good writer in history, a history he so strongly wished to defend, had, in order to ensure adequate expression, broken a range of rules laid down by previous writers. If Ganderax had been alive in Racine's day, Proust mockingly imagined that the Defender of the Language would have told even this embodiment of classical French that he couldn't write very well, because Racine had written slightly differently than those before him. He wondered what Ganderax would have made of Racine's lines in *Andromaque*:

I loved you fickle; faithful, what might I have done? . . .
Why murder him? What did he? By what right?
Who told you to?

Pretty enough, but didn't these lines break important laws of grammar? Proust pictured Ganderax delivering a rebuke to Racine:

> I understand your thought; you mean that since I loved you when you were fickle, what might that love have been if you had been faithful. But it's badly expressed. It could equally well mean that *you* would have been faithful. As official defender of the French language, I cannot let that pass.

"I'm not making fun of your friend, Madame, I assure you," claimed Proust, who hadn't stopped ridiculing Ganderax since the start of his letter. "I know how intelligent and learned he is. It's a question of 'doctrine.' This man who is so sceptical has grammatical certainties. Alas, Madame Straus, there are no certainties, even grammatical ones. . . . [O]nly that which bears the imprint of our choice, our taste, our uncertainty, our desire and our weakness can be beautiful."

And a personal imprint is not only more beautiful, it is also a good deal more authentic. Trying to sound like Chateaubriand or Victor Hugo when you are in fact the literary editor of *La Revue de Paris* implies a singular lack of concern with capturing what is distinctive about being Louis Ganderax, much as attempting to sound like the archetypal bourgeois Parisian young woman ("I don't have money to burn"; "You really are the limit!"), when you are in fact a particular young woman called Albertine, involves flattening your identity to fit a constrained social envelope. If, as Proust suggests, we are obliged to create our own language, it is because there are dimensions to ourselves absent from clichés, which require us to flout etiquette in order to convey with greater accuracy the distinctive timbre of our thought.

The need to leave a personal imprint on language is rarely more evident than in the personal sphere. The better we know someone, the more the standard name they bear comes to seem inadequate, and the greater the desire to twist theirs into a new one, so as to reflect our awareness of their particularities. Proust's name on his birth certificate was Valentin Louis Georges Eugène Marcel Proust, but because this was a dry mouthful, it was appropriate that those closest to him molded it into something more suited to who Marcel was for them. For his beloved mother, he was "*mon petit jaunet*" (my little yellow one), or "*mon petit serin*" (my little canary), or "*mon petit benêt*" (my little clod), or "*mon petit nigaud*" (my little oaf). He was also known as "*mon pauvre loup*" (my poor wolf), "*petit pauvre loup*" (poor little wolf), and "*le petit loup*" (the little wolf—Madame Proust called Marcel's brother, Robert, "*mon autre loup*," which gives us a sense of family priorities). To his friend Reynaldo Hahn, Proust was "Buncht" (and Reynaldo "Bunibuls"); to his friend Antoine Bibesco, Proust was "Lecram" and, when he got too friendly, "le Flagorneur" (the toady) or, when not straight enough, "le Saturnien." At home, he wanted his maid to refer to him as "Missou" and he would call her "Plouplou."

If Missou, Buncht, and the *petit jaunet* are endearing symbols of the way new words and phrases can be constructed to capture new dimensions of a relationship, then confusing Proust's name with someone else's looks like a sadder symbol of a reluctance to expand a vocabulary to account for the variety of the human species. To people who didn't know Proust very well, rather than making his name more personal, they had a depressing tendency to give him another name altogether, that of a far more famous contemporary writer, Marcel Prévost. "I am totally unknown," specified Proust in 1912. "When readers write to me at *Le Figaro* after an article, which happens rarely, the letters are forwarded to Marcel Prévost, for whom my name seems to be no more than a misprint."

Using a single word to describe two different things (the author of *In Search of Lost Time* and the author of *The Strong Virgins*) suggests a disregard for the world's real diversity which bears comparison with that shown by the cliché user. A person who invariably describes heavy rain with the phrase "*Il pleut des cordes*" can be accused of neglecting the real diversity of rain showers, much as the person who calls every writer whose name begin with *P* and ends in *t* Monsieur Prévost can be accused of neglecting the real diversity of literature.

So if speaking in clichés is problematic, it is because the world itself contains a far broader range of rainfalls, moons, sunshines, and emotions than stock expressions either capture or teach us to expect.

Proust's novel is filled with people who behave in un-stock ways. It is, for example, a conventional belief about family life that old aunts who love their family will entertain benevolent daydreams about them. But Proust's aunt Léonie loves her family greatly, and it doesn't stop her from deriving pleasure in involving them in the most macabre scenarios. Confined to her bed on account of a host of imaginary ailments, she is so bored with life that she longs for something exciting to happen to her, even if it should be something terrible. The most exciting thing she can imagine is a fire that would leave no stone of her house standing and would kill her entire family, but from which she herself would have plenty of time to escape. She would then be able to mourn her family affectionately for many years, and cause universal stupefaction in her village by getting out of bed to conduct the obsequies, crushed but courageous, moribund but erect.

Aunt Léonie would no doubt have preferred to die under torture rather than admit to harboring such "unnatural" thoughts—which does nothing to stop them from being very normal, if only rarely discussed.

Albertine has some comparably normal thoughts. She walks into the narrator's room one morning and experiences a rush of affection for him. She tells him how clever he is, and swears that she would rather die than leave him. If we asked Albertine why she had suddenly felt this rush of affection, one imagines her pointing to her boyfriend's intellectual or spiritual qualities—and we would of course be inclined to believe her, for this is a dominant societal interpretation of the way affection is generated.

However, Proust quietly lets us know that the real reason why Albertine feels so much love for her boyfriend is that he has had a very close shave this morning, and that she adores smooth skin. The implication is that his cleverness counts for little in her particular enthusiasm; if he refused to shave ever again, she might leave him tomorrow.

This is an inopportune thought. We like to think of love as arising from more profound sources. Albertine might vigorously deny that she had ever felt love because of a close shave, accuse you of perversion for suggesting it, and attempt to change the subject. It would be a pity. What can replace a clichéd explanation of our functioning is not an image of perversity but a broader conception of what is normal. If Albertine could accept that her reactions only demonstrated that a feeling of love can have an extraordinary number of origins, some more valid than others, then she might calmly evaluate the foundations of her relationship and identify the role which she wished good shaving to play in her emotional life.

In his descriptions both of Aunt Léonie and Albertine, Proust offers us a picture of human behavior that initially fails to match an orthodox account of how people operate, though it may in the end be judged to be a far *more* truthful picture than the one it has challenged.

The structure of this process may, rather obliquely, shed light on why Proust was so attracted to the story of the Impressionist painters.

In 1872, the year after Proust was born, Claude Monet exhibited a canvas entitled *Impression, Sunrise*. It depicted the harbor of Le Havre at dawn, and allowed viewers to discern, through a thick morning mist and a medley of unusually choppy brushstrokes, the outline of an industrial seafront, with an array of cranes, smoking chimneys, and buildings.

The canvas looked a bewildering mess to most who saw it, and particularly irritated the critics of the day, who pejoratively dubbed its creator and the loose group to which he belonged "impressionists," indicating that Monet's control of the technical side of painting was so limited that all he had been able to achieve was a childish daubing, bearing precious little resemblance to what dawns in Le Havre really looked like.

The contrast with the judgment of the art establishment a few years later could hardly have been greater. It seemed that not only could the Impressionists use a brush after all, but that their technique was masterful at capturing a dimension of visual reality overlooked by less talented contemporaries. What could explain such a dramatic reappraisal? Why had Monet's Le Havre been a great mess, then a remarkable representation of a Channel port?

The Proustian answer starts with the idea that we are all in the habit of

> giving to what we feel a form of expression which differs
> so much from, and which we nevertheless after a little time
> take to be, reality itself.

In this view, our *notion* of reality is at variance with actual reality, because it is so often shaped by inadequate or misleading accounts. Because we are surrounded by clichéd depictions of the world, our initial response to Monet's *Impression, Sunrise* may well be to balk and complain that Le Havre looks nothing like that, much as our initial response to Aunt Léonie and Albertine's behavior may be to think that such comportment lacks any possible basis in "reality." If Monet is a hero in this scenario, it is because he has freed himself from traditional, and in some ways limited, representations of Le Havre, in order to attend more closely to his own, uncorrupted impressions of the scene.

In a form of homage to the Impressionist painters, Proust inserted one into his novel, the fictional Elstir, who shares traits with Renoir, Degas, and Manet. In the seaside resort of Balbec, Proust's narrator visits Elstir's studio, where he finds canvases that, like Monet's Le Havre, challenge the orthodox understanding of what things look like. In Elstir's seascapes, there is no demarcation between the sea and the sky, the sky looks like the sea, the sea like the sky. In a painting of a harbor at Carquethuit, a ship that is out at sea seems to be sailing through the middle of the town, women gathering shrimps among the rocks look as if they were in a marine grotto overhung by ships and waves, a group of holidaymakers in a boat look like they were in a cariole riding up through sunlit fields and down through shady patches.

Elstir is not trying his hand at surrealism. If his work seems unusual, it is because he is attempting to paint something of what we *actually see* when we look around, rather than what we *know we see*. We know that ships don't sail through the middle of towns, but it can sometimes look as if this is happening when we see a ship against the backdrop of a town from a certain light at a certain angle. We know there is a demarcation between the sea and the sky, but it can on occasion be hard to tell whether an azure-colored band is in fact part of the sea or the sky, the confusion lasting only until our reason reestablishes a distinction between the two elements which had been missing at first glance. Elstir's achievement is to hang on to the original muddle, and to set down in paint a visual impression before it has been overruled by what he knows.

Proust was not implying that painting had reached its apotheosis in Impressionism, and that the movement had triumphantly captured "reality" in a way that previous schools of art had not. His appreciation of painting ranged further than this, but the works of Elstir illustrated with particular clarity what is arguably present in every successful work of art: an ability to restore to our sight a distorted or neglected aspect of reality. As Proust expressed it:

> Our vanity, our passions, our spirit of imitation, our
> abstract intelligence, our habits have long been at work, and it
> is the task of art to undo this work of theirs, making us travel

back in the direction from which we have come to the depths
where what has really existed lies unknown within us.

And what lies unknown within us includes such surprising things as ships
that go through towns, seas that are momentarily indistinguishable from
skies, fantasies that our beloved family will die in a major conflagration,
and intense feelings of love sparked by contact with smooth skin.

The moral? That life can be a stranger substance than cliché life, that
goldfinches should occasionally do things differently from their parents,
and that there are persuasive reasons for calling a loved one Plouplou,
Missou, or poor little wolf.

Learning from Eliot

SEAMUS HEANEY

The majority of poems one outgrows and outlives, as one outgrows and outlives the majority of human passions: Dante's is one of those which one can only just hope to grow up to at the end of life.

—T. S. Eliot

It was the middle of my own life before I began to grow up to T. S. Eliot, but the story necessarily starts far earlier. As a schoolboy in a Catholic boarding-school in Derry, I was daunted by the otherness of Eliot and all that he stood for. Nevertheless, when an aunt of mine offered to buy a couple of books for me, I requested his *Collected Poems*. It, and *Tales of Mystery and Imagination*, were the first 'grown-up' books I owned. Name and date—1955—were duly inscribed, so I was fifteen or sixteen years of age when the dark-blue linen-bound volume came into my possession: the British edition of *Collected Poems 1909–1935*, the one that ended with 'Burnt Norton' and had by then been reprinted fifteen times. It arrived in a food-parcel from home, and

it had an air of contraband about it, because the only reading matter we
were permitted, I am shocked to recollect, was what the sparsely stocked
college library held, or what our course syllabi required. So there I was
in 1955 with my forbidden book in my hand, with a literary reach that
exceeded my grasp, alone with the words on the page.

For a long time that book represented to me my distance from the
mystery and my unfittedness—as reader or writer—for the vocation it
represented. Over the years I could experience in its presence the onset
of a lump in the throat and a tightening of the diaphragm, symptoms
which until then had only affected me in maths class. Now my neu-
rotic symptoms in relation to advanced algebra and calculus extended to
encompass *Collected Poems*. And, later, during my first year at Queen's
University, when I read in E. M. Forster's *Howard's End* an account of
the character called Leonard Bast as somebody doomed forever to be
familiar with the outsides of books, my identification was not with the
privileged narrative voice but with Bast himself, pathetic scrambler on
the edge of literacy.

Do I exaggerate? Maybe. Maybe not. The fact that I would not then
have been able to put the matter to myself in exactly these terms does
not mean that the inarticulate ache towards knowing, towards adequacy, towards fitting oneself out as a reader of modern poetry did not
truly exist. It did exist and it ached all the more for being unrequited,
because one did not need to know any literary thing in particular in the
1950s in order to know that Eliot was the way, the truth and the light,
and that until one had found him one had not entered the kingdom of
poetry.

Even his name was a buzz-word for obscurity, and the word 'obscurity' was in turn suggestive of 'modern poetry', a term in those days
as compelling as the terms 'simony' and 'paralysis' were for the young
boy in Joyce's story 'The Sisters'. For the moment, however, the whole
burden of this mystery was confined in four pages of the school poetry
anthology, a bilious green compendium entitled *A Pageant of English
Verse*. About one quarter of the poems in this book were set each year as
part of the official syllabus for the Northern Ireland Senior Certificate
of Education, and in our year the syllabus included 'The Hollow Men'
and 'Journey of the Magi'. It was the first of these that made the truly

odd impression. It was impossible not to be affected by it, yet it is still impossible to say exactly what the effect was:

> Eyes I dare not meet in dreams
> In death's dream kingdom
> These do not appear:
> There, the eyes are
> Sunlight on a broken column
> There, is a tree swinging
> And voices are
> In the wind's singing
> More distant and more solemn
> Than a fading star.

Whatever happened within my reader's skin was the equivalent of what happens in an otherwise warm and well-wrapped body once a cold wind gets at its ankles. A shiver that fleetingly registered itself as more pertinent and more acutely pleasurable than the prevailing warmth. A cheese-wire exactness that revealed to you the cheesy nature of your own standards and expectations. But, of course, we were not encouraged to talk like that in English class, and anyhow, like the girl in *The Importance of Being Earnest* who was pleased to say she had never seen a spade, I had not then ever seen a cheese-wire.

All this is extremely interesting to remember now, for it persuades me that what is to be learned from Eliot is the double-edged nature of poetic reality: first encountered as a strange fact of culture, poetry is internalized over the years until it becomes, as they say, second nature. Poetry that was originally beyond you, generating the need to under-stand and overcome its strangeness, becomes in the end a familiar path within you, a grain along which your imagination opens pleasurably backwards towards an origin and a seclusion. Your last state is therefore a thousand times better than your first, for the experience of poetry is one which truly deepens and fortifies itself with reenactment. I now know, for example, that I love the lines quoted above because of the pitch of their music, their nerve-end tremulousness, their treble in the helix of the ear. Even so, I cannot with my voice make the physical sound that would be the equivalent of what I hear on my inner ear; and the ability to acknowledge that very knowledge, the confidence to affirm that there is a reality to poetry which is unspeakable and for that very reason all the more piercing, that ability and that confidence are largely based upon a reading of Eliot.

Of course, the rare music of 'The Hollow Men' was never mentioned in school. Disillusion was what we heard about. Loss of faith. The luke-warm spirit. The modern world. Nor do I remember much attention being given to the cadence, or much attempt being made to encourage us to hear rather than abstract a meaning. What we heard, in fact, was what gave us then a kind of herd laughter: the eccentric, emphatic enunciations of our teacher, who came down heavily on certain syllables and gave an undue weight to the HOLlow men, the STUFFED men. And needless to say, in a class of thirty boys, in an atmosphere of socks and sex and sniggers, stuffed men and prickly pears and bangs and whimpers did not elevate the mood or induce the condition of stillness which is the ideally desirable one if we are to be receptive to this poet's bat-frequency.

I was never caught up by Eliot, never taken over and shown to myself by his work, my ear never pulled outside in by what it heard in him. Numerous readers have testified to this sudden kind of conversion, when the whole being is flushed by a great stroke of poetry, and this did indeed happen to me when I read Gerard Manley Hopkins. From the start something in my make-up was always ready to follow the antique flute of sensuous writing, yet when this kind of writing made its appearance in Eliot—in *Ash-Wednesday*, for instance—its very plenitude was meant to render its beauty questionable. It signalled a distraction from the way of purgation:

> At the first turning of the third stair
> Was a slotted window bellied like the fig's fruit
> And beyond the hawthorn blossom and a pasture scene
> The broadbacked figure drest in blue and green
> Enchanted the maytime with an antique flute.
> Blown hair is sweet, brown hair over the mouth blown,
> Lilac and brown hair;

Distraction, music of the flute, stops and steps of the mind over
   the third stair,
Fading, fading; strength beyond hope and despair
Climbing the third stair.

The fact that within the finer tone and stricter disciplines of Eliot's
poetry, these lines represented what he would later call 'the deception
of the thrush' did not prevent me from being deceived into relishing
them. And in that relish two things were combined. First of all, a single
unbewildering image was presented. To read the passage was to look
across a deep lucidity towards a shaggy solidity, as if in a Renaissance
painting of the Annunciation the window of the Virgin's chamber
opened upon a scene of vegetal and carnal riot. Second, the language of
the lines called in a direct way, in a way that indeed skirted the parodic,
upon the traditional language of poetry. Antique figure. Maytime.
Hawthorn. Flute. Blue and green. The pleasures of recollection were all
there. The consolations of the familiar. So that combination of composed
dramatic scene and consciously deployed poetic diction appealed to
the neophyte reader in me. To express the appeal by its negatives, the
poetry was not obscure, neither in what it was describing nor in the
language that did the describing. It fitted happily my expectations of
what poetry might be: what unfitted it was all that other stuff in *Ash-
Wednesday* about leopards and bones and violet and violet. That scared
me off, made me feel small and embarrassed. I wanted to call on the
Mother of Readers to have mercy on me, to come quick, make sense of
it, give me the pacifier of a paraphrasable meaning and a recognizable,
firmed-up setting:

Lady, three white leopards sat under a juniper-tree
In the cool of the day, having fed to satiety
On my legs my heart my liver and that which had been
   contained
In the hollow round of my skull. And God said
Shall these bones live? shall these
Bones live?

My panic in the face of these lovely lines was not just schoolboy panic. It descended again in my late twenties when I had to lecture on *Ash-Wednesday* as part of a course for undergraduates at Queen's University, Belfast. I had no access to the only reliable source for such teaching, namely, the experience of having felt the poem come home, memorably and irrefutably, so the lecture was one of the most unnerving forty-five minutes of my life. I scrambled around beforehand, snatching at F. O. Matthiessen's *The Achievement of T. S. Eliot* and George Williamson's *A Reader's Guide to T. S. Eliot* and D. E. S. Maxwell's *The Poetry of T. S. Eliot.* But whatever they had to say in their commentaries had nothing to fall upon, or to combine with, on the ground of my reader's mind. The poem never quite became a gestalt. Nowadays I talk about it more freely because I am not as shy of the subject as I then was: purgation, conversion, the embrace of an air thoroughly thin and dry, joy in a vision as arbitrary and disjunct from the usual as the vision of the leopards and lady in a white gown—all this offers itself far more comprehensively and persuasively to someone in his late forties than to someone in his late twenties:

> The Lady is withdrawn
> In a white gown, to contemplation, in a white gown.
> Let the whiteness of bones atone to forgetfulness.
> There is no life in them. As I am forgotten
> And would be forgotten, so I would forget
> Thus devoted, concentrated in purpose. And God said
> Prophesy to the wind, to the wind only for only
> The wind will listen. And the bones sang chirping
> With the burden of the grasshopper, saying . . .

Those qualities which created resistance in the first place now seem to me the valuable things about this work. The sense that the poem stood like a geometry in an absence was what caused my original bewilderment. I sensed myself like a gross intrusion, all corporeality and blunder in the realm of grace and translucence, and this unnerved me.

Nowadays, however, what gratifies me most is this very feeling of being privy to an atmosphere so chastely invented, so boldly and unpredictably written. Things like bones and leopards—which pop into the scene without preparation or explanation and which therefore dis-combobulated me at first—these things I now accept not as the poet's mystifying whim but as his gift and visitation. They are not what I at first mistakenly thought them: constituent parts of some erudite code available to initiates. Nor are they intended to be counters for a can-nily secluded meaning. Rather, they arose airily in the poet's composing mind and reproduced themselves deliciously, with a playfulness and self-surprising completedness.

Of course, it is true that a reading of the Earthly Paradise cantos of Dante's *Purgatorio* prepares one for the rarefied air of Eliot's scene, just as some familiarity with Dante will take from the unexpectedness of the leopards that start up in the very first line of Section II of *Ash-Wednesday*. Yet it is wrong to see these things simply as references to Dante. They are not hostages taken from *The Divine Comedy* and held by Eliot's art in the ascetic compound of his poem. They actually sprang up in the pure mind of the twentieth-century poet and their in-placeness does not derive from their having a meaning transplanted from the iconography of the medieval one. It is true, of course, that Eliot's pure mind was greatly formed by the contemplation of Dante, and Eliot's dream processes fed upon the phantasmagoria of *The Divine Comedy* constantly, so the matter of Dante's poem was present to him, and Dante had thereby become *second nature* to him. Dante, in fact, belonged in the rag-and-bone shop of Eliot's middle-ageing heart, and it was from that sad organ, we might say, that all his lyric ladders started.

Given the habitual probity, severity and strenuousness of Eliot's mind, one has therefore no difficulty in crediting him with his right to those moments of release when his nerves threw patterns upon the screen of the language. Yet needless to say, back in that window-rattling classroom in Derry in 1956, with rain gusting up the Foyle Estuary and the sound of the chapel bell marking the beginning and end of each forty-minute period, these kinds of thoughts were far in the future for a candidate in A-Level English. All that fellow wanted was to be able to get a foothold on the slippery slope of the prescribed poems. In the case of 'The Hollow Men', his teacher gave him just such a foothold by driving into the poem a huge extraneous spike labelled 'Loss of Faith in

Modern World and Consequences for Modern Man'. There at least was one way of subduing the querulous, outcast melodies of the poem to the familiar tolling of the bell of Faith. The modernist canon was to be co-opted by the ideology that rang the college bell, and indeed it must be said that the rhetoric of the poem's distress connived with the complacencies of the college's orthodoxies. The fraying quotations from the Lord's Prayer and the general tone of litany (which was so much part of our daily round of prayers) all tended to co-opt the imaginative strangeness, formal distinctness and fundamental difference of this poetry into the emulsifying element of our doctrinally sound young heads.

Obviously, the domestication of 'Journey of the Magi' was easier still. The three wise kings had been part of the folk-life of our Catholicism, part of the Christmas crib, the Christmas gospel and the Christmas card itself. Moreover, the idea of conversion was also familiar to us. Losing your life to save it, abandoning self to begin the path of illumination— no problem there. And no problem for me in the reek of actual country when a horse rushes away or a dank green valley moisture generously irrigates the reader's nostrils. High modernism, high Anglicanism and the low-lying farmlands of County Derry came together in a pleasing exhalation or—as Eliot himself might have called it—an 'efflux' of poetry. No problem either when three trees on the skyline were said to prefigure the Crucifixion, or when the hands dicing among the empty wineskins prefigured the hands of the Roman soldier dicing for Christ's robe at the foot of the Cross. This poem required no spike driven into it to give us a grip. On the contrary, it seemed so generously provided with doctrinal spikes of its own that we could not help being pinned down by its images and its orthodoxy:

> Then at dawn we came down to a temperate valley,
> Wet, below the snow line, smelling of vegetation;
> With a running stream and a water-mill beating the darkness,
> And three trees on the low sky,
> And an old white horse galloped away in the meadow.
> Then we came to a tavern with vine-leaves over the lintel,
> Six hands at an open door dicing for pieces of silver,
> And feet kicking the empty wine-skins.

But there was no information, so we continued
And arrived at evening, not a moment too soon
Finding the place; it was (you may say) satisfactory.

The familiarity of the matter of this poem gave us the illusion of 'understanding'; or perhaps the 'understanding' was not an illusion, the illusion being that 'understanding' its content and the crisis it embodied was the equivalent of knowing it as a poem; a formal event in the language; an 'objective correlative'. We knew its correlation with conversion and with Christmas, but not its artistic objectivity. Those three trees were never allowed time to manifest themselves in the mind's eye as three trees before they were turned into images of Calvary; nor were the hands at the wine-skins allowed to be written hands-in-themselves before becoming inscribed symbols of the division of Christ's garments. It was a paradoxical destiny for a poet such as Eliot, whose endeavour had been to insist on the poetriness of poetry being anterior to its status as philosophy or ideas or any other thing.

At Queen's University I packed myself with commentaries and in particular advanced upon *The Waste Land* with what help I could muster in the library. I even read chunks of Jessie L. Weston's *From Ritual to Romance*. I began to hear the music and to attune myself, but chiefly I obeyed the directives of the commentaries and got prepared to show myself informed. Yet perhaps the most lasting influence from this time was Eliot's prose, all assembled and digested by John Hayward in a little purple-coloured Penguin book, the particular tint of purple being appropriately reminiscent of a confessor's stole. There I read and re-read 'Tradition and the Individual Talent', essays on the metaphysical poets, on Milton, on Tennyson's *In Memoriam*. On the music of poetry. On why *Hamlet* doesn't make it as a play, as an objective correlative. But most important of all, perhaps, was a definition of the faculty which he called 'the auditory imagination'. This was 'the feeling for syllable and rhythm, penetrating far below the conscious levels of thought and feeling, invigorating every word; sinking to the most primitive and forgotten, returning to the origin and bringing something back . . . [fusing] the most ancient and the most civilized mentality'.

It was not in the context of this definition that Eliot commented upon the dramatic efficacy of the lines from *Macbeth* spoken just before the murder of Banquo:

> Light thickens,
> And the crow makes wing to the rooky wood,
> Good things of day begin to droop and drowse.

Nor did he invoke it when he discussed the exquisitely direct yet profoundly suggestive line spoken by Othello 'Keep up your bright swords, for the dew will rust them.' Nevertheless, Eliot's revelation of his susceptibility to such lines, the physicality of his ear as well as the fastidiousness of its discriminations, his example of a poet's intelligence exercising itself in the activity of listening, all of this seemed to excuse my own temperamental incapacity for paraphrase and my disinclination to engage a poem's argument and conceptual progress. Instead, it confirmed a natural inclination to make myself an echo chamber for the poem's sounds. I was encouraged to seek for the contour of a meaning within the pattern of a rhythm.

In the 'Death by Water' section of *The Waste Land*, for example, I began to construe from its undulant cadences and dissolvings and reinings-in a mimetic principle which matched or perhaps even overwhelmed any possible meaning that might be derived from the story of Phlebas's fate. In the heft and largesse of the poem's music, I thought I divined an aural equivalent of the larger transcendental reality betrayed by the profit-and-loss people of the City of London, those merchants and clerks who come into the poem as a somnolent rhythmic flow of shades over London Bridge. I began to stop worrying about Phlebas's relation to the Drowned Man and the effigy of Osiris cast into the water; all that was important as a structural principle, but the breath of life was in the body of sound:

> Phlebas the Phoenician, a fortnight dead,
> Forgot the cry of gulls, and the deep sea swell
> And the profit and loss.
>   A current under sea

Picked his bones in whispers. As he rose and fell
He passed the stages of his age and youth
Entering the whirlpool.
            Gentile or Jew
O you who turn the wheel and look to windward,
Consider Phlebas, who was once handsome and tall as you.

At this stage of readiness to listen, I was also lucky enough to hear
Eliot's poetry read aloud by the actor Robert Speaight. I had made
an introductory foray into *Four Quartets* but was finding it difficult
to retain any impression unified and whole in my mind. The bigness
of the structure, the opacity of the thought, the complexity of the
organization of those poems held you at bay; yet while they daunted
you, they promised a kind of wisdom—and it was at this tentative
stage that I heard the whole thing read aloud. That experience taught
me, in the words of the poem, 'to sit still'. To sit, in fact, all through
an afternoon in Belfast, in an upstairs flat, with a couple of graduate
students in biochemistry, people with a less professional anxiety about
understanding the poetry than I had, since in their unprofessional but
rewarding way they still assumed that mystification was par for the
course in modern poetry.

What I *heard* made sense. In the opening lines of 'Burnt Norton', for
example, the footfall of the word 'time' echoes and repeats in a way that
is hypnotic when read aloud, yet can be perplexing when sight-read
for its meaning only. Similarly, the interweaving and repetition of the
words 'present', 'past' and 'future' goes round and round, like a linked
dance through the ear. Words going forward meet each other coming
back. Even the word 'echo' meets itself on the rebound. The effect is
one of a turning and a stillness. Neither from nor towards. At the still
point of the turning world:

Time present and time past
Are both perhaps present in time future,
And time future contained in time past.
If all time is eternally present
All time is unredeemable.

What might have been is an abstraction
Remaining a perpetual possibility
Only in a world of speculation.
What might have been and what has been
Point to one end, which is always present.
Footfalls echo in the memory
Down the passage which we did not take
Towards the door we never opened
Into the rose-garden. My words echo
Thus, in your mind.
                                   But to what purpose
Disturbing the dust on a bowl of rose leaves
I do not know.
                         Other echoes
Inhabit the garden. Shall we follow?
Quick, said the bird, find them, find them,
Round the corner. Through the first gate,
Into our first world, shall we follow
The deception of the thrush?

By its orchestration of theme and phrase, paraphrase and reprise, its premonitions of the end recoiling into the beginning, this passage is typical of the procedures of *Four Quartets* as a whole. The poetry comes through in a silent reading, of course, since (to quote again from Eliot's own definition of 'auditory imagination') it operates below the level of sense; but it operates much more potently when the words are spoken aloud. Gradually, therefore, I began in the early 1960s to take pleasure in the basement life of Eliot's ear and to teach myself 'to sit still' and let its underworkings work.

These were also years when I was trying to make a start as a poet, and searching for the charge that sets writing energy flowing in a hitherto unwriting system. Yet much as I was learning from Eliot about the right way to listen, he could not be the stimulator of poetry for me. He was more a kind of literary superego than a generator of the poetic libido, and in order for the libidinous lyric voice to get on with its business, it had to escape from his overseeing presence. So I turned towards more familiar, more engageable writers like Patrick Kavanagh, R. S. Thomas, Ted Hughes, John Montague, Norman MacCaig. All of a sudden I was making up for not having read contemporary British and Irish poetry; and that way, I got excited and got started.

Then I came upon C. K. Stead's book *The New Poetic*, with its revelation of Eliot as a poet who trusted the 'dark embryo' of unconscious energy. Stead revealed Eliot as a much more intuitive kind of writer than the commentaries had allowed one to believe. It is not that this lessened one's awareness of the strictness of his mind or the scrupulousness of his withholdings. Eliot was still a *rara avis*, one whose note was uniquely beyond the common scale, a thin pure signal that might not wash genially across the earthy reaches of one's nature but had the capacity to probe in the universe of spirit as far as Pluto. Yet one could grant this inimitable status to his achievement and still recognize the process that produced it as the usual, uncertain, hopeful, needy, half self-surrendering, half self-priming process which the rest of us also experienced.

What one learns ultimately from Eliot is that the activity of poetry is solitary, and if one is to rejoice in it, one has to construct something upon which to rejoice. One learns that at the desk every poet faces the same kind of task, that there is no secret that can be imparted, only resources of one's own that are to be mustered, or not, as the case may be. Many of the things Eliot says about poetic composition are fortifying because they are so authoritatively unconsoling:

> And what there is to conquer
> By strength and submission, has already been discovered
> Once or twice, or several times, by men whom one cannot hope
> To emulate—but there is no competition—
> There is only the fight to recover what had been lost
> And found and lost again and again: and now, under conditions
> That seem unpropitious. But perhaps neither gain nor loss.
> For us, there is only the trying. The rest is not our business.

So, to conclude. If Eliot did not help me to write, he did help me to learn what it means to read. The experience of his poetry is an unusually pure one. You begin and end with the words alone—which is admittedly always the case, but often in the work of other poets the reader can find respites and alibis. With Frost or Yeats or Hardy, for example, there is a corroborative relation between a landscape and a sensibility. The words on the page can function in a way that is supplementary to their primary artistic function: they can have a window effect and open the blinds of language on to subjects and places before or behind the words. But this kind of mutual help does not exist—and is not intended to exist—between the words of Eliot's poetry and the world that gave rise to them. When I visited Burnt Norton, for example, I did indeed find a rose garden and a dry concrete pool; but I also found this very documentary congruence between poem and place oddly disappointing. I realized that I did not really want a landscape to materialize, since I had long since internalized a soundscape.

Perhaps the final thing to be learned is this: in the realm of poetry, as in the realm of consciousness, there is no end to the possible learnings that can take place. Nothing is final, the most gratifying discovery is fleeting, the path of positive achievement leads to the *via negative*. Eliot forfeited his expressionist intensity when he renounced the lyric for philosophical song. It may even be truer to say that the lyric renounced Eliot. But in accepting the consequences of renunciation with such self-knowledge and in proceeding with such strictness of intent, he proved a truth that we want to believe not perhaps about all poets but about those who are the necessary ones. He showed how poetic vocation entails the disciplining of a habit of expression until it becomes fundamental to the whole conduct of a life.

Out of Kansas

SALMAN RUSHDIE

I wrote my first short story in Bombay at the age of ten. Its title was "Over the Rainbow." It amounted to a dozen or so pages, was dutifully typed up by my father's secretary on flimsy paper, and was eventually lost somewhere along my family's mazy journeyings between India, England, and Pakistan. Shortly before my father's death in 1987, he claimed to have found a copy moldering in an old file, but despite my pleadings he never produced it. I've often wondered about this incident. Maybe he never really found the story, in which case he had succumbed to the lure of fantasy, and this was the last of the many fairy tales he told me. Or else he did find it, and hugged it to himself as a talisman and a reminder of simpler times, thinking of it as his treasure, not mine—his pot of nostalgic, parental gold.

I don't remember much about the story. It was about a ten-year-old Bombay boy who one day happens upon the beginning of a rainbow, a place as elusive as any pot-of-gold end zone, and as rich in promise. The rainbow is broad, as wide as the sidewalk, and constructed like a grand staircase. Naturally, the boy begins to climb. I have forgotten almost everything about his adventures, except for an encounter with a talking pianola whose personality is an improbable hybrid of Judy Garland, Elvis Presley, and the "playback singers" of the Hindi movies, many of which made *The Wizard of Oz* look like kitchen-sink realism.

My bad memory—what my mother would call a "forgettery"—is probably a blessing. Anyway, I remember what matters. I remember that *The Wizard of Oz* (the film, not the book, which I didn't read as a child) was my very first literary influence. More than that: I remember that when the possibility of my going to school in England was mentioned, it felt as exciting as any voyage over rainbows. England felt as wonderful a prospect as Oz.

The wizard, however, was right there in Bombay. My father, Anis Ahmed Rushdie, was a magical parent of young children, but he was also prone to explosions, thunderous rages, bolts of emotional lightning, puffs of dragon smoke, and other menaces of the type also practiced by Oz, the great and terrible, the first Wizard Deluxe. And when the curtain fell away and we, his growing offspring, discovered (like Dorothy) the truth about adult humbug, it was easy for us to think, as she did, that our wizard must be a very bad man indeed. It took me half a lifetime to discover that the Great Oz's *apologia pro vita sua* fitted my father equally well; that he too was a good man but a very bad wizard.

I have begun with these personal reminiscences because *The Wizard of Oz* is a film whose driving force is the inadequacy of adults, even of good adults. At its beginning, the weaknesses of grown-ups force a child to take control of her own destiny (and her dog's). Thus, ironically, she begins the process of becoming a grown-up herself. The journey from Kansas to Oz is a rite of passage from a world in which Dorothy's parent-substitutes, Auntie Em and Uncle Henry, are powerless to help her save her dog, Toto, from the marauding Miss Gulch, into a world where the people are her own size, and in which she is never treated as a child but always treated as a heroine. She gains this status by accident, it's true, having played no part in her house's decision to squash the Wicked Witch of the East; but by the end of her adventure she has certainly grown to fill those shoes—or, rather, those famous ruby slippers. "Who'd have thought a girl like you could destroy my beautiful wickedness?" laments the Wicked Witch of the West as she melts—an adult becoming smaller than, and giving way to, a child. As the Wicked Witch of the West "grows down," so Dorothy is seen to have grown up. In my view, this is a much more satisfactory explanation for Dorothy's newfound power over the ruby slippers than the sentimental reasons offered by the ineffably soppy Good Witch Glinda, and then by Dorothy herself, in a cloying ending that I find untrue to the film's anarchic spirit. (More about this later.)

The helplessness of Auntie Em and Uncle Henry in the face of Miss Gulch's desire to annihilate Toto the dog leads Dorothy to think, childishly, of running away from home—of escape. And that's why, when the tornado hits, she isn't with the others in the storm shelter, and as a result is whirled away to an escape beyond her wildest dreams. Later, however, when she is confronted by the weakness of the Wizard of Oz, she doesn't run away but goes into battle—first against the Witch and then against the Wizard himself. The Wizard's ineffectuality is one of the film's many symmetries, rhyming with the feebleness of Dorothy's folks; but the difference in the way Dorothy reacts is the point.

The ten-year-old boy who watched *The Wizard of Oz* in Bombay's Metro cinema knew very little about foreign parts and even less about growing up. He did, however, know a great deal more about the cinema of the fantastic than any Western child of the same age. In the West, *The Wizard of Oz* was an oddball, an attempt to make a live-action version of a Disney cartoon feature despite the industry's received wisdom (how times change!) that fantasy movies usually flopped. There's little doubt that the excitement engendered by *Snow White and the Seven Dwarfs* accounts for MGM's decision to give the full, all-stops-out treatment to a thirty-nine-year-old book. This was not, however, the first screen version. I haven't seen the silent film of 1925, but its reputation is poor. It did, however, star Oliver Hardy as the Tin Man.

The Wizard of Oz never really made money until it became a television standard years after its original theatrical release, though it should be said in mitigation that coming out two weeks before the start of World War II can't have helped its chances. In India, however, it fitted into what was then, and remains today, one of the mainstreams of "Bollywood" film production.

It's easy to satirize the Indian commercial cinema industry. In James Ivory's film *Bombay Talkie*, a journalist (the touching Jennifer Kendal, who died in 1984) visits a studio soundstage and watches an amazing dance number featuring scantily clad nautch girls prancing on the keys of a giant typewriter. The director explains that this is no less than the Typewriter of Life, and we are all dancing out "the story of our Fate" upon that mighty machine. "It's very symbolic," the journalist suggests. The director, simpering, replies: "Thank you."

Typewriters of Life, sex goddesses in wet saris (the Indian equivalent of wet T-shirts), gods descending from the heavens to meddle in human affairs, magic potions, superheroes, demonic villains, and so on have always been the staple diet of the Indian filmgoer. Blond Glinda arriving in Munchkinland in her magic bubble might cause Dorothy to comment on the high speed and oddity of local transport operating in Oz, but to an Indian audience Glinda was arriving exactly as a god should arrive: *ex machina*, out of her divine machine. The Wicked Witch of the West's orange puffs of smoke were equally appropriate to her super-bad status. But in spite of all the similarities, there are important differences between the Bombay cinema and a film like *The Wizard of Oz*. Good fairies and bad witches might superficially resemble the deities and demons of the Hindu pantheon, but in reality one of the most striking aspects of the worldview of *The Wizard of Oz* is its joyful and almost complete secularism. Religion is mentioned only once in the film. Auntie Em, sputtering with anger at the gruesome Miss Gulch, reveals that she's waited years to tell her what she thinks of her, "and now, because I'm a good Christian woman, I can't do so." Apart from this moment, in which Christian charity prevents some old-fashioned plain speaking, the film is breezily godless. There's not a trace of religion in Oz itself. Bad witches are feared, good ones liked, but none are sanctified; and while the Wizard of Oz is thought to be something very close to all-powerful, nobody thinks to worship him. This absence of higher values greatly increases the film's charm and is an important aspect of its success in creating a world in which nothing is deemed more important than the loves, cares, and needs of human beings (and, of course, tin beings, straw beings, lions, and dogs).

The other major difference is harder to define, because it is, finally, a matter of quality. Most Hindi movies were then and are now what can only be called trashy. The pleasure to be had from such films (and some of them are extremely enjoyable) is something like the fun of eating junk food. The classic Bombay talkie uses scripts of dreadful corniness, looks tawdry and garish, and relies on the mass appeal of its star performers and musical numbers to provide a little zing. *The Wizard of Oz* also has movie stars and musical numbers, but it is also very definitely a Good Film. It takes the fantasy of Bombay and adds high production values and something more. Call it imaginative truth. Call it (reach for your revolvers now) art.

But if *The Wizard of Oz* is a work of art, it's extremely difficult to say who the artist was. The birth of Oz itself has already passed into legend: the author, L. Frank Baum, named his magic world after the letters O–Z on the bottom drawer of his filing cabinet. Baum had an odd, roller-coaster life. Born rich, he inherited a string of little theaters from his father and lost them all through mismanagement. He wrote one successful play and several flops. The Oz books made him one of the leading children's writers of his day, but all his other fantasy novels bombed. *The Wonderful Wizard of Oz*, and a musical adaptation of it for the stage, restored Baum's finances, but a financially disastrous attempt to tour America promoting his books with a "fairylogue" of slides and films led him to file for bankruptcy in 1911. He became a slightly shabby, if still frock-coated, figure, living on his wife's money at "Ozcot" in Hollywood, where he raised chickens and won prizes at flower shows. The small success of another musical, *The Tik-Tok Man of Oz*, improved his finances, but he ruined them again by setting up his own movie company, the Oz Film Company, and trying unsuccessfully to film and distribute the Oz books. After two bedridden years, and still, we are told, optimistic, he died in May 1919. However, as we shall see, his frock coat lived on into a strange immortality.

The Wonderful Wizard of Oz, published in 1900, contains many of the ingredients of the magic potion—all the major characters and events are here, as well as the most important locations, the Yellow Brick Road, the Deadly Poppy Field, the Emerald City. But *The Wizard of Oz* is that great rarity, a film that improves on the good book from which it came. One of the changes is the expansion of the Kansas section, which in the novel takes up precisely two pages before the tornado arrives, and just nine lines at the end. The story line in the Oz section is also simplified, by jettisoning several sub-plots, such as the visits to the Fighting Trees, the Dainty China Country, and the Quadlings that come, in the novel, just after the dramatic high point of the Witch's destruction and fritter away the story's narrative drive. And there are two even more important alterations: to the colors of the Wizard's city and of Dorothy's shoes.

Frank Baum's Emerald City was green only because everyone in it had to wear emerald-tinted glasses, whereas in the movie it really is a futuristic, chlorophyll green—except, that is, for the Horse of a Different Color You've Heard Tell Of. The Horse changes color in each successive shot, a change brought about by covering it in a variety of shades of powdered Jell-O.[1]

Frank Baum did not make up the ruby slippers. He called them Silver Shoes. Baum believed that America's stability required a switch from the gold to the silver standard, and the Shoes were a metaphor of the magical advantages of Silver. Noel Langley, the first of the film's three credited screenwriters, originally went along with Baum's idea. But in his fourth script, the script of May 14, 1938, known as the DO NOT MAKE CHANGES script, the clunky, metallic, and non-mythic footwear is jettisoned and the immortal jewel shoes are introduced for the first time, probably in response to the demand for color. (In Shot 114, "the ruby shoes appear on Dorothy's feet, glittering and sparkling in the sun.")

Other writers contributed important details to the finished screenplay. Florence Ryerson and Edgar Allan Woolf were probably responsible for "There's no place like home," which, to me, is, the least convincing idea in the film (it's one thing for Dorothy to want to get home, quite another that she can do so only by eulogizing the ideal state, which Kansas so obviously is not).[2] But there's some dispute about this, too. A studio memo implies that it could have been the associate producer Arthur Freed who came up with the cutesy slogan. And, after much quarreling between Langley and Ryerson-Woolf, it was the film's lyricist, Yip Harburg, who pulled the final script together and added the crucial scene in which the Wizard, unable to give the companions what they demand, hands out emblems instead, and to our satisfaction these symbols do the job. The name of the rose turns out to be the rose, after all.

Who, then, was the auteur of *The Wizard of Oz*? No single writer can claim that honor, not even the author of the original book. The producers, Mervyn LeRoy and Arthur Freed, both have their champions. At least four directors worked on the picture, most notably Victor Fleming; but he left before shooting ended (King Vidor was his uncredited replacement) to make *Gone With the Wind*, ironically enough the movie that dominated the Oscars while *The Wizard of Oz* won just three: Best Song ("Over the Rainbow"), Best Musical Score, and a Special Award for Judy Garland. The truth is that this great movie, in which the quarrels, sackings, and bungles of all concerned produced what seems like pure, effortless, and somehow inevitable felicity, is as near as dammit to that will-o'-the-wisp of modern critical theory: the authorless text.

—◆—

Kansas as described by L. Frank Baum is a depressing place, in which everything is gray as far as the eye can see—the prairie is gray and so is the house in which Dorothy lives. As for Auntie Em, "The sun and wind . . . had taken the sparkle from her eyes and left them a sober gray; they had taken the red from her cheeks and lips, and they were gray also. She was thin and gaunt, and never smiled now." Whereas: "Uncle Henry never laughed. He was gray also, from his long beard to his rough boots." And the sky? "It was even grayer than usual." Toto, though, was spared grayness. He "saved Dorothy from growing as gray as her surroundings." He was not exactly colorful, though his eyes twinkled and his hair was silky. Toto was black.

It is out of this grayness—the gathering, cumulative grayness of that bleak world—that calamity comes. The tornado is the grayness gathered together and whirled about and unleashed, so to speak, against itself. And to all this the film is astonishingly faithful, shooting the Kansas scenes in what we call black-and-white but what is in reality a multiplicity of shades of gray, and darkening its images until the whirlwind sucks them up and rips them into pieces.

—◆—

There is, however, another way of understanding the tornado. Dorothy has a surname: Gale. And in many ways Dorothy is the gale blowing through this little corner of nowhere. She demands justice for her little dog while the adults give in meekly to the powerful Miss Gulch. She is prepared to interrupt the gray inevitability of her life by running away but is so tenderhearted that she runs back again when Professor Marvel tells her that Auntie Em is distraught that she has fled. Dorothy is the life-force of this Kansas, just as Miss Gulch is the force of death; and perhaps it is Dorothy's turmoil, the cyclone of feeling unleashed by the conflict between Dorothy and Miss Gulch, that is made actual in the great dark snake of cloud that wriggles across the prairie, eating the world.

The Kansas of the film is a little less unremittingly bleak than that of the book, if only because of the introduction of the three farmhands and of Professor Marvel, four characters who will find their rhymes, their counterparts, in the Three Companions of Oz and the Wizard himself. Then again, the movie Kansas is also more terrifying, because it adds a presence of real evil: the angular Miss Gulch, with a profile that could carve a turkey, riding stiffly on her bicycle with a hat on her head like a plum pudding or a bomb, and claiming the protection of the Law for her campaign against Toto. Thanks to Miss Gulch, this cinematic Kansas is informed not only by the sadness of dirt-poverty but also by the badness of would-be dog murderers.

And *this* is the home that there's no place like? This is the lost Eden that we are asked to prefer (as Dorothy does) to Oz?

I remember (or I imagine I remember) that when I first saw this film, Dorothy's place struck me as being pretty much a dump. I was lucky, and had a good, comfortable home, and so, I reasoned to myself, if *I'd* been whisked off to Oz, I'd naturally want to get home again. But Dorothy? Maybe we should invite her over to stay. Anywhere looks better than *that*.

I thought one further thought, which I had better confess now, as it gave me a sneaking regard for Miss Gulch and her fantasy counterpart, the Wicked Witch, and, some might say, a secret sympathy for all persons of her witchy disposition, which has remained with me ever since: I couldn't stand Toto. I still can't. As Gollum says of the hobbit Bilbo Baggins in another great fantasy: "*Baggins*: we hates it to pieces."

Toto, that little yapping hairpiece of a creature, that meddlesome rug! L. Frank Baum, excellent fellow, gave the dog a distinctly minor role: it kept Dorothy happy, and when she was not, it had a tendency to "whine dismally"—not an endearing trait. Its only significant contribution to Baum's story came when it accidentally knocked over the screen behind which the Wizard of Oz was concealed. The film-Toto rather more deliberately pulls aside a curtain to reveal the Great Humbug, and in spite of everything I found this an irritating piece of mischief-making. I was not surprised to learn that the pooch playing Toto was possessed of a star's temperament, and even brought the shoot to a standstill at one point by staging a nervous breakdown. That Toto should be the film's one true object of love has always rankled. But such protest is useless, if satisfying. Nobody, now, can rid me of this turbulent toupee.

When I first saw *The Wizard of Oz* it made writer of me. Many years later, I began to devise the yarn that eventually became *Haroun and the Sea of Stories*. I felt strongly that—if I could only strike the right note—it must be possible to write the tale in such a way as to make it of interest to adults as well as children. The world of books has become a severely categorized and demarcated place, in which children's fiction is not only a kind of ghetto but one subdivided into writing for a number of different age-groups. The movies, however, have regularly risen above such categorizing. From Spielberg to Schwarzenegger, from Disney to Gilliam, the cinema has often come up with offerings before which kids and adults sit happily side by side. I watched *Who Framed Roger Rabbit* in an afternoon movie theater full of excited, rowdy children and went back to see it the next evening, at an hour too late for the kids, so that I could hear all the gags properly, enjoy the movie in-jokes, and marvel at the brilliance of the Toontown concept. But of all movies, the one that helped me most as I tried to find the right voice for *Haroun* was *The Wizard of Oz*. The film's influence is there in the text, plain to see. In Haroun's companions there are clear echoes of the friends who danced with Dorothy down the Yellow Brick Road.

And now I'm doing something strange, something that ought to destroy my love for the movie but doesn't: I'm watching a videotape with a notebook on my lap, a pen in one hand and a remote-control zapper in the other, subjecting *The Wizard of Oz* to the indignities of slow-motion, fast-forward, and freeze-frame, trying to learn the secret of the magic trick; and, yes, seeing things I'd never noticed before . . .

The film begins. We are in the monochrome "real" world of Kansas. A girl and her dog run down a country lane. *She isn't coming yet, Toto. Did she hurt you? She tried to, didn't she?* A real girl, a real dog, and the beginning, with the very first line of dialogue, of real drama. Kansas, however, is not real, no more real than Oz. Kansas is a painting. Dorothy and Toto have been running down a short stretch of "road" in the MGM studios, and this shot has been matted into a picture of emptiness. "Real" emptiness would probably not look empty enough. It's as close as makes no difference to the universal gray of Frank Baum's story, the void broken only by a couple of fences and the vertical lines of telegraph poles. If Oz is *nowhere*, then the studio setting of the Kansas scenes suggests that *so is Kansas*. This is necessary. A realistic depiction of the extreme poverty of Dorothy Gale's circumstances would have created a burden, a heaviness, that would have rendered impossible the imaginative leap into Storyland, the soaring flight into Oz. The Grimms' fairy tales, it's true, were often realistic. In "The Fisherman and His Wife," the eponymous couple live, until they meet the magic flounder, in what is tersely described as "a pisspot." But in many children's versions of the Grimms, the pisspot is bowdlerized into a "hovel" or some even gentler word. Hollywood's vision has always been of this soft-focus variety. Dorothy looks extremely well fed, and she is not really, but *unreally*, poor.

She arrives at the farmyard, and here (freezing the frame) we see the beginning of what will be a recurring visual motif. In the scene we have frozen, Dorothy and Toto are in the background, heading for a gate. To the left of the screen is a tree trunk, a vertical line echoing the telegraph poles of the scene before. Hanging from an approximately horizontal branch are a triangle (for calling farmhands to dinner) and a circle (actually a rubber tire). In mid-shot are further geometric elements: the parallel lines of the wooden fence, the bisecting diagonal wooden bar at the gate. Later, when we see the house, the theme of simple geometry is present once again; it is all right angles and triangles. The world of Kansas, that great void, is shaped into "home" by the use of simple, uncomplicated shapes; none of your citified complexity here. Throughout *The Wizard of Oz*, home and safety are represented by such geometrical simplicity, whereas danger and evil are invariably twisty, irregular, and misshapen.

The tornado is just such an untrustworthy, sinuous, shifting shape. Random, unfixed, it wrecks the plain shapes of that no-frills life.

The Kansas sequence invokes not only geometry but mathematics too. When Dorothy, like the chaotic force she is, bursts upon Auntie Em and Uncle Henry with her fears about Toto, what are they doing? Why do they shoo her away? "We're trying to count," they admonish her, as they take a census of the eggs, counting their metaphorical chickens, their small hopes of income, which the tornado will shortly blow away. So, with simple shapes and numbers, Dorothy's family erects its defenses against the immense, maddening emptiness; and these defenses are useless, of course.

Leap ahead to Oz and it becomes obvious that this opposition between the geometric and the twisty is no accident. Look at the beginning of the Yellow Brick Road: it's a perfect spiral. Look again at Glinda's carriage, that perfect, luminous sphere. Look at the regimented routines of the Munchkins as they greet Dorothy and thank her for squashing the Wicked Witch of the East. Move on to the Emerald City: see it in the distance, its straight lines soaring into the sky! And now, by contrast, observe the Wicked Witch of the West: her bent figure, her misshapen hat. How does she depart? In a puff of shapeless smoke . . . "Only bad witches are ugly," Glinda tells Dorothy, a remark of high political incorrectness that emphasizes the film's animosity toward whatever is tangled, claw-crooked, and weird. Woods are invariably frightening— the gnarled branches of trees are capable of coming to life—and the one moment when the Yellow Brick Road itself bewilders Dorothy is the moment when it ceases to be geometric (first spiral, then rectilinear) and splits and forks every which way.

⚬⚬⚬

Back in Kansas, Auntie Em is delivering the scolding that is the prelude to one of the cinema's immortal moments. *You always get yourself into a fret about nothing . . . find yourself a place where you won't get into any trouble!*

Some place where there isn't any trouble. Do you suppose there is such a place, Toto? There must be. Anybody who has swallowed the script-writers' notion that this is a film about the superiority of "home" over "away," that the "moral" of *The Wizard of Oz* is as sickly-sweet as an embroidered sampler—"East, West, home's best"—would do well to listen to the yearning in Judy Garland's voice as her face tilts up toward the skies. What she expresses here, what she embodies with the purity of an archetype, is the human dream of *leaving*, a dream at least as powerful as its countervailing dream of roots. At the heart of *The Wizard of Oz* is the tension between these two dreams; but as the music swells and that big, clean voice flies into the anguished longings of the song, can anyone doubt which message is the stronger? In its most potent emotional moment, this is unarguably a film about the joys of going away, of leaving the grayness and entering the color, of making a new life in the "place where there isn't any trouble." "Over the Rainbow" is, or ought to be, the anthem of all the world's migrants, all those who go in search of the place where "the dreams that you dare to dream really do come true." It is a celebration of Escape, a grand paean to the uprooted self, a hymn—*the* hymn—to Elsewhere.

E. Y. Harburg, the lyricist of "Brother, Can You Spare a Dime?" and Harold Arlen, who had written "It's Only a Paper Moon" with Harburg, made the songs for *The Wizard of Oz*, and Arlen actually did think of the melody line outside Schwab's drugstore in Hollywood. Aljean Harmetz records Harburg's disappointment with the music: too complex for a sixteen-year old to sing, too advanced by comparison with Disney hits like "Heigh Ho! Heigh Ho! It's Off to Work We Go." Harmetz adds: "To please Harburg, Arlen wrote the melody for the tinkling middle section of the song." *Where troubles melt like lemon drops / Away above the chimney tops / That's where you'll find me . . .* A little higher up, in short, than the protagonist of that other great ode to flight, "Up on the Roof."

That "Over the Rainbow" came close to being cut out of the movie is well known, and proof that Hollywood makes its masterpieces by accident, because it doesn't really know what it is doing. Other songs were dropped: "The Jitter Bug," after five weeks' filming, and almost all of "Lions and Tigers and Bears," which survives only as the chant of the Companions as they pass through the forest along the Yellow Brick Road: *Lions and Tigers and Bears—oh, my!* It's impossible to say if the film would have been improved or damaged by the addition of these songs; would *Catch-22* be *Catch-22* if it had been published under its original title of *Catch-18*? What we can say, however, is that Yip Harburg (no admirer of Judy) was wrong about Garland's voice.

The principal actors in the cast complained that there was "no acting" in the movie, and in the conventional sense they were right. But Garland singing "Over the Rainbow" did something extraordinary. In that moment she gave the film its heart. The force of her rendition is strong and sweet and deep enough to carry us through all the tomfoolery that follows, even to bestow a touching quality upon it, a vulnerable charm that is matched only by Bert Lahr's equally extraordinary interpretation of the role of the Cowardly Lion.

What is left to say about Garland's Dorothy? The conventional wisdom is that the performance gains in ironic force because its innocence contrasts so starkly with what we know of the actress's difficult later life. I'm not sure this is right, though it's the kind of remark movie buffs like making. It seems to me that Garland's performance succeeds on its own terms, and on the film's. She is required to pull off what sounds like an impossible trick. On the one hand she is to be the film's tabula rasa, the blank slate upon which the action of the story gradually writes itself—or rather, because this is a movie, after all, the blank screen upon which the action plays. Armed only with her look of wide-eyed innocence, she must be the object of the film as well as its subject, must allow herself to be the empty vessel that the movie slowly fills. And yet, on the other hand, she must—with a little help from the Cowardly Lion—carry the entire emotional weight, the whole cyclonic force of the film. That she achieves this is due not only to the mature depths of her singing voice but also to the odd stockiness, the physical gaucherie that endears us precisely because it is half unbeautiful, *jolie-laide*, instead of the posturing prettiness Shirley Temple would have brought to the role—and Temple was seriously considered for the part. The scrubbed, ever so slightly lumpy unsexiness of Garland's playing is what makes the movie work. One can only imagine the catastrophic flirtatiousness young Shirley would have insisted on employing, and be grateful that the MGM executives were persuaded to go with Judy.

The tornado that I've suggested is the product of the Gale in Dorothy's name was actually made of muslin stiffened with wire. A props man had to lower himself into the muslin tunnel to help pull the needles through and push them out again. "It was pretty uncomfortable when we reached the narrow end," he confessed. The discomfort was worth it, because that tornado, swooping down on Dorothy's home, creates the second genuinely mythic image of *The Wizard of Oz*: the archetypal myth, one might say, of moving house.

In this, the transitional sequence of the movie, when the unreal reality of Kansas gives way to the realistic surreality of the world of wizardry, there is, as befits a threshold moment, much business involving windows and doors. First, the farmhands open up the doors of the storm shelter, and Uncle Henry, heroic as ever, persuades Auntie Em that they can't afford to wait for Dorothy. Second, Dorothy, returning with Toto from her attempt at running away, struggles against the wind to open the screen door of the main house; this outer door is instantly ripped from its hinges and blows away. Third, we see the others closing the doors of the storm shelter. Fourth, Dorothy, inside the house, opens and shuts the doors of various rooms, calling out frantically for Auntie Em. Fifth, Dorothy goes to the storm shelter, but its doors are locked against her. Sixth, Dorothy retreats back inside the main house, her cries for Auntie Em now weak and fearful; whereupon a window, echoing the screen door, blows off its hinges and knocks her cold. She falls upon the bed, and from now on magic reigns. We have passed through the film's most important gateway.

This device—the knocking out of Dorothy—is the most radical and in some ways the worst of all the changes wrought to Frank Baum's original conception. For in the book there is no question that Oz is real, that it is a place of the same order, though not of the same type, as Kansas. The film, like the TV soap opera *Dallas*, introduces an element of bad faith when it permits the possibility that everything that follows is a dream. This type of bad faith cost *Dallas* its audience and eventually killed it off. That *The Wizard of Oz* avoided the soap opera's fate is a testament to the general integrity of the film, which enabled it to transcend this hoary cliché.

While the house flies through the air, looking in longshot like a tiny toy, Dorothy "awakes." What she sees through the window is a sort of movie—the window acts as a cinema screen, a frame within the frame—which prepares her for the new sort of movie she is about to step into. The effect shots, sophisticated for their time, include a lady knitting in her rocking chair as the tornado whirls her by, a cow standing placidly in the eye of the storm, two men rowing a boat through the twisting air, and, most important of all, the figure of Miss Gulch on her bicycle, which transforms, as we watch it, into the figure of the Wicked Witch of the West on her broomstick, her cape flying out behind her, and her huge cackling laugh rising above the noise of the storm.

———◦•◦———

The house lands. Dorothy emerges from her bedroom with Toto in her arms. We have reached the moment of color.

The first color shot, in which Dorothy walks away from the camera toward the front door, is deliberately dull, to match the preceding monochrome. But once the door is open, color floods the screen. In these color-glutted days it's hard to imagine a time when color films were still relatively new. Thinking back once again to my Bombay childhood in the 1950s, when Hindi movies were all in black-and-white, I can recall the excitement of the advent of color. In an epic about the Grand Mughal, the emperor Akbar, entitled *Mughal-e-Azam*, there was only one reel of color cinematography, featuring a dance at court by the fabled Anarkali. Yet this reel alone guaranteed the film's success, drawing in the crowds by the million.

The makers of *The Wizard of Oz* clearly decided they were going to make their color as colorful as possible, much as Michelangelo Antonioni, a very different sort of filmmaker, did years later in his first color feature, *Red Desert*. In the Antonioni film, color is used to create heightened, often surrealistic effects. *The Wizard of Oz* likewise goes for bold, expressionist splashes—the yellow of the Brick Road, the red of the Poppy Field, the green of the Emerald City and of the witch's skin. So striking were these colors that, soon after seeing the film as a child, I began to dream of green-skinned witches. Years afterward, I gave these dreams to the narrator of *Midnight's Children*, having completely forgotten their source:

"No colors except green and black the walls are green the sky is black . . . the Widow is green but her hair is black as black." In this stream-of-consciousness dream sequence a nightmare of Indira Gandhi is fused with the equally nightmarish figure of Margaret Hamilton: a coming together of the Wicked Witches of the East and West.

Dorothy, stepping into color, framed by exotic foliage with a cluster of dwarfy cottages behind her and looking like a blue-smocked Snow White, no princess but a good demotic American gal, is clearly struck by the absence of her familiar homey gray. *Toto, I have a feeling we're not in Kansas anymore.* That camp classic of a line has detached itself from the movie to become a great American catchphrase, endlessly recycled, even turning up as an epigraph to Thomas Pynchon's mammoth paranoid fantasy of World War II, *Gravity's Rainbow*, whose characters' destiny lies not "behind the moon, beyond the rain" but "beyond the zero" of consciousness, where lies a land at least as odd as Oz.

Dorothy has done more than step out of grayness into Technicolor. She has been *unhoused*, and her homelessness is underlined by the fact that, after all the door-play of the transitional sequence, she will not enter any interior at all until she reaches the Emerald City. From tornado to Oz, Dorothy never has a roof over her head.

Out there amid the giant hollyhocks, whose blooms look like old His-Master's-Voice gramophone trumpets; out there in the vulnerability of open space, albeit open space that isn't at all like the prairie, Dorothy is about to outdo Snow White by a factor of nearly fifty. You can almost hear the MGM studio chiefs plotting to put the Disney hit in the shade, not just by providing in live action almost as many miraculous effects as the Disney cartoonists created, but also in the matter of little people. If Snow White had seven dwarfs, then Dorothy Gale, from the star called Kansas, would have three hundred and fifty. There's some disagreement about how this many Munchkins were brought to Hollywood and signed up. The official version is that they were provided by an impresario named Leo Singer. John Lahr's biography of his father, Bert, tells a different tale, which I prefer for reasons Roger Rabbit would understand—i.e., because it is funny. Lahr quotes the film's casting director, Bill Grady:

Leo [Singer] could only give me 150. I went to a midget

monologist called Major Doyle. . . . I said I had 150 from
Singer. "I'll not give you one if you do business with that son-
of-a-bitch." "What am I gonna do?" I said. "I'll get you the
350." . . . So I called up Leo and explained the situation. . . .
When I told the Major that I'd called off Singer, he danced a
jig right on the street in front of Dinty Moore's.

The Major gets these midgets for me. . . . I bring them out West
in buses. . . . Major Doyle took the [first three] buses and arrived at
Singer's house. The Major went to the doorman. "Phone upstairs
and tell Leo Singer to look out the window." It took about ten minutes. Then Singer looked from his fifth-floor window. And there
were all those midgets in those buses in front of his house with
their bare behinds sticking out the window.

This incident became known as Major Doyle's Revenge.[3]

What began with a strip continued cartoonishly. The Munchkins were
made up and costumed exactly like 3-D cartoon figures. The Mayor of
Munchkinland is quite implausibly rotund, the Coroner (*and she's not
only merely dead / She's really most sincerely dead*) reads the Witch of
the East's death notice from a scroll while wearing a hat with an absurdly
scroll-like brim;[4] the quiffs of the Lollipop Kids, who appear to have
arrived in Oz by way of Bash Street and Dead End, stand up more stiffly
than Tintin's. But what might have been a grotesque and unappetizing
sequence—it is, after all, a celebration of death—instead becomes the
scene in which *The Wizard of Oz* captures its audience once and for all,
allying the natural charm of the story to brilliant MGM choreography,
which punctuates large-scale routines with neat little set-pieces like the
dance of the Lullaby League, or the Sleepy Heads awaking mobcapped
and benightied out of cracked blue eggshells set in a giant nest. And of
course there's also the infectious gaiety of Arlen and Harburg's exceptionally witty ensemble number, "Ding, Dong, the Witch Is Dead."

Arlen was a little contemptuous of this song and the equally memorable
"We're Off to See the Wizard," calling them his "lemon-drop songs"—
perhaps because in both cases the real inventiveness lies in Harburg's lyrics.
In Dorothy's intro to "Ding, Dong," Harburg embarks on a pyrotechnic
display of A-A-A rhyming (*the wind began to switch / the house to pitch*;

until at length we meet the *witch, to satisfy an itch / Went flying on her broomstick thumbing for a hitch*; and *what happened then was rich . . .*). As with a vaudeville barker's alliterations, we cheer each new rhyme as a sort of gymnastic triumph. Verbal play continues to characterize both songs. In "Ding, Dong," Harburg invents punning word-concertinas:

> Ding, Dong, the witch is dead!
> —*Whicholwitch?*
> —The wicked witch!

This technique found much fuller expression in "We're Off to See the Wizard," becoming the real "hook" of the song:

> We're off to see the Wizard,
> The wonderful *Wizzardavoz*,
> We hear he is a *Whizzavawiz*,
> If ever a *whizztherwoz*.
> If *everoever a whizztherwoz*
> The *Wizzardavoz* is one because . . .

Is it too fanciful to suggest that Harburg's use throughout the film of internal rhymes and assonances is a conscious echo of the "rhyming" of the plot itself, the paralleling of characters in Kansas with those in Oz, the echoes of themes bouncing back and forth between the monochrome and Technicolor worlds?

Few of the Munchkins could actually sing their lines, as they mostly didn't speak English. They weren't required to do much in the movie, but they made up for this by their activities off-camera. Some film historians try to play down the stories of sexual shenanigans, knife-play, and general mayhem, but the legend of the Munchkin hordes cutting a swathe through Hollywood is not easily dispelled. In Angela Carter's novel *Wise Children* there is an account of a fictitious version of *A Midsummer Night's Dream* that owes much to the Munchkins' antics and, indeed, to Munchkinland:

> The concept of this wood was scaled to the size of fairy folk, so
> all was twice as large as life. Larger. Daisies big as your head

and white as spooks, foxgloves as tall as the tower of Pisa that chimed like bells if shook. . . . Even the wee folk were real; the studio scoured the country for dwarfs. Soon, true or not, wild tales began to circulate—how one poor chap fell into the toilet and splashed around for half an hour before someone dashed in for a piss and fished him out of the bowl; another one got offered a high chair in the Brown Derby when he went out for hamburger.

Amidst all this Munchkining we are given two very different portraits of grown-ups. The Good Witch Glinda is pretty in pink (well, prettyish, even if Dorothy is moved to call her "beautiful"). She has a high, cooing voice, and a smile that seems to have jammed. She has one excellent gag-line. After Dorothy disclaims witchy status, Glinda inquires, pointing at Toto: *Well, then, is* that *the witch?* This joke apart, she spends the scene simpering and looking vaguely benevolent and loving and rather too heavily powdered. It is interesting that though she is the Good Witch, the goodness of Oz does not inhere in her. The people of Oz are naturally good, unless they are under the power of the Wicked Witch (as is shown by the improved behavior of her soldiers after she melts). In the moral universe of the film, only evil is external, dwelling solely in the dual devil-figure of Miss Gulch/Wicked Witch.

(A parenthetical worry about Munchkinland: is it not altogether too pretty, too kempt, too sweetly sweet for a place that was, until Dorothy's arrival, under the absolute power of the Wicked Witch of the East? How is it that this squashed Witch had no castle? How could her despotism have left so little mark upon the land? Why are the Munchkins so relatively unafraid, hiding only briefly before they emerge, and giggling while they hide? The heretical thought occurs: maybe the Witch of the East *wasn't as bad as all that*—she certainly kept the streets clean, the houses painted and in good repair, and, no doubt, such trains as there might have been running on time. Moreover, and again unlike her sister, she seems to have ruled without the aid of soldiers, policemen, or other regiments of oppression. Why, then, was she so hated? I only ask.)

Glinda and the Witch of the West are the only two symbols of power in a film which is largely about the powerless, and it's instructive to "unpack" them. They are both women, and a striking aspect of *The Wizard of Oz* is its lack of a male hero—because for all their brains, heart, and courage, it's impossible to see the Scarecrow, the Tin Man, and the Cowardly Lion as classic Hollywood leading men. The power center of the film is a triangle at whose corners are Dorothy, Glinda, and the Witch. The fourth point, at which the Wizard is thought for most of the film to stand, turns out to be an illusion. The power of men is illusory, the film suggests. The power of women is real.

Of the two witches, good and bad, can there be anyone who'd choose to spend five minutes with Glinda? The actress who played her, Billie Burke, the ex-wife of Flo Ziegfeld, sounds every bit as wimpy as her role (she was prone to react to criticism with a trembling lip and a faltering cry of "Oh, you're *browbeating* me!"). By contrast, Margaret Hamilton's Wicked Witch of the West seizes hold of the movie from her very first green-faced snarl. Of course Glinda is "good" and the Wicked Witch "bad," but Glinda is a trilling pain in the neck, while the Wicked Witch is lean and mean. Check out their clothes: frilly pink versus slim-line black. *No contest.* Consider their attitudes to fellow-women: Glinda simpers upon being called beautiful, and denigrates her unbeautiful sisters; whereas the Wicked Witch is in a rage because of her sister's death, demonstrating, one might say, a commendable sense of solidarity. We may hiss at her, and she may terrify us as children, but at least she doesn't embarrass us the way Glinda does. True, Glinda exudes a sort of raddled motherly safeness, while the Witch of the West looks, in this scene anyhow, curiously frail and impotent, obliged to mouth empty-sounding threats—*I'll bide my time. But you just try and keep out of my way*—but just as feminism has sought to rehabilitate old pejorative words such as "hag," "crone," "witch," so the Wicked Witch of the West could be said to represent the more positive of the two images of powerful womanhood on offer here.

Glinda and the Witch clash most fiercely over the ruby slippers, which Glinda magics off the feet of the late Witch of the East and onto Dorothy's feet, and which the Wicked Witch of the West is apparently unable to remove. But Glinda's instructions to Dorothy are oddly enigmatic, even contradictory. She tells Dorothy (1) "Their magic must be very powerful or she wouldn't want them so badly," and, later, (2)

"Never let those ruby slippers off your feet for a moment or you will be at the mercy of the Wicked Witch of the West." Statement One implies that Glinda is unclear about the nature of the ruby slippers' capabilities, whereas Statement Two suggests that she knows all about their protective powers. Nor does either statement hint at the slippers' later role in helping to get Dorothy back to Kansas. It seems probable that these confusions are hangovers from the long, dissension-riddled scripting process, during which the function of the slippers was the subject of considerable disagreement. But one can also see Glinda's obliqueness as proof that a good fairy or witch, when she sets out to be of assistance, never gives you everything. Glinda is not so unlike her own description of the Wizard of Oz: *oh, he's very good, but very mysterious.*

<hr />

Just follow the Yellow Brick Road, says Glinda, and bubbles off into the blue hills in the distance, and Dorothy, geometrically influenced, as who would not be after a childhood among triangles, circles, and squares, begins her journey at the very point from which the Road spirals outward. And as she and the Munchkins echo Glinda's instructions in tones both raucously high and gutturally low, something begins to happen to Dorothy's feet. Their motion acquires a syncopation, which in beautifully slow stages grows more noticeable. By the time the ensemble breaks into the film's theme song—*You're off to see the Wizard*—we see, fully developed, the clever, shuffling little skip that will be the journey's leitmotiv:

> *You're off to see the Wizard*
> (s-skip)
> *The wonderful Wizzardavoz*
> (s-skip)

In this way, s-skipping along, Dorothy Gale, already a National Hero of Munchkinland, already (as the Munchkins have assured her) History, a girl destined to be a *Bust in the Hall of Fame,* steps out along the road of destiny and heads, as Americans must, into the West.

Off-camera anecdotes about a film's production can be simultaneously delicious and disappointing. On the one hand there's an undeniable

Trivial Pursuit-ish pleasure to be had: did you know that Buddy Ebsen, later the patriarch of the Beverly Hillbillies, was the original Scarecrow, then switched roles with Ray Bolger, who didn't want to play the Tin Man? And did you know that Ebsen had to leave the film after his "tin" costume gave him aluminum poisoning? And did you know that Margaret Hamilton's hand was badly burned during the filming of the scene in which the Witch writes SURRENDER DOROTHY in smoke in the sky over Emerald City, and that her stunt double Betty Danko was even more badly burned during the scene's reshoot? Did you know that Jack Haley (the third and final choice for the Tin Man) couldn't sit down in his costume and could only rest against a specially devised "leaning board"? Or that the three leading men weren't allowed to eat their meals in the MGM refectory because their makeup was thought too revolting? Or that Margaret Hamilton was given a coarse tent instead of a proper dressing-room, as if she really was a witch? Or that Toto was a female and her name was Terry? Above all, did you know that the frock coat worn by Frank Morgan, playing Professor Marvel/the Wizard of Oz, was bought from a secondhand store, and had L. Frank Baum's name stitched inside? It turned out that the coat had indeed been made for the author; thus, in the movie, the Wizard actually wears his creator's clothes.

Many of these behind-the-scenes tales show us, sadly, that a film that has made so many audiences so happy was not a happy film to make. It is almost certainly untrue that Haley, Bolger, and Lahr were unkind to Judy Garland, as some have said, but Margaret Hamilton definitely felt excluded by the boys. She was lonely on set, her studio days barely coinciding with those of the one actor she already knew, Frank Morgan, and she couldn't even take a leak without assistance. In fact, hardly any-one—certainly not Lahr, Haley, and Bolger in their elaborate makeup, which they dreaded putting on every day—seems to have had any fun making one of the most enjoyable pictures in movie history. We do not really want to know this; and yet, so fatally willing are we to do what may destroy our illusions that we also do want to know, we do, we do.

As I delved into the secrets of the Wizard of Oz's drinking problem, and learned that Morgan was only third choice for the part, behind W. C. Fields and Ed Wynn, and as I wondered what contemptuous wildness

Fields might have brought to the role, and how it might have been if his female opposite number, the Witch, had been played by the first choice, Gale Sondergaard, not only a great beauty but also another Gale to set alongside Dorothy and the tornado, I found myself staring at an old color photograph of the Scarecrow, the Tin Man, and Dorothy posing in a forest set, surrounded by autumn leaves; and realized that I was looking not at the stars at all but at their stunt doubles, their stand-ins. It was an unremarkable studio still, but it took my breath away; for it, too, was both mesmerizing and sad. It felt like a perfect metaphor for the doubleness of my own responses.

There they stand, Nathanael West's locusts, the ultimate wanna-bes. Garland's shadow, Bobbie Koshay, with her hands clasped behind her back and a white bow in her hair, is doing her brave best to smile, but she knows she's a counterfeit, all right; there are no ruby slippers on her feet. The mock-Scarecrow looks glum, too, even though he has avoided the full-scale burlap-sack makeup that was Bolger's daily fate. If it weren't for the clump of straw poking out of his right sleeve, you'd think he was some kind of hobo. Between them, in full metallic drag, stands the Tin Man's tinier echo, looking miserable. Stand-ins know their fate: they know we don't want to admit their existence. Even when reason tells us that in this or that difficult shot—when the Witch flies, or the Cowardly Lion dives through a glass window—we aren't really watching the stars, still the part of us that has suspended disbelief insists on seeing the stars and not their doubles. Thus the stand-ins become invisible even when they are in full view. They remain off-camera even when they are on-screen.

This is not the only reason for the curious fascination of the stand-ins' photograph. It's so haunting because, in the case of a beloved film, *we are all the stars' doubles.* Imagination puts us in the Lion's skin, places the sparkling slippers on our feet, sends us cackling through the air on a broomstick. To look at this photograph is to look into a mirror. In it we see ourselves. The world of *The Wizard of Oz* has possessed us. We have become the stand-ins.

A pair of ruby slippers, found in a bin in the MGM basement, was sold at auction in May 1970 for the amazing sum of $15,000. The purchaser was, and has remained, anonymous. Who was it who wished so profoundly to possess, perhaps even to wear, Dorothy's magic shoes? Was it, dear reader, you? Was it I?

At the same auction the second highest price was paid for the Cowardly Lion's costume ($2,400). This was twice as much as the third largest bid, $1,200 for Clark Gable's trench coat. The high prices commanded by *Wizard of Oz* memorabilia testify to the power of the film over its admirers—to our desire, quite literally, to clothe ourselves in its raiment. (It turned out, incidentally, that the $15,000 slippers were too large to have fitted Judy Garland's feet. They had in all probability been made for her double, Bobbie Koshay, whose feet were two sizes larger. Is it not fitting that the shoes made for the stand-in to stand in should have passed into the possession of another kind of surrogate: a film fan?)

⟞⟐⟝

If asked to pick a single defining image of *The Wizard of Oz*, most of us would, I suspect, come up with the Scarecrow, the Tin Man, the Cowardly Lion, and Dorothy s-skipping down the Yellow Brick Road (actually, the skip grows more pronounced during the journey, becoming an exaggerated h-hop). How strange that the most famous passage of this very filmic film, a film packed with technical wizardry and effects, should be the least cinematic, the most "stagy" part of the whole! Or perhaps not so strange, for this is primarily a passage of surreal comedy, and we recall that the equally inspired clowning of the Marx Brothers was no less stagily filmed. The zany mayhem of the playing rendered all but the simplest camera techniques unusable.

"Where is Vaudeville?" Somewhere on the way to the Wizard, apparently. The Scarecrow and the Tin Man are both pure products of the burlesque theater, specializing in pantomime exaggerations of voice and movements, pratfalls (the Scarecrow descending from his post), improbable leanings beyond the center of gravity (the Tin Man during his little dance) and, of course, the smart-ass backchat of the cross-talk act:

> TIN MAN, *rusted solid*: (Squawks)
> DOROTHY: He said "oil can"!
> SCARECROW: Oil can what?

At the pinnacle of all this clowning is that comic masterpiece, Bert Lahr's Cowardly Lion, all elongated vowel sounds (*Put 'em uuuuuuup*), ridiculous rhymes (*rhinoceros / imposserous*), transparent bravado, and operatic, tail-tugging, blubbing terror. All three, Scarecrow, Tin Man, and Lion, are, in Eliot's phrase, hollow men. The Scarecrow actually does have a "headpiece filled with straw, alas"; but the Tin Man is no less empty—he even bangs on his chest to prove that his innards are missing, because "the Tinsmith," his shadowy maker, forgot to provide a heart. The Lion lacks the most leonine of qualities, lamenting:

> What makes the Hottentot so hot,
> What puts the ape in apricot,
> What have they got that I ain't got?
> Courage!

Perhaps it's because they are hollow that our imaginations can occupy them so easily. That is to say, it is their anti-heroism, their apparent lack of Great Qualities, that makes them our size, or even smaller, so that we can stand among them as equals, like Dorothy among the Munchkins. Gradually, however, we discover that along with their "straight man," Dorothy (who plays, in this part of the film, the part of the unfunny Marx Brother, the one who could sing and look hunky and do little else), they embody one of the film's "messages"—that we already possess what we seek most fervently. The Scarecrow regularly comes up with bright ideas, which he offers with self-deprecating disclaimers: The Tin Man can weep with grief long before the Wizard gives him a heart. And Dorothy's capture by the Witch brings out the Lion's courage, though he pleads with his friends to "talk me out of it."

For this message to have its full impact, however, we must learn the futility of looking for solutions outside ourselves. We must learn about one more hollow man: the Wizard of Oz himself. Just as the Tinsmith was a flawed maker of Tin Men—just as, in this secular movie, the Tin Man's god is dead—so too must our belief in Wizards perish, so that we may believe in ourselves. We must survive the Deadly Poppy Field, helped by a mysterious snowfall (why *does* snow overcome the poppies' poison?), and so arrive, accompanied by heavenly choirs, at the city gates.

Here the film changes convention once again. Now it's about hicks from the sticks arriving at the metropolis, one of the classic themes of American cinema, with echoes in *Mr. Deeds Goes to Town*, or even in Clark Kent from Smallville's arrival at the *Daily Planet* in *Superman*. Dorothy is a country bumpkin, "Dorothy the small and meek"; her companions are backwoods buffoons. Yet—this too is a familiar Hollywood trope—it is the out-of-towners, the country mice, who will save the day.

There never was a metropolis quite like the Emerald City. It looks from the outside like a fairy tale of New York, a thicket of skyscraping green towers. Inside its walls, though, it's the very essence of quaintness. It is startling that the citizens—many of them played by Frank Morgan, who adds the parts of the gatekeeper, the driver of the horse-drawn buggy, and the palace guard to those of Professor Marvel and the Wizard—speak with English accents that rival Dick Van Dyke's immortal cockney in *Mary Poppins. Tyke yer anyplace in the city, we does*, says the coachman, adding, *I'll tyke yer to a place where you can tidy up a bit, what?* Other members of the citizenry are dressed like Grand Hotel bellhops and glitzy nuns, and they say, or rather sing, things like *Jolly good fun!* Dorothy catches on quickly. At the Wash and Brush Up, a tribute to urban technological genius that has none of the dark doubts of a *Modern Times* or *City Lights*, our heroine even gets a little English herself:

> DOROTHY (*sings*): Can you even dye my eyes to
>   match my gown?
> ATTENDENTS (*in unison*): Uh-huh!
> DOROTHY: Jolly old town!

Most of the citizens are cheerful and friendly, and those that appear not to be—the gatekeeper, the palace guard—are quickly won over. (In this respect, once again, they are untypical city folk.) Our four friends gain entry to the Wizard's palace because Dorothy's tears of frustration un-dam a quite alarming reservoir of liquid in the guard, whose face is soon sodden with tears, and as you watch this Niagara you are struck by the number of occasions on which people cry in this film. Apart from Dorothy and the guard, there is the Cowardly Lion, who cries when

Dorothy bops him on the nose; the Tin Man, who almost rusts up again from weeping; and Dorothy again, captured by the Witch. (If the Witch had been closer at hand on one of these occasions and gotten herself wet, the movie might have been much shorter.)

So: into the palace we go, down an arched corridor that looks like an elongated version of the Looney Tunes logo, and at last we confront a Wizard whose illusions—giant heads, flashes of fire—conceal, but only for a while, his essential kinship with Dorothy. He, too, is an immigrant in Oz; indeed, as he will later reveal, he is a Kansas man himself. (In the novel, he came from Omaha.) These two immigrants, Dorothy and the Wizard, have adopted opposite strategies of survival in the new, strange land. Dorothy has been unfailingly polite, careful, courteously "small and meek," whereas the Wizard has been fire and smoke, bravado and bombast, and has hustled his way to the top—floated there, so to speak, on a current of his own hot air. But Dorothy learns that meekness isn't enough, and the Wizard—as his balloon gets the better of him for a second time—that his command of hot air isn't all it should be. It's hard for a migrant like myself not to see in these shifting destinies a parable of the migrant condition.

The Wizard's stipulation, that he will grant no wishes until the four friends have brought him the Witch's broomstick, ushers in the penulti-mate and least challenging (though most action-packed and "exciting") movement of the film, which is, in this phase, at once a buddy movie, a straightforward adventure yarn, and, after Dorothy's capture, a more or less conventional princess rescue story. After the great dramatic climax of the confrontation with the Wizard of Oz, the film sags for a while and doesn't really regain momentum until the equally climactic final struggle with the Wicked Witch of the West, ending with her melt-ing, her "growing down" into nothingness. The relative dullness of this sequence has something to do with the script's inability to make much of the Winged Monkeys, who remain ciphers throughout, whereas they could have been used (for example) to show us what the oppressed Munchkins might have been like under the power of the Witch of the East, before their liberation by Dorothy's falling house.

(One interesting detail. When the Witch dispatches the Winged Monkeys to capture Dorothy, she speaks a line that makes no sense at all. Assuring the chief Monkey that his prey will give him no trouble, the Witch explains, *I've sent a little insect on ahead to take the fight out of them.* But, as we cut down to the forest, we learn nothing further about this insect. It's simply not in the film. It was, though. The line of dialogue is left over from an earlier version of the film, and it refers to a ghost of the discarded musical sequence I mentioned earlier. The "little insect" was once a fully fledged song that took over a month to film. He is the Jitter Bug.)

Fast-forward. The Witch is gone. The Wizard has been unmasked and, in the moment after his unveiling, has succeeded in a spot of true magic, giving Dorothy's companions the gifts they did not believe they possessed until that instant. The Wizard has gone, too, and without Dorothy, their plans having been fouled up by (who else but) Toto. And here's Glinda, telling Dorothy she has to learn the meaning of the ruby slippers for herself . . .

> GLINDA: What have you learned?
> DOROTHY: If I ever go looking for my heart's desire again, I won't look further than my own back yard. And if it isn't there, I never really lost it to begin with. Is that right?
> GLINDA: That's all it is. And now those magic slippers will take you home in two seconds. Close your eyes . . . click your heels together three times . . . and think to yourself . . . there's no place like . . .

Hold it. Hold *it*.

How does it come about, at the close of this radical and enabling film, which teaches us in the least didactic way possible to build on what we have, to make the best of ourselves, that we are given this conservative little homily? Are we to believe that Dorothy has learned no more on her journey than that she didn't need to make such a journey in the first place? Must we accept that she now accepts the limitations of her home life, and agrees that the things she doesn't have there are no loss to her? "*Is that right?*" Well, excuse *me*, Glinda, but it isn't.

Home again in black-and-white, with Auntie Em and Uncle Henry and the rude mechanicals clustered round her bed, Dorothy begins her second revolt, fighting not only against the patronizing dismissals of her own folk but also against the scriptwriters, and the sentimental moralizing of the entire Hollywood studio system. *It wasn't a dream, it was a place*, she cries piteously. *A real, truly live place! Doesn't anyone believe me?*

Many, many people did believe her. Frank Baum's readers believed her, and their interest in Oz led him to write thirteen further Oz books, admittedly of diminishing quality; the series was continued, even more feebly, by other hands after his death. Dorothy, ignoring the "lessons" of the ruby slippers, went back to Oz, in spite of the efforts of Kansas folk, including Auntie Em and Uncle Henry, to have her dreams brainwashed out of her (see the terrifying electroconvulsive therapy sequence in the Disney film *Return to Oz*); and, in the sixth book of the series, she took Auntie Em and Uncle Henry with her, and they all settled down in Oz, where Dorothy became a princess.

So Oz finally *became* home; the imagined world became the actual world, as it does for us all, because the truth is that once we have left our childhood places and started out to make up our own lives, armed only with what we have and are, we understand that the real secret of the ruby slippers is not that "there's no place like home" but rather that there is no longer any such place *as* home: except, of course, for the home we make, or the homes that are made for us, in Oz, which is anywhere, and everywhere, except the place from which we began.

In the place from which I began, after all, I watched the film from the child's—Dorothy's—point of view. I experienced, with her, the frustration of being brushed aside by Uncle Henry and Auntie Em, busy with their dull grown-up counting. Like all adults, they couldn't focus on what was really important to Dorothy: namely, the threat to Toto. I ran away with Dorothy and then ran back. Even the shock of discovering that the Wizard was a humbug was a shock I felt as a child, a shock to the child's faith in adults. Perhaps, too, I felt something deeper, something I couldn't articulate; perhaps some half-formed suspicion about grown-ups was being confirmed.

Now, as I look at the movie again, I have become the fallible adult. Now I am a member of the tribe of imperfect parents who cannot listen to their children's voices. I, who no longer have a father, have become a father instead, and now it is my fate to be unable to satisfy the longings of a child. This is the last and most terrible lesson of the film: that there is one final, unexpected rite of passage. In the end, ceasing to be children, we all become magicians without magic, exposed conjurers, with only our simple humanity to get us through.

We are the humbugs now.

NOTES

[1] See Aljean Harmetz's definitive *The Making of The Wizard of Oz* (Pavilion Books, 1989).

[2] When I first published this essay in 1992, the idea of "home" had become problematic for me, for reasons I have little interest in rehearsing here. (But see Part II, "Messages from the Plague Years.") I won't deny that I did a great deal of thinking, in those days, about the advantages of a good pair of ruby shoes.

[3] According to some contemporary revisionists, Major Doyle never got the 350 Munchkins, and the filmmakers had to settle for 124.

[4] After the publication of an earlier version of this essay in *The New Yorker*, I received an appreciative letter from the Munchkin Coroner, Manfred Raabe, now living in a Penney Retirement Community in Fort Lauderdale, Florida. He liked what I had to say so much that he sent me a gift: a color photocopy of a picture of his big moment on the steps of the Town Hall, holding up that big scroll with its Gothic lettering reading "Certificate of Death." Under this lettering he had painstakingly filled out my name. I don't know what it means to have a Munchkin death certificate, but I've got one.

Portentous Evil

J. C. HALLMAN

"**P**ortentous evil—how was I to save that?" wrote Henry James, musing on his inspiration for *The Turn of the Screw* in the famous preface to the New York Edition of his work. Originally published in 1898 to a fanfare of publicity and some measure of condemnation, *Screw* has attracted as much critical attention as any book of the last hundred years, and the deluge that began not long after James died may make it seem an unlikely candidate for yet another treatment. But the nature of this criticism—Freudians raging against anti-Freudians and the likes of Edmund Wilson claiming that with *Screw* James had raped and murdered his inner girl—was so ridiculous that the real meaning of the book has been smothered. It's a murdered text.

When James says he wants to save evil, he's really talking about saving the ghost story genre itself. It was over, he said—all the good ghost stories had been told, and the new crop, presumably based on the science of psychical research in vogue at the time, were dispiriting because the popular study of a "real" phenomenon had damaged the genre. (Henry's brother William was active in the Society for Psychical

Research, which investigated a variety of phenomena, and Henry had on occasion delivered William's papers to the London branch for him.) No longer could the stories conjure up what James called "the dear old sacred terror." If he could save portentous evil, he decided in planning *Screw*, he would save the ghost story too.

You might be familiar with the story: a young governess in rural England relates an account of taking into her charge two privileged children, a boy and girl, orphans. Shortly after she arrives at the mansion where the children live, she begins to see ghosts of the previous governess and another servant on the property, both of whom had fallen into ill repute and died. Problem: the governess alone sees the apparitions. Although present at some of the sightings, the housekeeper and the children, who had spent an inordinate amount of time with the departed servants, deny seeing anything. The governess decides the ghosts are trying to "take hold" of the children (Truman Capote, in writing the Jack Clayton–directed screen version, *The Innocents*, portrays the ghost–children relationships as loosely homoerotic and sadomasochistic), and determines to save her charges by prodding them into admitting the nefarious relationships. A confrontation with the little girl fails when it causes her a panicked anxiety attack, and a second confrontation with the boy is judged a success by the governess even though it kills the boy. End of story.

In his preface, James claims that the source of the story was an evening not terribly different from the book's frame tale: a group has gathered on a holiday, the subject of ghost stories comes up one night round the fire, and someone tells this tale, notable for its dreadfulness. (James later attributed the details of *Screw* to the archbishop of Canterbury—a month after the prelate died. The archbishop's family denied that the story was part of their lore, and Leon Edel went on to discover a pulp story that James had read as a boy and that contained many of the elements of *Screw*.) But the story never returns to the original frame tale, and *Screw* leaves you with irreconcilable ambiguity—were the ghosts real or weren't they? Is the governess a savior or a murderer? At first, most readers agreed with Truman Capote. When the book was published they cared less about whether the ghosts were real than about the suggestions of sexual impropriety. Why did it have to be so awful, so evil? James wrote his preface after ten years of reaction to the story, and he complained, in a characteristically obtuse way, that it was not he who had put evil into the story, but his readers. This process, which he went on to describe, was the solution to portentous evil. He knew that *Screw* would hinge on readers suffering through the direst thing one could imagine, but he asked himself, "What would *be* then, on reflexion, this utmost conceivability?" Bad ghost stories, he knew, relied on "weak specifications," unambiguous supernatural presences, to carry them. (Think M. Night Shyamalan.) Better would be to rely on readers' imaginations, to draw an unfinished portrait that they would complete with whatever evil meant to them. "Only make the reader's general vision of evil intense enough, I said to myself . . . make him think it for himself, and you are released from weak specifications."

James repeated several times that this process was the one thing about the story that really interested him, but critics went on to display uncanny deafness to any part of the preface that did not fit with the interpretations that emerged once life had made a ghost of James. While most readers immediately sense that not all is right in the governess's account of her story, credit, in critical circles, for being the first to suggest the ghosts weren't real went to a woman named Edna Kenton, who posted a short notice to that effect in 1924. This feather was awarded by none other than Edmund Wilson, who with his own treatment of *Screw* became the standard-bearer for the text's Freudian reading. At best, this reading painted the governess as a poster child for Freudian repression—her love for the children's uncle manifested as a psychosexual derailing, leaving her delusional. At worst, according to Wilson, "There was always in Henry James an innocent little girl whom he cherished and loved and protected and yet whom he later tried to violate, whom he even tried to kill." In other words, *Screw* was James's attempt to throttle his inner lass.

Not all were happy with the Freudian read. On a *Screw* radio-show symposium, Allen Tate claimed that Henry James knew everything Freud knew before Freud knew it, and Katherine Anne Porter added that the same could be said of any major artist. But the Freudian read was potent enough that anti-Freudians were left arguing that the ghosts weren't delusions at all—they were real, and it was just a good ghost story. The reaction to the book stalled there—were the ghosts real or weren't they?—a pissing match that generated reams of criticism haggling over obscure points of fact within the text. Both sides ignored what James had called "my definite business."

It's remarkable how the story changes with James's intentions in mind. James wants to save the ghost story; the governess wants to save the children. James decides the way to save the ghost story is to enlist the reader's imagination; the governess, in coercing the children to admit salacious relationships, stumbles onto the same process. James insists that after he had pondered portentous evil, "the answer all admirably came" to him; the governess, pondering the children, says that "a sort of answer, after a time, had come to me." James longs for "the dear old sacred terror"; the governess says of the little boy that "I had seen in him the approach of immediate fear . . . which struck me indeed as perhaps the best thing to make him."

There are many parallels between the preface and the text, but the bottom line is that the story demonstrates the process James describes. His definite business was to present the governess as a kind of writer and the little boy as a kind of reader, and when the governess co-opts his imagination and frightens him to death, it's not so James can murder his inner child, but so he can show us, with portentous evil, the dear old sacred terror and the power of literature.

Unfortunately, criticism tends to decide which books are remembered and how they are remembered, and those critics influential enough to redirect a stream of interpretation seem disinclined to acknowledge a book that has garnered so much foolish attention. *The Turn of the Screw* has been handed over to mediocre critics, and better thinkers tend to ignore it. Harold Bloom, in an introduction to a collection of essays on *Daisy Miller* and *The Turn of the Screw*, somehow doesn't even mention the book—and neither do the essays. *Screw* will remain dead—and lost. Edmund Wilson, you sly old bat, you got away with murder.

The Other James

MICHAEL CHABON

I'll just come right out and say it: M. R. James's ghost story "Oh, Whistle, and I'll Come to You, My Lad" is one of the finest short stories ever written. The problematic term in that last sentence, of course, is not "finest" but "short stories." It's a mark of how radically we have changed our ideas of what a short story, and in particular a fine one, ought to be, that there should be something odd about ranking this masterpiece of the Other James in the same league with, say, "The Real Thing" or "Four Meetings." The ghost story has been consigned to the ghetto of subgenre. Rare is the contemporary anthology of "best short stories of all time" that includes even a token example of the form.

Once it was not so. Once, you could argue, the ghost story *was* the genre itself. Balzac, Poe, de Maupassant, Kipling—most of the early inventors—wrote ghost stories as a matter of course, viewing them as a fundamental of the storyteller's craft. Edith Wharton was an enthusiast and master of the "subgenre"; her ghost stories are the cream of her short fiction. And Henry James himself, of course, gave us the one ghost story whose status as literature is not open to debate: "The Turn of the

Screw." It was only the best of a good two dozen that he produced during the heyday of the form, in the latter half of the nineteenth century.

Maybe our taste has grown more refined, or our understanding of human psychology more subtle. Maybe we don't really believe in ghosts anymore. Or maybe for the past sixty years or so we've simply been cheating ourselves, we lovers of the short story, out of one of the genre's enduring pleasures.

A great ghost story is *all* psychology: in careful and accurate detail it presents 1) a state of perception, by no means rare in human experience, in which the impossible vies with the undeniable evidence of the senses; and 2) the range of emotions brought on by that perception. And then, by the quantum strangeness of literature, it somehow manages to engender these same emotions in the reader: the prickling nape, the racing heart, the sense of some person standing invisibly near. Everyone has felt such things, coming up the basement stairs with darkness at our backs, turning around at the sound of a footstep to find only an empty room. I once saw a face, intelligent and smiling, formed from the dappled shadow of a stucco ceiling in a Los Angeles bedroom. The face remained, perfectly visible to both my wife and me, until we finally turned out the light. The next morning it was gone. Afterward, no matter how we looked at the ceiling, in daylight or at night, the face failed to reappear. I have never to this day forgotten its mocking leer as it studied me.

It is tempting to say that, like his contemporaries Algernon Blackwood and Arthur Machen, Montague Rhodes James is something of a ghost himself, nowadays, at least in the United States. He haunts the pages of foxed anthologies with titles like *Classic Chilling Stories of Terror and Suspense*, his name lapsed into obscurity along with those of the authors of durable gems of the genre such as "The Beckoning Fair One" (Oliver Onions) and "The Monkey's Paw" (W. W. Jacobs). But in England he is still remembered, and even beloved. James is about as English as it is possible for an English writer to be. A hungry Anglophile, one with no interest whatever (if such a creature exists) in the ghosts that haunt old abbeys, dusty libraries, and the Saxon churches of leafy villages, could survive very happily on a steady diet of M. R. James. These are stories that venture to the limits of the human capacity for terror and revulsion, as it were, armed only with an umbrella and a very dry wit. They are still read aloud on the radio over there, in particular at Christmastime, when, as during the season that frames "The Turn of the Screw," it is apparently traditional to sit by a crackling yule fire and scare one's friends out of their wits. (And it would be hard to imagine anything more English than that.)

M. R. James presents a nearly unique instance in the history of supernatural literature—perhaps in the history of literature, period: he seems, for the entire duration of his life (1865–1936), to have considered himself the happiest of men. His biography, insofar as it has been written, is free of the usual writerly string of calamities and reversals, of intemperate behavior, self-destructive partnerings, critical lambasting, poverty, illness, bad luck. His childhood, though it sounds to modern ears to have been a tad heavy on devotional exercise, Christian study, and mindfulness of the sufferings of Jesus and his saints, was passed in material comfort and within the loving regard of his parents and older siblings; the candlelit gloom of the paternal church counterbalanced, if balance were needed, by ready access to the beauties of the East Anglian countryside that surrounded his father's rectory. His early school years were notable, if at all, only for the consistent excellence of his academic performance and for the popularity he attained among his fellow students, in part through a discovered knack for spinning a first-class frightening tale. At the age of fourteen he entered the world of Eton, and, though he spent the middle portion of his life as a laureate, fellow, and finally dean of King's College, Cambridge (itself a sister school to Eton), he never really left that sheltered, companionable green and gray world, assuming at last the mantle of provost of Eton in 1918, a position he held until he died. He was a brilliant, prize-winning, internationally known scholar of early Christian manuscripts who devoted his personal life to enlarging, slowly and knowledgeably, his circle of gentleman friends, a task made simpler by his brilliance, charm, wit, kindness, and affability. He took no interest in politics, involved his name in no controversy or cause, and traveled in comfort through Denmark, Sweden, France, and other tamer corners of the globe. The seeker after shadows who turns, in desperation, to discover what untold sufferings James, like H. C. Andersen or E. A. Poe, might have undergone for the love of a woman, will discover here a profound silence. James never married, and as far as we are allowed to determine, the complete absence of romantic attachments in his life caused him no pain or regret whatsoever.

And the childhood fascination with the tortures suffered by Christian martyrs, each date and gruesome detail of beheadings, immolations, and dismemberments lovingly memorized the way some boys memorize batting averages? And the spectral face at the garden gate, pale and wild-eyed and reeking of evil, that one evening peered back at the young James across the lawn as he looked out through the windows of the rectory? And the intimate eleven-year friendship with a man named McBryde, illustrator of some of James's best stories, traveling companion and inseparable confidant, whose rather late marriage, in 1903, was followed, scarcely a year later, by his untimely death? And the boys, the tens upon hundreds upon thousands of boys of Eton and King's, on whom James had lavished his great teacherly gifts, cut down in the battlefields of Belgium and France? And the empty lawns, deserted commons and dining halls, the utter desolation of Cambridge in 1918?

Over all of this speculation as to the origins of James's ghosts and horrors, over any hint of torment, shame, passion, remorse, or sorrow, the shutters have been drawn. The only evidence we have for the existence of such emotions in M. R. James is the disturbing tales he chose, over and over, to tell. Could they possibly be the work of a man whose life presented him with a nearly unbroken series of comfortable, satisfying, and gratifying days, from cradle to grave? Let us say that they could; let us stipulate that the stories are the work of a man whom life denied none of the fundamentals of mortal happiness. Violence, horror, grim retribution, the sudden revulsion of the soul—these things, then, are independent of happiness or suffering; a man who looks closely and carefully at life, whether pitiable as Poe or enviable as the provost of Eton, cannot fail to see them.

Along with A. E. Housman, Thomas Hardy, and even, we are told, Theodore Roosevelt, one of James's early admirers was the American horror writer H. P. Lovecraft (1890–1937). The two men shared a taste for old books and arcane manuscripts, for neglected museums and the libraries of obscure historical societies, and for ancient buildings, in particular those equipped with attics and crypts; they shared that requisite of any great writer of ghost stories: a hyperacute sense of the past. We all have this sixth human sense, to one degree or another, but in the case of Lovecraft and James the sense of the past is as evolved as the sense of smell in a professional *nez*. When it comes to their writing, however, Lovecraft and James could not differ more—in style, in scale, in temperament. Lovecraft's style is the despair of the lover of Lovecraft, at once shrill and vague, clotted, pedantic, hysterical, and sometimes out-and-out bad. James, on the other hand, writes the elegant English sentences, agile and reticent, that an excellent British education of his era both demanded and ensured. The contrast is particularly stark when it comes to their portrayal of the unportrayable. Lovecraft approaches Horror armed with adverbs, abstractions, and perhaps a too-heavy reliance on pseudopods and tentacles. James rarely does more than hint at the nature of his ghosts and apparitions, employing a few simple, select, revolting adjectives, summoning his ghosts into hideous, enduring life in the reader's mind in a bare sentence or two.

Evil, in Lovecraft, is universal, pervasive, and at least partially explicable in terms of notions such as Elder Races and blind idiot gods slobbering at the heart of creation. In James, Evil tends to have more of a local feel, somehow, assembling itself at times out of the most homely materials; and yet it remains, in the end, beyond any human explanation whatsoever. Evil is strangely rationalized in Lovecraft, irresistible but systematic; it can be sought, and found. In James it irrupts, is chanced upon, brushes against our lives irrevocably, often when we are looking in the other direction. But the chief difference between Lovecraft and James is one of temperament. Lovecraft, apart from a few spasmodic periods, including one in which he briefly married a Brooklyn Jew named Sonia Greene and formed a part of her salon, appears to have liked his own company best. He could be gloomy and testy, and was perhaps most appreciated by his friends at a distance, through his lively correspondence with them. M. R. James, on the other hand, was legendary for his conviviality, and loved nothing more than whiling away an afternoon over sherry and tobacco with his erudite friends. Indeed, friends—colleagues, companions—play an important role in James's stories, coming along to shore up the protagonist's courage at just the right moment, providing him with moral support, crucial information, or simply another soul with whom to share an unspeakable secret. In Lovecraft the protagonist has often cut himself off from his friends and companions, and must face the final moment of slithering truth alone.

Lovecraft wrote, in part, for money, often as little as one and a half cents a word; James was an avowed hobbyist of literature, and wrote many of his finest stories as Christmas entertainments of the sort already described, reading them aloud to his assembled friends by the light of a single candle. The stories are, nevertheless, unmistakably works of art, the products of a peculiar imagination, a moral sense at once keen and undogmatic, and an artist's scientific eye for shape and structure.

This brings us back to "Oh, Whistle, and I'll Come to You, My Lad," whose unlucky protagonist, Parkins, we first encounter in conversation with his fellow professors over dinner "in the hospitable hall of St. James's College." (James's stories never originate in cheap atmospherics, fogs or plagues or blasted landscapes, or with the creaky, dubious avowals of narratorial sanity so beloved of Lovecraft and Poe.) In the very first sentence[1] James displays the remarkable command that qualifies him as a great unrecognized master of point of view, which is the ultimate subject of any ghost story and, of course, of twentieth-century literature itself. For the narrator, or the author, or some indeterminate, playful amalgam of the two, reveals himself before we are twenty words into the story, and will continue to remind us of his presence throughout, right up to the final paragraph, when at last he takes leave, with a strange kind of cheerful pity, of the shattered Professor Parkins.

I don't think any writer has handled a narrator in quite the same way as James in "Oh, Whistle." For the narrator here is not merely a disembodied authorial voice in the classic nineteenth-century manner. He is *involved* in the lives of the characters he describes, he *knows* them, he sees them on a regular basis—he is, albeit invisibly, a character in the story, cut from the same cloth, as it were, as Professors Parkins and Rogers and the rest of the St. James faculty. There are portions of the story, he suggests, that *could* be told, that actually happened—most of them having to do with the game of golf—but which he gratefully lacks the expertise to set down. This accords with a fundamental operation of the supernatural story, from "The Facts in the Case of M. Valdemar" to *The Blair Witch Project*, which is to make the explicit point—generally implicit or finessed in "literary" fiction—that what is being given is a *factual account*. All ghost stories are "true" stories. We love them, if we love them, from the depth and antiquity of our willingness to believe them.

M. R. James, more than any other writer, explores the wobble, the shimmer of uncertainty that results when quotation marks are placed around the word "true." Because at the same time that the narrator of "Oh, Whistle" is implicating himself in his story—scrupulously telling us what he has seen for himself and what parts of the story he has only heard second- or third-hand—his supremely "authoritative" voice and evident easy control over the materials establish him as unmistakably the *writer* of the story, its inventor, hurrying us past characters we need not overly attend to, rendering the events with an impossible familiarity. This, in turn, calls into question the fictional status of the narrator, and hence that of the author himself.

All of this, I know, sounds dubiously postmodern. And indeed James, not merely in his approach, at once careful and cavalier, to point of view, but also in fitting out his stories with the full apparatus of scholarly research (footnotes, learned quotations from Latin, references to obscure medieval tracts), often anticipates Borges and the postmodernists—and with every iota of their self-conscious playfulness. But the playfulness is worn so lightly, and the experiments in point of view are undertaken with such a practical purpose—scaring you—in mind, that even a critical reader may scarcely be aware of them the first time through. James is like some casual, gentleman tinkerer yoking a homemade antigravity drive to the derailleurs of his bicycle because he is tired of being late to church every Sunday.

"Oh, Whistle, and I'll Come to You, My Lad" is, in many ways, the prototypical M. R. James story. It presents a man who stumbles, through benevolent motives, upon a historical puzzle that cannot fail to interest him and, poking innocently around in it, inadvertently summons—more literally here than in other stories—an unexpected revenant of a bygone time, with frightful results. Professor Parkins— "rather hen-like, perhaps, in his little ways; totally destitute, alas! of the sense of humour, but at the same time dauntless and sincere in his convictions, and a man deserving of the greatest respect"—kindly agrees to take time away from his golfing vacation on the Suffolk coast in order to investigate the ruins, in the neighborhood where he plans to stay, of an old Knights Templar church in which one of his colleagues takes a scholarly interest. Parkins, we have seen, is an avowed skeptic when it comes to the supernatural—to a fault, perhaps. Digging with his pocketknife in the earth around the ruins, he uncovers a strange metal flute bearing an enigmatic Latin inscription. When—as inevitably he must—Parkins plays a few notes on the flute, he calls up a series of increasingly terrifying disturbances, both atmospheric and psychic: winds, night terrors, and puzzling disarrangements or disturbances of the second, supposedly empty bed in his room at the Globe Inn. These disturbances culminate in the awful apparition—a marvel of James's gift for creating horror through understatement and suggestion—of a thing, some thing, with a woeful face of crumpled bed linens.

For this story is also prototypical James in that when at last we encounter the Horror, there is something about its manifestation, its physical attributes, its *habits*, that puts the reader in mind, however reluctantly, of sex. I say reluctantly in part because the cool, fleshy, pink, protruberant, furred, toothed, or mouthed apparitions one finds in M. R. James are so loathsome; and in part because James keeps his stories studiously free—swept clean—not merely of references to sexual behavior but of all the hot-and-heavy metaphor and overt Freudian paraphernalia with which supernatural fiction is so often encumbered. James is a hospitable writer, and one wishes not to offend one's host. But the fact remains that "Oh, Whistle, and I'll Come to You, My Lad" is a story about a man pursued into the darkness of a strange bedroom, and all of the terror is ultimately generated by a vision of a horribly disordered bed. The bodily horror, the uncanny, even repulsive nature of sex—a favorite theme of the genre from Stoker to Cronenberg—is a recurring element in the stories of M. R. James, rendered all the more potent because it feels so genuinely *unconscious*. Sex was undoubtedly the last thing on the mind of M. R. James as he sat down to compose his Christmas creepers, but it is often the first thing to emerge when the stays of reality are loosened.

At times, as in traditional ghost stories (e.g., "A Christmas Carol"), James's characters engender and deserve their ghastly fates, bringing them about through excesses of ambition, pride, or greed. Professor Parkins, one senses, does not entirely meet with the author's approval—he is priggish, skeptical, he plays golf—but in other stories the protagonists are men whose profession, temperament, and tastes barely distinguish them from their creator. Most of the time they are innocents, ignorant trippers and travelers who brush up against the omnipresent meaningless malevolence of the world, and the sins for which they are punished tend, likely as not, to be virtues—curiosity, honesty, a sympathy for bygone eras, a desire to do honor to one's ancestors. And, often, their punishment is far grimmer than the scare that Professor Parkins receives.

The secret power of James's work lies in his steadfast refusal to explain fully, in the end, the mechanisms that have brought about the local irruption of Evil he describes, and yet to leave us, time and again, utterly convinced that such an explanation is possible, if only we were in possession of all the facts. He makes us *feel* the logic of haunting, the residue of some inscrutable chain of ghostly causation, though we can't—though, he insists, we *never will be able to*—explain or understand that logic. In "Oh, Whistle" the elements—the Templars' ruined church, the brass flute with its fragmentary inscriptions, the blind pursuing figure in white, the whistled-up wind—all hang together seamlessly in the reader's imagination: they fit. And yet, in the end, we have no idea why. For the central story of M. R. James, reiterated with inexhaustible inventiveness, is ultimately the breathtaking fragility of life, of "reality," of all the structures that we have erected to defend ourselves from our constant nagging suspicion that underlying everything is chaos, brutal and unreasoning. It is hard to conceive of a more serious theme, or a more contemporary plot, than this.

It may be, in fact, that the ghost story, like the dinosaur, is still very much with us, transformed past the point of ready recognition into the feathered thing that we call "the modern short story." Perhaps all short stories can be understood as ghost stories, accounts of visitations and reckonings with the traces of the past. Were there ever characters in fiction more haunted by ghosts than Chekhov's or Joyce's?

The short story narrates the moment when a dark door, long closed, is opened, when a forgotten error is unwittingly repeated, when the fabric of a life is revealed to have been woven from frail and dubious fiber over top of something unknowable and possibly very bad. Ultimately all stories—ghost stories, mysteries, stories of terror or adventure or modern urban life—descend from the fireside tale, told with wolves in the woods all around, with winter howling at the window. After centuries of the refinements, custom fittings, and mutations introduced by artistry and the marketplace, the short story retains its fundamental power to frighten us with its recognition of the abyss at our backs, and to warm us with its flickering light.

NOTES

[1] "'I suppose you will be getting away pretty soon, now Full term is over, Professor,' said a person not in the story to the Professor of Ontography, soon after they had sat down next to each other at a feast in the hospitable hall of St James's College."

Truman Capote Reconsidered

CYNTHIA OZICK

Time at length becomes justice. A useful if obscure-sounding literary aphorism, just this moment invented. What it signifies is merely this: if a writer lives long enough, he may himself eventually put behind him the work that brought him early fame, and which the world ought to have put aside in the first place.

I remember reading somewhere not long ago a comment by Truman Capote on his first novel: it was written, he said, by somebody else.

Cruel time fleshes out this interesting, only seemingly banal, remark: who is this tiny-fingered flaccid man, with molasses eyes and eunuch's voice, looking like an old caricature of Aeolus, the puff-cheeked little god of wind? We see him now and then on television talk shows, wearing a hayseed hat, curling his fine feet, his tongue on his lip like a soft fly, genially telling dog stories. Or we read about the vast celebrity parties he is master of, to which whole populations of the famous come, in majestic array of might and mind. Or we hear of him in New Orleans some months ago, in the company of Princess Radziwill, observing the Rolling Stones and their congregations, with what secret thoughts print will soon make plain.

Or we catch him out as a cabal-sniffing inquisitor in *Playboy*, confiding in an interview how "other backgrounds" are not being "given a chance" because of the "predominance of the Jewish Mafia" in American letters. Or, back on television again, we learn from him about the psychology of criminals—which inadvertently lets us in a little on the psychology of people who are attracted to the psychology of criminals. Or we discuss, for months, his puzzling coinage "nonfiction novel," as if some new theory of literature had broken on the world—what he means, it turns out on publication, is the spawn of garden-variety interview journalism, only with this out: he is not to be held morally accountable for it.

(He is not even to be held accountable for his first non-nonfiction novel: it was written by Somebody Else.)

Were all these non-qualities implicit in that long-ago Somebody Else—that boy whose portrait on the back cover of *Other Voices, Other Rooms* became even more celebrated than the prose inside? Who can forget that boy?—languid but sovereign, lolling in the turn of a curved sofa in bow tie and tattersall vest, with tender mouth and such strange elf-cold eyes. Like everyone else whose youth we have memorized and who has had the bad luck to turn up on television afterward, he was bound to fatten up going toward fifty; and like everyone else who has made some money and gained some ease in the world, he was bound to lose that princely look of the furious dreamer.

On the face of it he was bound to become Somebody Else, in short: not only distant physically from the Dorian Gray of the memorable photograph, and not simply psychologically distant according to the chasm between twenty-three and forty-eight, and not merely (though this chiefly) distant from the sort of redolent prose craft that carried *Other Voices, Other Rooms* to its swift reputation. An even more radical distancing appears to intervene.

It's not only ourselves growing old that makes us into Somebody Else: it's the smell of the times too, the invisible but palpable force called *Zeitgeist*, which is something different from growth, and more capricious. Books change because we change, but no internal reasons, however inexorable, are enough to account for a book's turning to dust twenty-four years afterward. *Other Voices, Other Rooms* is now only dust—glass dust, a heap of glitter, but dust all the same.

Robert Gottlieb, editor-in-chief of Knopf, some time ago in *Publishers Weekly* took shrewd notice of how the life expectancy of books is affected: Solzhenitsyn, he said, can write as he does, and succeed at it, because in Russia they do not yet know that the nineteenth century is dead.

A century, even a quarter of a century, dies around a book; and then the book lies there, a shaming thing because it shows us how much worse we once were to have liked it; and something else too: it demonstrates exactly how the world seems to shake off what it does not need, old books, old notions of aesthetics, old mind-forms, our own included. The world to the eager eye is a tree constantly pruning itself, and writers are the first to be lopped off. All this means something different from saying merely that a book has dated. All sorts of masterpieces are dated, in every imaginable detail, and yet survive with all their powers. *Other Voices, Other Rooms* is of course dated, and in crucial ways: it would be enough to mention that its Southern family has two black retainers, an old man and his granddaughter, and that when he dies the old man is buried under a tree on the family property, the way one would bury a well-loved dog, and that the granddaughter, having gone north for a new life, is gang-raped on the way, and comes back to the white family's kitchen for love and safety. . . . In Harlem now, and in Washington, Watts, Detroit, Newark, and New Rochelle, they are dancing on the grave of this poetry. It was intolerable poetry then too, poetry of the proud, noble, but defective primitive, but went not so much unnoticed as disbelieved; and disbelief is no failing in an aesthetic confection. Even then no one thought Jesus Fever, the old man, and Zoo, the kitchen servant, any more real than the figures on a wedding cake; such figures are, however vulgar, useful to signify outright the fundamental nature of the enterprise. Dated matter in a novel (these signals of locale and wont) disposes of itself—gets eaten up, like the little sugar pair, who are not meant to outlive the afternoon. Dated matter in a novel is not meant to outlive the *Zeitgeist*, which can last a long time, often much longer than its actual components, digesting everything at hand.

But *Other Voices, Other Rooms* is not a dead and empty book because Zoo is, in today's understanding, the progenitrix of black militancy, or because the times that appeared to welcome its particular sensibility are now lost. Indeed, the reason "dated matter" has so little effect on *Other*

Voices, Other Rooms is that it is a timeless book, as every autonomous act of craft is intended to be. A jug, after all, is a jug, whether bought last week at the five-and-dime or unearthed at Knossos: its meaning is self-contained—it has a shape, handles, a lip to pour. And *Other Voices, Other Rooms* has a meaning that is similarly self-contained: Subjectivity, images aflash on a single mind, a moment fashioned with no reference to society, a thing aside from judgment. One can judge it as well made or not well made; but one cannot judge it as one judges a deed.

And this is why it is not really possible to turn to the *Zeitgeist* to account for *Other Voices, Other Rooms'* present emptiness. In fiction in the last several years there have been two clearly recognizable drives: to shake off the final vestiges of narration as a mechanism to be viewed seriatim, and to achieve an autonomous art—"where characters," William Gass explains in a remark derived from Gnosticism in general and from MacLeish in particular, "unlike ourselves, freed from existence, can shine like essence, and purely Be." The atmosphere of our most recent moments—Gass's sentence is their credo—ought both to repulse and retrieve *Other Voices, Other Rooms*: it begins deep in narrative like Dickens (a boy setting out on his own to find the father he has never seen), but ends in Being, and shines like "essence," which I take to be, like Tao or satori, recognizable when you have it but otherwise undefinable—and not, surely, accessible, like a deed, to judgment.

The literary *Zeitgeist* is, to use the famous phrase, Against Interpretation; and it is into such a philosophy, freed from existence, and above all freed from the notion of the morally accountable Deed, that *Other Voices, Other Rooms* ought almost flawlessly to glide. For just as its outmoded Negroes do not matter—essence transcends history—so also does the impediment of its rusty narrative works vanish in the dazzle of its prose-poem Being. *Other Voices, Other Rooms* is, as we always boringly say, a vision: a vision apart from its components, which include a paralyzed father who signals by dropping red tennis balls, a Panlike twin, a midget, a transvestite cousin, the aforementioned sad-happy darkies, not one but two decaying manses (one of which is called the Cloud Hotel), and the whole apparatus of a boy's *rite de passage* into probable homosexuality. But the vision is not the sum of any combination of its parts, no more than some or all of the churches of the world add up to the idea of a planet redeemed. Joel Knox, the boy who comes to Skully's Landing in search of his father, is nevertheless after a redemption that has nothing to do with the stuff of the story he passes through; and at the close of the novel he *is* redeemed, because the novel itself is his redemption, the novel is a sacrament for both protagonist and novelist.

A less fancy way of saying all this is that *Other Voices, Other Rooms* is the novel of someone who wanted, with a fixed and single-minded and burning will, to write a novel. The vision of *Other Voices, Other Rooms* is the vision of capital-A Art—essence freed from existence. And what is meant by the cant phrase "the novel ought to be about itself" is this: the will to write a novel expresses the novel itself; the will to make art expresses art itself—"expresses" not in the sense that one is equivalent to the other, but that the fulfillment of desire is itself a thing of value, or enough for literature. This is so much taking the imagining to signify the thing itself (which is, after all, *literature*) that quotidian life—acts followed by their consequences—is left behind at the Cloud Hotel. To quote the theoretician Gass again: "Life is not the subject of fiction."[1] One would be willing to broaden this comment to strike a more percipient grain: life is not the subject of the sort of fiction that is at home in the American *Zeitgeist* at this moment—despite some beginning strands of dissent. The novel that is said to be "about itself," or "about its own language," belongs not to the hard thing we mean when we say "life," but rather to transcendence, incantation, beatification, grotesquerie, epiphany, rhapsody and rapture—all those tongues that lick the self: a self conceived of as sanctified (whether by muses or devils or gods) and superhuman. When life—the furious web of society, manners, institutions, ideas, tribal histories, and the thicket of history-of-ideas itself—when life is not the subject of fiction, then magic is. Not fable, invention, metaphor, the varied stuff of literature—but *magic*. And magic is a narcissistic exercise, whether the magic is deemed to be contained within language or within psychology: in either case the nub is autonomous inwardness.

The *Zeitgeist* is just now open to all this. Yet *Other Voices, Other Rooms*—a slim, easy, lyrical book—can no longer be read. Dead and empty. And what of 1948, the year of its publication? What was that time like, the time that sped Capote and his novel to a nearly legendary celebrity that has not since diminished?

In 1948, cruising the lunchbag-odorous Commons of Washington Square College, I used to keep an eye out for *Other Voices, Other Rooms*. That place and that time were turbulent with mainly dumb, mainly truculent veterans in their thirties arrived under the open enrollment of the GI Bill, and the handful of young aesthetes, still dewy with high-school Virgil (*O infelix Dido!*), whose doom it was to wander through that poverty-muttering postwar mob in hapless search of Beauty, found one another through Truman Capote. Other voices, other rooms—ah, how we felt it, the tug of somewhere else, inchoate, luminous, the enameled radiance of our eternal and gifted youth. Instead, here were these veterans, responsible clods, jerks, and dopes, with their preposterous eye-wrinkles, their snapshots of preposterous wives and preposterous little children, the idiotic places they lived in, dopey Quonset huts on some dopey North Brother Island, slow-witted all, unable to conjugate, full of angry pragmatic questions, classroom slumberers grinding their joyless days through English and history and language, coming alive only for Marketing and Accounting, sniggering at Sheats and Kelley, hating Thomas Wolfe, with every mean money-grubbing diaper-stinking aging bone hating Poetry and Beauty and Transfiguration. . . .

Capote was the banner against this blight. To walk with Capote in your grasp was as distinctive, and as dissenting from the world's values, as a monk's habit. Capote: that is what the pseudonym signified: a concealing cloak, to be worn by enraptured adepts.

If *Other Voices, Other Rooms* was written by Somebody Else, it was, even more so, read by Somebody Else. Who made Capote famous? I, said the fly, with my covetous eye—I and all those others who clung to him and made him our cult, I and my fellow cabalists for whom he embodied Art Incarnate (among them the late Alfred Chester, who, priestlike, claimed to have Capote's unlisted telephone number). He was not much older than we were, and had already attained what we longed for: the eucharist of the jacket biography. So we seized the book, the incongruous moment, the resplendent and ecstasy-stung words:

> . . . the run of reindeer hooves came crisply tinkling down
> the street, and Mr. Mystery, elegantly villainous in his black
> cape, appeared in their wake riding a most beautiful boatlike

sleigh: it was made of scented wood, a carved red swan graced
its front, and silver bells were strung like beads to make a sail:
swinging, billowing-out, what shivering melodies it sang as the
sleigh, with Joel aboard and warm in the folds of Mr. Mystery's
cape, cut over snowdeep fields and down unlikely hills.

Whereupon the room commenced to vibrate slightly, then more
so, chairs overturned, the curio cabinet spilled its contents, a
mirror cracked, the pianola, composing its own doomed jazz,
held a haywire jamboree: down went the house, down into the
earth, down, down, past Indian tombs, past the deepest root,
the coldest stream, down, down, into the furry arms of horned
children whose bumblebee eyes withstand forests of flame.

Who could withstand these forests of flaming prose? In the generation
of his own youth Capote was the shining maggot in the fiction of the
young.

The *Zeitgeist* then had nothing to do with it. The *Zeitgeist* now
ought to have everything to do with it, but masses of the young do not
now read the early Capote; the new cults form around anti-stylists like
Vonnegut and Brautigan.

Something needs to be explained. It is not that the novel was written,
and read, by Somebody Else; after twenty years all novels are. It is not
that the mood of the era is now against Poetry and Transfiguration; the
opposite is true. Above all, it is not that *Other Voices, Other Rooms* is
dead and empty only now; it always was.

What needs to be explained is the whole notion of the relation of
Zeitgeist to fiction. In fact there is none, yet there is no fallacy more uni-
versally swallowed. For what must be understood about an era's moods
is this: often they are sham or nostalgia or mimicry, and they do not
always tell the truth about the human condition; more often than not
the *Zeitgeist* is a lie, even about its own data. If, as Gottlieb persuades us,
Solzhenitsyn comes to us with all the mechanism of the Tolstoyan novel
intact, and yet comes to us as a living literary force, it is not because the
nineteenth century is not yet dead in the Russian mind, although that
may be perfectly true. It is because, whatever its mechanics, the idea of

the novel is attached to life, to the life of deeds, which are susceptible of both judgment and interpretation; and the novel of Deed is itself a deed to be judged and interpreted. But the novel that is fragrant with narcissism, that claims essence sans existence, that either will not get its shoes drekky or else elevates drek to cultishness—the novel, in short, of the aesthetic will—*that* novel cannot survive its cult.

Further: one would dare to say that the survival of the novel as a form depends on this distinction between the narcissistic novel and the novel of Deed.

On the surface it would seem that Capote's progress, over a distance of seventeen years, from *Other Voices, Other Rooms* to *In Cold Blood*—from the prose-poetry of transfiguration to the more direct and plain, though still extremely artful, prose of his narrative journalism—is a movement from the narcissistic novel to the novel of Deed; Capote himself never once appears in the pages of his crime story. But there is no forward movement, it is all only a seeming; both the novel and the "nonfiction novel" are purely aesthetic shapes. In *Other Voices, Other Rooms* it is the ecstasy of language that drives the book; in *In Cold Blood* it is something journalists call "objectivity," but it is more immaculate than that. "My files would almost fill a whole small room up to the ceiling," Capote told an interviewer; for years he had intertwined his mind and his days with a pair of murderers—to get, he said, their point of view. He had intertwined his life; he was himself a character who impinged, in visit after visit, on the criminals; and yet, with aesthetic immaculateness, he left himself out. Essence without existence; to achieve the alp of truth without the risk of the footing. But finally and at bottom he must be taken at his word that *In Cold Blood* has the blood of a novel. He cannot have that *and* the journalist's excuse for leaving himself out of it—in the end the "nonfiction novel" must be called to account like any novel. And no novel has ever appeared, on its face, to be more the novel of Deed than this narrative of two killers—despite which it remains judgment-free, because it exempts itself from its own terms. Chekhov in "Ward No. 6," one of the most intelligent short novels ever written, understood how the man who deals with the fate of the imprisoned begins to partake of the nature of the imprisoned; this is the great moral hint, the profound unholy question, that lurks in *In Cold Blood*. But it is evaded, in the name of objectivity, of journalistic distance, all those things that the novel has no use for. In the end *In Cold Blood* is, like *Other Voices, Other Rooms*, only another design, the pattern of a hot desire to make a form; one more aesthetic manipulation. It cannot go out of itself—one part of it leads only to another part. Like *Other Voices, Other Rooms*, it is well made, but it has excised its chief predicament, the relation of the mind of the observer to the mind of the observed, and therefore it cannot be judged, it escapes interpretation because it flees its own essential deed. Such "objectivity" is as narcissistic as the grossest "subjectivity": it will not expose itself to an accounting.

Despite every appearance, every modification of style, Capote is at the root *not* Somebody Else. The beautiful reclining boy on the jacket of *Other Voices, Other Rooms* and the middle-aged television celebrity who tells dog stories are one, more so than either would imagine; nothing in Capote as writer has changed. If the world has changed, it has not touched Capote's single and persistent tone. Joel Knox in the last sentence of *Other Voices, Other Rooms* looks back "at the boy he had left behind." False prophecy. Nothing has been left behind—only, perhaps, the younger writer's habit of the decorated phrase. What continues in Capote, and continues in force, is the idea that life is style, and that shape and mood are what matter in and out of fiction. That is the famous lie on which aesthetics feeds the centuries. Life is not style, but what we do: Deed. And so is literature. Otherwise Attic jugs would be our only mentors.

NOTES

[1] It ought to be noted, though, that much of Gass's fiction brilliantly contradicts his theory of fiction. Yet as the prevailing embodiment of this type of aesthetic formulation, Gass's credo is significant currency, representative enough to warrant its appearance elsewhere in this volume. [See Ozick's *Art & Ardor*, "Toward a New Yiddish," p. 151.]

What Chekhov Meant by Life

JAMES WOOD

What did Chekhov mean by "life"? I wondered this while uncomfortably watching a Broadway production of *A Doll's House*. Mild, slippery Chekhov once told Stanislavsky, with soft surprise as if it were something too obvious to say: "But listen, Ibsen is no playwright! . . . Ibsen just doesn't know life. In life it simply isn't like that." No, in life it simply isn't like that, even while sitting in a theater. It was summer. Outside, the Broadway traffic sounded like an army that is getting close but never arrives. The fantastic heat was sensual, the air conditioners dripping their sap, their backsides thrust out of the window like Alisoun, who does the same in Chaucer. Everything was the usual noisy obscurity. Yet inside, here was Ibsen ordering life into three trim acts, and a cooled audience obediently laughing and tutting at the right moments, and thinking about drinks at the interval—the one moment of Chekhovian life being that in the lobby the barman could be heard putting out glasses, tuning up his little cocktail orchestra. The clinking was disturbing Ibsen's simpler tune.

A Doll's House tells the story of a woman's subjection to, and eventual escape from, her husband. Ibsen is not clumsy; he does not make Nora's husband, Torvald, monstrous so much as uncomprehending. And yet he cannot resist telling us how foolishly uncomprehending is Torvald. Nora deceives her husband in order to protect him; he discovers the deception and is furious. Toward the end of the play, Nora tells him that she is leaving him because she has never been more than his toy. Torvald "forgives" her for her deception. Nora cries because Torvald cannot understand. "Why are you crying?" asks Torvald. "Is it because I have forgiven you for your deception?" At this moment, the audience snickered knowingly. Poor, foolish Torvald, who thinks he can make things all right by forgiving his wife! Ibsen wants no part of Torvald's foolishness to escape us. Surely Chekhov's objection to Ibsen was founded in the feeling that Ibsen is like a man who laughs at his own jokes. He relishes the *dramatic* "ironies" of the situation; indeed, he can think only in dramatic ironies, like someone who can write only on one kind of wide-margin paper. Ibsen's people are too comprehensible. We comprehend them as we comprehend fictional entities. He is always tying the moral shoelaces of his characters, making everything neat, presentable, knowable. The secrets of his characters are knowable secrets, not the true privacies of Chekhov's people. They are the bourgeois secrets: a former lover, a broken contract, a blackmailer, a debt, an unwanted relative.

But Chekhov's idea of "life" is a bashful, milky complication, not a solving of things. We can get a good understanding of this from the notebook he kept. This notebook was, in effect, the mattress in which he stuffed his stolen money. It is full of enigmas in which nothing adds up, full of strange squints, comic observations, and promptings for new stories.

Instead of sheets—dirty tablecloths.

The dog walked in the street and was ashamed of its crooked legs.

They were mineral water bottles with preserved cherries in them.

In the bill preserved by the hotel-keeper was, among other things: "Bugs—fifteen kopecks."

He picked his teeth and put the toothpick back into the glass.

A private room in a restaurant. A rich man, tying his napkin round his neck, touching the sturgeon with his fork: "At least I'll have a snack before I die"—and he has been saying this for a long time, daily.

If you wish women to love you, be original; I know a man who used to wear felt boots summer and winter, and women fell in love with him.

What is noticeable is that Chekhov thinks of detail, even visual detail, as a story, and thinks of story as an enigma. He was not interested in noticing that the roofs of a town look like armadillo shells, or that he was confused about God, or that the Russian people represented the world-spirit on a troika. He was drawn neither to the statically poetic nor to the statically philosophical. Detail is hardly ever a stable entity in Chekhov's work; it is a reticent event. He found the world to be as deeply evasive as he was himself—life as a tree of separate hanging stories, of dangling privacies. For him a story did not merely begin in enigma, but ended in enigma too. He had a character in "Concerning Love" complain that "decent Russians like ourselves have a passion for problems that have never been solved." Chekhov had such a passion for problems, but only if solution might stay unrequited. The writer Ivan Bunin said that Chekhov loved to read out random oddities from the newspapers: "Babkin, a Samara merchant, left all his money for a memorial to Hegel!" The attraction of such tales, one suspects, was that a newspaper imagines that it has explained a story when all it has done is told one. Bunin supplied a true anecdote about a deacon who ate all the caviar at a funeral party; Chekhov used this at the beginning of "In the Ravine." His writing, which is strewn with unsolved details, is a kind of newspaper of the intimate fantastic. In this respect, his stories are like tales of crime in which nobody is a criminal.

There is no introspection in Chekhov's notebook. Everything has the same hard, found, random quality. We can infer as much of Chekhov's personality from one entry as from all of them together. A friend said that he "lacked gaiety, and his fine, intelligent eyes always looked at everything from a distance." From the various memoirs by relatives and friends, we can imagine a man who always seemed a little older than himself, and older than anyone he met, as if he were living more than one life. He would not make himself transparent: he was approachable but unknowable. He had an arbitrary smile, and a comic's ability to make strange things seem inevitable. When an actor asked him to explain what kind of writer Trigorin is, in *The Seagull*, he replied: "But he wears checkered trousers." He had a horror of being the center of attention. He delivered his judgments in a tone of weary generosity, as if they were so obvious that he had simply missed someone else saying them earlier. He was deeply charming; seasonally, a different woman fell in love with him. On this picture has been built the Anglo-American vision of Chekhov, in which the writer resembles the perfect literary Englishman—a writer of the religion of no religion, of instincts rather than convictions, a governor of ordinary provinces whose inhabitants may be unhappy or yearning for change but who eventually learn to calm down and live by the local laws. D. S. Mirsky, a Russian critic who lived in England, argued that Chekhov was popular in England because of his "unusually complete rejection of what we may call the heroic values." This idea of Chekhov as the nurse of the prosaic is far from the truth, and Chekhov's writing, which is odd, brutal, despairing, and unhappily comic, gives no excuse for it.

The fullest biography to appear in English, by Donald Rayfield, clouds the soft Anglo-American idea of Chekhov, which is a good thing. In this account Chekhov is still charming, tactful, and decent. He is still the man who bought new books for the library of his hometown, who dispensed free medicine and became a hospital inspector near his farm at Melikhovo. But we also see that Chekhov's life was a long flight into his work. He ran from human connections. There is something cruel, even repulsive in a man who was so sensitive to pain, about the way Chekhov encouraged women to fall in love with him, and then, month by month, canceled their ardor. He would reply scantily or not at all to their letters. His most productive writing years, between 1892 and 1900, were spent on his Melikhovo estate, about fifty miles south of Moscow, where he lived with his dutiful sister, Masha, and his parents. Here he tried to ration unnecessary involvement with people. Chekhov had the temperament of a philanderer. Sexually, he preferred brothels or swift liaisons. (This picture overpowers with superior evidence V. S. Pritchett's benign suggestion that Chekhov lacked sexual appetite.)

His one loyalty was to his family, for whom he became the breadwinner while at medical school in Moscow. He was born in Taganrog, in southern Russia, in 1860. His father, Pavel, may be seen as the original of all Chekhov's great portraits of hypocrites. Pavel was a grocer, but he failed at everything he touched except religious devotion. In between flogging his children—he was exceptionally cruel—he became *kappelmeister* of the cathedral choir, where his love of the liturgy made services interminable. In church, "Pavel never compromised over his favorite quality, splendor." He was horribly pious. There is the story of Pavel finding a rat in a barrel of olive oil in his shop. "He was too honest to say nothing, too mean to pour the oil away, too lazy to boil and re-filter it. He chose consecration: Father Pokrovsky conducted a service in the shop."

Chekhov would become a writer who did not believe in God, hated physical cruelty, fought every sign of "splendor" on the page, and filled his fiction with hypocrites. The ghost of Pavel can be found everywhere in Chekhov, in the complacent Dr. Ragin in "Ward 6," who lectures his abused patients at the local asylum about Marcus Aurelius and the importance of stoicism, and in the fatuous priest in "In the Ravine" who, at dinner, comforts a woman who has just lost her baby while pointing at her with "a fork with a pickled mushroom on the end of it." Yet the son did not abandon the father. Once the Chekhovs had moved to Moscow, Anton calmly assumed the sustenance of his whole family. He checked his dissolute elder brothers with that strange, sourceless maturity of his, which sometimes gives him the air of being the sole possessor of a clandestine happiness. There are eight rules by which "well-bred people" live, he told his brother Nikolai in a long letter. You restrain yourself sexually; you do not brag. "The truly gifted are always in the shadows, in the crowd, far from exhibitions." Until

Donald Rayfield gained access to previously censored archives, the last line of this letter has always been soothed into English as: "You have to relinquish your pride: you are not a little boy anymore." But the actual version runs: "You must drop your fucking conceit . . ." It is good to tear our idea of Chekhovian perfection with these little hernias. We should see the lapses, the mundanities, the coarseness, the sexual honesty which Russian censors and English worshipers removed. Chekhov is still philo-Semitic and a supporter of women's rights. But every so often his letters fall, show a little bulge of prejudice—"Yids" appear from time to time, and women are verbally patted.

The Chekhov family lived off Anton's literary earnings. These were small at first. Chekhov wrote hackishly for six years—comic stubs, sketches, cartoons and colorings for newspapers. (His mature work, of course, has a briskness, and sometimes a slapping, educative motion reminiscent of the form of a cartoon or sketch.) His meeting with Alexei Suvorin, the owner of the newspaper *Novoye Vremya*, was the foundation of his greatest writing. Suvorin had had his eye on Chekhov's writing. From 1887 until 1900, he was Chekhov's patron and deepest correspondent. He was also the writer's opposite; thus Chekhov had to function like Suvorin's kidney, extracting the businessman's poisons—his anti-Semitism (they quarreled over the Dreyfus affair when Chekhov announced himself a Dreyfusard), his artistic conservatism, his wariness of the slightest political radicalism. Suvorin was reviled by most enlightened thinkers, and Chekhov's alliance with him was often scorned. But then Chekhov also became friendly with Gorki, and his fiction was sometimes simultaneously claimed by both right and left: the pantomime horse of politics fighting inside itself for front and back legs, and then collapsing on stage.

"The Steppe" (1888) was the first story to appear in a "thick journal": Chekhov was a renowned writer for the rest of his life. He was only twenty-eight, and the story has it hesitations, such as a weakness for lurid theatrical gargoyles (Moses and Solomon, the Jewish traders), which seem Dickensian but which are obviously lifted from Gogol. But much of the beauty of mature Chekhov is here; it is just an early footprint made by a lighter man. In particular, the bashful pace of the writing, which moves at the aimless, random speed of the imagination.

We follow a little boy, Yegorushka, who is going to a new school, and who has hitched a ride with two men—a wool trader called Kuzmichov, and a priest called Father Christopher. As they leave the boy's home village, at the start of the journey, they pass the cemetery in which his father and his grandmother are buried. Chekhov's description drifts.

> From behind the wall cheerful white crosses and tombstones peeped out, nestling in the foliage of cherry trees and seen as white patches from a distance. At blossom time, Yegorushka remembered, the white patches mingled with the cherry blooms in a sea of white, and when the cherries had ripened the white tombs and crosses were crimson-spotted, as if with blood. Under the cherries behind the wall the boy's father and his grandmother Zinaida slept day and night. When Grandmother had died she had been put in a long, narrow coffin, and five-copeck pieces had been placed on her eyes, which would not stay shut. Before dying she had been alive, and she had brought him soft poppy-seed bun rings from the market, but now she just slept and slept.

Woolf and Joyce admired Chekhov, and faced with little Yegorushka's drifting thought, one sees why. (Just as, watching the didactic *A Doll's House*, one sees why George Bernard Shaw admired Ibsen.) For this is a form of stream of consciousness, more natural and less showy than Anna Karenina's mania at the end of Tolstoy's novel. "Before dying, she had been alive . . . but now she just slept and slept." This is not only how a small boy thinks, but how all of us think about the dead, privately: *Before dying, she had been alive.* It is one of those obviously pointless banalities of thought, an accidental banality which, being an accident, is not banal, is never banal. But something deeper about Chekhov's art is revealed a page later, when Yegorushka cries because he misses his mother, and Father Christopher comforts him. "Never mind, son," the priest says. "Call on God. Lomonosov once traveled just like this with the fishermen, and he became famous throughout Europe. Learning conjoined with faith yields fruit pleasing to God. What does the prayer say? 'For the glory of the Creator, for our parents' comfort, for the benefit of church and country.' That's the way of it." Of course, Father Christopher is offering no comfort at all; he is self-involved. His solace has no dramatic point, in the Ibsen sense. He is speaking his mind, literally. He speaks in the same apparently arbitrary manner as the boy thinks. This use of stream of consciousness would, in later years, become the basis of Chekhov's innovation in stagecraft; it is also his innovation in fiction. Chekhov sees the similarities between what we say to ourselves and what we say to others: both are failed privacies. Both are lost secrets, the former lost somewhere between our minds and our souls, the latter lost somewhere between each other. Naturally, this kind of mental speech, whether turned inward or outward, has the arbitrary quality of memory or dream. It *is* memory or dream. And this is why it seems comic, because watching a Chekhov character is like watching a lover wake up in bed, half awake and half dreaming, saying something odd and private which means nothing to us because it refers to the preceding dream. In life, at such moments, we sometimes laugh and say: "You're not making any sense, you know." Chekhov's characters live in these two states.

Sometimes his characters turn their thought outward, and speak it; sometimes their thought remains inward, and Chekhov describes it for us—and very often these two ribbons of revelation are indistinguishable from each other, as in Yegorushka's remembrance of his grandmother. "The Bishop," a late story which Chekhov completed in 1902, two years before he died, is a good example of this new fluency in storytelling. A dying cleric starts to think about his childhood . . . and suddenly he is adrift. He remembers "Father Simeon, who was very short and thin, but who had a terribly tall son (a theological student). . . . Once his son lost his temper with the cook and called her 'Ass of Jehudiel,' which made Father Simeon go very quiet, for he was only too ashamed of not being able to remember where this particular ass was mentioned in the Bible." Such richness, such healthy secularism of detail! Yet the great novelty of Chekhov is not in discovering or inventing such details and anecdotes, for we can find details as good in Tolstoy and Leskov. It is in their placement, their sudden flowering, their lack of apparent point, as if Chekhov's characters were coming across something unwanted, certainly unexpected. The thought seems to be thinking the characters.

It is the movement of free consciousness in literature for perhaps the first time: neither Austen nor Sterne, neither Gogol nor Tolstoy, allows a character quite this relationship to memory.

The great pleasure of seeing Chekhov develop as a writer, from "The Steppe" to "The Lady with the Dog" eleven years later, is to see the way he discovers and enlarges this idea of apparently arbitrary detail. For it is not merely Chekhov's characters who think in sudden lunges and bites of detail. It becomes the very principle of Chekhov's prose style. Nabokov once complained about Chekhov's "medley of dreadful prosaisms, ready-made epithets, repetitions." Nabokov was certainly wrong. Chekhov's metaphors, nature scenes, and visual details are often finer than Nabokov's (and invariably finer than Tolstoy's) because they have an unexpectedness that seems to break away from literature. He sees the world not as a writer might see it but as one of his characters might. This is the case even when he is telling a story as "Chekhov," apparently from outside a character's head. "From somewhere far off came the mournful, indistinct cry of a bittern, sounding just like a cow locked up in a shed." This is not an obviously poetic likeness; it is how a villager might think of a bittern's cry. "A cuckoo seemed to be adding up someone's age, kept losing count and starting again." A girl about to burst into tears, "her face oddly strained as if her mouth were full of water." (The key there is the word "oddly." Oddly to whom? To the other characters in the room, one of whom is Chekhov: he is no longer a writer.) The noise, in a poor village, of "an expensive-sounding accordion."

More completely than any writer before him Chekhov became his characters. A great story like "Gusev" is impossible without this identification. It is set on a boat returning to Russia. In the sick bay, a stupid peasant called Gusev is dying. The other patients make fun of his primitive imagination—he thinks that the winds are chained up somewhere like dogs to a wall, and that it is stormy because they have been let loose. As Gusev lies in the ship, he recalls his home village, and we see that his imagination is not primitive. Soon he dies and is buried at sea, wrapped in a sail. "Sewn up in the sailcloth," writes Chekhov, "he looked like a carrot or radish: broad at the head and narrow at the feet." As he falls into the sea, clouds are massing. Chekhov writes that one cloud looks like a triumphal arch, another like a lion, a third like a pair of scissors. Suddenly we realize that Chekhov sees the world as Gusev does. If Gusev is foolish, then so is Chekhov! Why is it more foolish to think of the wind as a chained dog, as Gusev does, than to think of a cloud as a lion or a corpse as a radish, as Chekhov does? Chekhov's very narration disappears into Gusev's.

Stupendously, Chekhov's fullest biographer has little time for Chekhov's writing. It appears to obstruct the siege of biographical "fact." Donald Rayfield tells us in his preface that Chekhov's works are discussed "inasmuch as they emerge from his life and as they affect it, but less as material for critical analysis. Biography is not criticism." Of course, this separation of life and work, as a butcher might use separate knives for raw meat and for cooked, is primitive. Biography is criticism, especially in the case of Chekhov, who so often evaded life to strengthen his work. Undoubtedly, Rayfield offers a newly full idea of Chekhov's life—he is more brutal, more cruel, more ordinary, more lonely. But his book is only grayly rich: a massive diary of travel and letters and meetings. About the writer, he tells us almost nothing, and in several places disarms facts of their literary context. On the whole, it would be better if he never mentioned Chekhov's work, because his brief comments seem merely mandatory. "Gusev," he tells us, "is an awesome portrayal of nature's indifference to death. . . . Chekhov's post-Sakhalin phase had begun." "Ward 6" is "a bleak allegory of the human condition. There is no love interest." Of "The Student" (Chekhov's own favorite), he comments: "This is 'late Chekhov,' where . . . all is evoked, not stated." And so on. Most of the stories are brushed off in a line or two. He forces stories into biographical cells, distorting many of them. At other times, he takes comments by Chekhov and skins them of the literary. For example, in January 1901, Chekhov was in Rome with his friend M. M. Kovalevsky. Chekhov, according to Rayfield, was ill and depressed. He had three years to live. Offered as evidence of Chekhov's state of mind is his response to a penitential procession that he saw with Kovalevsky at St. Peter's. Rayfield comments: "Anton's mood grew grim: he told Kovalevsky he was writing nothing long, because he would soon die. [He] watched a penitential procession in St. Peter's. Asked how he would describe it, he replied, 'A stupid procession dragged past.'" But Kovalevsky's memoir (most recently reprinted in Andrei Turkov's book *Anton Chekhov and His Times*, which was published in Moscow in 1990) makes clear that Chekhov's was a literary response. Kovalevsky discusses Chekhov's dismissal in the light of his "avoidance of any kind of unnecessary detail" as a writer. When they had watched the procession go by, Kovalevsky suggested that "for a belletrist," what they had seen was "not without a certain attraction." "Not the slightest," replied Chekhov. "The modern novelist would be obliged to satisfy himself with the phrase: 'A silly procession dragged on.'" The literary context is not only truer and more interesting than the wrongly biographical reading; it tells us more about the "biographical" Chekhov.

In 1890, Chekhov made a long journey to Sakhalin, a prison island off the coast of Siberia. Chekhov saw Russia's human leavings on Sakhalin, a kind of living death camp. Near the end of the book-length report he published in 1895, Chekhov describes seeing a murderer being given ninety lashes. Then this Chekhovian detail—a whining military medical assistant who asks a favor. "Your worship, please let me see how they punish a prisoner." There were times, wrote Chekhov, when "I felt that I saw before me the extreme limits of man's degradation." Chekhov believed in the importance of good schools and medicine. But Sakhalin heated his meliorism. At Melikhovo, the estate he bought in 1892, he helped to build a new school, gave freely of his medical expertise. His greatest stories became darker, more absolving. Prisons are everywhere in them: even the lovers in "The Lady with the Dog," published in 1899 while Chekhov was first involved with his future wife, Olga Knipper, feel trapped in a cage, "and it was impossible to escape from it, just as though you were in a lunatic asylum or a convict chain-gang!" The bleak "Gusev" (1890) was seeded when Chekhov saw two men die on board the ship bringing him back from Sakhalin. "Ward 6" (1892) is set in an asylum. A complacent doctor, who has ignored the sufferings of his patients, finds that his own mind is lapsing. He in turn is thrown into the asylum. From the window, he can see the town prison: "There's reality for you!" thinks the doctor. He dies in the asylum, and as he leaves consciousness he goes on a mental safari, and Chekhov awards him one of those lunges, one of those random aerations or white apertures that are so distinctive a feature of his work: "A herd of deer, extraordinarily beautiful and graceful, which he had been reading about on the previous day, raced past him, then a peasant woman stretched out a hand to him with a registered letter. . . ." These stories have a rather frantic humanism: Chekhov wrote to Suvorin in 1898 that the writer's task was to "stand up for the guilty if they have already been condemned and punished." This was a year after he made his first public stand, in behalf of Dreyfus.

What did Chekhov believe in? In his essay on the writer, the philosopher Lev Shestov suggested (approvingly) that Chekhov had "no ideal, not even the ideal of ordinary life." His work, he said, murmurs a quiet "I don't know" to every problem. Certain Soviet critics decided that Chekhov's "hopeless" characters were not prophetic enough about the imminent revolution—too pessimistic about Russia's future. But because Chekhov's stories confound philosophy they do not necessarily lack it. Susan Sontag is surely right when she suggests that Chekhov's writing is a dream of freedom—"an absolute freedom," wrote Chekhov, "the freedom from violence and lies." And freedom is not merely political or material in his work. It is a neutral saturate, like air or light. How often he describes a village, and then, at the village's edge—"the open fields." The narrator of "Man in a Case" remembers the freedom of being a child, when his parents went out, "and we would run around the garden for an hour or so, reveling in perfect freedom." And because Chekhov is truthful, because he is not a Tolstoy, who will shuffle his characters toward the freedom of the Godhead, or a Gorki, who will lead his characters to instinctive socialism, he must admit that freedom is not always attractive to us, and that it frightens us. Perhaps freedom is only the freedom not to exist? "Oh how nice not to exist," cries Chebutykin in *Three Sisters*. Often we notice that his characters long to escape into a freedom whose vastness depends on its nonexistence. Moscow is not just an impossibility for the three sisters. It does not exist, and their desire for it has made it disappear. Perhaps the gap between yearning for a new life—the most familiar gesture of Chekhov's characters, and one the writer saw firsthand among his own family—and yearning for no life, is small. But whatever happens to Chekhov's characters, however they yearn, they have one freedom that flows from his literary genius: they act like free consciousnesses, and not as owned literary characters. This is not a negligible freedom.

For the great achievement of Chekhov's beautifully accidental style, his mimicking of the stream of the mind, is that it allows forgetfulness into fiction. Buried deep in themselves, people forget themselves while thinking, and go on mental journeys. Of course, they do not exactly forget to be themselves. They forget to act as *purposeful fictional characters*. They mislay their scripts. They stop being actors, Ibsen's envoys.

Chekhov's characters forget to be Chekhov's characters. We see this most beautifully in one of his earliest stories, "The Kiss," written when he was twenty-seven. A virginal soldier kisses a woman for the first time in his life. He hoards the memory of it, and bursts to tell his fellow soldiers about his experience. Yet when he does tell them, he is disappointed because his story takes only a short minute to tell, yet "he had imagined it would take until morning." One notices that many of Chekhov's characters are disappointed by the stories they tell, and somewhat jealous of other people's stories. But to be disappointed by one's own story is an extraordinarily subtle freedom in literature, for it implies a character's freedom to be disappointed not only by his own story but, by extension, by the story Chekhov has given him. Thus he wriggles out of Chekhov's story into the bottomless freedom of disappointment. He is always trying to make his own story out of the story Chekhov has given him, and even this freedom of disappointment will be disappointing. (That this freedom is awarded and managed by the author is of course a trivial paradox: how else could it arise?) And yet it *is* a freedom. We see this so finely in "The Kiss." The soldier forgets that he is in Chekhov's story because he has become so involved in his own. His own story is bottomless, and yearns to last all night; yet Chekhov's story "takes only a minute to tell." In Chekhov's world, our inner lives run at their own speed. They are laxly calendared. They live in their own gentle almanac, and in his stories the free inner life bumps against the outer life like two different time-systems, like the Julian calendar against the Gregorian. This was what Chekhov meant by "life." This was his revolution.

Herman Melville's *Moby Dick*

D. H. LAWRENCE

Moby Dick, *or the White Whale.*

A hunt. The last great hunt.

For what?

For Moby Dick, the huge white sperm whale: who is old, hoary, monstrous, and swims alone; who is unspeakably terrible in his wrath, having so often been attacked; and snow-white.

Of course he is a symbol.

Of what?

I doubt if even Melville knew exactly. That's the best of it.

He is warm-blooded, he is loveable. He is lonely Leviathan, not a Hobbes sort. Or is he?

But he is warm-blooded and loveable. The South Sea Islanders, and Polynesians, and Malays, who worship shark, or crocodile, or weave endless frigate-bird distortions, why did they never worship the whale? So big!

Because the whale is not wicked. He doesn't bite. And their gods had to bite.

He's not a dragon. He is Leviathan. He never coils like the Chinese dragon of the sun. He's not a serpent of the waters. He is warm-blooded, a mammal. And hunted, hunted down.

It is a great book.

At first you are put off by the style. It reads like journalism. It seems spurious. You feel Melville is trying to put something over you. It won't do.

And Melville really is a bit sententious: aware of himself, self-conscious, putting something over even himself. But then it's not easy to get into the swing of a piece of deep mysticism when you just set out with a story.

Nobody can be more clownish, more clumsy and sententiously in bad taste, than Herman Melville, even in a great book like *Moby Dick*. He preaches and holds forth because he's not sure of himself. And he holds forth, often, so amateurishly.

The artist was so *much* greater than the man. The man is rather a tiresome New Englander of the ethical mystical-transcendentalist sort: Emerson, Longfellow, Hawthorne, etc. So unrelieved, the solemn ass even in humour. So hopelessly *au grand sérieux*, you feel like saying: Good God, what does it matter? If life is a tragedy, or a farce, or a disaster, or anything else, what do I care! Let life be what it likes. Give me a drink, that's what I want just now.

For my part, life is so many things I don't care what it is. It's not my affair to sum it up. Just now it's a cup of tea. This morning it was wormwood and gall. Hand me the sugar.

One wearies of the *grand sérieux*. There's something false about it. And that's Melville. Oh dear, when the solemn ass brays! brays! brays!

But he was a deep, great artist, even if he was rather a sententious man. He was a real American in that he always felt his audience in front of him. But when he ceases to be American, when he forgets all audience, and gives us his sheer apprehension of the world, then he is wonderful, his book commands a stillness in the soul, an awe.

In his "human" self, Melville is almost dead. That is, he hardly reacts to human contacts any more; or only ideally: or just for a moment. His human-emotional self is almost played out. He is abstract, self-analytical and abstracted. And he is more spell-bound by the strange slidings and collidings of Matter than by the things men do. In this he is like Dana. It is the material elements he really has to do with. His drama is with them. He was a futurist long before futurism found paint. The sheer naked slidings of the elements. And the human soul experiencing it all. So often, it is almost over the border: psychiatry. Almost spurious. Yet so great.

It is the same old thing as in all Americans. They keep their old-fashioned ideal frock-coat on, and an old-fashioned silk hat, while they do the most impossible things. There you are: you see Melville hugged in bed by a huge tattooed South Sea Islander, and solemnly offering burnt offering to this savage's little idol, and his ideal frock-coat just hides his shirt-tails and prevents us from seeing his bare posterior as he salaams, while his ethical silk hat sits correctly over his brow the while. That is so typically American: doing the most impossible things without taking off their spiritual get-up. Their ideals are like armour which has rusted in, and will never come off. And meanwhile in Melville his bodily knowledge moves naked, a living quick among stark elements. For with sheer physical vibrational sensitiveness, like a marvellous wireless-station, he registers the effects of the outer world. And he records also, almost beyond pain or pleasure, the extreme transitions of the isolated, far-driven soul, the soul which is now alone, without any real human contact.

The first days in New Bedford introduce the only human being who really enters into the book, namely, Ishmael, the "I" of the book. And then the moment's heart's-brother, Queequeg, the tattooed, powerful South Sea harpooner, whom Melville loves as Dana loves "Hope". The advent of Ishmael's bedmate is amusing and unforgettable. But later the two swear "marriage", in the language of the savages. For Queequeg has opened again the flood-gates of love and human connexion in Ishmael.

"As I sat there in that now lonely room, the fire burning low, in that mild stage when, after its first intensity has warmed the air, it then only glows to be looked at; the evening shades and phantoms gathering round the casements, and peering in upon us silent, solitary twain: I began to be sensible of strange feelings. I felt a melting in me. No more my splintered heart and maddened hand were turned against the wolfish world. This soothing savage had redeemed it. There he sat, his very indifference speaking a nature in which there lurked no civilized hypocrisies and bland deceits. Wild he was; a very sight of sights to see; yet I began to feel myself mysteriously drawn towards him."—So they smoked together, and are clasped in each other's arms. The friendship is finally sealed when Ishmael offers sacrifice to Queequeg's little idol, Gogo.

"I was a good Christian, born and bred in the bosom of the infallible Presbyterian Church. How then could I unite with the idolater in worshipping his piece of wood? But what is worship?—to do the will of God—*that* is worship. And what is the will of God?—to do to my fellow man what I would have my fellow man do to me—*that* is the will of God."—Which sounds like Benjamin Franklin, and is hopelessly bad theology. But it is real American logic. "Now Queequeg is my fellow man. And what do I wish that this Queequeg would do to me? Why, unite with me that this Quecqueg would do to me? Why, unite with me in my particular Presbyterian form of worship. Consequently, I must unite with him; ergo, I must turn idolater. So I kindled the shavings; helped prop up the innocent little idol; offered him burnt biscuit with Queequeg; salaamed before him twice or thrice; kissed his nose; and that done, we undressed and went to bed, at peace with our own consciences and all the world. But we did not go to sleep without some little chat. How it is I know not; but there is no place like bed for confidential disclosures between friends. Man and wife, they say, open the very bottom of their souls to each other; and some old couples often lie and chat over old times till nearly morning. Thus, then, lay I and Queequeg—a cosy, loving pair——"

You would think this relation with Queequeg meant something to Ishmael. But no. Queequeg is forgotten like yesterday's newspaper. Human things are only momentary excitements or amusements to the American Ishmael. Ishmael, the hunted. But much more Ishmael the hunter. What's a Queequeg? What's a wife? The white whale must be hunted down. Queequeg must be just "KNOWN", then dropped into oblivion.

And what in the name of fortune is the white whale?

Elsewhere Ishmael says he loved Queequeg's eyes: "large, deep eyes, fiery black and bold." No doubt like Poe, he wanted to get the "clue" to them. That was all.

The two men go over from New Bedford to Nantucket, and there sign on to the Quaker whaling ship, the *Pequod*. It is all strangely fantastic, phantasmagoric. The voyage of the soul. Yet curiously a real whaling voyage, too. We pass on into the midst of the sea with this strange ship and its incredible crew. The Argonauts were mild lambs in comparison. And Ulysses went *defeating* the Circes and overcoming the wicked hussies of the isles. But the *Pequod*'s crew is a collection of maniacs fanatically hunting down a lonely, harmless white whale.

As a soul history, it makes one angry. As a sea yarn, it is marvellous: there is always something a bit over the mark, in sea yarns. Should be. Then again the masking up of actual seaman's experience with sonorous mysticism sometimes gets on one's nerves. And again, as a revelation of destiny the book is too deep even for sorrow. Profound beyond feeling.

You are some time before you are allowed to see the captain, Ahab: the mysterious Quaker. Oh, it is a God-fearing Quaker ship.

Ahab, the captain. The captain of the soul.

"I am the master of my fate,
 I am the captain of my soul!"

Ahab!

"Oh, captain, my captain, our fearful trip is done."

The gaunt Ahab, Quaker, mysterious person, only shows himself after some days at sea. There's a secret about him! What?

Oh, he's a portentous person. He stumps about on an ivory stump, made from sea-ivory. Moby Dick, the great white whale, tore off Ahab's leg at the knee, when Ahab was attacking him.

Quite right, too. Should have torn off both his legs, and a bit more besides.

But Ahab doesn't think so. Ahab is now a monomaniac. Moby Dick is his monomania. Moby Dick must DIE, or Ahab can't live any longer. Ahab is atheist by this.

All right.

This *Pequod*, ship of the American soul, has three mates.

1. Starbuck: Quaker, Nantucketer, a good responsible man of reason, forethought, intrepidity, what is called a dependable man. At the bottom, *afraid*.

2. Stubb: "Fearless as fire, and as mechanical." Insists on being reckless and jolly on every occasion. Must be afraid too, really.

3. Flask: Stubborn, obstinate, without imagination. To him "the wondrous whale was but a species of magnified mouse or water-rat———"

There you have them: a maniac captain and his three mates, three splendid seamen, admirable whalemen, first-class men at their job.

America!

It is rather like Mr. Wilson and his admirable, "efficient" crew, at the Peace Conference. Except that none of the Pequodders took their wives along.

A maniac captain of the soul, and three eminently practical mates.

America!

Then such a crew. Renegades, castaways, cannibals: Ishmael, Quakers.

America!

Three giant harpooners, to spear the great white whale.

1. Queequeg, the South Sea Islander, all tattooed, big and powerful.

2. Tashtego, the Red Indian of the sea-coast, where the Indian meets the sea.

3. Daggoo, the huge black negro.

There you have them, three savage races, under the American flag, the maniac captain, with their great keen harpoons, ready to spear the white whale.

And only after many days at sea does Ahab's own boatcrew appear on deck. Strange, silent, secret, black-garbed Malays, fire-worshipping Parsees. These are to man Ahab's boat, when it leaps in pursuit of that whale.

What do you think of the ship *Pequod*, the ship of the soul of an American?

Many races, many peoples, many nations, under the Stars and Stripes. Beaten with many stripes.

Seeing stars sometimes.

And in a mad ship, under a mad captain, in a mad, fanatic's hunt.

For what?

For Moby Dick, the great white whale.

But splendidly handled. Three splendid mates. The whole thing practical, eminently practical in its working. American industry!

And all this practicality in the service of a mad, mad chase.

Melville manages to keep it a real whaling ship, on a real cruise, in spite of all fantastics. A wonderful, wonderful voyage. And a beauty that is so surpassing only because of the author's awful flounderings in mystical waters. He wanted to get metaphysically deep. And he got deeper than metaphysics. It is a surpassingly beautiful book, with an awful meaning, and bad jolts.

It is interesting to compare Melville with Dana, about the albatross—Melville a bit sententious. "I remember the first albatross I ever saw. It was during a prolonged gale in waters hard upon the Antarctic seas. From my forenoon watch below I ascended to the overcrowded deck, and there, lashed upon the main hatches, I saw a regal feathered thing of unspotted whiteness, and with a hooked Roman bill sublime. At intervals it arched forth its vast, archangel wings—wondrous throbbings and flutterings shook it. Though bodily unharmed, it uttered cries, as some King's ghost in supernatural distress. Through its inexpressible strange eyes methought I peeped to secrets not below the heavens—the white thing was so white, its wings so wide, and in those for ever exiled waters, I had lost the miserable warping memories of traditions and of towns. I assert then, that in the wondrous bodily whiteness of the bird chiefly lurks the secret of the spell——"

Melville's albatross is a prisoner, caught by a bait on a hook.

Well, I have seen an albatross, too: following us in waters hard upon the Antarctic, too, south of Australia. And in the Southern winter. And the ship, a P. and O. boat, nearly empty. And the lascar crew shivering.

The bird with its long, long wings following, then leaving us. No one knows till they have tried, how lost, how lonely those Southern waters are. And glimpses of the Australian coast.

It makes one feel that our day is only a day. That in the dark of the night ahead other days stir fecund, when we have lapsed from existence.

Who knows how utterly we shall lapse.

But Melville keeps up his disquisition about "whiteness". The great abstract fascinated him. The abstract where we end, and cease to be. White or black. Our white, abstract end!

Then again it is lovely to be at sea on the *Pequod*, with never a grain of earth to us.

"It was a cloudy, sultry afternoon; the seamen were lazily lounging about the decks, or vacantly gazing over into the lead-coloured waters. Queequeg and I were mildly employed weaving what is called a sword-mat, for an additional lashing to our boat. So still and subdued, and yet somehow preluding was all the scene, and such an incantation of reverie lurked in the air that each silent sailor seemed resolved into his own invisible self——"

In the midst of this preluding silence came the first cry: "There she blows! there! there! there! She blows!" And then comes the first chase, a marvellous piece of true sea-writing, the sea, and sheer sea-beings on the chase, sea-creatures chased. There is scarcely a taint of earth—pure sea-motion.

"'Give way, men,' whispered Starbuck, drawing still further aft the sheet of his sail; 'there is time to kill a fish yet before the squall comes. There's white water again!—Close to!—Spring!' Soon after, two cries in quick succession on each side of us denoted that the other boats had got fast; but hardly were they overheard, when with a lightning-like hurtling whisper Starbuck said: 'Stand up!' and Queequeg, harpoon in hand, sprang to his feet.—Though not one of the oarsmen was then facing the life and death peril so close to them ahead, yet, their eyes on the intense countenance of the mate in the stern of the boat, they knew that the imminent instant had come; they heard, too, an enormous wallowing sound, as of fifty elephants stirring in their litter. Meanwhile the boat was still booming through the mist, the waves curbing and hissing around us like the erected crests of enraged serpents.

"'That's his hump. *There! There*, give it to him!' whispered Starbuck.—A short rushing sound leapt out of the boat; it was the darted iron of Queequeg. Then all in one welded motion came a push from astern, while forward the boat seemed striking on a ledge; the sail collapsed and exploded; a gush of scalding vapour shot up near by; something rolled and tumbled like an earthquake beneath us. The whole crew were half-suffocated as they were tossed helter-skelter into the white curling cream of the squall. Squall, whale, and harpoon had all blended together; and the whale, merely grazed by the iron, escaped——"

Melville is a master of violent, chaotic physical motion; he can keep up a whole wild chase without a flaw. He is as perfect at creating stillness. The ship is cruising on the Carrol Ground, south of St. Helena.——"It was while gliding through these latter waters that one serene and moonlight night, when all the waves rolled by like scrolls of silver; and by their soft, suffusing seethings, made what seemed a silvery silence, not a solitude; on such a silent night a silvery jet was seen far in advance of the white bubbles at the bow——"

Then there is the description of brit. "Steering northeastward from the Crozetts we fell in with vast meadows of brit, the minute, yellow substance upon which the Right Whale largely feeds. For leagues and leagues it undulated round us, so that we seemed to be sailing through boundless fields of ripe and golden wheat. On the second day, numbers of Right Whales were seen, who, secure from the attack of a Sperm Whaler like the *Pequod*, with open jaws sluggishly swam through the brit, which, adhering to the fringing fibres of that wondrous Venetian blind in their mouths, was in that manner separated from the water that escaped at the lip. As moving mowers who, side by side, slowly and seethingly advance their scythes through the long wet grass of the marshy meads; even so these monsters swam, making a strange, grassy, cutting sound; and leaving behind them endless swaths of blue on the yellow sea. But it was only the sound they made as they parted the brit which at all reminded one of mowers. Seen from the mast-heads, especially when they paused and were stationary for a while, their vast black forms looked more like lifeless masses of rock than anything else——"

This beautiful passage brings us to the apparition of the squid.

"Slowly wading through the meadows of brit, the *Pequod* still held her way northeastward towards the island of Java; a gentle air impelling her keel, so that in the surrounding serenity her three tall, tapering masts mildly waved to that languid breeze, as three mild palms on a plain. And still, at wide intervals, in the silvery night, that lonely, alluring jet would be seen.

"But one transparent-blue morning, when a stillness almost preternatural spread over the sea, however unattended with any stagnant calm; when the long burnished sunglade on the waters seemed a golden finger laid across them, enjoining secrecy; when all the slippered waves whispered together as they softly ran on; in this profound hush of the visible sphere a strange spectre was seen by Daggoo from the mainmast head.

"In the distance, a great white mass lazily rose, and rising higher and higher, and disentangling itself from the azure, at last gleamed before our prow like a snow-slide, new slid from the hills. Thus glistening for a moment, as slowly it subsided, and sank. Then once more arose, and silently gleamed. It seemed not a whale; and yet, is this Moby Dick? thought Daggoo——"

The boats were lowered and pulled to the scene.

"In the same spot where it sank, once more it slowly rose. Almost forgetting for the moment all thoughts of Moby Dick, we now gazed at the most wondrous phenomenon which the secret seas have hitherto revealed to mankind. A vast pulpy mass, furlongs in length and breadth, of a glancing cream-colour, lay floating on the water, innumerable long arms radiating from its centre, and curling and twisting like a nest of anacondas, as if blindly to clutch at any hapless object within reach. No perceptible face or front did it have; no conceivable token of either sensation or instinct; but undulated there on the billows, an unearthly, formless, chance-like apparition of life. And with a low sucking it slowly disappeared again."

The following chapters, with their account of whale hunts, the killing, the stripping, the cutting up, are magnificent records of actual happening. Then comes the queer tale of the meeting of the *Jeroboam*, a whaler met at sea, all of whose men were under the domination of a religious maniac, one of the ship's hands. There are detailed descriptions of the actual taking of the sperm oil from a whale's head. Dilating on the smallness of the brain of a sperm whale, Melville significantly remarks—"for I believe that much of a man's character will be found betokened in his backbone. I would rather feel your spine than your skull, whoever you are——" And of the whale, he adds:

"For, viewed in this light, the wonderful comparative smallness of his brain proper is more than compensated by the wonderful comparative magnitude of his spinal cord."

In among the rush of terrible, awful hunts, come touches of pure beauty.

"As the three boats lay there on that gently rolling sea, gazing down into its eternal blue noon; and as not a single groan or cry of any sort, nay not so much as a ripple or a thought, came up from its depths; what landsman would have thought that beneath all that silence and placidity the utmost monster of the seas was writhing and wrenching in agony!"

Perhaps the most stupendous chapter is the one called *The Grand Armada*, at the beginning of Volume III. The *Pequod* was drawing through the Sunda Straits towards Java when she came upon a vast host of sperm whales. "Broad on both bows, at a distance of two or three miles, and forming a great semicircle embracing one-half of the level horizon, a continuous chain of whale-jets were up-playing and sparkling in the noonday air." Chasing this great herd, past the Straits of Sunda, themselves chased by Javan pirates, the whalers race on. Then the boats are lowered. At last that curious state of inert irresolution came over the whales, when they were, as the seamen say, gallied. Instead of forging ahead in huge martial array they swam violently hither and thither, a surging sea of whales, no longer moving on. Starbuck's boat, made fast to a whale, is towed in amongst this howling Leviathan chaos. In mad career it cockles through the boiling surge of monsters, till it is brought into a clear lagoon in the very centre of the vast, mad, terrified herd. There a sleek, pure calm reigns. There the females swam in peace, and the young whales came snuffing tamely at the boat, like dogs. And there the astonished seamen watched the love-making of these amazing monsters, mammals, now in rut far down in the sea—"But far beneath this wondrous world upon the surface, another and still stranger world met our eyes, as we gazed over the side. For, suspended in these watery vaults, floated the forms of the nursing mothers of the whales, and those that by their enormous girth seemed shortly to become mothers. The lake, as I have hinted, was to a considerable depth exceedingly transparent; and as human infants while sucking will calmly and fixedly gaze away from the breast, as if leading two different lives at a time; and while yet drawing moral nourishment, be still spiritually feasting upon some unearthly reminiscence, even so did the young of these whales seem looking up towards us, but not at us, as if we were but a bit of gulf-weed in their newborn sight. Floating on their sides, the mothers also seemed quietly eyeing us.—Some of the subtlest secrets of the seas seemed divulged to us in this enchanted pond. We saw young Leviathan amours in the deep. And thus, though surrounded by circle upon circle of consternation and affrights, did these inscrutable creatures at the centre freely and fearlessly indulge in all peaceful concernments; yea, serenely revelled in dalliance and delight——"

There is something really overwhelming in these whale-hunts, almost superhuman or inhuman, bigger than life, more terrific than human activity. The same with the chapter on ambergris: it is so curious, so real, yet so unearthly. And again in the chapter called *The Cassock*— surely the oldest piece of phallicism in all the world's literature.

After this comes the amazing account of the Try-works, when the ship is turned into the sooty, oily factory in mid-ocean, and the oil is extracted from the blubber. In the night of the red furnace burning on deck, at sea, Melville has his startling experience of reversion. He is at the helm, but has turned to watch the fire: when suddenly he feels the ship rushing backward from him, in mystic reversion—"Uppermost was the impression, that whatever swift, rushing thing I stood on was not so much bound to any haven ahead, as rushing from all havens astern. A stark bewildering feeling, as of death, came over me. Convulsively my hands grasped the tiller, but with the crazy conceit that the tiller was, somehow, in some enchanted way, inverted. My God! What is the matter with me, I thought!"

This dream-experience is a real soul-experience. He ends with an injunction to all men, not to gaze on the red fire when its redness makes all things look ghastly. It seems to him that his gazing on fire has evoked this horror of reversion, undoing.

Perhaps it had. He was water-born.

After some unhealthy work on the ship, Queequeg caught a fever and was like to die. "How he wasted and wasted in those few, long-lingering days, till there seemed but little left of him but his frame and tattooing. But as all else in him thinned, and his cheek-bones grew sharper, his eyes, nevertheless, seemed growing fuller and fuller; they took on a strangeness of lustre; and mildly but deeply looked out at you there from his sickness, a wondrous testimony to that immortal health in him which could not die, or be weakened. And like circles on the water, which as they grow fainter, expand; so his eyes seemed rounding and rounding, like the circles of Eternity. An awe that cannot be named would steal over you as you sat by the side of this waning savage———"

But Queequeg did not die—and the *Pequod* emerges from the Eastern Straits, into the full Pacific. "To any meditative Magian rover, this serene Pacific once beheld, must ever after be the sea of his adoption. It rolls the midmost waters of the world———"

In this Pacific the fights go on: "It was far down the afternoon, and when all the spearings of the crimson fight were done, and floating in the lovely sunset sea and sky, sun and whale both stilly died together; then such a sweetness and such a plaintiveness, such inwreathing orisons curled up in that rosy air, that it almost seemed as if far over from the deep green convent valleys of the Manila isles, the Spanish landbreeze had gone to sea, freighted with these vesper hymns. Soothed again, but only soothed to deeper gloom, Ahab, who had sterned off from the whale, sat intently watching his final wanings from the now tranquil boat. For that strange spectacle, observable in all sperm whales dying—the turning of the head sunwards, and so expiring—that strange spectacle, beheld of such a placid evening, somehow to Ahab conveyed wondrousness unknown before. 'He turns and turns him to it; how slowly, but how steadfastly, his homage-rendering and invoking brow, with his last dying motions. He too worships fire . . .'"

So Ahab soliloquizes: and so the warm-blooded whale turns for the last time to the sun, which begot him in the waters.

But as we see in the next chapter, it is the Thunder-fire which Ahab really worships: that living sundering fire of which he bears the brand, from head to foot; it is storm, the electric storm of the *Pequod*, when the corposants burn in high, tapering flames of supernatural pallor upon the masthead, and when the compass is reversed. After this all is fatality. Life itself seems mystically reversed. In these hunters of Moby Dick there is nothing but madness and possession. The captain, Ahab, moves hand in hand with the poor imbecile negro boy, pip, who has been so cruelly demented, left swimming alone in the vast sea. It is the imbecile child of the sun hand in hand with the northern monomaniac, captain and master.

The voyage surges on. They meet one ship, then another. It is all ordinary day-routine, and yet all is a tension of pure madness and horror, the approaching horror of the last fight. "Hither and thither, on high, glided the snow-white wings of small unspecked birds; these were the gentle thoughts of the feminine air; but to and fro in the deeps, far down in the bottomless blue, rushed mighty leviathans, sword-fish and sharks; and these were the strong, troubled, murderous thinkings of the masculine sea———" On this day Ahab confesses his weariness, the weariness of his burden. "But do I look very old, so very, very old, Starbuck? I feel deadly faint, and bowed, and humped, as though I were Adam staggering beneath the piled centuries since Paradise———" It is the Gethsemane of Ahab, before the last fight: the Gethsemane of the human soul seeking the last self-conquest, the last attainment of extended consciousness—infinite consciousness.

At last they sight the whale. Ahab sees him from his hoisted perch at the masthead—"From this height the whale was now seen some mile or so ahead, at every roll of the sea revealing his high, sparkling hump, and regularly jetting his silent spout into the air."

The boats are lowered, to draw near the white whale. "At length the breathless hunter came so nigh his seemingly unsuspectful prey that his entire dazzling hump was distinctly visible, sliding along the sea as if an isolated thing, and continually set in a revolving ring of finest, fleecy, greenish foam. He saw the vast involved wrinkles of the slightly projecting head, beyond. Before it, far out on the soft, Turkish rugged waters, went the glistening white shadow from his broad, milky forehead, a musical rippling playfully accompanying the shade; and behind, the blue waters interchangeably flowed over the moving valley of his steady wake; and on either side bright bubbles arose and danced by his side. But these were broken again by the light toes of hundreds of gay fowl softly feathering the sea, alternate with their fitful flight; and like to some flagstaff rising from the pointed hull of an argosy, the tall but shattered pole of a recent lance projected from the white whale's back; and at intervals one of the clouds of soft-toed fowls hovering, and to and fro shimmering like a canopy over the fish, silently perched and rocked on this pole, the long tail-feathers streaming like pennons.

"A gentle joyousness—a mighty mildness of repose in swiftness, invested the gliding whale———"

The fight with the whale is too wonderful, and too awful, to be quoted apart from the book. It lasted three days. The fearful sight, on the third day, of the torn body of the Parsee harpooner, lost on the previous day, now seen lashed on to the flanks of the white whale by the tangle of harpoon lines, has a mystic dream-horror. The awful and infuriated whale turns upon the ship, symbol of this civilized world of ours. He smites her with a fearful shock. And a few minutes later, from the last of the fighting whale-boats comes the cry: "'The ship! Great God, where is the ship?' Soon they, through dim, bewildering mediums, saw her sidelong fading phantom, as in the gaseous Fata Morgana; only the uppermost masts out of the water; while fixed by infatuation, or fidelity, or fate, to their once lofty perches, the pagan harpooners still maintained their sinking lookouts on the sea. And now concentric circles seized the lone boat itself, and all its crew, and each floating oar, and every lance-pole, and spinning, animate and inanimate, all round and round in one vortex, carried the smallest chip of the *Pequod* out of sight——"

The bird of heaven, the eagle, St. John's bird, the Red Indian bird, the American, goes down with the ship, nailed by Tashtego's hammer, the hammer of the American Indian. The eagle of the spirit. Sunk!

"Now small fowls flew screaming over the yet yawning gulf; a sullen white surf beat against its steep sides; then all collapsed; and the great shroud of the sea rolled on as it rolled five thousand years ago."

So ends one of the strangest and most wonderful books in the world, closing up its mystery and its tortured symbolism. It is an epic of the sea such as no man has equaled; and it is a book of esoteric symbolism of profound significance, and of considerable tiresomeness.

But it is a great book, a very great book, the greatest book of the sea ever written. It moves awe in the soul.

The terrible fatality.

Fatality.

Doom.

Doom! Doom! Doom! Something seems to whisper it in the very dark trees of America. Doom!

Doom of what?

Doom of our white day. We are doomed, doomed. And the doom is in America. The doom of our white day.

Ah, well, if my day is doomed, and I am doomed with my day, it is something greater than I which dooms me, so I accept my doom as a sign of the greatness which is more than I am.

Melville knew. He knew his race was doomed. His white soul, doomed. His great white epoch, doomed. Himself, doomed. The idealist, doomed. The spirit, doomed.

The reversion. "Not so much bound to any haven ahead, as rushing from all havens astern."

That great horror of ours! It is our civilization rushing from all havens astern.

The last ghastly hunt. The White Whale.

What then is Moby Dick? He is the deepest blood-being of the white race; he is our deepest blood-nature.

And he is hunted, hunted, hunted by the maniacal fanaticism of our white mental consciousness. We want to hunt him down. To subject him to our will. And in this maniacal conscious hunt of ourselves we get dark races and pale to help us, red, yellow, and black, east and west, Quaker and fire-worshipper, we get them all to help us in this ghastly maniacal hunt which is our doom and our suicide.

The last phallic being of the white man. Hunted into the death of upper consciousness and the ideal will. Our blood-self subjected to our will. Our blood-consciousness sapped by a parasitic mental or ideal consciousness.

Hot-blooded sea-born Moby Dick. Hunted by monomaniacs of the idea.

Oh God, oh God, what next, when the *Pequod* has sunk?

She sank in the war, and we are all flotsam.

Now what next?

Who knows? *Quien sabe? Quien sabe, señor?*

Neither Spanish nor Saxon America has any answer.

The *Pequod* went down. And the *Pequod* was the ship of the white American soul. She sank, taking with her negro and Indian and Polynesian, Asiatic and Quaker and good, businesslike Yankees and Ishmael: she sank all the lot of them.

Boom! as Vachel Lindsay would say.

To use the words of Jesus, IT IS FINISHED.

Consummatum est!

But *Moby Dick* was first published in 1851. If the Great White

Whale sank the ship of the Great White Soul in 1851, what's been happening ever since?

Post-mortem effects, presumably.

Because, in the first centuries, Jesus was Cetus, the Whale. And the Christians were the little fishes. Jesus, the Redeemer, was Cetus, Leviathan. And all the Christians all his little fishes.

An Excerpt from *Out of Sheer Rage*

GEOFF DYER

When Laura came back from her assignment we spent our afternoons under that sky, sunbathing on the roof, and our evenings hanging out at the Calisto. I had a few articles to write, simple things, but time-consuming enough to make me lose what little momentum I had built up on my study of Lawrence. It was because these articles were so simple, in fact, that I stalled on the Lawrence book. What was the point flogging my guts out writing a study of Lawrence that no one would want to read when I could bang out articles that paid extremely well and took only a fraction of the effort? Especially since Lawrence himself felt the same way: 'I feel I never want to write another book. What's the good! I can eke out a living on stories and little articles, that don't cost a tithe of the output a book costs. Why write novels any more!' He expressed similar sentiments on numerous occasions; at one point he reckoned he was losing his 'will to write altogether', meaning, on this occasion, that he no longer even felt like writing letters. I was so heartened by this that my interest in writing about Lawrence revived to the extent that I started in on Rilke's letters again. By now, I had persuaded myself, reading Rilke was part and parcel of working on my study of Lawrence. '*Il faut travailler, rien que travailler.*' It was a shame, Rilke thought, that we had so many seductive memories of idleness; if only we had 'work-memories' then perhaps, without recourse to compulsion or discipline, it would be possible to find 'natural contentment' in work, in 'that one thing which nothing else touches'. The worst thing, for Rilke, was that he had these two kinds of memory, both these impulses, in himself: a longing, on the one hand, to devote himself to art and, on the other, to set up a simple shop with 'no thought for the morrow'. Laura's version of this normal life was—and still is—to run a *pensione*. She had mentioned it in Taormina and several times since coming back she had talked about the pride she would take in keeping it clean. *My* version of this was to live in England and watch telly. The ideal situation for us both would have been to have watched a series about an Italian *pensione* on telly. Rilke did more or less the same thing, reconciling these impulses by making his vision of contentment the subject of a poem, 'Evening Meal'. More broadly, this tension between life and work remained one of the dominant preoccupations of his life—and work. 'Either happiness or art,' he declared, struggling to assimilate the example of Rodin. 'All the great men have let their lives get overgrown like an old path and have carried everything into their art. Their life is stunted like an organ they no longer use.' Yeats offered the same choice: perfection of the man or the work.

For some writers there has scarcely been any friction between the demands of the life and the demands of the work. John Updike arranged his circumstances to his liking fairly early on and then simply got on with his writing, book after book, day after day. At the opposite extreme there was John Berger who only managed such extreme changes in his writing by corresponding changes in how and where he lived. For Rilke, too, the real work was to organise his existence, to will himself a life that would create the ideal conditions in which to work. Allowing life to atrophy so that he might work was itself a way of enhancing his life—even though the demands this made on his life, on his life-capacity, were immense and unremitting. To make *things* he had constantly to re-make himself: '*Du mußt dein Leben ändern*' ('i.e., find a different princess to live off' was Larkin's sardonic gloss).

And to what end, this subordination of life to work? There may be an 'ancient enmity between our daily life and the great work' but this relationship is more fluid, more complex, than the aphoristic formula from 'Requiem for a Friend' allows. 'For one human being to love another human being: that,' Rilke conceded, 'is perhaps the most difficult task that has been given to us, the ultimate final problem and proof, the work for which all other work is merely preparation.'

Lawrence was untroubled by any of this. All the work of his maturity was built on his relationship with Frieda. 'Fidelity to oneself means fidelity single and unchanging, to one other one.' His adult life begins with the unalterable fact of his marriage. As for work, he wrote when he felt like it, didn't when he didn't. Idleness seems to have held no attraction for him as a seductive ideal: the division between work and rest seems to have been as natural as that between sleeping and waking. Writing the novels took an enormous toll, obviously, but to Lawrence, the miner's son who had grown up amidst the ravages of gruelling physical labour, living by his pen was not such a bad option. He spent no time agonising over the rival claims of work and life because the two were inextricably bound together. 'I don't sacrifice myself for anything but I do devote myself to something.' And to what did he devote himself? To writing? No. To living ('not the work I shall produce, but the real Me I shall achieve, that is the consideration'). To say this is to reiterate one of the most hackneyed aspects of the Lawrence myth but it is difficult to improve upon, or at least his own version of it is: 'I *don't* think that to work is to live. Work is all right in proportion: but one wants to have a certain richness and satisfaction in oneself, which is more than anything produced. One wants to *be*.'

That was all very well but I had no richness and satisfaction in myself, more like a poverty and dissatisfaction. I had made progress on my study, that is, I had made progress in my mental preparation but now I had stalled. My lassitude was irritating me a good deal and this meant that Rome irritated me a good deal too. There had been several mornings when the Caffè Farnese had not had the *cornetti integrali* that I depended on for my breakfast. Without these *integrali*—more accurately *with* the disappointment of not having had my *integrali*—I found it difficult to get started on my work. I sulked, I went on a tacit strike as a protest against the Farnese and its undependable supply of *integrali*. I picked up books and put them down, thought about doing some writing and then did the washing-up instead. I recognised all these signs of unfocused anxiety and began to wonder if it might not be a good idea to move somewhere else to write my study of Lawrence. Laura's apartment should have been the perfect place to work but I couldn't get any work done there. I recognised *that* feeling too. Over the years I had come across several places that offered the ideal conditions to work. The room in Montepulciano, for example, with the lovely wooden bed and white sheets, the window gazing out over the Tuscan countryside, the terrace formed by what had once been a little bridge connecting our building to the one next door. Or the house in Lauzun with the room overlooking a field of wheat, facing west so that in the evenings the paper on the desk was bathed red. Or my apartment on Rue Popincourt with the floor-to-ceiling window from which you could see right down Rue de la Roquette, as far as the Bastille almost.

What they all had in common, these ideal places for working, was that I never got any work done in them. I would sit down at my desk and think to myself *What perfect conditions for working*, then I would look out at the sun smouldering over the wheat, or at the trees gathering the Tuscan light around themselves, or at the Parisians walking through the twilight and traffic of Rue de la Roquette, and I would write a few lines like 'If I look up from my desk I can see the sun smouldering over the wheat'; or 'Through my window: crowded twilight on the Rue de la Roquette'; and then, in order to make sure that what I was writing was capturing exactly the moment and mood, I would look up again at the sun smouldering over the flame-red wheat or the crowds moving through the neon twilight of Rue de la Roquette and add a few more words like 'flame-red' or 'neon', and then, in order to give myself over totally to the scene, would lay down my pen and simply gaze out at the scene, thinking that it was actually a waste to sit here writing when I could be looking and by looking—especially on Rue de la Roquette where the pedestrians hurrying home in the neon twilight would look up and see a figure at his desk, bathed in the yellow light of the anglepoise—actually become a part of the scene, whereas writing involved not an immersion in the actual scene but its opposite, a detachment from it. After a very short time I would grow bored by contemplating the scene, would leave my desk and go for a walk in the wheatfield sunset or leave my apartment and walk down to the Bastille so that I could become one of the people walking back through the neon twilight of the Rue de la Roquette, looking up at the empty desk, bathed in the light of the anglepoise . . .

When I thought of the ideal conditions for working, in other words, I looked at things from the perspective of someone not working, of someone on holiday, of a tourist in Taormina. I always had in mind the view that my desk would overlook, thereby overlooking the fact that the view from the desk is invisible when you are actually working, and forgetting that of the many genres of sentence I dislike there is none that I despise more than ones which proceed along the lines of 'If I look up from my desk . . .' The ideal conditions for working were actually the worst possible conditions for working.

And in any case maybe all this fuss about the conditions for working was irrelevant. After all, did it matter so much *where* you lived? The important thing, surely, was to find some little niche where you could work; to settle into a groove and get your work done. Logically, yes, but once, in north London, I had found myself walking along the road where Julian Barnes lived. I didn't see him but I knew that in one of these large, comfortable houses Julian Barnes was sitting at his desk, working, as he did every day. It seemed an intolerable waste of a life, *of a writer's life especially*, to sit at a desk in this nice, dull street in north London. It seemed, curiously, a betrayal of the idea of the writer. It made me think of a picture of Lawrence, sitting by a tree in the blazing afternoon, surrounded by the sizzle of cicadas, notebook on his knees, writing: an image of the ideal condition of the writer.

Or so it had appeared in memory. When I actually dug it out it turned out that there was no notebook on his knees. Lawrence is not writing, he is just sitting there: which is why, presumably, it is such an idyllic image of the writer.

He is wearing a white shirt, sitting with his back to a tree. (What kind of tree? Had he been looking at a photograph of someone else sitting there, Lawrence would have been able to identify it immediately. He was one of those writers who knew the names of trees.) Everything is still, but, sculpted by the absent wind, the branches record its passing. A hot, hot day. Lawrence sitting by the tree, the fingers of both hands laced together over his left knee. Schiele fingers. Thin wrists, thick trousers. Freshly laundered, pressed, his white shirt is full of the sun in which it has dried. Like the shirt of the prisoner facing execution in Goya's *The Third of May 1808*, it is the bright focus of all the light—and there is a *lot* of light—in the photograph.

Lawrence's jacket is rolled up beside him on the grass. The sleeves of his shirt are rolled down, buttoned around his bony wrists, lending a formal quality to the picture. By the 1920s photographs no longer required the interminable exposure times of the Victorian era (when heads and limbs had to be clamped in place to prevent blurring), but they were nearer to that unwieldy stage of photographic culture than to the Instamatic images of the post-war era. In early portraits, as part of the preparation for having a photograph taken, people focused their lives 'in the moment rather than hurrying past it'. Here, too, there is a strong sense of Lawrence *sitting* for a photograph. As far as formality is concerned the final touch is provided by the way that Lawrence's shirt is buttoned up to the collar. Why does that collar hold not just Lawrence's shirt but the photograph itself together?

Because even here, in the midst of this audible heat, Lawrence has to be careful to keep warm. He feels the cold, has to be careful not to catch a chill (the thick jacket is close to hand). His mother's concern for the sickly child—years of being told to keep warm, to keep his jacket on—have been internalised. By now, in the heat, it is second nature to cover up his skinniness, to keep himself warm.

His feet are invisible, buried in the grass, creating the impression—emphasised by the way that his body was surrounded by the trunk of the tree ('the tree's life penetrates my life, and my life the tree's')—that Lawrence is growing out of the ground. 'Thank God I am not free,' he wrote from Taos in 1922, 'any more than a rooted tree is free.' This line caused Larkin some astonishment. 'It is hard to see how he could have been less encumbered in the affairs of life,' he wrote from Leicester almost thirty years later. 'Put him down in salaried employment or with a growing family or an ageing one—why, he didn't even own a house & furniture!'

This is not strictly true: Lawrence *did* own some furniture (Brodsky was right: there is 'no life without furniture'), much of which he made himself. And while he may not have owned a house, the Lawrences' constant moving obliged them to keep *making* home. It is typical of Lawrence that, on the one hand, he became more and more anxious about finding a place to settle and, on the other, achieved the ideal condition of being at home anywhere: 'I feel a great stranger, but have got used to that feeling, and prefer it to feeling "homely". After all, one is a stranger, nowhere so hopelessly as at home.' That was from Taos in 1922; three years later the emphasis had changed: 'One can no longer say: I'm a stranger everywhere, only "everywhere I'm at home".'

He had found a home within himself and in what he did, in his *being*. Rilke had admired the same thing in Rodin who lived in a house that 'meant nothing to him' [Rodin] because 'deep within him he bore the darkness, peace and shelter of a house and he himself had become the sky above it and the wood around it and the distance and the great river that always flowed past'. Lawrence had likened himself to a rooted tree; sunk in himself, Rodin, according to Rilke, was 'fuller of sap than an old tree in autumn'. He had 'grown deep'. This idea, of being at home in yourself as a way of being at home in the world, was to receive its most exalted expression in the final lines of the last of the *Sonnets to Orpheus*:

> Whisper to the silent earth: I'm flowing.
> To the flashing water say: I am.

I'd torn the photo of Lawrence by the tree out of a biography published by the University of New Mexico Press. Before doing so I had tried to find where and when it was taken but there was no information. It was the only uncaptioned photo in the book. Had there been a caption I might have felt more reluctant about committing that small act of bibliographical vandalism. As it was, there had been no text to anchor the photo to the book, nothing to keep it in place. It seemed apposite that this, the only uncaptioned image in the book, was now free of the only context—the physical one of the book—available. If the bust made by Jo Davidson showed Lawrence what he would become in death, when—as suggested earlier—the loose pages of his life were bound and dated, then this picture showed Lawrence unbound, alive.

A photograph's meaning is bound up closely with its caption. As the photograph frames the subject, so the caption frames the photograph. Without a caption a photograph is not quite developed, its meaning not fixed. With a little research I could have found out—could still find out—where and when it was taken but I preferred, and prefer, not to: it seemed fitting that this photograph of Lawrence sitting there, 'happy as a cicada', should elude place and time. Like this it was a photo of Lawrence in the state evoked by Rilke in his sonnet; like this I *could* identify the tree: it is a photo of Lawrence sitting by a bho tree.

Buddha was sitting under a bho tree when he achieved enlightenment and in the spring of 1926 Lawrence told Brewster that he was 'convinced that every man needs a bho tree of some sort in his life. What ails us is, we have cut down all our bho trees . . . Still, here and there in the world a solitary bho tree must be standing . . . And I'm going to sit right down under one, to be American about it, when I come across one.'[1]

Another picture of Lawrence, the one I always hoped to come across in bookshops, the one that I had seen when I was seventeen, showed him—if I remember rightly—standing towards the edge of a vast horizontal landscape. Clouds streamed across the sky. I forget which book I saw it in all those years ago but I remember thinking that the caption— 'A fine wind is blowing the new direction of Time'—had been chosen so perfectly that the picture seemed less a photograph of Lawrence (a tiny figure in the corner, recognisable only by his beard) than an illustration of this line. At the time I did not know where it was from: a quotation from Lawrence, presumably, but beyond that I had no idea. I wanted to track that quotation down—or, to put it more passively and accurately, I hoped to come across it—and the prospect was intriguing precisely because there was nothing to go on. From the start, in other words, I read Lawrence in order to make sense of—to better understand—a photograph of him.

The urge to discover the source of this caption also explains my pleasure in reading Lawrence's letters in what might seem to be the ludicrously complete Cambridge edition. Or, to make the same point the opposite way, perhaps my pleasure in reading Lawrence's letters is the culmination of an urge, the first pulse of which was felt twenty years ago when I saw what I later discovered was a line from 'Song of a Man Who Has Come Through'. From that moment on, part of the incentive to read Lawrence was to discover the source of this line, to read it in the original, as it were, without quotation marks. I came across it in the Penguin *Selected Poems* (the edition that I still had with me in Rome, the one that I didn't take to Alonissos) but my satisfaction was qualified (or so it seems to me now) because everything in a 'Selected' format comes in tacit quotation marks: those provided by the editor's choice of material. When we read a 'selection' we are, so to speak, in the realm of massively extended quotation. When we read the author's work in definitive or collected editions, however, we are *there*: nothing comes between us and the writer (the often cumbersome editorial apparatus serves, paradoxically, to facilitate the intimacy between reader and writer). Like this I can read Lawrence *unquoted*.

'You mustn't look in my novel for that old stable ego of the character . . . the ordinary novel would trace the history of the diamond—but I say "diamond, what! This is carbon".' *Those* lines, even if we read them in the collected edition of Lawrence's letters, seem like a citation. Their true context is in a book about Lawrence—this one, for example! When we see them in Volume 2 of the *Collected Letters* it almost seems as if Lawrence lifted them from one of the hundreds of critical studies of him. And *so* much of my early reading of Lawrence came in quotation marks. At a very early stage 'doing' English became synonymous with reading criticism, most of it by academics. Go into any university bookshop and you will see stacks and stacks of books on Lawrence by academics. Such books form the basis of literary study in universities and none of them has anything to do with literature.

In my final year at university there was a great deal of fuss about course reform. Instead of ploughing through everything from *Beowulf* to Beckett, academics like Terry Eagleton were proposing a 'theory' option. I didn't know what theory was but it sounded radical and challenging. Within a few years 'theory', whatever it was, had achieved a position of dominance in English departments throughout Britain. Synoptic works of theory were pouring from the presses. Fifteen years down the line these texts still appear radical and challenging except in one or two details, namely that they are neither radical nor challenging. One Christmas when I was about ten my parents gave me a *Beryl the Peril* annual which included some of Beryl's answers to difficult exam questions. Asked to construct a sentence using the word 'discourse' she wrote '"Discourse is too hard for me," said the golfer.' How quaint! Twenty years on she would probably have no trouble coming up with a whole paper on 'The Self and its Others'. In no time at all theory had become more of an orthodoxy than the style of study it sought to overthrow. Any lecturer worth his weight in corduroy was fluent in discoursese, could signify-and-signified till the cows came home.

Hearing that I was 'working on Lawrence', an acquaintance lent me a book he thought I might find interesting: *A Longman Critical Reader on Lawrence*, edited by Peter Widdowson. I glanced at the contents page: old Eagleton was there, of course, together with some other state-of-the-fart theorists: Lydia Blanchard on 'Lawrence, Foucault and the Language of Sexuality' (in the section on 'Gender, Sexuality, Feminism'), Daniel J. Schneider on 'Alternatives to Logocentrism in D. H. Lawrence' (in the section featuring 'Post-Structuralist Turns'). I could feel myself getting angry and then I flicked through the introductory essay on 'Radical Indeterminacy: a post-modern Lawrence' and became angrier still. How could it have happened? How could these people with no feeling for literature have ended up *teaching* it, writing about it? I should have stopped there, should have avoided looking at any more, but I didn't because telling myself to stop always has the effect of urging me on. Instead, I kept looking at this group of wankers huddled in a circle, backs turned to the world so that no one would see them pulling each other off. Oh, it was too much, it was too stupid. I threw the book across the room and then I tried to tear it up but it was too resilient. By now I was blazing mad. I thought about getting Widdowson's phone number and making threatening calls. Then I looked around for the means to destroy his vile, filthy book. In the end it took a whole box of matches and some risk of personal injury before I succeeded in deconstructing it.

I burned it in self-defence. It was the book or me because writing like that kills everything it touches. That is the hallmark of academic criticism: it kills everything it touches. Walk around a university campus and there is an almost palpable smell of death about the place because hundreds of academics are busy killing everything they touch. I recently met an academic who said that he taught German literature. I was aghast: to think, this man who had been in universities all his life was teaching Rilke. *Rilke!* Oh, it was too much to bear. You don't teach Rilke, I wanted to say, you kill Rilke! You turn him to dust and then you go off to conferences where dozens of other academic-morticians gather with the express intention of killing Rilke and turning him to dust. Then, as part of the cover-up, the conference papers are published, the dust is embalmed and before you know it literature is a vast graveyard of dust, a dustyard of graves. I was beside myself with indignation. I wanted to maim and harm this polite, well-meaning academic who, for all I knew, was a brilliant teacher who had turned on generations of students to the *Duino Elegies*. Still, I thought to myself the following morning when I had calmed down, the general point stands: how can you know anything about literature if all you've done is read books?

Now, criticism is an integral part of the literary tradition and academics can sometimes write excellent works of criticism but these are exceptional: the vast majority, the overwhelming majority of books by academics, especially books like that Longman Reader are *a crime against literature*. If you want to see how literature lives then you turn to writers, and see what they've said about each other, either in essays, reviews, in letters or journals—and in the works themselves. 'The best readings of art are art,' said George Steiner (an academic!); the great books add up to a tacit 'syllabus of enacted criticism'. This becomes explicit when poets write a poem about some great work of art—Auden's 'Musée des Beaux Arts'—or about another poet: Auden's elegy for Yeats, Brodsky's elegy for Auden, Heaney's elegy for Brodsky (the cleverly titled 'Audenesque'). In such instances the distinction between imaginative and critical writing disappears.

When it comes to reviews and essays in which writers address other writers and other books, on the other hand, it would seem that they are engaged in something indistinguishable from academic criticism. But this formal narrowing of difference in kind enhances the difference in spirit. Brodsky has gone through certain poems of Auden's with the finest of combs; Nabokov has subjected Pushkin to forensic scrutiny.

The difference is that these works of Pushkin's and Auden's were not just studied: they were lived through in a way that is anathema to the academic . . .

Except this is nonsense of course. Scholars live their work too. Leon Edel—to take one example from hundreds—embraced Henry James's life and work as perilously intimately as any writer ever has. I withdraw that claim, it's ludicrous, it won't stand up to any kind of scrutiny. I withdraw it unconditionally—but I also want to let it stand, conditionally. Scholarly work on the texts, on preparing lovely editions of Lawrence's letters is one thing but those critical studies that we read at university . . . Research! Research! The very word is like a bell, tolling the death and the imminent turning to dust of whichever poor sod is being researched. Spare me. Spare me the drudgery of systematic examinations and give me the lightning flashes of those wild books in which there is no attempt to cover the ground thoroughly or reasonably. While preparing to write *Etruscan Places* Lawrence thanked a friend for sending an authoritative book on the subject by Roland Fell who was

> very thorough in washing out once more the few rags of
> information we have concerning the Etruscans: but not a thing
> has he to say. It's really disheartening: I shall just have to start
> in and go ahead, and be damned to all authorities! There really
> is next to nothing to be said, *scientifically*, about the Etruscans.
> Must take the imaginative line.

That's why Lawrence is so exciting: he took the imaginative line in all his criticism, in the *Study of Thomas Hardy* or the *Studies in Classic American Literature*, or the 'Introduction to his Paintings'. Each of them is an electrical storm of ideas! Hit and miss, illuminating even when hopelessly wide of the mark ('the judgment may be all wrong: but this was the impression I got'). Bang! Crash! Lightning flash after lightning flash, searing, unpredictable, dangerous.

In truth I prefer these books to the novels which I have kept putting off re-reading. I re-read *The Rainbow* in Rome and I could have forced myself to re-read *Women in Love*, could have forced myself to sit down and peer at every page—or so I like to believe: who knows if, when it came to the crunch, I really had it in me?—but, I thought, why should I? Why should I re-read this book that I not only had no desire to re-read but which I actively wanted not to re-read. I had no desire to re-read *The Rainbow* but, unwilling to give myself the benefit of the doubt, sat down and re-read it, just to be on the safe side. I re-read the same copy that I had read first time around: part of the uniform Penguin editions of Lawrence with photographs on the cover (roosters or hens in this case) and, on the back, a sepia photo of Lawrence with beard (naturally) and centre parting. When I re-read *The Rainbow* I had thought I might discover, like a flower pressed between the pages, the dried remains of my younger self preserved within it. In the most literal sense I was there, the underlinings and annotations, made when we did the book at Oxford (i.e. when we read a load of dreary critical studies about it), were still there but in any kind of metaphorical sense—no, there was nothing, no traces of my earlier self, no memories released by the act of re-reading the same page that I had read years before one particular afternoon wherever and whenever that was.

My impressions of the book were more or less unaltered. It remained a book which I had no desire to re-read; as soon as I had finished re-reading *The Rainbow* it reverted to being what it was *before* I re-read it: a book which I had read and which I had no desire to re-re-read. It was a closed book: even when it was open and being re-read it was somehow still a closed book. As for *Women in Love*, I read it in my teens and, as far as I am concerned, it can stay read.

If we're being utterly frank, I don't want to re-read *any* novels by Lawrence. And not only do I not want to *re*-read some of Lawrence's books I don't even want to *read* all of them. I want to keep some in reserve—I want to know that there are bits and pieces of Lawrence that are still out there, still fresh, waiting to be discovered (by me at least), waiting to be read for the first time.

In this respect I made a serious mistake in Rome, a mistake of such magnitude, in fact, as to jeopardise any chance of going on with—let alone completing—my study of Lawrence. From the start I'd known that I had to write my book as I went along. There are people who like to complete all the reading, all the research, and then, when they have read everything that there is to read, when they have attained complete mastery of the material, *then* and only then do they sit down and write it up. Not me. Once I know enough about a subject to begin writing about it I lose interest in it immediately. In the case of Lawrence I knew I'd have to make sure that I finished writing my book at exactly the moment that I had satisfied my curiosity, and to do this the writing had to lag fractionally behind the reading. Especially when it came to Lawrence's letters. The letters were Lawrence's life and I knew I had to ration my reading of them, not get too far ahead of myself. They were my main resource, a source so rich I knew I'd squander them if I just burrowed away at them from beginning to end. I knew that I could not be closer to Lawrence than I was while reading his letters for the first time. Ideally, if I were going to spend eighteen months writing my book about D. H. Lawrence I would be reading those letters for sixteen or even seventeen months, for a year at the very least.

But what did I do? I read them, all seven volumes, cover to cover, in two months. It's my parents' fault. When I was a child they rationed out my sweets too slowly and so I grew up to be a gobbler. That's what I did with Lawrence's letters: I gobbled them all down and in no time at all there were none left, the bag was empty. I couldn't stop myself, couldn't help it. I loved reading them too much. I read Volume 2, then 3, then 5, then 4, then 6, then 1 (which I had no real interest in, whizzing through it in a day and a half). That left Volume 7. Whatever you do, I said to myself, keep Volume 7 in reserve: under no circumstances read Volume 7 because then you will have nothing left to read. It should have been relatively easy because there were so many other books to read—I could have re-read *Women in Love* (which I couldn't face re-reading), or one of the numerous critical books on Lawrence (which I had decided were a waste of anyone's time to read) or the poems or plays but instead I kept *glancing at* Volume 7, touching it, holding it, opening a few pages, reading the introduction. Finally I thought I would read just the first few letters even though I knew that reading the first few was exactly what I had to avoid because I would not be able to stop after three or four letters. After three or four I would keep reading another one or two until I had read so many that it would be pointless to stop reading the book and before I knew it I would have read all the Lawrence letters. And so the important thing was to avoid even opening the book: I knew it would be easier to avoid starting to read the book than it would be to stop reading the book once I had started. I knew all this but I opened it anyway, thinking to myself that I would read the first few letters. Which I did. But since these letters were pretty insignificant in themselves, harmless, I read one or two more which were also pretty innocuous and I thought I would keep reading until I came to a significant letter and *then* stop. It went on like that until I realised with a shock that I was in danger of finishing all of Lawrence's letters. I read one after another and the more I read the less there were *to* read and although I knew part of the reason for reading the letters of Lawrence was to put off the moment when I had to write about him I also realised that by reading the letters like this, by failing to moderate my consumption of the letters, I was caught up in the gathering momentum of his death. I was running out of letters to read just as Lawrence was running out of life. The nearer I got to the end of the book the shorter and more insignificant the letters became, little gasps of anger where before there had been long, thousand-word rants, and so the pace of decline accelerated. Even insignificant communications—'Blair has been kind as an angel to me. Here is £10 for housekeeping'—became something to cherish against the coming end.

And then, abruptly, there were no more letters. It was the end: oblivion. There were no more letters. If only, I found myself thinking, if only there had been Volumes 8, 9, 10 or 11. I had read four thousand pages of letters by Lawrence and I wanted thousands of pages more . . . I wanted them not to end. And yet, at the same time that I was wishing they would not come to an end, I was hurrying through these books because however much you are enjoying a book, however much you want it never to end, you are always eager for it *to* end. However much you are enjoying a book you are always flicking to the end, counting to see how many pages are left, looking forward to the time when you can put the book down and have done with it. At the back of our minds, however much we are enjoying a book, we come to the end of it and some little voice is always saying, 'Thank Christ for that!'

Still, better reading than writing. One of the reasons I was enjoying reading the Lawrence letters so much, and the main reason I wished that there were more Lawrence letters to read, was because they were a perfect excuse for not writing my book about Lawrence. Whereas now I had no choice, no choice at all.

It was a terrible prospect since although I had read the Lawrence letters and was therefore obliged to begin writing about Lawrence I had also read his letters in such a way that I was actually in no state to begin writing about Lawrence. Not only had I read them too fast, I'd also read them out of sequence, as they became available at the British Council Library in Rome, so that all sense of chronology, of development had been lost. One moment Lawrence was in New Mexico, the next he was eighteen months younger, in Italy, putting off going to America. If I had done it properly I would have read them sequentially and paced it so that my reading of the letters kept pace with the writing but now a huge six-volume gap had opened between my reading and my writing. I was like an out-of-condition athlete in a race who had lost touch with the front runners and the group in the middle: it was too much of a haul to get back in touch. I was out of the race, finished. The only alternative to giving up was to keep plodding round the track for the sake of finishing, grinding it out, metre by metre, page by page.

Not only had I read the Lawrence letters too fast and out of sequence, I had also failed to take notes. I had intended doing so as I went along, transcribing any particularly important passages and keeping a careful record of where these passages occurred, but I had been in such a hurry to gobble down the letters that, except on a few occasions, I had not done so. Not only that, I realised as I glanced back through the volumes of letters that I had already read, but there were many that, in my eagerness and impatience to get through all seven volumes, I had taken no notice of. The more I looked, the more letters there were that I had no recollection of. I could read the letters again because I had read them so badly the first time around. In fact, I realised with a sinking heart, I was practically obliged to re-read the Lawrence letters which I had longed to go on reading but which, now that I *had* to go on reading them, I wished to God I was shot of.

In no time at all, though, I was back under their spell. There were actually hundreds of letters which I had not read at all, which I saw for the first time as I re-read them. Like this one from November 1916 when, in the course of a letter to Kot, Lawrence remembered a time when he had seen an adder curled up in the spring sunshine, asleep. The snake was not aware of Lawrence's presence until he was very close and then 'she lifted her head like a queen to look' and moved away. 'She often comes into my mind, and I think I see her asleep in the sun, like a Princess of the fairy world. It is queer, the intimation of other worlds, which one catches.'

Queer, too, the intimation of future works which one catches so often in the letters. In this case the writing of the famous poem 'Snake' was still several years distant but here we have, as it were, a first draft of the experience which will later form the basis of the poem. This is one of the pleasures of the letters: one has the very first touch of a poem. It is like watching a fire and seeing the first lick of flame along a log: you think it is about to catch but then it vanishes. You watch and wait for the flame to come back. It doesn't—and then, after you have stopped looking, the flame flickers back again and the log catches.

Lawrence began writing his greatest poem, 'The Ship of Death', in the autumn of 1929. According to Keith Sagar, the opening image of the poem—

> Now it is autumn and the falling fruit
> and the long journey towards oblivion

—was suggested by a visit to Rottach in late August when he noticed the 'apples on tall old apple-trees, dropping so suddenly'. But the first intimation of the poem actually comes as early as New Year's Eve, 1913, in a letter to Edward Garnett: 'it is just beginning to look a bit like autumn—acorns and olives falling, and vine leaves going yellow'. I *had* made a note of that, and of the occasion a few months later when I felt the rhythm of the image pulsing into life long, long before Lawrence began working on the poem: 'the apples blown down lie almost like green lights in the grass'. It was like cadential draft of a poem that was nowhere near being written, and as I went through the letters for the second time I noticed more and more pre-echoes like this. As Sagar points out, the immediate source for the image of the ship of death was a 'little bronze' one he saw in Cerveteri in April 1927. Already by the summer of 1925, however, the opening image is redolent with the atmosphere of departure and journeying that will make up the poem's narrative: 'seems already a bit like autumn, and there is feeling of going away in the air'.

Who can say when a poem begins to stir, to germinate, in the soil of the writer's mind? There are certain experiences waiting to happen: like the snake at Lawrence's water trough, the poem is already there, waiting for him. The poem is waiting for circumstance to activate it, to occasion its being written.

NOTES

[1] What Lawrence intended to sit under, Rilke, in the first of the *Duino Elegies*, was content merely to glimpse and speculate upon: 'Perhaps there remains for us some tree on a hillside . . .'

Robert Frost

CZESLAW MILOSZ

I write about him, who is recognized as the greatest American poet of the twentieth century, not with admiration, but rather with amazement that such a figure is possible. Because it is difficult to understand how one country could produce three such different poets as Walt Whitman, Emily Dickinson, and Robert Frost.

Born in 1874, a contemporary, more or less, of Paul Valéry (b. 1871), Leopold Staff (b. 1878), and Bolesław Lesmian (b. 1878), he was already formed intellectually when the twentieth century began. America at that time was far removed from Europe, whose cultural capital was Paris. I can think about Frost comparatively, knowing, as I do, poets who are very different from him—French and Polish poets. Not only Europeans thought of America then as a country of shallow materialism; her citizens did, too, and if they valued culture they looked longingly across the Atlantic. Frost, too, when he was a young man, spent a couple of years in England, where he published *North of Boston* (1914), which also earned him recognition in America. But he built his entire, unusual career after his return to the land of the golden calf. How did he do it?

He changed his clothes and donned a mask. He put himself forward as a rube, a New England farmer, writing in a simple language, full of colloquialisms, about his environs and the people who lived there. A real American, digging in the soil, and not from any big city! A self-made talent, a country sage in daily contact with nature and the seasons! Helped by his acting and declamatory talents, he carefully maintained that image, playing on the appeal of the simple country philosopher. His readings attracted large crowds. I saw that bard with my own eyes when he was already an old man: blue eyes, a white mane, sturdily built, deserving of sympathy and trust with his openness and simplicity.

In fact, he was someone entirely different. His childhood was spent in San Francisco, not in the country outside of Boston. Among his various means of earning his living there were also a couple of years of managing a farm in New England—the oldest part of the American continent to have been colonized by whites. He felt the landscape there, the people, the language; he knew their work because he had done it himself—mower, digger, lumber-jack. His readers valued him, however, for his idyllic mood, which was only a disguise. Beneath it was concealed a grim, hopeless vision of man's fate.

A powerful intellect, unusual intelligence, well-read in philosophy, and such enormous deceptiveness that he was capable of hiding his skepticism behind his constant ambivalence, so that his poems deceived with their supposedly wise affability. I am amused by the thought of a French poet reading Frost—for instance, Paul Valéry. He would probably have snorted contemptuously at those little story-plays taken from life and written down with the pen of, you know, a simpleton, a cowboy. At the same time, one should remember that both poets, despite their will and their knowledge, were connected to the language's moment, to its current—descending, in the case of the French, and ascending, in the case of American English.

Frost struggled with the scientific worldview of the nineteenth century, enthusiastically reading Darwin, who was, *nota bene*, not only a scientist but a thinker, aware of the influence of his discoveries on his contemporaries. For Frost, this meant a break with Emerson, with American faith in the benign power of nature, and acceptance of the ungrounded nature of individual life, which is caused solely by chance. That is to say, he pondered evolution, and also borrowed from his reading of Bergson's *Creative Evolution*, but I won't delve into his philosophy. All I want to say is that Lesmian's poetry has a similar underpinning of skepticism, and that his balladic simplicity is also different from what it appears to be on the surface. His gods and other worlds are a conscious description of the Buddhist veil of maya. Like him in his skeptical worldview, Paul Valéry promoted constructions of the self-creating mind which admires its own creations. In Lesmian, however, Nature takes on fairy-tale shapes; it swarms with fantastic creatures, and an almost Christian Heaven opens out into a universe of poetic imagination, redeemed by its own beauty. Constructed out of crystals, the autonomous edifice of intellect in Valéry also finds its ultimate realization in the perfection of metric verse, and several lines from *Le Cimetière marin* have always remained with me. Why then, I ask, do I find Frost so disturbing and depressing?

It is not that he dissembled. He decided to become a great poet, mercilessly condemned his rivals, but also knew that he would not achieve greatness pursuing his philosophical bent. Quite simply, he discerned what would be his strengths: rural New England and his superb ear, registering the variants of colloquial English. He had to limit himself to what he knew well, cling to his seeming provincialness. His poetry is not lyrical but tragic, for his narrative poems about the ties between people are mini-tragedies; or else it is descriptive, or, more accurately, moralistic. I feel that it is cold.

To think at one and the same time about that poetry and the biography concealed behind it is to descend into a bottomless well. No one will learn about Frost's own wounds and tragedies by reading his poetry; he left no clues. An appalling chain of misfortunes, numerous deaths in the family, madness, suicides, and silence about this, as if confirming his Puritan heritage, which demands that one conceal what is private behind a stoic façade. The worst part of all this is that in concerning oneself with him one is menaced by a sense of one's own particular existence. If the boundaries of the human personality are so fluid that we truly do not know who we are and are constantly trying on different changes of costume, how did Frost manage? It is impossible to grasp who he really was, aside from his unswerving striving toward his goal of fame, in an attempt to exact revenge for his own defeats in life.

I confess that I do not like his poetry and that in calling him great I am only repeating what others, Joseph Brodsky included, have written about him. Brodsky seems to have valued him as a master of metrical poetry. Frost said of free verse that it is like a game of tennis without a net. I, however, am absolutely on Walt Whitman's side.

In Frost's defense, I should add that he did not soften the cruel truth about human life, as he perceived it, and if his readers and listeners did not understand that very well, all the better for them. There is, for example, one poem about how very alone man is in relation to nature, which is absolutely indifferent to him, even though he wishes to receive some sign of understanding. Alone, not only in relation to nature, because each "I" is isolated from all others, as if it were the sole ruler of the universe, and seeks love in vain, while what it takes to be a response is only the echo of his own hope. I cite this poem because it also demonstrates Frost's allegorical and moralistic methods:

THE MOST OF IT

He thought he kept the universe alone;
For all the voice in answer he could wake
Was but the mocking echo of his own
From some tree-hidden cliff across the lake.
Some morning from the boulder-broken beach
He would cry out on life, that what it wants
Is not its own love back in copy speech,
But counter-love, original response.
And nothing ever came of what he cried
Unless it was the embodiment that crashed
In the cliff's talus on the other side,
And then in the far distant water splashed,
But after a time allowed for it to swim,
Instead of proving human when it neared
And someone else additional to him,
As a great buck it powerfully appeared,
Pushing the crumpled water up ahead,
And landed pouring like a waterfall,
And stumbled through the rocks with horny tread,
And forced the underbrush—and that was all.

An Excerpt from
The Year of Reading Proust
P H Y L L I S R O S E

> *"We guess as we read, we create; everything starts from an*
> *initial error. . . . A large part of what we believe to be true . . .*
> *with an obstinacy equalled only by our good faith, springs from*
> *an original mistake in our premises."*
>
> —The Fugitive

For a long time I used to try to read Proust. At first I could not. Like a heavy car with a tiny engine, I charged up the hill again and again only to stall around page 50, somewhere within the exhausting story of young Marcel's getting to sleep one night in Combray. Who can have reached adulthood in our times in literate circles without knowing how much Marcel wanted his mother to come upstairs and kiss him good night? But fewer people may know the subsequent, perverse emotion: that when Marcel's whining succeeds in getting his father to send his mother to spend the night in his room, he feels somewhat discomforted. To have his mother with him all night is too great a gift, a humiliating sign his father thinks him a sickly child who might as well be indulged. Moreover, having secured his mother, Marcel no longer wants her so much. As he will discover over and over in love, what is imagined and yearned for is more exciting than what is possessed; anticipation is a more pleasurable state than occupation. Almost all the love affairs in Proust are variations on Groucho Marx's insight that any club that wants you is not a club you want to join.

The opening section of *Swann's Way* seemed so slow, so static, so filled with tedious description and irritating embellishment, I was always so fatigued by the immense work of reading which evidently lay ahead of me, that either I would fall asleep myself reading how Marcel did or I would put the book aside with a mixture of irritation at Proust's demands on me, shame at my own feeble powers of response, and the whoopdedoo exhilaration of a schoolkid at recess, only to pick it up and try again, perhaps in a different paperback edition, a different translation, years later, and have the same thing recur.

Once or twice, however, with my foot pressed even harder on the accelerator, I would chug uphill to the story of Uncle Adolphe, between pages 99 and 110. There I stalled again, but for a different reason. Worldly Uncle Adolphe, knowing that his family disapproved of the actresses and courtesans he enjoyed entertaining, contrived to keep their visits strictly separate from the visits of his family, but young Marcel, eager to meet such women, managed to burst in on his uncle on one of the forbidden days. So he got to meet the adorable lady in pink, and although his uncle suggested he keep news of this meeting from his parents, Marcel was so excited that he told them all about it, causing a rift between them and Uncle Adolphe. Later Marcel encountered his uncle on the street, riding in his carriage, and he was so moved by his uncle's kindness and so remorseful for having caused the family rift that he considered merely raising his hat to him an inadequate gesture. So he did nothing, turning his head away. Uncle Adolphe, concluding that Marcel was acting on his parents' instructions, never forgave them, and Marcel never saw his uncle again.

To be so moved that you don't even make a gesture of common courtesy is a morsel of typically Proustian paradox: it is normal to express your feelings by gestures which seem to express their exact opposite. Anyone who has never answered a letter that especially pleased them will understand. You might think from my stopping my reading at Uncle Adolphe that I wasn't enjoying it, as had been the case earlier on, when I read about Marcel's efforts to go to sleep. But it was exactly the opposite. I savored the moment so much that I could not continue. The result was the same—I stalled—but the process was different, for in the second case I was re-enacting the perverse logic of Marcel's snub of his uncle: I felt too much to make the simple gesture of continuing to read. If I moved on, I would leave behind the section I so much enjoyed. Yet if I didn't abandon the beloved part, how would I ever come to know the whole of the novel? I was like a traveler who arrives in Rome in the first days of a lengthy tour of Italy, falls in love with the city, and is tempted to cancel the rest of his travel plans, even though he knows he would thereby deprive himself of the certain delights of Venice and Florence; he finally continues his trip, but never experiences exactly the same pleasure, always feels a certain regret, comparing the joys of the next city to the joys he knew in Rome, which are augmented by memory, and finding the subsequent pleasures lesser.

Well, I exaggerate. I went on to experience the same joys I had in reading about Uncle Adolphe and more in my year of reading Proust. Just now, writing, I got carried away by my exercise in Proustian style, of whose chief elements—paradox, inclusiveness, and simile—simile was the horse that took me off on that wild ride to Rome, Venice, and Florence. I will try to rein him in. But in discussing the pain caused by moving forward in enterprises we love, I might have gone on to mention the regret of the mother who, no matter how much she loves her grown son, always suffers from the loss of the adorable baby he once was and which, of the successive incarnations that form what we call for convenience a person, was the one she first fell in love with. Had I done so, I would have made a complete Proustian circuit—from a solitary mental event (reading) to a physical activity (in this case travel, which for Proust is often an enactment of desire) to a human relationship (the feelings of mother for son) considered in time. Such spirals replace in Proust the straight-line narrative of the traditional novel.

>—◆—=

Yes, I read Proust for a year. More than a year. In fact, as I write this, I am still reading him. I have not yet begun the final volume of *In Search of Lost Time*, the sixth, which contains, I know, Proust's account of sitting down to write his masterpiece and the final party, given by the new Princesse de Guermantes, highest-ranking member of the most exclusive circle in Paris, whom we first meet as middle-class, affected Madame Verdurin. No one reads Proust for the plot. Still, I maintain a kind of skepticism that substitutes for narrative momentum. Madame Verdurin becomes the Princesse de Guermantes? I'll believe it when I read it.

Unpropelled by narrative, caught in the spirals or circles of reference which generate his depth and amplitude, every reader of Proust has to find his or her own reason for moving ahead. I myself began by ignoring what was unique to Proust, reading him as though he were a nineteenth-century novelist, like Tolstoy or George Eliot or Stendhal, with whom I already felt comfortable. So I read quickly and as if with half-closed eyes those sections in *Swann's Way* about sleep and landscape which I found static and woke up when I got to the "story" (for story it blessedly was) of Swann's obsession with Odette ("Swann in Love"). Swann is among the most refined men in Paris, and Odette is no better than a high-class call girl. (She will turn out to have been Uncle Adolphe's lady in pink.) Swann loves Odette almost because she is not his type, his love fueled by jealousy. This was matter I could understand, more paradoxical than Madame Bovary's love affair or Julien Sorel's or Fabrice del Dongo's, but still in the great French tradition of writing about love.

And so I arrived, panting and gasping as from a long-distance race, at volume 2. On a practical note, I must add that I would never have reached this level of achievement had I not made the reading of Proust the central business of my life, the work I turned to when I first got up in the morning. I had begun, as usual, doing my own writing in the morning and reading Proust in the afternoon or in bed before I went to sleep. That proved impossible. Proust declined my peripheral attention. He wanted, he demanded, he got my best thought, my best energy, the best of my day.

I had read *Swann's Way* so conscious of my own pleasure or lack of it that I could hardly enjoy it. I was so amazed to be reading the book at all, to have moved beyond Uncle Adolphe, that the feeling of amazement overwhelmed all my other responses, as when a person who for the first time skis or drives a car is too astonished to find himself successfully propelled through space, too absorbed by the difficulties of movement, to take in the scenery. Focused on the success or failure of my own activity, I was largely unable to study the verbal scenery of volume 1. But by volume 2, I was steady enough on my feet to look around.

What I noticed first, unfashionably enough, was Proust's wisdom. Generations of critics have told us we are not supposed to read novels for what they have to tell us about life, but Proust seemed to have many things he wanted to say, or rather to explain, about human nature, and I wanted to hear. At the start of *Within a Budding Grove*, we find Swann, who had been the model of tact, friend of duchesses and princesses who prized his discretion, now married to Odette and become a vulgarian who boasts when some junior government official's wife pays a visit to his. Proust is eager to explain why. Have we noticed the way artists, as they age, pride themselves on their secondary talents? A great writer will imagine he pleases his friends with gifts of his mediocre paintings, or a brilliant theoretical chemist will want to be admired for his efforts at poetry. The principle is the same in social life. We know the standards of the arts we practice. Outside our own area, our taste and discretion go astray and we ascribe to our least efforts, all the more precious to us because marginal, an importance they don't have. So Swann, who would never have boasted of his friendship with duchesses, boasts of his wife's visits from Madame Bontemps.

To my astonishment Proust, who I'd been led to expect looked always into himself, seemed to be looking at other people's behavior, explaining, understanding, generalizing from particular cases, or predicting the particular from an understanding of the general. In the first section of *Within a Budding Grove*, Marcel is obsessed with getting to know Madame Swann and Gilberte, her daughter. When he meets the diplomat, the Marquis de Norpois, who is a friend of Madame Swann, he steers the conversation around to her, gets the marquis to say that he will mention him to Madame Swann, and has the ridiculous urge, instantaneously suppressed, to kiss Monsieur de Norpois's hand in gratitude. He is so embarrassed at having almost done this that he convinces himself Monsieur de Norpois didn't notice. But Monsieur de Norpois had noticed, even remembers the gesture years later and recalls it to Marcel. And of course, seeing how important it is to Marcel that he mention him to Madame Swann, he resolves by no means to do so.

This small, well-observed transaction becomes the subject of a discourse on the effects of magnification. How could Marcel have convinced himself his gesture was too small to be seen? We often think we are invisible, either because we underestimate our size in other people's eyes or because we overestimate the number of gestures—the size of the world—most people take in. Proust moves easily from Marcel and the Marquis de Norpois to "we" or "people" or "one," the level of generalization.

Generalizations about "we" are so thick throughout *Lost Time* that for the sport of the thing in discussing them I will limit myself to volume 2, where my notes were not so voluminous as they later became. Very often these generalizations are cast in an epigrammatic form that links Proust to Montaigne: "The time which we have at our disposal every day is elastic; the passions that we feel expand it, those that we inspire contract it, and habit fills up what remains." (p. 257) "We understand the characters of people we are indifferent to." (p. 648) "Pleasure is like photography. What we take, in the presence of the beloved object, is merely a negative which we develop later, when we are back at home, and have once again found at our disposal that inner darkroom the entrance to which is barred to us so long as we are with other people." (pp. 616–617) "The true secret of giving ourselves pleasure . . . is not to aspire to it but merely to help ourselves pass the time less boringly." (p. 728) Sometimes, rarely, there's a hortatory note, and epigram shades into essay, as in his portrait of the friendship of Marcel and the aristocratic Saint-Loup and the ensuing discussion of the rewards of friendship versus those of art. Sometimes the generalizations take the form of references to human traits we are all presumed to know about, references that breathe a French worldliness, like similar references in Colette, as when he mentions "that subservience of refinement to vulgarity" which is the rule in many households (p. 126), or "that anxiety . . . that desire for something more, which destroys in us, in the presence of the person we love, the sensation of loving." (p. 139)

It was no surprise to me, it confirmed what I'd been sensing, when Marcel refers to himself toward the end of *Budding Grove* as a "human

naturalist." Darwin, during his travels on the *Beagle*, collected speci-
mens of bird and animal life which later, a housebound recluse in
England, he sifted mentally in order to write *The Origin of Species*.
So too Proust, in his years of social observation and activity, collected
examples of human behavior which later, immured in his cork-lined
bedroom in Paris, he sifted and studied in order to find general, uni-
fying laws. The title of Proust's masterpiece, *A la recherche du temps
perdu*, currently translated into English as *In Search of Lost Time*,
has inspired a good deal of talk about time (*temps*)—time lost, time
scanned, time recovered—but critics have paid less attention to Proust's
recherche, which evokes for me research as well as searching. Proust is
a researcher, happiest when, between two sensations, experiences, or
pieces of behavior he finds a common element, when, beneath particular examples, he discerns a connective law. After all, what is simile, that
cornerstone of Proust's style, but a way of finding a connection between
two seemingly dissimilar things?

Proust is hardly alone among epic writers in obtaining denseness
of texture, denseness of reference, a sense of felt life, from those surprising, sometimes far-fetched similes which have been used to deepen
description as far back in western literature as Homer and which are
therefore called "Homeric." By comparing something to something
very different, you incorporate two layers of life in your work within
one description. So in Homer one finds soldiers in ambush compared to
wolves preying on sheep, and thereby the reader has both the farmyard
and the battlefield called to mind. By the same token, Proust describes
the way the Marquis de Norpois listens motionless when someone talks
to him in the manner of people who are used to controlling conversations and who are often asked for advice. Then suddenly he "falls on
you like an auctioneer's hammer." In one sentence you have the world
of the salon and the world of the auction. Monsieur de Norpois sends
Marcel to pay a visit on a writer whom he very much admires but little
thought to meet, plunging him into as great anxiety "as if he had told
me I was to embark the next day as cabin boy on a windjammer." Salon
widens into seaport. The degree to which Proust relies on simile to open
out his work is, I think, unprecedented in the novel, merely hinted at
even in so insistently comparative a work as *Middlemarch*, and is the

point at which his aesthetic impulses, that is, his impulses as a writer of poetic prose, and his scientific impulses, his way of proceeding as a "researcher" into human nature, intersect and reinforce each other..

⬥

The final step in any scientific investigation is, of course, the application of the principles discovered to new data—in other words, further experiments. Rapidly, I began applying the fruits of Proust's research to my own life.

An old friend, a man who had felt compelled to side with my husband's first wife when they were divorced but continued to wish us well, visiting our town, pleasantly accepted an invitation to dinner at our house then canceled a day or so later on a notably feeble pretext. Was I puzzled? No. Proust had explained his behavior: "The Princess never liked to tell people that she would not go to their houses. Every day she would write to express her regret at having been kept away—by the sudden arrival of her husband's mother, by an invitation from her brother-in-law."

Another friend would taunt me periodically with the names of people she'd been seeing, people who didn't seem so eager to see me. It made it easier to bear to know that Madame Swann, too, had collected friends as though she were conducting a colonial campaign of annexation. I told myself that if my friend bothered to taunt me with her new colonies, at least that made me Germany to her France or Spain to her Netherlands.

A new couple came to town and made their way with unprecedented swiftness into our little circle of writers and painters. Although their impact as artists and their charm as friends was considerable, a distinguishing feature of these newcomers was their wealth. But you'd never have known this from hostesses who invited them to parties and then extolled their talents to the other guests. I understood because Proust had revealed that when people were admitted to the witty Guermantes circle because they were wellborn, as happened now and then, the Guermantes would always protest that the initiates were really very witty.

Increasingly I saw similarities between our town and Balbec, the seaside resort where Marcel goes in the second half of *Budding Grove* (and where I'd been reluctant to follow him, so entranced was I by the matter of Marcel and Madame Swann, Marcel, and Gilberte). Proust explained the social dynamics of places like Balbec, Martha's Vineyard, and Key West. According to the Proustian paradox that what should be marginal to people is often central to them, life in vacation spots matters more to many people than life in the city. And this is true to such an extent that some will cultivate in the city individuals they would otherwise not have bothered with in order to see them in the vacation spot, where, because of local hierarchies, they enjoy much greater status.

Proust had shown me the underlying laws. Like the Marxist who boasts that if you really understand history you can predict it and sneers at those who, not understanding it, are condemned to repeat it, like the Freudian smug in the face of human aberration because he thinks he can explain what produced it, I felt privileged, exempt, suddenly the master of the life I was observing. I had been given a key, a free subscription to some hitherto locked-out cable channel which in front of my eyes lost its frustrating distortion and transformed itself from blurred, wavy, taffy-pull mystery shapes into a clear and enjoyable picture.

When my son complained about a feeling of oppression upon starting his first job, despite the fact that he liked the job very much, I sent him, hoping to do for him what Proust had done for me, a Xerox of two paragraphs about Marcel's anxiety when his father agrees to let him abandon diplomacy and devote himself to literature, saying to Marcel's mother, among other things, "He's no longer a child. He knows pretty well now what he likes." The passage explored various anxieties his father's response aroused in Marcel, starting with the question of whether his writing deserved that much generosity. More deeply, he had always thought of himself as standing on the threshold of life, with that life before him. Now, it appeared, it had already begun. When would the fun start? Time had him in its grip. Soon he would be old. My son had a hard time with the passage, whose complexity and length I cannot reproduce without quoting the whole thing and disastrously tearing the fabric of my own discussion (Proust is deeply competitive: it's always a choice between yourself and him), but eventually he understood it and appreciated the consolation that parallel experience provides.

By the start of volume 3, I felt so solid on my sea legs that I could even—and easily—distinguish between "good Proust" and "bad Proust." The opening of *The Guermantes Way* was bad Proust. The sentences were short and jumpy, lacking associative flow. The similes, of which I now considered myself a connoisseur, seemed conspicuously forced and arid, comparing Marcel's experience not to other experience, but to Greek myth or the Bible—literary events not lived ones. A person having to return to his seat after the intermission at the theater, parting the crowd, is compared to the Hebrews in the Red Sea. Boo! Marcel's idea that a certain gentleman in the audience was the Prince of Saxony on his way to see the Duchesse de Guermantes accompanied this gentleman like a deity who, invisible to everyone else, accompanies a Greek soldier in battle. Hiss!

As I review these opening sections of *The Guermantes Way* now, I see no lapse. Marcel and his family have moved to Paris and are living in the same building as the Guermantes. Marcel begins his ascent into the Guermantes circle. The somewhat stilted similes I noted are there, but so is much else that is marvelous. Why did I focus on the glitches? To signify that a new stage had been reached in my reading of Proust? That I was not merely capable of enjoyment but of discernment as well? Because, in the continuing underlying competition between us, a competition in which I'd had to begin by ceding him the supremacy, not just reading him entirely on his terms but giving over my life to him, I could regain power over Proust by rejecting parts of him? In this ostensibly responsive but subconsciously hostile mode, I conceded ("Even I have to admit") that by page 108, Proust was back in form. This was, I noted, "prime Proust," condescending praise which while seeming to award the Artist five points awards the Critic ten. The passage I liked so much described—remembrance of things past—Marcel falling asleep. See how far I had come? I might have flunked that exam the first time around, but this time I would get an A+!

Falling asleep now, Marcel is older, no longer a child at Combray longing for his mother, but a young man visiting his friend Saint-Loup, who is with his regiment in a town called Doncières. Marcel has gone there to escape from his obsession with the Duchesse de Guermantes but also to solicit Saint-Loup's help in arranging an introduction to her. The regimental band plays outside his window, sometimes interfering with sleep, sometimes absorbed into the process. The description of falling asleep is about 1,500 words long, that is about the length of this chapter up to the paragraph starting, "I had read *Swann's Way* so conscious of my own pleasure or lack of it that I could hardly enjoy it." It presents the gradual detachment of the mind from everyday reality and its entry into another world where problems that have been addressed over and over by the conscious mind throughout the day are solved in another way.

Sometimes the experience of reading Proust is like the experience— were we ever to subject ourselves to it—of watching a feature-length movie in slow motion. He pays such minute attention to the sequence of emotions and experiences which constitute any psychological event, he breaks down all psychological movement to so many component parts that all motion seems suspended, and what we see, however fascinating, is no longer sequential action but a series of static gestures. A visual analogy exists in the photographs of Eadweard Muybridge, showing, for example, a woman walking up a ramp or a horse running in frames of split seconds, each allowing us to understand locomotion in a way we never had before. Describing how the mind blurs, softens, and distorts as we fall asleep, gradually escaping from the world of reality into the world of dreams, Proust isolates the moment at which we notice with glee a sudden lapse in logic in our own obsessive thoughts. This moment signals the opening of a door into the other world. His description of it makes me recall the famous freeze-frame in Muybridge's study of animal locomotion by which he proved Leland Stanford's hunch that at some point a running horse has all four legs off the ground. I think, too, of Harold Edgerton's strobe photo of a milk spill, proving that a splash, random and sloppy to the unassisted eye, forms a perfect circle in scientific reality. I have known that moment of glee at the advent of illogic, but I've never read about it, never seen it reconstituted as literature, and hence have never really been sure of its existence outside my own experience. Thanks to the literary equivalent of the freeze-frame, one has the exhilarating feeling over and over in reading Proust of coming into undiscovered country, of reading about experiences never written about before, even though the experiences he writes about—falling asleep or falling in love—are about as basic as human experience gets.

Although most literature represents a radically condensed and speeded-up version of life, so that the baby of page 1 is the dying old man of the final chapter of a book we read in a month at most, the pace of life is generally faster than the pace of Proust and generally more even. I had been reading Proust for four months before I reached the end of volume 3, with the Guermantes' party especially slow going. I zipped through the opening of *Sodom and Gomorrah*, which introduces Charlus as a homosexual, takes us back to Balbec, describes Marcel's affair with Albertine as well as Charlus's affair with the violinist Morel. But it took me five months to read the account of Monsieur and Madame Verdurin's party in that volume. Admittedly that was a bit much: I was distracted; I had other work to do; I went on some travels. But I defy anyone to read that section in the matter of hours which the Verdurins' party in reality might have occupied. No more than *Ulysses* can be read in a day. Like other modernist innovators in the novel—James Joyce and Virginia Woolf—Proust compressed the time of the "action" (Bloom's day in Dublin leading up to his meeting with Stephen, Mrs. Dalloway's day in London leading up to her party) in order to anchor the narrative while the prose line wandered in time and space, with any moment in the present acting as a kind of diving platform offering access to a lake of memory, anticipation, and association.

⬗◈⬔

Roger Shattuck, in his "Modern Masters Series" book on Proust, frankly lists the parts of *Lost Time* he thinks you can skip. He wants to suggest a kind of minimal investment that will nonetheless allow you to experience Proust's masterpiece. I think this is brave of him and kindly meant. Sometimes I consult his list to check my progress and the coming attractions. According to Shattuck, you must read most of *Swann's Way* and part 2 of *Within a Budding Grove*. In *The Guermantes Way*, he finds essential only chapter 1 of part 2. In *Sodom and Gomorrah*, only the first thirty and the last thirty pages. In *The Captive*, only the first thirty pages and the two hundred pages on the concert.

Ahead of me I saw next to *The Fugitive* the single, uncompromising word "omit."

Omit? Omit the whole volume? What was the problem? I could hardly wait to get to *The Fugitive* and see for myself. Perhaps unsurprisingly, given what we know about perversity and paradox, this was among my favorite sections of *Lost Time*. Albertine, the zesty young woman who becomes Marcel's mistress, lives in his Paris apartment in a state of virtual captivity created by his jealousy. Eventually she leaves him and dies soon after in a riding accident. Even better than the brilliant section on Marcel's grandmother's death, *The Fugitive* describes what it is like to have a loved one die. In Proustian detail, which is to say slowly, patiently, imaginatively, thoroughly, bringing everything in his mind to bear on each observation, comparing, contrasting, contextualizing, historicizing, drawing out of his inner darkness the precise words needed to render the emotion in all its particularity as it's never been rendered in words before, he presents the stages of Marcel's grief and the process of recovery.

I was so taken with this section that, whenever a conversation could be crowbarred around to Proust or death or literature, I would recount whole chunks of it, citing in pedantic detail what Proust had to say about the process of detachment. "Proust says you have to trace your steps backward to where you were before you knew the person who died. That is, you have to forget them in order to accept that they're dead. If you still actively love them, it's too painful."

"I don't feel that way about Jimmy," said Alison Lurie one day over lunch in Key West, applying what I'd said Proust said to the death of her friend, the poet James Merrill. "I just feel that he's gone some place very far away. Like Australia."

I felt foolish, so reasonable was Alison's attitude. My own explanation of mourning seemed labored and tortuous compared to "I just feel he's in Australia." To excuse myself, I can only say I was thinking of my father, whose death, unlike James Merrill's, was no surprise and whom I could in no way imagine as having gone to Australia. At his age? In his state of health? Without my mother?

Still, I was beginning to wonder if I had a mind of my own or if I was just a puppet speaking for Proust. If a friend consulted me on a question of human behavior, I would search my notes and my memory to see if Proust had anything to say about it. Was there anyone in literature, Wendy asked, who could make sense of her friend Irene? Was there any character who varied as much as Irene did between charm and relentless vindictiveness? Yes. In Charlus, as Proust explains, the desire to charm produced extreme alternations between affection (if you were charmed) and hatred (if you seemed immune). What should my son do about the downstairs neighbor, who constantly and unreasonably complained about noise? Neurotics, Proust counseled, are irritated at the slightest provocation by inoffensive enemies, but as soon as anyone takes the offensive against them, they become meek. So I advised my son, who had gone out of his way to be polite, to change tactics and stand up to the neighbor. The harrassing calls stopped.

I was twelve months into my project, almost through volume 5, which contains *The Captive* and *The Fugitive*, and reading Proust had become as much a way of life as a literary pastime, closer to a religious practice than to the usual discrete encounter with a single work of art. I retreated into my communion with the text as a way of vacationing from daily life, as a Sunday worshipper might put aside routine concerns on entering a church, returning to the way I'd read as a fifteen-year-old, when, since I had no date for New Year's Eve, to bury my chagrin, to keep from thinking of the fun I was missing, I immersed myself in *Gone With the Wind* and finished it in one long celebratory night. Now, if I was distracted by social demands, household chores, bills to pay, calls to return, supplies to restock, I could momentarily suspend my obligations to the world of the living by picking up Proust, the essential escapism of what I was doing neutralized by the belief that I was enlarging my understanding of the world as well as renewing my zest for it. Proust was solving my problems, structurally, by providing an alternative activity, and substantively, by functioning as a sourcebook, the Whole Earth Catalogue of Human Emotions, the sacred text that seers consult for answers, the chicken entrails they read. Moreover, Proust's style had permeated my mind and changed my literary taste. A mixed blessing: everything I'd written before, whose chief virtues were clarity and brevity, now seemed pinched and parsimonious.

At the start of my project, I had turned down the corners of pages to mark passages I especially liked or wanted to remember: I would come back to them some time in the future. With volume 2, I started writing notes in the blank pages at the back of the book, jotting down page numbers, saying to myself, "Quote this," but not writing down what I wanted to quote. By volume 5, my notes were so extensive that I ran out of blank pages at the back of the book and then at the front of it, too. I was copying out whole passages. Passage after passage. I responded so thoroughly to Proust by this point that there was almost nothing I didn't think worth coming back to. I had to start reading at the computer, so I could transcribe the beloved passages quickly enough to move on.

Eventually it struck me that nothing less than total transcription of the text would do. Anything more condensed was inadequate tribute, inadequate understanding, unworthy of its subject. Like the hero of Borges's story, "Pierre Menard, Author of the Quixote," I didn't want to write a contemporary appreciation of Proust, or my version of Proust, I wanted to write Proust over from the beginning, word for word, and have it be mine. I had run into the fundamental problem of criticism as an account of literature, and it reproduced the problem of literature as an account of life. A translation, a reduction, a condensation, an approximation, a metaphor is the best that can be achieved in art, no matter how inclusive, as an account of life, and the same is true for criticism as an account of art. No matter how full we make our accounts of reading, no matter how hard we try to make our style sympathetic to the work under discussion and not to violate it by analysis, what we produce is less than the text it describes. Just as there is no way to live a life except minute by minute, there is no way to experience a novel except word by word, and when I reach the end of Proust, the only thing for me to do will be to start to re-read.

The Humble Animal

RANDALL JARRELL

I have read Marianne Moore's poetry too many years and too many times not to be afraid that both the poems and my feelings about them will be poorly represented by anything I write. It might be better to say, like Graves's Augustus, "Words fail me, my lords," and to go through *What Are Years* pointing. This is Miss Moore's own method of criticism, as anyone who has read one of her reviews will remember; it would be a rude kind of justice to make a criticism of her poetry quotations and a few conjunctions.

One critic has said that Miss Moore's poetry is not poetry at all, but criticism—actually even her criticism is not criticism but an inferior sort of poetry. She not only can, but must, make poetry out of everything and anything: she is like Midas, or like Mozart choosing unpromising themes for the fun of it, or like one of those princesses whom wizards force to manufacture sheets out of nettles. And yet there is one thing Miss Moore has a distaste for making poetry of: the Poetic. She has made a principle out of refusing to believe that there is any such thing as the antipoetic; her poems restore to poetry the "business documents and school books" that Tolstoy took away.

Pound wrote one famous sentence of advice which—to judge from the practice of most of the poets who read it—was understood as: *Poetry must be just as badly written as prose.* Miss Moore understood it more as it was meant to be understood: her poetry, not satisfied with the difficulties of verse, has added to them those of prose. Her poems have the virtues—form, concentration, emotion, observation, imagination, and so on—that one expects of poetry; but one also finds in them, in supersaturated solution, some of the virtues of good prose. Miss Moore's language fits Wordsworth's formula for the language of poetry surprisingly well—something that will disquiet lovers of either of the two poets, though not lovers of both; but I am sure Wordsworth would have looked at it with uncomfortable dislike, and have called it the language of extraordinary women. This would be true: Miss Moore, in spite of a restraint unparalleled in our time, is a natural, excessive, and magnificent eccentric. (On a small scale, of course; like all cultivated Americans, she is afraid of size.) Eccentricity has been to her a first resort, an easy but inescapable refuge.

Miss Moore's forms have the lacy, mathematical extravagance of snowflakes, seem as arbitrary as the prohibitions in fairy tales; but they work as those work—disregard them and everything goes to pieces. Her forms, tricks and all, are like the aria of the Queen of the Night: the intricate and artificial elaboration not only does not conflict with the emotion but is its vehicle. And her machinery—bestiary, rather— fits both the form and final content of her poems as precisely as if all three were pieces of some extraordinary puzzle. Another of the finest American poets, Wallace Stevens, is as addicted to exotic properties; but his often get in the way of what he has to say, or hide from him the fact that he does not, this time, care to say anything much. The things *are* what Miss Moore wants to say, and express her as naturally and satisfactorily as the Lamb and the Tyger did God. (Some true wit—Miss Moore, I suppose—put an index at the back of *Observations*, the early collection of her poems.) A style ought to make it easy for you to say all that you have to say, not, as most do, make it impossible for you to get free from one narrowed range of experience and expression; Miss Moore's style, whether it seems to or not, does the first—this is proved by the fact that her poetry is richer, more balanced, and more objective than her prose. Nobody else's mechanism and mannerisms come so close to being independently satisfactory—like the Cheshire Cat's smile, which bewitched one for some time after the cat was gone. (Sometimes the smile is almost better than the cat: I once read, in a college newspaper's account of a lecture, that poets put "real toes in imaginary gardens, as Mary Ann Moore says.")

It would be stupid not to see Miss Moore in all her protective creatures—"another armored animal," she once reflects, or confesses. Patience, honesty, the courage that is never conscious of itself because it has always taken itself for granted—all the qualities she distils from, or infuses into, the real pastoral of natural history books, she is at last able to permit even to man, looking at him (in the beautiful "The Pangolin") as equably, carefully, and affectionately as she ever looked at any animal. "The Pangolin" may be her best poem; it is certainly one of the most moving, honest, and haunting poems that anyone has written in our century.

Miss Moore realizes that there is no such thing as the *Ding an Sich*, that the relations *are* the thing; that the outside, looked at hard enough, is the inside; that the wrinkles are only the erosion of habitual emotion. She shows that everything is related to everything else, by comparing everything to everything else; no one has compared successfully more disparate objects. She has as careful and acute an eye as anybody alive, and almost as good a tongue: so that when she describes something, a carrot, it is as if she had taken the carrot's cries in some final crisis, cries that hold in themselves a whole mode of existence. One finds in her poems so much wit and particularity and observation; a knowledge of "prosaic" words that reminds one of *Comus*; a texture that will withstand any amount of rereading; a restraint and delicacy that make many more powerful poems seem obvious. And, over and above the love and care and knowledge she has lavished on the smallest details of the poems, Miss Moore is an oddly moral writer, one who coalesces moralities hardly ever found together; she is even, extraordinarily enough in our time, a writer with a happy ending—of a kind.

One could make a queer economic-historical analysis of Miss Moore, as the representative of a morality divorced both from religion and from economics, of a class-segment that has almost been freed either from power or from guilt—whose cultivation, because of its helplessness and poverty, is touching. One might say that Miss Moore is, fragmentarily, Henry James in pure crystalline form. (Sometimes James's morality, in its last extravagance, is one more Great Game, a species of ethical hydroponics.) In Miss Moore's poems religion and economics are ghosts. Clergymen are spare cultivated old men, friends of your father, living scrupulously off dwindling incomes, who on the lawn tell you occasionally, not without a dry and absent impressiveness, about unfrequented hallways of the Old Testament. Business, the West, furnish you with no more than an odd quotation about the paper of an encyclopedia, and in the colonies of the West there are neither workers nor hunger, only pandas. Society is the incredible monster you inhabit, like the whale in Lucian; for many years, long before your birth even, there has been nothing anyone could do—so while you wait under the shade of that great doom you do well and, whether any bless you or not, are blessed. Alone in your civility, precariously safe and beautiful in the enforced essential privacy of late individualism, you are like the reed which escapes, perhaps, the storm that wrecks the forest; or like the humble, the children and sparrows, who served as models for salvation in the similar convulsions of an earlier world. And what an advantage it is to be poor and humble, to have lost your stake in the game that corrupts even if you play unwillingly and without belief! It is you who can sit still—no need to wish to—and keep your mouth shut, or speak so softly and dryly it is as good as silence.

Miss Moore has great limitations—her work is one long triumph of them; but it was sad, for so many years, to see them and nothing else insisted upon, and Miss Moore neglected for poets who ought not to be allowed to throw elegies in her grave. I have read that several people think So-and-So the greatest living woman poet; anybody would dislike applying so clumsy a phrase to Miss Moore—but surely she is. Her poems, at their unlikely best, seem already immortal, objects that have endured their probative millenia in barrows; she has herself taken from them what time could take away, and left a skeleton the years can only harden. People have complained about the poems, in the words of the poems: "Why dissect destiny with instruments which are more specialized than the tissues of destiny itself?" But nothing is more specialized than destiny. Other people have objected, "They are so small." Yes, they are as small as those animals which save the foolish heroes of fairy tales—which can save only the heroes, because they are too small not to have been disregarded by everyone else.

Loving Dostoyevsky

SUSAN SONTAG

The literature of the second half of the twentieth century is a much traversed field, and it seems unlikely that there are still masterpieces in major, intently patrolled languages waiting to be discovered. Yet some ten years ago, rifling through a bin of scruffy-looking used paperbacks outside a bookshop on London's Charing Cross Road, I came across just such a book, *Summer in Baden-Baden*, which I would include among the most beautiful, exalting, and original achievements of a century's worth of fiction and parafiction.

The reasons for the book's obscurity are not hard to fathom. To begin with, its author was not by profession a writer. Leonid Tsypkin was a doctor, a distinguished medical researcher, who published nearly a hundred papers in scientific journals in the Soviet Union and abroad. But—discard any comparison with Chekhov and Bulgakov—this Russian doctor-writer never saw a single page of his literary work published during his lifetime.

Censorship and its intimidations are only part of the story. Tsypkin's fiction was, to be sure, a poor candidate for official publication. But it did not circulate in samizdat either, for Tsypkin remained—out of pride, intractable gloom, unwillingness to risk being rejected by the unofficial literary establishment—wholly outside the independent or underground literary circles that flourished in Moscow in the 1960s and 1970s, the era when he was writing "for the drawer." For literature itself.

Actually, it is something of a miracle that *Summer in Baden-Baden* survived at all.

Leonid Tsypkin was born in 1926 in Minsk of Russian-Jewish parents, both physicians. The medical specialty of his mother, Vera Polyak, was pulmonary tuberculosis. His father, Boris Tsypkin, was an orthopedic surgeon, who was arrested at the start of the Great Terror, in 1934, on the usual fanciful charges and then released, through the intervention of an influential friend, after he tried to commit suicide by jumping down a prison stairwell. He returned home on a stretcher, with a broken back, but he did not become an invalid and went on with his surgical practice until his death (at sixty-four) in 1961. Two of Boris Tsypkin's sisters and a brother were also arrested during the Terror, and perished.

Minsk fell a week after the German invasion in 1941, and Boris Tsypkin's mother, another sister, and two little nephews were murdered in the ghetto. Boris Tsypkin, his wife, and fifteen-year-old Leonid owed their escape from the city to the chairman of a nearby collective farm, a grateful ex-patient, who ordered several barrels of pickles taken off a truck to accommodate the esteemed surgeon and his family.

A year later Leonid Tsypkin began his medical studies, and when the war was over, he returned with his parents to Minsk, where he graduated from medical school in 1947. In 1948 he married Natalya Michnikova, an economist. Mikhail, their only child, was born in 1950. By then Stalin's anti-Semitic campaign, launched the year before, was racking up victims, and Tsypkin hid out on the staff of a rural psychiatric hospital. In 1957 he was allowed to settle with his wife and son in Moscow, where he had been offered a post as a pathologist at the prestigious Institute of Poliomyelitis and Viral Encephalitis. He became part of the team that introduced the Sabin polio vaccine in the Soviet Union; his subsequent work at the institute reflected a variety of research interests, among them the response of tumor tissues to lethal viral infections and the biology and pathology of monkeys.

Tsypkin had always been fervent about literature, had always written a little for himself, both prose and poetry. In his early twenties, when he was nearing the completion of his medical studies, he considered quitting medicine in order to study literature, with the idea of devoting himself entirely to writing. Riven by the nineteenth-century Russian soul questions (how to live without faith? without God?), he had idolized Tolstoy, who eventually was replaced by Dostoyevsky. Tsypkin also had cine-loves: Antonioni, for example, but not Tarkovsky. In the early 1960s he had thought about enrolling in night classes at the Institute of Cinematography to become a film director, but the necessity of supporting his family, he said later, made him pull back.

It was also in the early 1960s that Tsypkin began a more committed spate of writing: poems that were strongly influenced by Tsvetayeva and Pasternak; their photographs hung above his small work table. In September 1965 he decided to chance showing some of his lyrics to Andrei Sinyavsky, but Sinyavsky was arrested a few days before their appointment. Tsypkin and Sinyavsky, who were virtually the same age, were never to meet, and Tsypkin became even more cautious. ("My father," says Mikhail Tsypkin, "was not inclined to talk or even to think much about politics. In our family, it was assumed without discussion that the Soviet regime was Evil incarnate.") After several unsuccessful attempts to publish some of his poems, Tsypkin stopped writing for a while. Much of his time was devoted to finishing "A Study of the Morphological and Biological Properties of Cell Cultures of Trypsinized Tissues," his dissertation for a doctor of science degree. (His earlier dissertation, for a Ph.D., was on growth rates of brain tumors that had been subjected to repeated surgeries.) After the successful defense of his second dissertation, in 1969, Tsypkin received an increase in salary, which freed him from moonlighting as a part-time pathologist in a small hospital. Already in his forties, he began writing again—not poetry but prose.

In the thirteen years he had left to live, Tsypkin created a small body of work of ever larger reach and complexity. After a handful of short sketches came longer, more plotted stories, two autobiographical novellas, *The Bridge Across the Neroch* and *Norartakir*, and then his last and longest work of fiction, *Summer in Baden-Baden*, a kind of dream novel, in which the dreamer, who is Tsypkin himself, conjures up his own life and that of Dostoyevsky in a streaming, passionate narration. Writing was engorging, isolating. "Monday through Friday," relates Mikhail Tsypkin, "my father left at a quarter to eight sharp for his work at the Institute of Poliomyelitis and Viral Encephalitis, which was situated in a distant suburb of Moscow, not far from the Vnukovo airport. He came back home at 6 p.m., had dinner, took a short nap, and sat down to write—if not his prose, then his medical research papers. Before going to bed, at 10 p.m., he sometimes took a walk. He usually spent his weekends writing as well. My father craved every opportunity to write, but writing was difficult, painful. He agonized over each word and endlessly corrected his handwritten manuscripts. Once finished with editing, he typed his prose on an ancient, shiny German typewriter, an Erika—Second World War loot that an uncle gave him in 1949. And in that form his writings remained. He did not send his manuscripts to publishers, and did not want to circulate his prose in samizdat because he was afraid of problems with the KGB and of losing his job." Writing without hope or prospect of being published—what resources of faith in literature does that imply? Tsypkin's readership was never much larger than his wife, his son, and a couple of his son's Moscow University classmates. He had no real friends in any of the Moscow literary worlds.

There was one literary personage in Tsypkin's immediate family, his mother's younger sister, the literary critic Lydia Polyak, and readers of *Summer in Baden-Baden* make her glancing acquaintance on the very first page. Aboard a train bound for Leningrad, the narrator opens a book, a precious book whose binding and decorative bookmark are lovingly described before we learn that it is the *Diary* of Dostoyevsky's second wife, Anna Grigoryevna Dostoyevsky, and that this copy, flimsy and almost falling apart when it came into Tsypkin's hands, belongs to an unnamed aunt who can only be Lydia Polyak. Since, Tsypkin writes, "in my heart of hearts I had no intention of returning the book borrowed from my aunt who possessed a large library," he has had it trimmed and rebound.

According to Mikhail Tsypkin, several of his father's stories contain a cranky reference to Polyak. A well-connected member of the Moscow intelligentsia for half a century, she held a research position at the Gorky Institute of World Literature since the 1930s, and even when she was fired from her teaching post at Moscow University during the anti-Semitic purges of the early 1950s, she managed to keep her position at the institute, where Sinyavsky eventually became a junior colleague of hers. Although it was she who arranged the aborted meeting with Sinyavsky, Polyak apparently disapproved of her nephew's writings and condescended to him, for which he never forgave her.

In 1977 Tsypkin's son and daughter-in-law decided to apply for exit visas. Natalya Michnikova, fearing that her employment, for which a security clearance was needed, would prejudice her son's chances, resigned from her job in the division of the State Committee for Material and Technical Supplies (GOSSNAB) that allocated heavy road-building and construction equipment to practically all sectors of the Soviet economy, including the military. The visas were granted, and Mikhail and Elena Tsypkin left for the United States. As soon as the KGB relayed this information to Sergei Drozdov, the director of the Institute for Poliomyelitis and Viral Encephalitis, Tsypkin was demoted to junior researcher—a position for someone without an advanced degree (he had two) and his starting rank of more than twenty years earlier. His salary, now the couple's only source of income, was cut by seventy-five percent. He continued to go to the institute every day but was excluded from laboratory research, which was always conducted by teams; not one of his colleagues was willing to work with Tsypkin, for fear of being tainted by contact with an "undesirable element." There would have been no point in seeking a research position elsewhere, since in every job application he would have had to declare that his son had emigrated.

In June 1979 Tsypkin, his wife, and his mother applied for exit visas. They then waited for almost two years. In April 1981 they were informed that their requests were "inexpedient" and had been denied. (Emigration from the USSR virtually stopped in 1980, when relations with the United States deteriorated as a result of the Soviet invasion of Afghanistan; it became obvious that, for the time being, no favors from Washington would be forthcoming in exchange for permitting Soviet Jews to leave.) It was during this period that Tsypkin wrote most of *Summer in Baden-Baden.*

He started the book in 1977 and completed it in 1980. The writing was preceded by years of preparation: consulting archives and photographing places associated with Dostoyevsky's life as well as those frequented by Dostoyevsky's characters during the seasons and at the times of day mentioned in the novels. (Tsypkin was a dedicated amateur photographer and had owned a camera since the early 1950s.) After finishing *Summer in Baden-Baden*, he presented an album of these photographs to the Dostoyevsky museum in Leningrad.

However inconceivable it was that *Summer in Baden-Baden* could be published in Russia, there was still the option of publishing it abroad, as the best writers were then doing with their work. Tsypkin decided to attempt just this and asked Azary Messerer, a journalist friend who had received permission to leave in early 1981, to smuggle a copy of the manuscript and some of the photographs out of the Soviet Union. Messerer was able to arrange this through the good offices of two American friends, a married couple, who were Moscow-based correspondents for UPI.

At the end of September 1981 Tsypkin, his wife, and his mother reapplied for exit visas. On October 19, Vera Polyak died at the age of eighty-six. The refusal of all three visa applications came a week later; this time, the decision had taken less than a month.

In early March 1982 Tsypkin went to see the head of the Moscow visa office, who told him, "Doctor, you will never be allowed to emigrate." On Monday, March 15, Sergei Drozdov informed Tsypkin that he would no longer be kept on at the institute. The same day Mikhail Tsypkin, who was in graduate school at Harvard, called Moscow to announce that on Saturday his father had finally become a published writer. Azary Messerer had succeeded in placing *Summer in Baden-Baden* with a Russian-émigré weekly in New York, *Novaya Gazeta*, which would be serializing the novel. The first installment, illustrated by some of Tsypkin's photographs, had appeared on March 13.

Early on Saturday, March 20, his fifty-sixth birthday, Tsypkin sat down at his desk to continue work on the translation of a medical text from English into Russian—translating being one of the few possibilities of eking out a living open to refuseniks (Soviet citizens, usually Jews, who had been denied exit visas and fired from their jobs). He suddenly felt unwell (it was a heart attack), lay down, called out to his wife, and died. He had been a published author of fiction for exactly seven days.

———◆———

For Tsypkin, it was a matter of honor that everything of a factual nature in *Summer in Baden-Baden* be true to the story and the circumstances of the real lives it evokes. This is not, like J. M. Coetzee's wonderful *The Master of Petersburg*, a Dostoyevsky fantasy. Neither is it a docu-novel, although Tsypkin was obsessed with getting everything "right." (In his son's words, he was, in all matters, "very systematic.") It is possible that Tsypkin imagined that if *Summer in Baden-Baden* were ever published as a book, it should include some of the photographs he had taken, thereby anticipating the signature effect of the work of W. G. Sebald, who, by seeding his books with photographs, infused the plainest idea of verisimilitude with enigma and pathos.

What kind of a book is *Summer in Baden-Baden*? From the start, it proposes a double narrative. It is wintertime, late December, no date given: a species of "now." The narrator is on a train going to Leningrad (former and future St. Petersburg). And it is mid-April 1867. The newly married Dostoyevskys, Fyodor ("Fedya") and his young wife, Anna Grigoryevna, have left St. Petersburg and are on their way to Dresden. The account of the Dostoyevskys' travels—for they will be mostly abroad in Tsypkin's novel, and not only in Baden-Baden—has been scrupulously researched. The passages where the narrator—Tsypkin—describes his own doings are wholly autobiographical. Since imagination and fact are easily contrasted, we tend to draw genre lessons from this and segregate invented stories (fiction) from real-life narratives (chronicle and autobiography). That's one convention—ours. In Japanese literature the so-called I-novel (*shishōsetsu*), a narrative that is essentially autobiographical but contains invented episodes, is a dominant novel form.

In *Summer in Baden-Baden* several "real" worlds are evoked, described, re-created in a hallucinatory rush of associations. The originality of Tsypkin's novel lies in the way it *moves*, from the displacements of the never-to-be-named narrator, embarked on his journey through the bleak contemporary Soviet landscape, to the life of the peripatetic Dostoyevskys. In the cultural ruin that is the present, the feverish past shines through. Tsypkin is traveling *into* Fedya's and Anna's souls and bodies, as he travels *to* Leningrad. There are prodigious, uncanny acts of empathy.

Tsypkin will stay in Leningrad for a few days: it is a Dostoyevsky pilgrimage (surely not the first), a solitary one (no doubt as usual), that will end in a visit to the house where Dostoyevsky died. The Dostoyevskys are just beginning their impecunious travels; they will remain in Western Europe for four years. (It is worth recalling that the author of *Summer in Baden-Baden* was never allowed outside the Soviet Union.) Dresden, Baden-Baden, Basel, Frankfurt, Paris—their lot is to be constantly agitated by the confusions and humiliations of cramping financial misery, while having to negotiate with a chorus of presumptuous foreigners (porters, coachmen, landladies, waiters, shopkeepers, pawnbrokers, croupiers), and by gusts of whim and of volatile emotions of many kinds. The gambling fever. The moral fevers. The fever of illness. The sensual fevers. The fever of jealousy. The penitential fevers. The fear . . .

The principal intensity depicted in Tsypkin's fictional re-creation of Dostoyevsky's life is not gambling, not writing, not Christing. It is the searing, generous absoluteness (which is not to pronounce on the satisfactoriness) of conjugal love. Who will forget the image of the couple's lovemaking as swimming? Anna's all-forgiving but always dignified love for Fedya rhymes with the love of literature's disciple, Tsypkin, for Dostoyevsky.

Nothing is invented. Everything is invented. The framing action is the trip the narrator is making to the sites of Dostoyevsky's life and novels, part of the preparation (as we come to realize) for the book we hold in our hands. *Summer in Baden-Baden* belongs to a rare and exquisitely ambitious subgenre of the novel: a retelling of the life of a real person of accomplishment from another era, it interweaves this story with a story in the present, the novelist mulling over, trying to gain deeper entry into, the inner life of someone whose destiny it was to have become not only historical but monumental. (Another example, and one of the glories of twentieth-century Italian literature, is *Artemisia* by Anna Banti.)

Tsypkin leaves Moscow on the first page and two-thirds of the way through the book arrives at the Moscow Station in Leningrad. Although aware that somewhere near the station is the "ordinary, grey Petersburg dwelling-house" where Dostoyevsky spent the last years of his life, he walks onward with his suitcase in the icy nocturnal gloom, crossing the Nevsky Prospect to pass by other places associated with Dostoyevsky's last years, then turns up where he always stays in Leningrad, a portion of a dilapidated communal apartment occupied by a tenderly described intimate of his mother, who welcomes him, feeds him, makes up a broken sofa for him to sleep on, and asks him, as she always does, "Are you still as keen on Dostoyevsky?" When she goes to bed, Tsypkin sinks into a volume plucked at random out of the prerevolutionary edition of Dostoyevsky's collected works in her bookcase, *Diary of a Writer*, and falls asleep musing about the mystery of Dostoyevsky's anti-Semitism.

After a morning spent chatting with his affectionate old friend, and hearing more stories of the horrors endured during the Leningrad Blockade, Tsypkin sets off—the short winter day is already darkening—to roam about the city, "taking photographs of the Raskolnikov House or the Old Moneylender's House or Sonechka's House or buildings where their author had lived during the darkest and most clandestine period of his life in the years immediately following his return from exile." Walking on, "led by a kind of instinct," Tsypkin manages to reach "exactly the right spot"—"my heart was pounding with joy and some other vaguely sensed feeling"—opposite the four-story corner building where Dostoyevsky died, now the Dostoyevsky museum; and the description of the visit ("An almost churchlike silence reigned in the museum") segues into a narrative of a dying that is worthy of Tolstoy. It is through the prism of Anna's excruciating grief that Tsypkin re-creates the long deathbed hours in this book about love, married love and the love of literature—loves that are in no way linked or compared, but each given its due, each contributing its infusing fire.

<hr/>

Loving Dostoyevsky, what is one to do—what is a Jew to do—with the knowledge that he hated Jews? How to explain the vicious anti-Semitism of "a man so sensitive in his novels to the suffering of others, this jealous defender of the insulted and injured"? And how to understand "this special attraction which Dostoyevsky seems to possess for Jews"?

The most intellectually powerful of the earlier Jewish Dostoyevsky-lovers is Leonid Grossman (1888–1965), who heads a long list of such figures cited by Tsypkin. Grossman is an important source for Tsypkin's reimagining of Dostoyevsky's life, and one of the books mentioned at the beginning of *Summer in Baden-Baden* is the product of Grossman's scholarly labors. It was he who edited the first selection of Anna Dostoyevsky's *Reminiscences*, which was published in 1925, seven years after her death. Tsypkin speculates that the absence of "loathsome little Jews" and other such expectable phrases in the memoirs of Dostoyevsky's widow may be explained by the fact that she wrote them, on the eve of the Revolution, after she had made Grossman's acquaintance.

Tsypkin must have known Grossman's many influential essays on Dostoyevsky, such as *Balzac and Dostoyevsky* (1914) and *Dostoyevsky's Library* (1919). He may have come across Grossman's novel, *Roulettenburg* (1932), a gloss on Dostoyevsky's novella about the gambling passion. (*Roulettenburg* was the original title of *The Gambler*.) But he couldn't have read Grossman's *Confession of a Jew* (1924), which had gone completely out of circulation. *Confession of a Jew* is an account of the life of the most enthralling and pathetic of the Jewish Dostoyevskyists, Arkady Uri Kovner (1842–1909), brought up in the Vilna ghetto, with whom Dostoyevsky entered an epistolary relationship. A reckless autodidact, Kovner had fallen under the writer's spell and was inspired by reading *Crime and Punishment* to commit a theft to succor an ailing impoverished young woman with whom he was in love. In 1877, from his cell in a Moscow jail, before being transported to serve a sentence of four years of hard labor in Siberia, Kovner wrote to Dostoyevsky to challenge him on the matter of his antipathy to Jews. (That was the first letter; the second was about the immortality of the soul.)

In the end, there is no resolution of the anguishing subject of Dostoyevsky's anti-Semitism, a theme that comes surging into *Summer in Baden-Baden* once Tsypkin reaches Leningrad. It seemed, he writes, "strange to the point of implausibility . . . that this man should not have come up with even a single word in the defense or justification of a people persecuted over several thousand years . . . and he did not even refer to the Jews as a people, but as a tribe . . . and to this tribe I belonged and the many friends and acquaintances of mine with whom I had discussed the subtlest problems of Russian literature." Yet this hasn't kept Jews from loving Dostoyevsky. How to explain that?

Tsypkin has no better explanation than the fervor of Jews for the greatness of Russian literature—which might remind us that the German worship of Goethe and Schiller was in large part a Jewish affair, right up to the time Germany started murdering its Jews. Loving Dostoyevsky means loving literature.

A crash course on all the great themes of Russian literature, *Summer in Baden-Baden* is unified by the ingenuity and velocity of its language, which moves boldly, seductively, between first and third person—the doings, memories, musings of the narrator ("I") and the Dostoyevsky scenes ("he," "they," "she")—and between past and present. But this is not a unitary present (of the narrator Tsypkin on his Dostoyevsky pilgrimage), any more than it is a unitary past (the Dostoyevskys from 1867 to 1881, the year of Dostoyevsky's death). Dostoyevsky, in the past, submits to the undertow of remembered scenes, passions from earlier moments in his life; the narrator, in the present, summons up memories of his past.

Each paragraph indent begins a long, long sentence whose connectives are "and" (many of these) and "but" (several) and "although" and "and so" and "whereas" and "just as" and "because" and "as if," along with many dashes, and there is a full stop only when the paragraph ends. In the course of these ardently protracted paragraph-sentences, the river of feeling gathers up and sweeps along the narrative of Dostoyevsky's life and of Tsypkin's: a sentence that starts with Fedya and Anna in Dresden might flash back to Dostoyevsky's convict years or to an earlier bout of gambling mania linked to his romance with Polina Suslova, then thread onto this a memory from the narrator's medical-student days and a rumination on some lines by Pushkin.

Tsypkin's sentences call to mind José Saramago's run-on sentences, which fold dialogue into description and description into dialogue, and are spiked by verbs that refuse to stay consistently in either the past or the present tense. In their incessantness, Tsypkin's sentences have something of the same force and hectic authority as those of Thomas

Bernhard. Obviously, Tsypkin could not have known the books of Saramago and Bernhard. He had other models of ecstatic prose in twentieth-century literature. He loved the early (not the late) prose of Pasternak—*Safe Conduct*, not *Doctor Zhivago*. He loved Tsvetayeva. He loved Rilke, in part because Tsvetayeva and Pasternak had loved Rilke; he read very little foreign literature and only in translation. Of what he had read, his greatest passion was Kafka, whom he discovered by way of a volume of stories published in the Soviet Union in the mid-1960s. The amazing Tsypkin sentence was entirely his own invention.

Reminiscing about his father, Tsypkin's son describes him as obsessed by detail and compulsively neat. His daughter-in-law, commenting on his choice of medical specialty—pathology—and his decision never to practice as a clinical physician, recalls that "he was very interested in death." Perhaps only an obsessive, death-haunted hypochondriac, such as Tsypkin seems to have been, could have devised a sentence-form that is free in so original a way. His prose is an ideal vehicle for the emotional intensity and abundance of his subject. In a relatively short book, the long sentence bespeaks inclusiveness and associativeness, the passionate agility of a temperament steeped, in most respects, in adamancy.

Besides the account of the incomparable Dostoyevsky, Tsypkin's novel offers an extraordinary mental tour of Russian reality. Taken for granted, if that is not too odd a way of putting it, are the sufferings of the Soviet era, from the Great Terror of 1934–37 to the present of the narrator's quest: the book pulses with them. *Summer in Baden-Baden* is also a spirited and plangent account of Russian literature—the whole arc of Russian literature. Pushkin, Turgenev (there is a scene of fierce confrontation between Dostoyevsky and Turgenev), and the great figures of twentieth-century literature and ethical struggle—Tsvetayeva, Solzhenitsyn, Sakharov, and Bonner—also enter, are poured into the narration.

One emerges from reading *Summer in Baden-Baden* purged, shaken, fortified, breathing a little deeper, grateful to literature for what it can harbor and exemplify. Leonid Tsypkin did not write a long book. But he made a great journey.

An Excerpt from *How to Read a Poem and Fall in Love with Poetry*

EDWARD HIRSCH

Look closely into the poetry of our century and you find history warming up its sacrificial victims, preparing its martyrdoms: Osip Mandelstam, Miguel Hernández, César Vallejo ("I will die in Paris, on a rainy day," he prophesied, "On some day I can already remember"). Somewhere it is 1914 and George Trakl, a dispensing chemist in the Austrian army, has found the wherewithal to craft his magisterial poem "Grodek," the name of a town in Galicia, Poland, where the Austrians were defeated and he was left to care for ninety wounded men, most of whose suffering he could not relieve, some of whom committed suicide in his presence. Soon he would follow with a self-administered overdose of cocaine. "O prouder grief!" Trakl cries out,

> You brazen altars,
> Today a great pain feeds the hot flame of the spirit,
> The grandsons yet unborn.

> *(translated by Michael Hamburger)*

The dream of the concluding poem. It is the sacrificial hour of abandonment and prayer, of ritualized grief before brazen altars, of the last determined quest for a consoling unity. These are threshold poems. That's why they so often begin with nightfall (Trakl writes: "At nightfall the autumn wind cries out / With deadly weapons and golden plains") and take place in the absolute field of night (Yeats's hour, like Cavafy's and Desnos's, was jubilant midnight). Just as often they conclude in the eerie blue light of dawn ("the cauldron of morning," as Plath called it). These poems take place at whatever moment evokes the transition between worlds. They have the gravity of a light forever changing, of visionary imagination. They are written in the presence of what Heidegger called "being-to-death." The poet is performing the last rites in advance of death, and thus the poem is delivered back to us with a certain formal sense of ceremonial procession.

Poems are presences. They ventriloquize voices. Many dramatic poems have the quality of soliloquy: the act of speaking to oneself in or as if in solitude. A final soliloquy is the last version of such a speech. In some sense, every poem is about time, but the final soliloquy is posed against death in a particular way. It is a boundary poem that inscribes a last wish about vanishing, a concluding trope of disappearance. It is furiously crafted against the contingencies of time. It had better be, for the poet is vanishing and human life must be breathed into the poem. There is no other way: the words are all. Such life can be instilled in poetry through style. Style both creates the surface and calls upon— calls up—the deep unconscious life.

Remember everything is at stake in this conclusive last utterance, this rising self-elegy, and yet no actor is getting ready to dramatize the words, no costumed thespian is preparing to strut across a scenic stage for an appreciative communal audience. This ritual enacts another kind of magical transference and imaginative exchange. There was a writer who became a book, there is a reader leaning over the page to decipher the letters, to meet the written characters . . .

The art of last things is an art pared away to what is absolutely essential, an art of making language at the edge of a void where everything is undone, unmade. Language was put to a grave test on October 31, 1944, when the Hungarian poet Miklós Radnóti somehow found it within himself to write the last of his four "Postcard" poems in the midst of a forced march westward across Hungary.

Postcard
4

I fell next to him. His body rolled over.
It was tight as a string before it snaps.
Shot in the back of the head—"This is how
you'll end." "Just lie quietly," I said to myself.
Patience flowers into death now.
"Der springt noch auf," I heard above me.
Dark filthy blood was drying on my ear.

Szentskirályszabadja
October 31, 1944
(*translated by Steven Polgar, Stephen Berg, and S. J. Marks*)

Radnóti speaks to the unspeakable in these seven lines, to the horrific death he knew was coming. The poem inscribes a suffering unimaginably intense, a consciousness of death unbearably palpable. It is a poem nearly literally rising up from a mass grave. Near the town of Abda, sometime between November 6 and November 10, Radnóti was one of twenty-two prisoners murdered and tossed into a collective grave. He was thirty-five years old. After the war his widow had his body exhumed and his last poems were found in his field jacket, written in pencil in a small Serbian exercise book. They display the classical poise of an Orphic art that comes back from the underworld to give testimony.

All the poems written during Radnóti's internment appeared in a posthumous volume, *Clouded Sky* (1946), which is one of the pinnacles of Central European poetry in this century. I have sometimes wondered if Radnóti's commitment to classical values as well as his immense labor in translation (his 1942 volume *In the Footsteps of Orpheus* ranges across two thousand years of European poetry) was a way of keeping alive an ideal of Europe as a place of Enlightenment during a time when it had clearly become a site of barbarism.

Radnóti's poems are filled with disquieting premonitions of the horrors to come. Characterizing the times, he wrote, "I lived on this earth in an age / when man fell so low / he killed willingly, for pleasure, without orders." He was doom-ridden and had an uncanny sense of his own impending destruction. "I am the one they'll kill finally / because I myself never killed," he prophesied in 1939 for a new edition of *Steep Road*, the last individual collection of his poetry published while he was still alive. One high-water mark of his work is a series of eight eclogues, written in hexameters, that refashion the pastoral form to address an era when morality is turned upside down and right and wrong have changed places. He calls on the pastoral muse to assist him in trying to preserve the values of civilization. These poems sing to overcome terror, invoking the splendor of memory, the landscape of childhood, and the necessity of love at a time when "reason falls apart."

Radnóti's descriptive powers never faltered. Until the end, he was able to characterize with poignant accuracy the nightmare he experienced. I'm struck by the fact that he entitled his last poems "Postcards." Here the jauntiness of the title belies the gravity of the content. It's an offering characterized as much by what is left out as by what is put in, and its brevity (its self-acknowledged communicative inadequacy) speaks volumes to what must be left unsaid. The informality of the postcard (dashed off, superficial) is also belied by the scrupulousness with which Radnóti re-creates the scene with a few dramatic brushstrokes.

Radnóti's poem is not an exact transcription of experience but a made thing. It is not a work of reportage but of art, and therefore it enters art psyche, art time. It has the moonglow of a poem made halfway to Hades. There are minds that can split themselves off and still have utterance, minds that show uncanny stoicism on the edge of the grave. It takes a particular kind of involvement and detachment both to speak and to stand beside oneself, to engage oneself as an artist with a dead person lying next to you. I think of Wilfred Owen, Robert Graves, Siegfried Sassoon, or Keith Douglas.

There may be no name for the kind of speaker we have in a poem like Radnóti's last "Postcard." It doesn't seem entirely accurate to call him either a fictive construction or a mere witness, though he has elements of both. Rather, Radnóti's speaker is both completely personal and somehow beyond the personal, at once a historical self and a transcendental self. I would call him "transpersonal." Radnóti's classical training and his psychological insight come together here under the stimulus of his own finality, and he uses art to pull himself up to some higher level, to change consciousness. Maybe he dreamed that by imagining his own end he could somehow be saved from it.

The fourth "Postcard" begins drastically with two sharp staccato sentences that fuse together in one line broken in the middle: "I fell next to him. His body rolled over." The speaker has fallen out of time into the netherworld (no time for elaboration now) and immediately we're inside the experience of someone who has fallen, or been thrown down, next to a dead body. That body is compared to a string so taut it's about to snap. I can't stop thinking of him lying there next to someone who had been shot in the back of the head. Something has got to give, and Radnóti seems to be desperately trying to hold on to reason, to fend off madness, which terrified him. Remember his poem "Maybe . . .":

> But don't leave me, delicate mind!
> Don't let me go crazy.
> Sweet wounded reason, don't
> leave me now.

> Don't leave me. Let me die, without fear,
> a clean lovely death,
> like Empedocles, who smiled as he fell
> into the crater.
> (*translated by Steven Polgar, Stephen Berg, and S. J. Marks*)

These pleading lines echo as I listen to the voice in "Postcard" that comes to the still-living man with a flat warning, a matter-of-fact declaration: "This is how you'll end." A threat made good. The poet counsels himself to hold still, to accept what is happening to him. He says it aloud to calm himself, to enact it for us. There's a terrifying stoicism to the line "Patience flowers into death now." A blossoming into oblivion. Then he hears an unattributed voice floating over him in German, the language of death. There's remarkable richness in the phrase "Der springt noch auf," which means something like "Wait till you see this guy break open." It has a nasty colloquial edge. But the verb *aufspringen*, which means "to break or pop open," is usually used to describe a bud or a flower. It's an image of germination, and so perhaps there's a hidden tenderness here, as if the poet ventriloquized the German to say, "Wait till you see him blossom." He is breaking free of his fetters; and death has become a liberation. After this, the last statement of the poem (a memory made more forceful by the way the sentence and the line coincide) has an eerie calmness: "Dark filthy blood was drying on my ear." Radnóti was also thinking associatively here, and the sound of German links to the image of blood coagulating on his ear. The one who listens and observes is still alive, speaking from the earth.

I cling to the fact that a postcard is a message directed to another person. It has a particular reader in mind. But its openness suggests that it can be read by anyone. The poem in the guise of a postcard is a testimony back to life, a signal that Radnóti has pushed back the silence long enough to embody a final experience. This postcard peels off his body. He has taken us all the way into the shadowy hushed space of death itself.

———❖———

There are elegies for the self—poems of self-commemoration—that move into lyric time, religious space. These poems are written from the far side of alienation, from the vanishing point of life, and thus they seek consolation in closing the circle. They are poems of the deepest initiated awe.

Think for a moment of the sixteenth-century anthology piece "Tichborne's Elegy." The title was supplied by an early publisher.

> My prime of youth is but a frost of cares,
> My feast of joy is but a dish of pain,
> My crop of corn is but a field of tares,
> And all my good is but vain hope of gain;
> The day is past, and yet I saw no sun,
> And now I live, and now my life is done.

My tale was heard and yet it was not told,
My fruit is fallen and yet my leaves are green,
My youth is spent and yet I am not old,
I saw the world and yet I was not seen;
My thread is cut and yet it is not spun,
And now I live, and now my life is done.

I sought my death and found it in my womb,
I looked for life and saw it was a shade,
I trod the earth and know it was my tomb,
And now I die, and now I was but made;
My glass is full, and now my glass is run,
And now I live, and now my life is done.

This simple three-part lyric monumentalizes a fleeting instant of consciousness, a springboard or threshold moment. It bears some similarity to other commemorative inscriptions scratched or carved into the walls of the Tower of London, but its dizzying circularity creates a different sense of time and space than other last statements ("Here was . . ."). Its incantatory structure and balanced repetitions make a different proposition about eternity. Reading it I'm reminded of Peter Sacks's claim in his fine book *The English Elegy* that "Repetition creates a sense of continuity, of an unbroken pattern such as one may oppose to the extreme discontinuity of death." The rhythm of lament expresses and controls the experience of unbounded grief.

"Tichbome's Elegy" relies entirely on the language of paradox to create a sense of reconciliation between opposites. Its reiterations are a creative response to psychological trauma. Note the progression of tenses throughout the poem: how it begins in the present (stanza 1), moves to the past (stanza 2), and fuses past and present together (stanza 3). Note, too, that each refrain becomes more literal and thus brings the speaker closer to actual death. The poem presses back against that literalism by symbolically closing the circle: "I sought my death and found it in my womb." The Renaissance poet who wrote this shows his kinship with his pre-Christian Celtic inheritance now overlaid with a redemptive Christian immortality.

"Tichborne's Elegy" ritualizes a moment of slippage between past and present, present and future, and thus between death and immortality. Sharon Cameron points out that Tichborne's paradigmatic scheme looks very much like the one proposed by Emily Dickinson:

> Behind Me—dips Eternity—
> Before Me—Immortality—
> Myself—the Term between—

The lyric poem itself becomes the term between, its form a consolation that would deliver us into a primal unity, a deep fusion experience of the world. The lyric delivered at the edge of the earth puts me in mind of the Sufi maxim, "The Beloved and I are one."

———◆———

On February 5, 1963, just one week before her suicide, Sylvia Plath completed two poems. One of these is "Edge." "Edge" has that absolute certainty which we associate with poetry that has been dictated from the deepest sources. Contact has been made. The poem has a sense of recognition and inevitability so complete it suggests a dream life has been fulfilled.

> **Edge**
> The woman is perfected.
> Her dead
>
> Body wears the smile of accomplishment,
> The illusion of a Greek necessity
>
> Flows in the scrolls of her toga,
> Her bare
>
> Feet seem to be saying:
> We have come so far, it is over.
>
> Each dead child coiled, a white serpent,
> One at each little

Pitcher of milk, now empty.
She has folded

Them back into her body as petals
Of a rose close when the garden

Stiffens and odors bleed
From the sweet, deep throats of the night flower.

The moon has nothing to be sad about,
Staring from her hood of bone.

She is used to this sort of thing.
Her blacks crackle and drag.

I still remember the mounting revulsion and horror, the near physical nausea, I felt when I first read this poem thirty years ago. I almost had to raise up an arm to fend off its harsh white light. I saw how the suicide imagined herself—she created a space which she would soon enter and occupy—and it terrified me. Suddenly, I could view my own body laid out dead. I saw the naked feet pointing upward on the metal table and felt the chill of the morgue. I recoiled from the lifeless object I'd become, from what I was forced to see and acknowledge. Such a shock of recognition opens up a grave region, a profound religious hush, within the reader.

There is something deeply eerie about the way Plath has split and textualized herself in this poem which hits the unconscious with an age-old horror. The fury of its self-estrangement, its self-detachment, is immense. It's a poem with a performing stoicism. A poem of easeful death. It also pushes back the silence in a way that's hard to get a grip on. Like other minimalist successes—a de Chirico painting, a Beckett one-act play, a Japanese scroll painting—it threatens to distill itself away from you. It shakes you off. No wonder then that most of Plath's commentators have turned away from it, averting their gaze. It's unbearable. An enormous artistic victory.

"Edge" looks dramatic on the page: the severe black lines surrounded by empty white space. The first line is utterly foreseen, propositional, indicative, implacable: "The woman is perfected." The narrative of the living body is over (it now "wears the smile of accomplishment") and the rest of the poem has the mystery and clarity of a mournful procession. Its language is stark, spare, stately: the language of essential things. There's purposefulness to the couplets in a poem filled with twinnings—the joining of life and death, of a mother gathering back her two children. The elasticity of short and long lines unfolding across the two-line stanzas gives the poem a dirgelike movement, the finality of a funeral. Each of the stanzas is enjambed until the final four lines of the poem, and this also creates a sense of movement within stasis. The language has the severity of "doing something" which we associate with ritual. "Edge" takes place not in narrative but in nonlinear time, timeless space. It has the character of the last act of a classical Greek tragedy.

Plath went to school on other poetry. She took from Robert Lowell the breakthrough fire of personal material, the fever of confession. She internalized the power of other modern poets who had used archaic methods to give their poems ritual power: Yeats, Graves, Lawrence, Roethke, Hughes. And she appropriated the uncanny gothic imagination of Emily Brontë and Mary Shelley: *Wuthering Heights* and *Frankenstein* were both books that circulated in her blood. That's how a so-called confessional poet could become a mythological one, a personal history transform itself under the sign of eternity.

The modern woman who has died in "Edge" is barefoot and dressed in a simple Greek toga, like a figure on a sarcophagus. She has become her own tragic and completed work: a corpse, a corpus. I have a sense that Plath is moving back through Christian into pre-Christian or pagan rites in this lyric stripped down to an elemental black and white. "Edge" was called "Nuns in Snow" in an early draft. Its title and some of its imagery arose when she was writing her earlier poem "Mystic." But the "Greek necessity" refers to Greek tragedy and the notion that suicide was an honorable release from dishonor. It returns one to the religious rites of death.

I find a dark tribalism in the way the dead woman clutches to her breasts her two dead children, each a coiled white serpent. Plath is thinking symbolically here: the whiteness appears as a sign of ritual purity, the serpent a consort of the great goddess who could induce trance and prophesy, who takes on pre-Christian power. (It was at a relatively late date that the serpent was reappropriated as a Christian emblem of evil.) Plath is also thinking metaphorically since each breast becomes a little "pitcher of milk, now empty." It's as if by folding her children back into her body (a terrifying reversal of childbirth) she is participating in a primitive vegetation rite.

She is also asserting an age-old mother right, an awesome maternal power. The Medusa element is shocking, and we should not shrink from the horror of the sacrifice being enacted here. We should also remember that there is catharsis in liturgy, in symbolic action. Perhaps the poet was acting out this sacrifice on a symbolic level precisely so that she wouldn't have to do it literally. She could not save herself, but she could spare her children.

The symbolic legacy of the dead woman in "Edge" is a thwarted personal inheritance, but also a trope of sexual and maternal power returned to the earth. She enacts a sacrifice that will bloom forth, like Whitman's lilacs, in the elegiac flowers of poetry. The last two couplets hit a complex register:

> The moon has nothing to be sad about,
> Staring from her hood of bone.

The moon's indifference is expressed colloquially, but her blank gaze is a bleak romantic image that goes up a linguistic notch. The pattern is repeated in the last two lines:

> She is used to this sort of thing.
> Her blacks crackle and drag.

The fact that this kind of sacrifice is now so common that the moon has become accustomed to it is expressed colloquially, but the final line hits a note that is below or above speech, and therefore visionary. The moon is engendered and hooded, she is wearing funeral attire, the clothes of mourning. She's a white figure in black robes. It's as if the moon is grieving despite herself, and this reluctant mourning, this form of animism gives the poem its final feeling of catharsis and incarnation, of a transcendent numinous power. "Edge" embodies a final desire to be completed, to be reborn into the deepest unity.

A Slight Sound at Evening

E. B. WHITE

Allen Cove, Summer, 1954

In his journal for July 10–12, 1841, Thoreau wrote: "A slight sound at evening lifts me up by the ears, and makes life seem inexpressibly serene and grand. It may be in Uranus, or it may be in the shutter." The book into which he later managed to pack both Uranus and the shutter was published in 1854, and now, a hundred years having gone by, *Walden*, its serenity and grandeur unimpaired, still lifts us up by the ears, still translates for us that language we are in danger of forgetting, "which all things and events speak without metaphor, which alone is copious and standard."

Walden is an oddity in American letters. It may very well be the oddest of four distinguished oddities. For many it is a great deal too odd, and for many it is a particular bore. I have not found it to be a well-liked book among my acquaintances, although usually spoken of with respect, and one literary critic for whom I have the highest regard can find no reason for anyone's giving *Walden* a second thought. To admire the book is, in fact, something of an embarrassment, for the mass of men have an indistinct notion that its author was a sort of Nature Boy.

I think it is of some advantage to encounter the book at a period in one's life when the normal anxieties and enthusiasms and rebellions of youth closely resemble those of Thoreau in that spring of 1845 when he borrowed an ax, went out to the woods, and began to whack down some trees for timber. Received at such a juncture, the book is like an invitation to life's dance, assuring the troubled recipient that no matter what befalls him in the way of success or failure he will always be welcome at the party—that the music is played for him, too, if he will but listen and move his feet. In effect, that is what the book is—an invitation, unengraved; and it stirs one as a young girl is stirred by her first big party bid. Many think it a sermon; many set it down as an attempt to rearrange society; some think it an exercise in nature-loving; some find it a rather irritating collection of inspirational puffballs by an eccentric show-off. I think it none of these. It still seems to me the best youth's companion yet written by an American, for it carries a solemn warning against the loss of one's valuables, it advances a good argument for traveling light and trying new adventures, it rings with the power of positive adoration, it contains religious feeling without religious images, and it steadfastly refuses to record bad news. Even its pantheistic note is so pure as to be noncorrupting—pure as the flute-note blown across the pond on those faraway summer nights. If our colleges and universities were alert, they would present a cheap pocket edition of the book to every senior upon graduating, along with his sheepskin, or instead of it. Even if some senior were to take it literally and start felling trees, there could be worse mishaps: the ax is older than the Dictaphone and it is just as well for a young man to see what kind of chips he leaves before listening to the sound of his own voice. And even if some were to get no farther than the table of contents, they would learn how to name eighteen chapters by the use of only thirty-nine words and would see how sweet are the uses of brevity.

If Thoreau had merely left us an account of a man's life in the woods or if he had simply retreated to the woods and there recorded his complaints about society, or even if he had contrived to include both records in one essay, *Walden* would probably not have lived a hundred years. As things turned out, Thoreau, very likely without knowing quite what he was up to, took man's relation to Nature and man's dilemma in society and man's capacity for elevating his spirit and he beat all these matters together, in a wild free interval of self-justification and delight, and produced an original omelette from which people can draw nourishment in a hungry day. *Walden* is one of the first of the vitamin-enriched American dishes. If it were a little less good than it is, or even a little less queer, it would be an abominable book. Even as it is, it will continue to baffle and annoy the literal mind and all those who are unable to stomach its caprices and imbibe its theme. Certainly the plodding economist will continue to have rough going if he hopes to emerge from the book with a clear system of economic thought. Thoreau's assault on the Concord society of the mid-nineteenth century has the quality of a modern Western: he rides into the subject at top speed, shooting in all directions. Many of his shots ricochet and nick him on the rebound, and throughout the melee there is a horrendous cloud of inconsistencies and contradictions, and when the shooting dies down and the air clears, one is impressed chiefly by the courage of the rider and by how splendid it was that somebody should have ridden in there and raised all that ruckus.

When he went to the pond, Thoreau struck an attitude and did so deliberately, but his posturing was not to draw the attention of others to him but rather to draw his own attention more closely to himself. "I learned this at least by my experiment: that if one advances confidently in the direction of his dreams, and endeavors to live the life which he has imagined, he will meet with a success unexpected in common hours." The sentence has the power to resuscitate the youth drowning in his sea of doubt. I recall my exhilaration upon reading it, many years ago, in a time of hesitation and despair. It restored me to health. And now in 1954 when I salute Henry Thoreau on the hundredth birthday of his book, I am merely paying off an old score—or an installment on it.

In his journal for May 3–4, 1838—Boston to Portland—he wrote: Midnight—head over the boat's side—between sleeping and waking—with glimpses of one or more lights in the vicinity of Cape Ann. Bright moonlight—the effect heightened by seasickness." The entry illuminates the man, as the moon the sea on that night in May. In Thoreau the natural scene was heightened, not depressed, by a disturbance of the stomach, and nausea met its match at last. There was a steadiness in at least one passenger if there was none in the boat. Such steadiness (which in some would be called intoxication) is at the heart of *Walden*—confidence, faith, the discipline of looking always at what is to be seen, undeviating gratitude for the life-everlasting that he found growing in his front yard. "There is nowhere recorded a simple and irrepressible satisfaction with the gift of life, any memorable praise of God." He worked to correct that deficiency. *Walden* is his acknowledgment of the gift of life. It is the testament of a man in a high state of indignation because (it seemed to him) so few ears heard the uninterrupted poem of creation, the morning wind that forever blows. If the man sometimes wrote as though all his readers were male, unmarried, and well connected, it is because he gave his testimony during the callow years. For that matter, he never really grew up. To reject the book because of the immaturity of the author and the bugs in the logic is to throw away a bottle of good wine because it contains bits of the cork.

Thoreau said he required of every writer, first and last, a simple and sincere account of his own life. Having delivered himself of this chesty dictum, he proceeded to ignore it. In his books and even in his enormous journal, he withheld or disguised most of the facts from which an understanding of his life could be drawn. *Walden*, subtitled "Life in the Woods," is not a simple and sincere account of a man's life, either in or out of the woods; it is an account of a man's journey into the mind, a toot on the trumpet to alert the neighbors. Thoreau was well aware that no one can alert his neighbors who is not wide awake himself, and he went to the woods (among other reasons) to make sure that he would stay awake during his broadcast. What actually took place during the years 1845–47 is largely unrecorded, and the reader is excluded from the private life of the author, who supplies almost no gossip about himself, a great deal about his neighbors and about the universe.

As for me, I cannot in this short ramble give a simple and sincere account of my own life, but I think Thoreau might find it instructive to know that this memorial essay is being written in a house that, through no intent on my part, is the same size and shape as his own domicile on the pond—about ten by fifteen, tight, plainly finished, and at a little distance from my Concord. The house in which I sit this morning was built to accommodate a boat, not a man, but by long experience I have learned that in most respects it shelters me better than the larger dwelling where my bed is, and which, by design, is a manhouse not a boathouse. Here in the boathouse I am a wilder and, it would appear, a healthier man, by a safe margin. I have a chair, a bench, a table, and I can walk into the water if I tire of the land. My house fronts a cove. Two fishermen have just arrived to spot fish from the air—an osprey and a man in a small yellow plane who works for the fish company. The man, I have noticed, is less well equipped than the hawk, who can dive directly on his fish and carry it away, without telephoning. A mouse and a squirrel share the house with me. The building is, in fact, a multiple dwelling, a semidetached affair. It is because I am semidetached while here that I find it possible to transact this private business with the fewest obstacles.

There is also a woodchuck here, living forty feet away under the wharf. When the wind is right, he can smell my house; and when the wind is contrary, I can smell his. We both use the wharf for sunning, taking turns, each adjusting his schedule to the other's convenience. Thoreau once ate a woodchuck. I think he felt he owed it to his readers, and that it was little enough, considering the indignities they were suffering at his hands and the dressing-down they were taking. (Parts of *Walden* are pure scold.) Or perhaps he ate the woodchuck because he believed every man should acquire strict business habits, and the woodchuck was destroying his market beans. I do not know. Thoreau had a strong experimental streak in him. It is probably no harder to eat a woodchuck than to construct a sentence that lasts a hundred years. At any rate, Thoreau is the only writer I know who prepared himself for his great ordeal by eating a woodchuck; also the only one who got a hangover from drinking too much water. (He was drunk the whole time, though he seldom touched wine or coffee or tea.)

Here in this compact house where I would spend one day as deliberately as Nature if I were not being pressed by the editor of a magazine, and with a woodchuck (as yet uneaten) for neighbor, I can feel the companionship of the occupant of the pond-side cabin in Walden woods, a mile from the village, near the Fitchburg right of way. Even my immediate business is no barrier between us: Thoreau occasionally batted out a magazine piece, but was always suspicious of any sort of purposeful work that cut into his time. A man, he said, should take care not to be thrown off the track by every nutshell and mosquito's wing that falls on the rails.

There has been much guessing as to why he went to the pond. To set it down to escapism is, of course, to misconstrue what happened. Henry went forth to battle when he took to the woods, and *Walden* is the report of a man torn by two powerful and opposing drives—the desire to enjoy the world (and not be derailed by a mosquito wing) and the urge to set the world straight. One cannot join these two successfully, but sometimes, in rare cases, something good or even great results from the attempt of the tormented spirit to reconcile them. Henry went forth to battle, and if he set the stage himself, if he fought on his own terms and with his own weapons, it was because it was his nature to do things differently from most men, and to act in a cocky fashion. If the pond and the woods seemed a more plausible site for a house than an in-town location, it was because a cowbell made for him a sweeter sound than a churchbell. *Walden*, the book, makes the sound of a cowbell, more than a churchbell, and proves the point, although both sounds are in it, and both remarkably clear and sweet. He simply preferred his churchbell at a little distance.

I think one reason he went to the woods was a perfectly simple and commonplace one—and apparently he thought so, too. "At a certain season of our life," he wrote, "we are accustomed to consider every spot as the possible site of a house." There spoke the young man, a few years out of college, who had not yet broken away from home. He hadn't married, and he had found no job that measured up to his rigid standards of employment, and like any young man, or young animal, he felt uneasy and on the defensive until he had fixed himself a den. Most young men, of course, casting about for a site, are content merely to draw apart from their kinfolks. Thoreau, convinced that the greater part of what his neighbors called good was bad, withdrew from a great deal more than family: he pulled out of everything for a while, to serve everybody right for being so stuffy, and to try his own prejudices on the dog.

The house-hunting sentence above, which starts the chapter called "Where I Lived, and What I Lived For," is followed by another passage that is worth quoting here because it so beautifully illustrates the offbeat prose that Thoreau was master of, a prose at once strictly disciplined and wildly abandoned. "I have surveyed the country on every side within a dozen miles of where I live," continued this delirious young man. "In imagination I have bought all the farms in succession, for all were to be bought, and I knew their price. I walked over each farmer's premises, tasted his wild apples, discoursed on husbandry with him, took his farm at his price, at any price, mortgaging it to him in my mind; even put a higher price on it—took everything but a deed of it—took his word for his deed, for I dearly love to talk—cultivated it, and him too to some extent, I trust, and withdrew when I had enjoyed it long enough, leaving him to carry it on." A copy-desk man would get a double hernia trying to clean up that sentence for the management, but the sentence needs no fixing, for it perfectly captures the meaning of the writer and the quality of the ramble.

"Wherever I sat, there I might live, and the landscape radiated from me accordingly." Thoreau, the home-seeker, sitting on his hummock with the entire State of Massachusetts radiating from him, is to me the most humorous of the New England figures, and *Walden* the most humorous of the books, though its humor is almost continuously subsurface and there is nothing deliberately funny anywhere, except a few weak jokes and bad puns that rise to the surface like the perch in the pond that rose to the sound of the maestro's flute. Thoreau tended to write in sentences, a feat not every writer is capable of, and *Walden* is, rhetorically speaking, a collection of certified sentences, some of them, it would now appear, as indestructible as they are errant. The book is distilled from the vast journals, and this accounts for its intensity: he picked out bright particles that pleased his eye, whirled them in the kaleidoscope of his content, and produced the pattern that has endured—the color, the form, the light.

On this its hundredth birthday, Thoreau's *Walden* is pertinent and timely. In our uneasy season, when all men unconsciously seek a retreat from a world that has got almost completely out of hand, his house in the Concord woods is a haven. In our culture of gadgetry and the multiplicity of convenience, his cry "Simplicity, simplicity, simplicity!" has the insistence of a fire alarm. In the brooding atmosphere of war and the gathering radioactive storm, the innocence and serenity of his summer afternoons are enough to burst the remembering heart, and one gazes back upon that pleasing interlude—its confidence, its purity, its deliberateness—with awe and wonder, as one would look upon the face of a child asleep.

"This small lake was of most value as a neighbor in the intervals of a gentler rain-storm in August, when, both air and water being perfectly still, but the sky overcast, midafternoon had all the serenity of evening, and the wood-thrush sang around, and was heard from shore to shore." Now, in the perpetual overcast in which our days are spent, we hear with extra perception and deep gratitude that song, tying century to century.

⟫⟪

I sometimes amuse myself by bringing Henry Thoreau back to life and showing him the sights. I escort him into a phone booth and let him dial Weather. "This is a delicious evening," the girl's voice says, "when the whole body is one sense, and imbibes delight through every pore." I show him the spot in the Pacific where an island used to be, before some magician made it vanish. "We know not where we are," I murmur. "The light which puts out our eyes is darkness to us. Only that day dawns to which we are awake." I thumb through the latest copy of *Vogue* with him. "Of two patterns which differ only by a few threads more or less of a particular color," I read, "the one will be sold readily, the other lie on the shelf, though it frequently happens that, after the lapse of a season, the latter becomes the most fashionable." Together we go outboarding on the Assabet, looking for what we've lost—a hound, a bay horse, a turtledove. I show him a distracted farmer who is trying to repair a hay baler before the thunder shower breaks. "This farmer," I remark, "is endeavoring to solve the problem of a livelihood by a formula more complicated than the problem itself. To get his shoestrings he speculates in herds of cattle."

I take the celebrated author to Twenty-One for lunch, so the waiters may study his shoes. The proprietor welcomes us. "The gross feeder," remarks the proprietor, sweeping the room with his arm, "is a man in the larva stage." After lunch we visit a classroom in one of those schools conducted by big corporations to teach their superannuated executives how to retire from business without serious injury to their health. (The shock to men's systems these days when relieved of the exacting routine of amassing wealth is very great and must be cushioned.) "It is not necessary," says the teacher to his pupils, "that a man should earn his living by the sweat of his brow, unless he sweats easier than I do. We are determined to be starved before we are hungry."

I turn on the radio and let Thoreau hear Winchell beat the red hand around the clock. "Time is but the stream I go a-fishing in," shouts Mr. Winchell, rattling his telegraph key. "Hardly a man takes a half hour's nap after dinner, but when he wakes he holds up his head and asks, 'What's the news?' If we read of one man robbed, or murdered, or killed by accident, or one house burned, or one vessel wrecked, or one steamboat blown up, or one cow run over on the Western Railroad, or one mad dog killed, or one lot of grasshoppers in the winter—we need never read of another. One is enough."

I doubt that Thoreau would be thrown off balance by the fantastic sights and sounds of the twentieth century. "The Concord nights," he once wrote, "are stranger than the Arabian nights." A four-engined airliner would merely serve to confirm his early views on travel. Everywhere he would observe, in new shapes and sizes, the old predicaments and follies of men—the desperation, the impedimenta, the meanness—along with the visible capacity for elevation of the mind and soul. "This curious world which we inhabit is more wonderful than it is convenient; more beautiful than it is useful; it is more to be admired and enjoyed than used." He would see that today ten thousand engineers are busy making sure that the world shall be convenient even if it is destroyed in the process, and others are determined to increase its usefulness even though its beauty is lost somewhere along the way.

At any rate, I'd like to stroll about the countryside in Thoreau's company for a day, observing the modern scene, inspecting today's snowstorm, pointing out the sights, and offering belated apologies for my sins. Thoreau is unique among writers in that those who admire him find him uncomfortable to live with—a regular hairshirt of a man.

A little band of dedicated Thoreauvians would be a sorry sight indeed: fellows who hate compromise and have compromised, fellows who love wildness and have lived tamely, and at their side, censuring them and chiding them, the ghostly figure of this upright man, who long ago gave corroboration to impulses they perceived were right and issued warnings against the things they instinctively knew to be their enemies. I should hate to be called a Thoreauvian, yet I wince every time I walk into the barn I'm pushing before me, seventy-five feet by forty, and the author of *Walden* has served as my conscience through the long stretches of my trivial days.

Hairshirt or no, he is a better companion than most, and I would not swap him for a soberer or more reasonable friend even if I could. I can reread his famous invitation with undiminished excitement. The sad thing is that not more acceptances have been received, that so many decline for one reason or another, pleading some previous engagement or ill health. But the invitation stands. It will beckon as long as this remarkable book stays in print—which will be as long as there are August afternoons in the intervals of a gentle rainstorm, as long as there are ears to catch the faint sounds of the orchestra. I find it agreeable to sit here this morning, in a house of correct proportions, and hear across a century of time his flute, his frogs, and his seductive summons to the wildest revels of them all.

Good-Bye, Holden Caulfield. I Mean It. Go! Good-Bye!

WALTER KIRN

It was a great book and I understood it. How great could it really be? I wondered. Mr. Durkee read whole chapters aloud, stirring his mustache and beard with puffs of air when he grew especially enthused. His impersonation of Holden Caulfield involved a compromise between his own voice—flat, midwestern, and modest in its vowels—and a lavish, nasal New England overdub that came in and out like a marginal radio signal. The effort of such complex enunciation dried his lips and forced him to keep licking them, which I found hard to watch. I gazed out the window at an old custodian weed-whacking tall grass around the flagpole.

My eighth-grade English teacher, Mr. Durkee, wore sandals with bumpy massage-nub soles and held the paperback inches from his glasses as he paced in front of the blackboard and performed, embarrassing us, as usual, with his commitment to raising our horizons above the ballfields and Lutheran steeples of eastern Minnesota. Between his readings, he spoke on themes and images. The word "nonconformist" was big, and so was "Christlike." I felt uncomfortable. He was trying to convert us, a couple of dozen unresponsive teens, to some sort of new philosophy or outlook that would set us at odds with our parents and our towns while granting us no clear benefits in return. *The Catcher in the Rye*, as he explained it, had helped to "radicalize" American culture and represented an artistic "watershed" in its portrayal of disillusioned youth.

Mr. Durkee so loved the book (the "text," he called it; another term that made me squirm and worry) that he insisted we read it twice—once at home, by ourselves, and a second time at school, together. His picture of our home lives was mistaken, though. Our houses were full of dogs and cats and siblings and noisy TVs and radios and telephones. There were lawns to mow and horse stalls to scrape clean and shirts to fold and even cows to milk. Flipping through *The Catcher in the Rye* and jotting our thoughts in the margins would not be possible for all but a few of us, and maybe none of us. Sure, our parents encouraged homework—technically—but only when it involved digesting science facts or wrestling with numbers. Our homework, if we were to be indulged in it, had to look like homework, and lazing around with a slim red paperback about a high-school dropout just wouldn't cut it.

Instead we depended on Mr. Durkee to read the book for us, and then tell us what it meant. This was a better plan all around. For one thing, there were curse words in the book, and it eased my conscience quite a bit to let someone else be responsible for speaking them. There were penalties for such language, I'd been taught, and I was in enough trouble as it was. The usual sex sins, the usual petty thefts, the usual forbidden dreams and longings. Mr. Durkee, on the other hand, with his nicotine-stained skin and his slouch and his odd clothes, struck me as someone who'd shot his wad, salvation-wise. A little potty talk couldn't hurt him further.

"Holden accepts nothing at face value," he told us after finishing one chapter. "He questions the value of basic institutions. He sees through social roles. The America of the 1950s was different from the nation of today—fearful about change, conventional, preferring stability over free expression."

Stability sounded pretty good to me. I was a raging conservative that year; I'd lived through about as much change as I could take. 1975, in

the St. Croix River valley, was a plague year of divorces and teenage suicides and gas shortages and drug busts and mental breakdowns. The '60s
had finally made it to the boonies and it felt as though my small town
had been invaded by a swarm of psychedelic locusts. The Vietnam War
was ending, but someone had spraypainted dripping, blood-red peace
signs all over the library and the general store. The antique bandstand
on the village green hosted a round-the-clock miniature Woodstock of
blaring FM rock and stolen six-packs and screaming matches with the
constable. The last thing I wanted to hear about in school was the case
for free expression and more chaos.

Not only didn't I welcome Mr. Durkee's ideas about Holden as a
proto-hippie, I didn't believe them. This Holden character was a good
kid; a privileged softy. Sure he drank and smoked a little and was given
to moody, irritable funks, but he also fretted about his family and tried
to do the right thing more often than not. Mostly, he just seemed bored
and very tired. Funny, too, though I dared not laugh at him out of
respect for Serious Literature. This was grave business, Holden's nonconformism, and when Mr. Durkee finally closed the book, he asked
the class whether Holden was insane or if his "repressive era" was at
fault—for being so hypocritical, so bland, so dull, so intolerant. The
"era," we said, since we knew a test was coming.

To me, though, the era sounded, well, beautiful. The tidy parks with
their flocks of fluffy ducks. The glamorous restaurants that served
drinks to minors. The museums. The trains. The crime-free avenues.
New York, as pictured on the evening news, was a hellhole of muggers
and uncollected garbage, of sidewalks strewn with junkies' hypo-
dermics, and to think that there had been this golden decade when
teenagers could roam about at night there, checking in to hotels and
blithely wandering—repressive? Hardly. It sounded like a blast.

———❖———

My first college roommate was a Long Island Quaker who spent the
evenings playing acoustic guitar while I sat on my bunk bed and drank
beer and tried to sing along. The songs were mournful, idealistic, sensitive. Neil Young. James Taylor. The hits from *Godspell*. When my
roommate's fingers got tired, we played the radio—a New York folk

rock station, mellow and uplifting—while discussing, oh I don't know, nuclear disarmament. We were terribly liberal, out to save the world, though secretly lonesome for our homes and families. The important big books we pretended to admire weren't sinking in as deeply as they should have been and I, for one, felt like a phony amid the ivy.

One night it came in over the radio, into our smoggy little Princeton dorm room with its paisley batiks and Jimmy Hendrix poster and towering stereo speakers and two-foot bong, that John Lennon, the Beatle, had been assassinated outside his apartment building near Central Park. My roommate collapsed. He genuinely grieved. I envied his responsiveness to tragedy and figured that it was due to his ability to picture the scene of the crime, which I found difficult, having never visited Manhattan.

All I knew of Central Park and its environs came from Salinger and Mr. Durkee. It seemed like such a cheerful place, full of strollers and charming eccentrics and young families. I decided to refresh my memory by opening *The Catcher in the Rye* for the first time since junior high. This was a big mistake. A Lennon mourner caught me in the act, grabbed the paperback away from me, and tossed it across the dining hall. Only later did I find out why. Lennon's killer, according to the news, had been fixated on the novel, and in its pages had discerned some sort of secret message authorizing his crime.

Now I was really intrigued. I'd gotten the book wrong again, it seemed. The first time around I'd missed its radical message about nonconformism and so on, and this time I'd missed its advocacy of violence toward multimillionaire rock musicians. I read it again, but I couldn't find the part that compelled Mark David Chapman to blaze away. This novel that had seemed to me once so breezy and straightforward—a couple of days in the life of a glum wisecracker who couldn't quite figure out where he was going and ached for all the people he'd left behind. But I had to admit the book had power. Wow! What power! To throw an entire generation into a social and philosophical uproar, as Mr. Durkee had taught, and then to whisper evilly in the ear of a grandiose music fan with a loaded pistol.

I knew by now that Salinger was a recluse, but I also happened to know that one of his children, a son, was somewhere on the campus, a

Princeton student. I had someone point him out to me one day. He was tall and athletic and handsome. This baffled me. I expected an odder, less conventional creature. Someone with wrinkled slacks. So much for looking to life to help with books. Still, it was exciting to see the guy and have secondhand proof of his father's physicality.

My literature classes didn't help me deepen my understanding of the novel. The Princeton English Department, just then, was in a phase of high obscurity, and readable modern American authors such as Salinger weren't part of the syllabus. Desperate to take on the snobbery of my teachers, I came to regard the old hermit's books as classy young-adult fiction in a league with *Old Yeller*, *Black Beauty*, and *A Separate Peace*. The pleasure I took in Holden's voice (once I learned to distinguish it from Mr. Durkee's) was Exhibit A in the case against his greatness.

—————

I published my first book in my late twenties, a collection of stories on modest hometown subjects that featured several teenage narrators and reminded some reviewers of Salinger. This wasn't the wonderful compliment it seemed. Write about a white male under twenty in this country and you're sure to be compared to Salinger—never wholly favorably, even when the critic likes the book, and even when he makes it clear that he considers Salinger himself dated, minor, light, or overrated. Comparing young male writers to Salinger is code for saying they have a way to go before they become important, mature, profound.

The comparisons made no sense to me. My reactions to Holden Caulfield had always been personal, despite others' urgings to view him as an artifact of cultural, not actual, history. To me he was, above all else, an Easterner, and privileged in ways that I had never been. A gifted family, artistic, cosmopolitan. An expensive private education. Exposure to Broadway, to world-class museums. The learning, sophistication, and experience that Holden threw away in a few days would have lit up my small-town high school for a year.

The kid was sent to a madhouse, for heaven's sake, and madhouses were for rich folks. The farmers and Mormon kids I was writing about wouldn't have known who to go to for a reference to a respectable madhouse. What baloney.

But I picked up the book again, anyway. Just curious. It had been years and I'd forgotten most of it, which is always how it happens with novels I love. People tell me that the mark of a great book is the way it sticks with you, stays vivid over time, but I disagree. The best books fade into the scenery, dissolve into instant backdrop, return to dust. But that dust is never the same, it's changed forever. The book hangs on like a spore inside soil, and now and then it's suddenly reactivated by certain conditions of temperature and moisture.

The book had been reactivated in me every eight years or so. This was our third round. I fully expected that it would be our last. My intention was to erase whatever influence it might have had on my own beginner's fiction. Either that or determine that it had no influence; that my stories were as original as I'd hoped.

I sat on a porch in Montana, where I lived, far, far away from the scenes of Holden's delinquency, and sought to clear my head of Mr. Durkee, the dead John Lennon, and my Princeton professors. Too much static. I wanted a clear signal. Holden and I would meet out in the open, shake hands, and—I hoped—be finished with each other.

The edition was not the one I'd read before. Its cover was illustrated, not solid red, and featured a kid in a trench coat and hunting cap against a blurred background that looked like New York City. And though it showed Holden as Salinger described him and as most careful readers surely picture him, the image bewildered me. It was too fixed, too specific, too inert. Where was Mr. Durkee's young radical? Chapman's dark muse? The author's handsome son? Where was my own preferred vision of the character, the exhausted, cranky, preppy softy?

I read the book in one sitting, as usual, and forgot it even faster than in the past. I'd turn a page and look up from the porch, across the street at the neighbor's station wagon and his yard full of rusty tricycles and crabgrass, and the preceding page would vaporize. Good-bye slobby roommate. Good-bye old pederast. Good-bye ducks. Good-bye Central Park. Good-bye kid sister. At the end, Holden says how he misses everyone, a stroke that always comes as a surprise to me and seems both too broad and sloppy and too brilliant. I said good-bye to that, too, then shut my eyes. My conscious, definitive reading was over, leaving me with . . . what? As a writer myself, it was time I pegged this book, assessed its technique, its style, its larger context. But nothing came. Just self-centered memories. Watching a school custodian mow grass. Singing Neil Young songs in a filthy dorm room. Hearing a radio bulletin: "Former Beatle . . ." Standing next to a mailbox in Montana, reading the first reviews of my own stories.

The best books vanish. I don't know where they go. One looks for them and only finds one's self. And then, under strange new circumstances, they're back. An editor phones and tells me he's compiling a book on Salinger, and though I thought I was rid of that damned novel, here it is once more, open on my desk. How maddening. It's as if I'm being stalked. I'm sure that it's gone, that I'm free, but then I turn . . .

Mr. Durkee, was it the same for you?

Mr. Pater's Last Volume

OSCAR WILDE

When I first had the privilege—and I count it a very high one—of meeting Mr. Walter Pater, he said to me, smiling, "Why do you always write poetry? Why do you not write prose? Prose is so much more difficult."

It was during my undergraduate days at Oxford; days of lyrical ardours and of studious sonnet-writing; days when one loved the exquisite intricacy and musical repetitions of the ballade, and the villanelle with its linked long-drawn echoes and its curious completeness; days when one solemnly sought to discover the proper temper in which a triolet should be written; delightful days, in which, I am glad to say, there was far more rhyme than reason.

I may frankly confess now that at the time I did not quite comprehend what Mr. Pater really meant; and it was not till I had carefully studied his beautiful and suggestive essays on the Renaissance that I fully realised what a wonderful self-conscious art the art of English prose-writing really is, or may be made to be. Carlyle's stormy rhetoric, Ruskin's winged and passionate eloquence, had seemed to me to spring from enthusiasm rather than from art. I don't think I knew then that even prophets correct their proofs. As for Jacobean prose, I thought it too exuberant; and Queen Anne prose appeared to me terribly bald, and irritatingly rational. But Mr. Pater's essays became to me "the golden book of spirit and sense, the holy writ of beauty." They are still this to me. It is possible, of course, that I may exaggerate about them. I certainly hope that I do; for where there is no exaggeration there is no love, and where there is no love there is no understanding. It is only about things that do not interest one, that one can give a really unbiassed opinion; and this is no doubt the reason why an unbiassed opinion is always absolutely valueless.

But I must not allow this brief notice of Mr. Pater's new volume to degenerate into an autobiography. I remember being told in America that whenever Margaret Fuller wrote an essay upon Emerson the printers had always to send out to borrow some additional capital "I's," and I feel it right to accept this transatlantic warning.

"Appreciations," in the fine Latin sense of the word, is the title given by Mr. Pater to his book, which is an exquisite collection of exquisite essays, of delicately wrought works of art—some of them being almost Greek in their purity of outline and perfection of form, others mediæval in their strangeness of colour and passionate suggestion, and all of them absolutely modern, in the true meaning of the term modernity. For he to whom the present is the only thing that is present, knows nothing of the age in which he lives. To realise the nineteenth century, one must realise every century that has preceded it, and that has contributed to its making. To know anything about oneself, one must know all about others. There must be no mood with which one cannot sympathise, no dead mode of life that one cannot make alive. The legacies of heredity may make us alter our views of moral responsibility, but they cannot but intensify our sense of the value of Criticism; for the true critic is he who bears within himself the dreams and ideas and feelings of myriad generations, and to whom no form of thought is alien, no emotional impulse obscure.

Perhaps the most interesting, and certainly the least successful, of the essays contained in the present volume is that on "Style." It is the most interesting because it is the work of one who speaks with the high authority that comes from the noble realisation of things nobly conceived. It is the least successful, because the subject is too abstract. A true artist like Mr. Pater, is most felicitous when he deals with the concrete, whose very limitations give him finer freedom, while they necessitate more intense vision. And yet what a high ideal is contained in these few pages! How good it is for us, in these days of popular education and facile journalism, to be reminded of the real scholarship that is essential to the perfect writer, who, "being a true lover of words for their own sake, a minute and constant observer of their physiognomy," will avoid what is mere rhetoric, or ostentatious ornament, or negligent misuse of terms, or ineffective surplusage, and will be known by his tact of omission, by his skilful economy of means, by his selection and self-restraint, and perhaps above all by that conscious artistic structure which is the expression of mind in style. I think I have been wrong in saying that the subject is too abstract. In Mr. Pater's hands it becomes very real to us indeed, and he shows us how, behind the perfection of a man's style, must lie the passion of a man's soul.

As one passes to the rest of the volume, one finds essays on Wordsworth and on Coleridge, on Charles Lamb and on Sir Thomas Browne, on some of Shakespeare's plays and on the English kings that Shakespeare fashioned, on Dante Rossetti, and on William Morris. As that on Wordsworth seems to be Mr. Pater's last work, so that on the singer of the "Defence of Guenevere" is certainly his earliest, or almost his earliest, and it is interesting to mark the change that has taken place in his style. This change is, perhaps, at first sight not very apparent. In 1868 we find Mr. Pater writing with the same exquisite care for words, with the same studied music, with the same temper, and something of the same mode of treatment. But, as he goes on, the architecture of the style becomes richer and more complex, the epithet more precise and intellectual. Occasionally one may be inclined to think that there is, here and there, a sentence which is somewhat long, and possibly, if one may venture to say so, a little heavy and cumbersome in movement. But if this be so, it comes from those side-issues suddenly suggested by the idea in its progress, and really revealing the idea more perfectly; or from those felicitous after-thoughts that give a fuller completeness to the central scheme, and yet convey something of the charm of chance;

or from a desire to suggest the secondary shades of meaning with all their accumulating effect, and to avoid, it may be, the violence and harshness of too definite and exclusive an opinion. For in matters of art, at any rate, thought is inevitably coloured by emotion, and so is fluid rather than fixed, and, recognising its dependence upon moods and upon the passion of fine moments, will not accept the rigidity of a scientific formula or a theological dogma. The critical pleasure, too, that we receive from tracing, through what may seem the intricacies of a sentence, the working of the constructive intelligence, must not be overlooked. As soon as we have realised the design, everything appears clear and simple. After a time, these long sentences of Mr. Pater's come to have the charm of an elaborate piece of music, and the unity of such music also.

I have suggested that the essay on Wordsworth is probably the most recent bit of work contained in this volume. If one might choose between so much that is good, I should be inclined to say it is the finest also. The essay on Lamb is curiously suggestive; suggestive, indeed, of a somewhat more tragic, more sombre figure, than men have been wont to think of in connection with the author of the Essays of Elia. It is an interesting aspect under which to regard Lamb, but perhaps he himself would have had some difficulty in recognising the portrait given of him. He had, undoubtedly, great sorrows, or motives for sorrow, but he could console himself at a moment's notice for the real tragedies of life by reading any one of the Elizabethan tragedies, provided it was in a folio edition. The essay on Sir Thomas Browne is delightful, and has the strange, personal, fanciful charm of the author of the "Religio Medici"; Mr. Pater often catching the colour and accent and tone of whatever artist, or work of art, he deals with. That on Coleridge, with its insistence on the necessity of the cultivation of the relative, as opposed to the absolute spirit in philosophy and in ethics, and its high appreciation of the poet's true position in our literature, is in style and substance a very blameless work. Grace of expression, and delicate subtlety of thought and phrase, characterise the essays on Shakespeare. But the essay on Wordsworth has a spiritual beauty of its own. It appeals, not to the ordinary Wordsworthian with his uncritical temper, and his gross confusion of ethical with æsthetical problems, but rather to those who desire to separate the gold from the dross, and to reach at the true Wordsworth through the mass of tedious and prosaic work that bears his name, and that serves often to conceal him from us. The presence of an alien element in Wordsworth's art, is, of course, recognised by Mr. Pater but he touches on it merely from the psychological point of view, pointing out how this quality of higher and lower moods gives the effect in his poetry "of a power not altogether his own, or under his control"; a power which comes and goes when it wills, "so that the old fancy which made the poet's art an enthusiasm, a form of divine possession, seems almost true of him." Mr. Pater's earlier essays had their *purpurei panni*, so eminently suitable for quotation, such as the famous passage on Monna Lisa, and that other in which Botticelli's strange conception of the Virgin is so strangely set forth. From the present volume it is difficult to select any one passage in preference to another as specially characteristic of Mr. Pater's treatment. This, however, is worth quoting at length. It contains a truth eminently useful for our age:—

> That the end of life is not action but contemplation—*being* as distinct from *doing*—a certain disposition of the mind: is, in some shape or other, the principle of all the higher morality. In poetry, in art, if you enter into their true spirit at all, you touch this principle in a measure; these, by their very sterility, are a type of beholding for the mere joy of beholding. To treat life in the spirit of art is to make life a thing in which means and ends are identified: to encourage such treatment, the true moral significance of art and poetry. Wordsworth, and other poets who have been like him in ancient or more recent times, are the masters, the experts, in this art of impassioned contemplation. Their work is not to teach lessons, or enforce rules, or even to stimulate us to noble ends, but to withdraw the thoughts for a while from the mere machinery of life, to fix them, with appropriate emotions, on the spectacle of those great facts in man's existence which no machinery affects, "on the great and universal passions of men, the most general and interesting of their occupations, and the entire world of nature"—on "the operations of the elements and the

appearances of the visible universe, on storm and sunshine, on the revolutions of the seasons, on cold and heat, on loss of friends and kindred, on injuries and resentments, on gratitude and hope, on fear and sorrow." To witness this spectacle with appropriate emotions is the aim of all culture; and of these emotions poetry like Wordsworth's is a great nourisher and stimulant. He sees nature full of sentiment and excitement; he sees men and women as parts of nature, passionate, excited, in strange grouping and connection with the grandeur and beauty of the natural world:—images, in his own words, "of man suffering, amid awful forms and powers."

Certainly the real secret of Wordsworth has never been better expressed. After having read and re-read Mr. Pater's essay—for it requires re-reading—one returns to the poet's work with a new sense of joy and wonder, and with something of eager and impassioned expectation. And perhaps this might be roughly taken as the test or touchstone of the finest criticism.

Finally, one cannot help noticing the delicate instinct that has gone to fashion the brief epilogue that ends this delightful volume. The difference between the classical and romantic spirits in art has often, and with much over-emphasis, been discussed. But with what a light sure touch does Mr. Pater write of it. How subtle and certain are his distinctions! If imaginative prose be really special art of this century, Mr. Pater must rank amongst our century's most characteristic artists. In certain things he stands almost alone. The age has produced wonderful prose styles, turbid with individualism, and violent with excess of rhetoric. But in Mr. Pater, as in Cardinal Newman, we find the union of personality with perfection. He has no rival in his own sphere, and he has escaped disciples. And this, not because he has not been imitated, but because in art so fine as his there is something that, in its essence, is inimitable.

Into Some Wild Places with Hemingway

FRED SETTERBERG

> *He was always a little frightened of the woods at night. He opened the flap of the tent and undressed and lay very quietly between the blankets in the dark. . . . He was not afraid of anything definite as yet. But he was getting very afraid. Then suddenly he was afraid of dying.*
>
> —Ernest Hemingway, "Indian Camp"

When Ann proposed that we escape for a long weekend in the country, I turned to a volume of Hemingway short stories to set my bearings. The story I had in mind was "Big Two-Hearted River," an old favorite featuring Nick Adams, Hemingway's fictional World War I veteran, recently returned from the Italian front.

Nothing much happens in "Big Two-Hearted River." Nick tramps several miles into the forest somewhere in Michigan's Upper Peninsula. He makes camp, fishes, cleans the fish, cooks dinner; before folding himself up in a blanket to sleep, he extinguishes a hapless mosquito that has lit upon the canvas flap of his tent. The mosquito hisses and flares into oblivion upon the nub of a match.

A summary of the story's plot falls desperately short of the excitement contained in the "big" Hemingway novels—say, Robert Jordan blowing up Spanish bridges in *For Whom the Bell Tolls*. Yet the small moments in "Big Two-Hearted River" have always meant a good deal to me. Ten years ago, when it seemed that everybody was logging sacramental time outdoors, I inserted a mental bookmark in my own memory, reminding me to consult "Big Two-Hearted River" whenever I began to lose track of the best reasons for spending a few days in the woods. I recognize that it sounds pretty foolish when a guy needs a book to remind him to go outside. But "Big Two-Hearted River" is one of American literature's most practical outdoor guides. It's also Hemingway at his zenith: not the swaggering bully of our worst recollections, slaughtering animals carelessly, boozing suicidally, squandering his great talent and years in self-parody. Rather, the story reveals what Alfred Kazin has called "the fierce love that Hemingway, beyond anyone else of this time and place, brought to Nature in America." It's this fierceness that has always drawn me to Hemingway, particularly when it's suitably rooted within the natural world, rather than paired to the domestic brutalities of the author's later life and lesser books. But despite the worst that anybody can say about Hemingway, the precision of every gesture in "Big Two-Hearted River" rings eternally true. Every time I read the story, I stumble upon something new. Or even better, I recall something I've forgotten, thanks to the distractions of everyday life in the city.

From his earliest moments in the woods, Hemingway's hero, Nick Adams, thwarts all distractions. Nick makes a study of his campsite, his careful discipline emphasizing a passion for order, the rigor for detail that is the mark of a true outdoorsman. Nick's routine even compels us to believe that a tin of coffee boiling over the morning campfire should taste snugly delicious. Nobody drinks boiled coffee today. But the image of the white-hot metal pot steaming over the flames reminds me pleasantly of a dozen sloppy excursions of my own into the woods and mountains with my buddies as a teenager and young man. I recall now that we always let the coffee boil, burned the dinner over the campsite's stone-rimmed ring of uncontrollable flames, and woke up in a haze of black flies spread across

316 | The Story About the Story

a landscape of sand bogs. We weren't outdoorsmen. And really, that's the point of once again leafing through the pages of "Big Two-Hearted River": it's sweet to take a fluttery glance back at our own first stumblings out into the wilderness. I can see three or four of us now—rawboned, rangy, obscene teenagers—standing upon the curl of some granite ledge, flushed with heat and discovery. We're perched up there on that stony lip, out of the house at last and far from safety, combing the woods for signs of life, maybe catching sight of something small and puny like a rabbit or lizard—maybe ridiculously bumping into a cow if we've strayed off the trail onto grazing land. And yet we're thrilled to be there, callow and puny ourselves, sharing the view with creatures we can mostly only imagine, trodding upon the vegetation that we can't begin to identify.

It's the dirt-real feeling of this memory, coupled forever to one of my favorite short stories, that I'll always cherish. And that's one reason I agreed with Ann that we should leave the city as soon as possible and get out into the woods.

Another good reason to leave the city was that the city we were visiting was Detroit.

We'd just passed a week in the suburbs, handling some unexpected family business. At the end of each day we circled back around the city to locate our hotel, skirting Detroit's burned-out core of crumbling redbrick tenements and the flattened, flame-scorched lots that lay corner-to-side like chains of fractured dominos.

On our last night in town, Ann traced our escape route along the AAA road map spread across the hotel carpet, speculating which highway would lead us the farthest fastest. Ann advocated a trip to the Porcupine Mountains Wilderness, mainly on the strength of its name. She improvised a vision of friendly porcupine armies swarming out of the forest to surround our tent in the evening like trench fortifications. (In the spooky woods that neither of us knew, some spiky line of defense would have suited me too.) But a trip to the Upper Peninsula's western mountains could cost us another day, requiring passage that looped the far way around Wisconsin. Instead we shot past Saginaw Bay City, Grayling, and Mackinaw City, straight across the gleaming arch of the Mackinac Bridge. I had another reason for urging us due north. If we headed to the Upper Peninsula's farthest coast, we'd eventually strike the territory described in "Big Two-Hearted River." Finally, we'd hit the Two-Hearted River itself.

Over the years, I'd told Ann more than she wanted to hear about "Big Two-Hearted River." I'd last read Hemingway on a solo camping trip to Northern California's Mount Lassen the summer before. And I had returned home from the forest full of praise for the same old story.

While it's true that many of Mount Lassen's cold-water lakes and wooded ridges resemble the territory described in "Big Two-Hearted River," I was otherwise treading upon shaky ground. Lassen is most noticeably a geothermal region, offering a ragged smorgasbord of topographical bewilderments not found anywhere in Hemingway: painted sand dunes, sage flats settled upon river canyons, alpine meadows melting into lava beds, gurgling fumaroles, bubbling mud pots, and devilish pools of boiling water. Patched together, it's a boggled landscape; no wonder the camper hordes haven't yet got a handle on what the place offers. Unlike Yosemite, which stands only 150 miles to the southeast, Lassen boasts no celebrated vacation valley clogged with ardent hikers, no famous luxury lodge, no afternoon gridlock. Neither is there any justifiable reason for me to have inserted Hemingway where he surely never stood, but that's how stubbornly the story could pull me back into its pages. It may sound silly, but it's true: whenever I found myself alone in the woods, I conjured up visions of Hemingway the Outdoorsman, patron saint to incompetent campers like me.

As we drove across the Straits of Mackinac and slid onto the Upper Peninsula, I droned on pedantically about the flora and fauna to be found up in Michigan—at least, as I understood it from my latest reading of "Big Two-Hearted River" the night before back in Detroit. Off the road, past Epoufette, we passed the charred remains of the previous year's forest fires, the poor-shave stubble of blackened tree stumps that brought to mind the devastation Nick Adams encountered when he hopped off the train near Seney to trudge past hillsides of burnt timber. In the story, Nick notices that even the grasshoppers were "all turned black from living in the burned-over land." The fire traces we encountered among the stands of sugar maple and yellow birch were not as severe, but they echoed the same hollow note of devastation—the persistent theme, as Nick Adams understands only too well, that wild country signifies "tragic adventure."

In truth, most wild places offer a great deal more tragic adventure than city visitors can digest. Back in Lassen, I recalled, the rocky flats spit vaporous sulphur and the mudholes bubbled up like campfire goulash. But Michigan's Upper Peninsula is a more subtle landscape. The forest throngs of trees, shrubs, ferns, and flowers press forward from the choppy, low-sloping hills and shaded river banks, not in a sweeping uniform assault upon the senses but rather as a succession of mysterious layers, peeled back at the corners or fanned like a fistful of playing cards. First you notice the immense bouquets of hemlock and jack pine, and then the interspersed stands of black ash or balsam fir, and somewhere deeper into the woods you might finally stumble upon black spruce rising up amid the floating mats of murky-vert lake vegetation that the pioneering species had originally colonized. The dark forest is a thickset, lively place, and who can say what you'll find there?

In "Big Two-Hearted River," Nick finds a moment of peace amid a world of hazards. "His muscles ached and the day was hot, but Nick felt happy. He felt he had left everything behind, the need for thinking, the need to write, other needs. It was all back of him."

Ford Madox Ford rightly observed that Hemingway's "words strike you as if they were pebbles fetched fresh from a brook. They live and shine, each in its place. So one of his pages has the effect of a brook-bottom into which you look down through the floating water." In "Big Two-Hearted River," Nick also sees straight through our most popular illusions about nature. He has spent enough time in the Michigan woods to know that they're merely a temporary hedge against the outside world. Hemingway could never shake from his adult imagination the dark forest of his boyhood.

Even after he had finished the working draft of "Big Two-Hearted River," the unforgettable texture of the land forced him to confess to Gertrude Stein his desire "to write about the country so it would be there like Cézanne had done it in painting." Of course, the Upper Peninsula's devastated area, both in the story and from what Ann and I now saw spread before us, could never have been justly contained by the gauzy impressionists. Burned-over land demands Bosch or Brueghel, painters whom Hemingway also admired; all three artists were interested in fierce places. But in his longing to set it down on paper, I suspect that Hemingway was expressing the understandable urge of a man who both loves and dreads nature. He wanted to round up the wild things and draw borders around their persistent threat; he'd feel safer if he could wrap the wilderness in a printed page. I think many people feel this way. If not on canvas or in a story to be retold to the folks back home, then at least in our own indelible memories we desire to contain nature, though we know damn well that we can't. I suppose that's what *I'm* trying to do now: double-wrapping the wilderness in newsprint as I swab together recollections of my last stay in the woods with expectations for the next—with both dreams of the outdoors lashed into a single piece upon the fictional frame of "Big Two-Hearted River."

I know it feels tempting sometimes to bundle up the wilderness and carry it back home. But I also think it's an unsound practice and doomed to fail. The wilderness isn't just an idea. For the present, at least, it's still an actual place that demands our respect the minute we set foot there. That's what Dave Foreman, founder of Earth First! and an unusually rough-hewn environmentalist, straight out of Hemingway, is growling to whoever will listen these days. "It's not really wilderness," explains Foreman, "unless there's something bigger and meaner than you in there."

Hemingway was forever concerned about the lurkings of bigger, meaner things out in the world. In his fiction and throughout his life, this lasting anxiety led him to ask incessantly: Am I a brave man? It seems an odd question for a writer—by definition, a bookish person. Certainly the matter of physical courage doesn't come up much in evaluations of Faulkner, Steinbeck, Dos Passos, and the rest. But the unique relationship between Hemingway's work and the Hemingway myth makes it hard to ignore the question.

Was Hemingway a brave man? And if so, why does Nick Adams seem so frightened out in the woods?

Zelda Fitzgerald took an instant dislike to Hemingway, advising her husband Scott that the blustery young man from Michigan was "bogus" and "phony as a rubber check." Gertrude Stein, after being repeatedly wounded by the writer's legendary ingratitude, struck back in *The Autobiography of Alice B. Toklas* by calling him yellow "just like the flat-boat men on the Mississippi river described by Mark Twain"—a particularly nasty turn of the knife, given Hemingway's contention that American literature owed everything to *The Adventures of Huckleberry Finn*.

Of course, the rest of the world generally held a closer course to the Hemingway myth, the supermasculine re-creation of the writer as warrior, hunter, athlete, patriarch, and tribal chieftain. "He has the most profound bravery that it has ever been my privilege to see," wrote Dorothy Parker, in an uncharacteristically breathless and profoundly inaccurate piece of reporting for the *New Yorker* in 1929. Parker had fallen hard for Hemingway's war stories. Wounded by shrapnel in a trench shelling, Hemingway had amplified his injuries with nonexistent machine-gun fire. By the time he returned home to Oak Park, Illinois, he was telling friends, family, and reporters that he had been hit thirty-two times by .45-caliber bullets (he hadn't); that he was the first American wounded in Italy (he knew that he wasn't); and that he had fought in three crucial battles as an officer with the *Arditi*, Italy's crack shock troops (he had never even tried to join). All these fictitious reports survived in various scholarly and popular accounts of the author's life until Kenneth Lynn's debunking biography, published in the 1980s.

Yet Parker was right in essence, if not detail. Hemingway was a courageous person not because of the foolhardy risks he took all his life, but more because of the fact, as Norman Mailer once speculated, "that his inner landscape was a nightmare, and he spent his nights wrestling with the gods . . . that he carried a weight of anxiety with him which would have suffocated any man smaller than himself."

"As to Ernest as a boy," Fitzgerald confided in correspondence to a friend, "it is undeniable that the dark was peopled for him."

In rare circumstances, Hemingway could even admit it. In 1976, the great writer's son Gregory revealed that his father told him "about the times he'd been scared as a boy, how he used to dream about a furry monster who would grow taller and taller every night and then, just as it was about to eat him, would jump over the fence. He said fear was perfectly natural and nothing to be ashamed of. The trick to mastering it was controlling your imagination."

<hr />

We run to the woods to see what we can't imagine at home—or perhaps what we fear to observe too closely. But we still have to pack up and carry into the dark forest our old city selves.

By the time Ann and I cut a path to the Fox River through the bright flush of speckled alder thickets and the flowering bramble of blue flag, I had already been chattering away for several hours about Hemingway, Nick Adams, and all the devious ways that nature both comforted and terrorized the two of them. Ann had heard just about enough of that. She slid her pack straps off her shoulders, plopped the heavy bundle onto the ground, and rocked back against it like an overturned tortoise. She had her own book to stick her nose into.

Ann had come fully armed with a stack of terrain guides, each bountifully illustrated with trail photographs and precise, blazing-color identification plates, those *Baedekers* of birds and flowers. She studied her guidebooks and noted the profusion of wildflowers. She announced that seven hundred species of ferns, herbs, shrubs, grasses, and trees were gathered in Michigan's Upper Peninsula. They represented about seventy-five plant families. Even trying to separate one from another was hopeless. Wildlife fared somewhat better. The most common mammals were the low-slung, stealthy rodents whose relatives we'd just left back in Detroit. Alert and persistent, we might catch a glimpse of a rat, mouse, mole, vole, or shrew. A truly fortunate sighting would be a snowshoe hare or red fox, or, at night, perhaps a pine marten or lynx. There were black bears prowling and reports of moose and timber wolf.

The author of Ann's best guidebook expressed an expert's detachment from this profusion of wildlife. And he took even greater pains to mark his distance from the common two-legged mammals—specifically, the outsiders and know-nothings, city people like us. We should not get too excited, he cautioned, too *poetic*, about the outdoors and its accumulation of creatures who were, after all, only natural. His authoritative voice took relish in driving home the stiffest facts about the natural world's real character: the grisly truth was that all of the delightful creatures inhabiting our outdoors playground, this peaceable kingdom stretching from pine barren to sylvan glade, were at bottom hungry creatures, and they dined unmercifully each day upon one another's flesh, muscle, and bone.

We sentimentalize nature. But nature is no more a peaceable kingdom than Detroit: that is another message to be gleaned from "Big Two-Hearted River" with its burned-back woods and burned-black grasshoppers. As more explicit evidence, Ann read aloud an outdoors parable from her guidebook about the last bright morning of an inverte-brate leafhopper residing along the Upper Peninsula's shore. It seemed that at sunrise this leafhopper fully achieved his own tragic adventure: he was eaten by a water scorpion who was then devoured by a lake trout who was immediately snapped up by a large garter snake who was sub-sequently gobbled down whole by a great blue heron.

Of course, all this murder and devouring is another reason we enjoy the outdoors. Close to the massacre, we can exercise our own rudest human nature. Naturally, we want to peep and gawk: it's *interesting* to stumble upon one creature munching up another. (I am always keen for campers' stories about how they were unable to turn away from the spectacle of a wolf disemboweling a fallen deer with its furious paws.) And that's because it's hard to justify this kind of curiosity back in the city. After a few days spent in the barbarous woods, I think most of us are glad to return home to the relative peace of urban life. The city is a safe haven where our position at the top of the food chain remains taste-fully obscured by the convenience of Safeway's meat market; where our trout, unstuffed with scorpion, is wrapped in a sheaf of microwavable plastic.

How smug and bloodless our own dinners must be—how distracted the munching and crunching. Maybe that's why we find ourselves a bit hungry after a time for all the bloody stuff.

Earlier in the week, before leaving Detroit, Ann and I had watched a family friend perform in the ghoulish Stephen Sondheim musical *Sweeney Todd*. In one of the most affecting scenes, Sweeney, the mad, throat-slitting demon barber of Fleet Street, who stuffed *his* victims into the worst meat pies in London, stepped to the front of the stage and sang with piquant affection: "The history of the world, my sweet . . . Is who gets eaten and who gets to eat." This line, noted our actor friend, always got a great rise of recognition and revulsion from the audience. Danger, everywhere, danger.

We venture into the woods because it's a great, dangerous place. That's what Ann's guidebook, "Big Two-Hearted River," and our own instincts insist we understand. And when we emerge safely, we're pleased and confident. Maybe we're even a little astonished.

As Ann and I stumbled through a stand of dark-crowned hemlock, sweating pleasantly in the cool shade amid the calls of warblers, woodpeckers, and chickadees, Ann told me about an old boyfriend whom years ago she had dragged through the northern California redwoods. Fit and ruggedly athletic, the former Marine protested that he feared the peaceable kingdom. She thought he must be joking. When they hiked along the fern-patched trails, shaded over even at noon by the camouflage of the redwoods' cathedral bowers, he got shaky. Fallen branches crackled underfoot: he wanted to turn back. Scampish ground squirrels ricocheted across their path, bouncing furiously from tree trunk to burrow, rolling across the layered mulch carpet like hoppity grenades. Her ex-Marine boyfriend blanched and refused to take another step; and then he explained: Vietnam.

We slip into the woods for peace and quiet, and we find that. But we also find the world at war with itself. Nature's wonderous complexity turns out to be a code word for the constant state of siege. Ground squirrels and the sharp report of branches cracking underfoot remind us that we're easy targets.

"Big Two-Hearted River" got that right too. Nick Adams, veteran of the Italian front, finally cannot distract himself from his own bloody experiences beyond the wilderness. In fact, the accumulated pressure of World War I has long been held up as a critical key to unlocking the deeper meaning of the Hemingway story. Kazin explains that "Big Two-Hearted River" is really about "a soldier back from the First World War, seeking on a fishing trip to empty his troubled mind." Nick's recollection of the war causes him to become "obsessively concerned with every detail as he makes camp in a section of burned land." It leads him to "the swamp" where "fishing was tragic adventure." Edmund Wilson talked about Nick Adams's "touch of panic" in the Michigan woods; he attributed the flaw in Nick's calm to "the wholesale shattering of human beings in which he has taken part." Hemingway himself plainly stated that the story was about "coming back from the war but there was no mention of the war in it."

The story informs us that the woods—and the world—are wilder places than we like to admit. We can find wilderness, places containing "something bigger and meaner" than ourselves, wherever we go.

There's always something worth fearing out there, and it is by our own terrors that we come to know ourselves.

And yet, sometimes our terror is thrilling.

I'm thinking right now about some fellows I knew years ago from Deadwood, South Dakota, who scrambled through urban landscapes as though our cities were the wildest places on earth. I first met the Deadwood boys at a dull professional meeting in Salt Lake City. Warding off Sunday morning blue laws, they had imported several cases of beer for a wide-open hotel-room bash. Later they showed up in Oakland: hicks on the loose, they bragged. Most exhilarating to these rustics, veterans of the South Dakota high plains and prairies who professed admiration for the worst and wildest that the peaceable kingdom could throw at them, was the prospect of being killed in the city. They might be mangled on the busy freeway, fall off a skyscraper, run into the point of a mugger's knife because of their incautious hick detours. The jungle of cities offered them risks that home could not provide. During the winter, buried in snow back in Deadwood, they would lull themselves into dangerous dreams about the kind of wildness they missed on a daily basis. No longer on the loose, the hicks studied Bellow, Roth, Nelson Algren, and James T. Farrell for insight into the urban badlands.

Of course, books should open up all kinds of experience. They should pry us loose, nudge us into the country, cast us off into the city. But books cannot contain the whole story. When we try to preserve what we feel most deeply, most *suddenly*, between the pages of a book—a slick technique for smoothing out the fearful creases—we also run the risk of pressing flat the experience once the book is finally slapped shut.

Experience should leap out at us.

<hr />

A yellow-mottled cat leapt out at us on the two-lane blacktop skirting the Two-Hearted River. It had scrambled out from the brush and slipped under my car's left front wheel. I could feel the car roll up, then over, the cat's body. We pulled to the side.

Years ago, I hit a slick black Labrador retriever near my home. At the time, I drove a 1963 Chevy Impala. The dog glanced off its bumper, sailing wonderfully across the street. His haunches curled up towards his gaping jaws, his white eyes throbbed, and his pink tongue flapped with enthusiasm; he looked like a great heap of animated coal merrily cannonaded. When the Labrador retriever hit the dirt with a dusty scrape, he yelped once, galloped into his front yard, and frothed like a braggart while whipping his tail around the legs of his nonchalant master. The dog was okay, his owner assured me, no problem, no sweat, happens all the time.

Now, like everybody else, I drive a little Japanese four-banger: lucky for the cat up in Michigan.

She picked herself up from the road and shot back into the woods. It seemed impossible that she wasn't dead. Finally, Ann located her among the seven hundred species of ferns, shrubs, and grasses. She bled from the hind legs. I think she recognized us as her assailants: her eyes cried alarm, and she flitted back across the field, slipping into a drainage pipe. Maybe now she could nurse her hindquarters in the darkness, or die privately, miserably, from unseen wounds.

Our duty was clear. We had hit her, though of course, it had been an accident. But we were the cause of her pain, and now we had to make the pain stop. We had to rescue her. Or if the injury proved too grave, we had to kill her; in any case, we needed to stop her pain. But I think we both knew that, as city people, we might not measure up to the task; we weren't used to killing, even in kindness. And *how* would we do it? Ann might stomp upon the infestation of garden snails that each morning trailed across her flowerboxes back home, but how would we dispatch a creature that might have otherwise fit warm and purring in our arms? Finally, the cat proved impossible to aid. She had scudded into the pipe, knowing that two big creatures like us would never even try to fit inside. She would suffer in peace, her pain unmolested.

But something else sat in the road, fluffy and barely squeaking. A kitten. Its neck was wet, where the mother had latched on to carry it—before she slipped under my car wheels, before the kitten sailed to perfect safety like the fortunate black Labrador of years past. I scooped up the kitten and carried it down the road. There was a fishing lodge situated about a quarter mile into the woods.

The woman who managed the lodge speculated that I had hit a feral cat. We discussed taking the kitten back to the pipe, where the mother might return for it. But then, the mother also might die.

"Don't you want a nice little cat?" the lodge manager demanded feebly. We didn't even have to make excuses about living two thousand miles away. The woman was obviously a big softie. She cradled the kitten in her flat, open palms. It was hers already.

I have to admit that my guidebook, "Big Two-Hearted River," failed to prepare me for the tragic adventure of the cat and her kitten. Nick Adams never displays any fondness for the wild animals whose company he shares in the woods. The fish he pulls from the water can't be garnished with sentimentality; they're slated for dinner over the campfire griddle. Yet Nick Adams's creator, the hardboiled Hemingway, was a notorious big softie in some special cases. Although he butchered countless wonderful wild beasts throughout his life, more often for amusement than any good reason, he was ridiculously touched by—what else?—household cats. Throughout his later years, in Cuba at the Finca Vigia, Hemingway lived with fifty-two cats. Years earlier, during one of his black moods in Paris, the young writer confessed to a friend that he had "just one consolation" in life—and that consolation was "my kitty."

Even in the wilderness, even among the wildest creatures, sometimes we strike upon an errant kindness, unreasonable and unexpected, but right and necessary too. I am sorry I ran over the cat. I am glad the woman took the kitten.

Sometimes we go out into the wild places and find ourselves not only enlivened, but also softer and more vulnerable, even more sentimental than at home in the cities that have hardened us. Unprotected by routine, we see that anything can happen. We witness little lives snuffed out with hideous regularity: the mosquito blazing upon the flame of Nick Adams's matchstick, that poor cat, us too, eventually. It's hard not to think about our own inevitable end out there among the wild things.

In the evening, after the cat, Ann and I hiked back to the Two-Hearted River and briskly circled the perimeter before bedding down to sleep the night by the shore. Trout flipped in and out of the water, sewing together the sky and the river's broken surface with their comic, blunt needle-faces.

At dusk a family of deer boldly crept into the meadow. It was meteorite season, and the sky should have been laced with falling stars, but we forgot to look up. Instead we lost ourselves in belting out

Broadway show tunes to the doe and its four fawns, an absurd salute to Michigan's Upper Peninsula, the big Two-Hearted River, and I suppose to Hemingway too. We sang corny songs from *My Fair Lady* and *Guys and Dolls*. Ann knew all the words to "Embraceable You." We both made a run at some cannibalism numbers from *Sweeney Todd*. We sang out with threats and admiration to the deer, who paid almost no attention to us at all. Occasionally the doe would look up, wagging her head with anthropomorphic disdain. Then she cast an eye over her family and returned to her feed in the high grass.

Lowell's Graveyard

ROBERT HASS

It's probably a hopeless matter, writing about favorite poems. I came across "The Lost Son," "The Quaker Graveyard in Nantucket" and "Howl" at about the same time. Some of the lines are still married in my head and they still have talismanic power: *snail, snail, glister me forward; Mohammedan angels staggering on tenement roofs illuminated; this is the end of running on the waves.* I see now that they are all three lost son poems, but at the time I didn't see much of anything. I heard, and it was the incantatory power of the poems that moved me. Enchantment, literally. I wandered around San Francisco demolishing the twentieth century by mumbling to myself, *blue-lunged combers lumbered to the kill* and managed to mix up Roethke's *ordnung! ordnung! papa's coming* with the Lord who survived the rainbow of his will.

⎯⎯◆⎯⎯

You can analyze the music of poetry but it's difficult to conduct an argument about its value, especially when it's gotten into the blood. It becomes autobiography there. The other night in a pub in Cambridgeshire (named The Prince Regent and built just before the regency in the year when the first man who tried to organize a craft union among weavers was whipped, drawn, quartered and disemboweled in a public ceremony in London) the subject of favorite poems came up and a mild-looking man who taught high school geology treated us to this:

> For it's Din! Din! Din!
> You limpin' lump o' brick dust, Gunga Din!
> Though I've belted you and flayed you,
> By the livin' Gawd that made you,
> You're a better man than I am, Gunga Din!

And he began to talk about his father's library in a summer cottage in Devon. I thought of how my older brother had loved that poem, how we had taken turns reading Vachel Lindsay and Kipling aloud on summer nights in California, in our upstairs room that looked out on a dusty fig orchard and grapevines spilling over the wooden fence.

Poems take place in your life, or some of them do, like the day your younger sister arrives and replaces you as the bon enfant in the bosom of the family; or the day the trucks came and the men began to tear up the wooden sidewalks and the cobblestone gutters outside your house and laid down new cement curbs and asphalt streets. We put paper bags on our feet to walk back and forth across the road which glistened with hot oil. That was just after the war. The town was about to become a suburb in the postwar boom. The fig orchard went just after the old road. I must have been six. Robert Lowell had just published in the *Partisan Review* a first version of "The Quaker Graveyard in Nantucket."

———◆———

Thinking about this a long time later made me realize that "The Quaker Graveyard" is not a political poem. I had assumed that it was, that its rage against the war and Puritan will and the Quakers of Nantucket who financed the butchery of whales was an attack on American capitalism. But a political criticism of any social order implies both that a saner one can be imagined and the hope or conviction that it can be achieved. I had by then begun to have a way of describing such an order, got out of a melange of Paul Goodman, Camus and *To the Finland Station*, but what lay behind it was an imagination of early childhood, dusty fig leaves and sun and fields of wild fennel. Nostalgia locates desire in the past where it suffers no active conflict and can be yearned toward pleasantly. History is the antidote to this. When I saw that my paradise was Lowell's hell, I was forced to see that it was not a place in time I was thinking of, but a place in imagination. The fury of conflict is in "The Quaker Graveyard" but I went back to the poem looking for the vision of an alternative world. There is none. There's grief and moral rage but the poem imagines the whole of human life as sterile violence:

> All you recovered from Poseidon died
> With you, my cousin, and the harrowed brine
> Is fruitless on the blue beard of the god . . .

and it identifies finally with the inhuman justice of God:

> You could cut the brakish waters with a knife
> Here in Nantucket, and cast up the time
> When the Lord God formed man from the sea's slime
> And breathed into his face the breath of life,
> And blue-lunged combers lumbered to the kill.
> The Lord survives the rainbow of his will.

There are no choices in this history of the experiment of evolution and so there can be no politics. "The Lost Son," all inward animal alertness and numbed panic, contains the possibility of a social order by imagining return. And "Howl" wants to imagine a fifth international of angels.

It struck me then that the poem was closer in sensibility to someone like Robinson Jeffers than to most of the poets whom I had come to associate with Lowell. Both poets are forced to step outside the human process and claim the vision of some imperturbable godhead in which the long violence of human history looks small. But in "The Quaker Graveyard" it is important to say that is the position the poem *finally* arrives at because it is a poem of process, and of anguish. Warren Winslow drowns, the Quakers drown, the wounded whale churns in an imagination of suffering and violence which it is the imperative of the poem to find release from, and each successive section of the poem is an attempt to discover a way out. When I was beginning to read poetry to learn what it was and what it could be, this seemed the originality of the poem and its greatness.

———•◦•———

And it's still hard for me to dissociate it from the excitement of that first reading. The poem leapt off the page. Its music, its fury and grief, haunted me:

> where the bones
> Cry out in the long night for the hurt beast
> Bobbing by Ahab's whaleboats in the East

By that time Lowell was writing in the later, more influential style, then controversial, now egregious orthodoxy:

> These are the tranquilized fifties
> and I am forty . . .

But I didn't know that, and I still find myself blinking incredulously when I read—in almost anything written about the poetry—that those early poems "clearly reflect the dictates of the new criticism," while the later ones are "less consciously wrought and extremely intimate." This is the view in which it is "more intimate" and "less conscious" to say "my mind's not right" than to imagine the moment when

> The death-lance churns into the sanctuary, tears
> The gun-blue swingle, heaving like a flail,
> And hacks the coiling life out . . .

which is to get things appallingly wrong.

———•◦•———

Years later I heard a part of this judgment echoed in a curious way. I was listening to Yvor Winters, just before his death, lecturing on George

Herbert. He was talking about Herbert's enjambments and, in one of his rare excursions into the present, he said in a bass grumble, "Young Lowell has got a bad enjambment which he got from Allen Tate who probably got it from Herbert." I thought of "The Quaker Graveyard":

> Light
> Flashed from his matted head and marble feet

> Seagulls blink their heavy lids
> Seaward

It lit up the poem all over again. Lowell had just published this in one of the fashionable journals:

> Only man thinning out his kind
> sounds through the Sabbath noon, the blind
> swipe of the pruner and his knife
> busy about the tree of life . . .

Non est species, but plenty of *decor*. I'm still not sure what I think about these lines. There is enormous, ironic skill in the octosyllabic couplets, and terrible self-laceration in their poise. It is probably great writing in the sense that the state of mind couldn't be rendered more exactly. But I wondered about the state of mind and said a small prayer to the small gods—hilarity and carnality—that I could escape it. The writer, among other things, is getting a certain magisterial pleasure from seeming to be outside the picture. The writer of these lines is in it:

> And rips the sperm-whale's midriff into rags,
> Gobbets of blubber spill to wind and weather,
> Sailor, and gulls go round the stoven timbers
> Where the morning stars sing out together . . .

———◈———

It is possible, I suppose, to object to the brilliance of the writing. Charles Olson is said to have complained that Lowell lacquered each of his poems and hung it in a museum. But this judgment, like the "confessional" revolution envisaged by the professoriat, seems to be based on the sociology of Kenyon College or the fact of meter or Lowell's early models, on everything but a reading of the poems. Finish in poetry is, as Olson insisted, a question of form following function. "The Quaker Graveyard" is brilliantly written, and in a decade of amazing poetry: the *Pisan Cantos*, the first books of *Paterson*, *Four Quartets*, HD's *War Trilogy*, Stevens' "Credences of Summer," Roethke's "The Lost Son." But its brilliance seems neither dictated nor wrought; it is headlong, furious, and casual. There are moments that hover near grandiloquence—"Ask for no Orphean lute . . ." but they didn't bother me then and don't much now.

Everything about the sound of the poem seemed gorgeous on first reading. "A brakish reach of shoal off . . ." sounded like an impossible Russian word, sluggish and turbulent; the Indian-Yankee "Madaket" bit it off with wonderful abruptness. I still like to say it:

A brakish reach of shoal off Madaket,—

In the second line, the oddness of the sound, which is a substitution in the third foot, has a slightly startling effect:

The sea was still breaking violently . . .

The rhythm breaks "breaking," makes a violence out of slackness in a way that I had never seen before, and it was clearly intended because *still* is an extra syllable:

The sea was still breaking violently and night

From here to the end of the stanza, the energy of the poem allows no rest—

Had steamed into our North Atlantic fleet,
When the drowned sailor clutched the drag-net. Light
Flashed from his matted head and marble feet,

> He grappled at the net
> With the coiled hurdling muscles of his thighs:

I loved the nervous restlessness of the rhyming, the way you accept "net" as the rhyme for "fleet" and "Madaket," then get the off-rhyme "light," so that when you arrive at "feet" it is hardly an arrival and you are pushed toward "net" again. It's like a man shooting at a target with such random desperation that the hits count for no more than the misses. This effect, together with "young Lowell's bad enjambment," transmute an acquired skill into articulate rage. And the colon after "thighs" is not a rest; it insists on the forward hurtle of the lines:

> The corpse was bloodless . . .

<hr>

Warren Winslow or not, it has always seemed to me that Lowell himself was the drowned sailor, just as Roethke is the lost son. Otherwise the sudden moments of direct address make no sense:

> Sailor, will your sword
> Whistle and fall and sink into the fat?
> In the great ash-pit of Jehoshaphat
> The bones cry for the blood of the white whale,
> The fat flukes arch and whack about its ears,
> The death-lance churns into the sanctuary . . .

It is having it both ways to be the young man drowned in the "slush," in the "bilge and backwash," "the greased wash," "the sea's slime" where "the whale's viscera go and the roll of its corruption overruns the world" and to be at the same time the young poet who identifies with the vengeance of the earth-shaker, "green, unwearied, chaste" whose power outlasts the merely phallic brutality of the guns of the steeled fleet, but the impacted writing permits this and it is psychologically true. Distrust of birth is the beginning of one kind of religious emotion.

In the speed of the writing, the syntax comes apart; it dissolves into emotion, into music and the subterranean connections among images.

Throughout the poem it is characteristic that the important associations occur in subordinate clauses or compounds so breathless that you have to sort your way back quite consciously to the starting point. This resembles the syntactical strategies of the French surrealists, particularly Desnos and Peret. The main clause is a pushing off place and the poem makes its meaning out of its momentum. It's a way of coming to terms with experience under pressure and not some extrinsic decision about style. Even the lines about the shark—

> Where the heelheaded dogfish barks its nose
> On Ahab's void and forehead

are not Clevelandizing; they are not even—in the period phrase—a metaphysical image because their force is not intellectual. The lines depend on our willingness to let barking dogs marry scavenging sharks in the deep places where men void and are voided. To complain about this is not to launch an attack on "consciously wrought" but the reverse.

The current taste is for the explicit, however weird. Surrealism comes to mean the manufacture of peculiar imagery and not something in the sinews of a poem. The fish in "For the Union Dead" are a midpoint in this leveling process. They are transformed into sharks and then into cars as "a savage servility slides by on grease," but the delivery is slower, the context narrative and topographical. It is pretty much the same image as in "The Quaker Graveyard," but it has been clarified like broth, a fish stock served up as clam chowder to the peremptory gentleman in the cartoon who likes to see what he's eating.

And this won't do for Lowell because the power of his imagery has always been subliminal; it exists as the nervous underside of the thing said. Look at this, for example, from "Fourth of July in Maine." The poet is addressing Harriet Winslow:

> Dear Cousin, life is much the same,
> though only fossils know your name
> here since you left this solitude,
> gone, as the Christians say, for good.
> Your house, still outwardly in form

lasts, though no emissary comes
to watch the garden running down,
or photograph the propped-up barn.

If memory is genius, you
had Homer's, enough gossip to
repeople Trollope's Barchester,
nurses, Negro, diplomat, down-easter,
cousins kept up with, nipped, corrected,
kindly, majorfully directed,
though family furniture, decor,
and rooms redone meant almost more.

How often when the telephone
brought you to us from Washington,
we had to look around the room
to find the objects you would name—
lying there, ten years paralyzed,
half-blind, no voice unrecognized,
not trusting in the afterlife,
teasing us for a carving knife.

High New England summer, warm
and fortified against the storm
by nightly nips you once adored,
though never going overboard,
Harriet, when you used to play
your chosen Nadia Boulanger
Monteverdi, Purcell, and Bach's
precursors on the Magnavox.

This is affectionate, even cozy. And beneath that first sensation is deep
pathos; and beneath that is something like terror, so that the force of
the phrase "life is much the same" keeps changing—for the worse—as
you read. The imagery of a life with fossil memory, a run-down garden,
a propped-up barn, a devastated Troy and cursed Mycenae, a Barchester

that needs repeopling, people who need to be nipped and corrected, or redone, a half-blind paralyzed woman (the syntax has a way of paralyzing her objects as well), the need to be fortified against summer (with nips: the carving knife lying suddenly across both the cozy drinking and the corrected behavior) all issue in, among time's other wreckage, a Magnavox, the great voice which reproduces a great religious passion in the form of a performer's art. Everything dwindles, is rendered. Boulanger's Monteverdi. Lowell's Harriet. It's easy to explicate poems and hard to get their tone. The tone here has one moment of extraordinary pathos which is deeper than the catlike movement through entropy and corrosion:

> half-blind, no voice unrecognized,
> not trusting in the afterlife,
> teasing us for a carving knife.
> High New England summer . . .

But in the end the tone has to do with rendering; the whole passage is majorfully directed. It is not the experience but a way of handling the experience. The imagery accumulates its desolating evidence, but in such a way that the terror in the poetry is perceived while the novelistic pathos is felt. The subterranean images, whether "consciously wrought" or not, are intellectual. In this way, it is exactly a metaphysical poem as nothing in *Lord Weary's Castle* is.

In the second section of "The Quaker Graveyard" there's not much that could be called development. Four sentences, three of which use syntax only as a line of energy, do little more than elaborate an instance of what used to be called the pathetic fallacy, but they confront the experience of grief, of terror at the violence of things, directly:

> Whenever winds are moving and their breath
> Heaves at the roped-in bulwarks of this pier,
> The terns and seagulls tremble at your death
> In these home waters. Sailor, can you hear
> The Pequod's sea-wings, beating landward, fall

Headlong and break on our Atlantic wall
Off 'Sconset, where the yawing S-boats splash
As the entangled screeching mainsheet clears
The blocks: off Madaket, where lubbers lash
The heavy surf and throw their long lead squids
For blue-fish? Seagulls blink their heavy lids
Seaward. The wind's wings beat upon the stones,
Cousin, and scream for you and the claws rush
At the sea's throat and wring it in the slush
Of this old Quaker Graveyard where the bones
Cry out in the long night for the hurt beast
Bobbing by Ahab's whaleboats in the East.

The effect here is not simple, but for me it is the most beautiful moment in the poem. The whole of that first sentence relaxes. The lines break deliberately as if they were trying to hold the emotion in place. But the content is terrible and the perception is extraordinarily intense. The feathers of the gulls ruffling in the wind are made to hurt. And it's such an ordinary perception. "Whenever winds are moving," to my Pacific grounding, is almost always, so that the image registers the steady pain of merely seeing. For some reason this connected in my mind with a thing Lévi-Strauss says near the end of *Tristes Tropiques*: "What I see is an affliction to me, what I cannot see a reproach." The power of this image connects all the description in the poem with the eyes of the dead sailor and the gulls' eyes and the profoundly becalmed eyes of the Virgin of Walsingham. It connects the wind's breath with the breath of the poet which accelerates into violence again in the next sentence. And that sentence is a good example of the expressive power of syntax in the poem. In its fierce accumulation of images, you lose any sense that it began, rather gently, as a rhetorical question. This is a way of being lost, of drowning in the dissolution of syntax. Surrealism, I'm tempted to say, is syntax: not weird images but the way the mind connects them. Here they swell and gather toward violence, toward a continuous breaking like the breaking of waves on the shore, and the effort of control is conveyed by the way "the entangled screeching mainsheet clears the blocks."

So the poem must slow down again: "Seagulls blink their heavy lids /

Seaward." This fixity, the imperturbable consciousness of the gull whose feathers a moment before were trembling in "home waters," is an enormous relief. It is not the dead staring eyes of the drowned sailor and it is not yet the seeing of Our Lady of Walsingham. That heavy-lidded blinking of gulls seems to have a wonderful Buddhalike somnolent alertness when you look at it. It accepts things as they are. It's when gulls are perched on piers, heads tucked in a little, eyes blinking matter-of-factly, that I'm suddenly aware they have no arms, no hands. Even if they don't like what they see, they're not going to do anything about it. And this is a relief. But gulls are also scavengers. Their seeing doesn't hope for much, but it belongs to the world of appetite and their appetites are not very ambitious. That is why the sailors, grasping at straws in section IV, are only three-quarters fools. They want something, have heard news "of IS, the whited monster." So the lines accelerate again. The sea, godly in the first section, is consumed in the general violence in this one and the section ends in a long wail for Moby Dick, the object of desire, monster and victim.

Almost all of "The Quaker Graveyard" works in this way. It's hard to get at without a lot of tedious explication, but look at the third section of the poem. If you ask yourself how the language or the thought proceeds, it's not easy to say. First sentence: All you recovered died with you. Second sentence: Guns blast the eelgrass. Third sentence: They died . . . ; only bones abide. Characteristically, the Quaker sailors appear at the extremity of a dependent clause; then their fate is seized on, midway through the section, as a subject, and the stanza unravels again into violence as the sailors drown proclaiming their justification. And it does not seem arbitrary. It seems inevitable, because this hopelessly repeated unraveling into violence is both the poem's theme and the source of its momentum. Hell is repetition and the structure of anger is repetition. In this poem history is also repetition, as it is the structure of religious incantation. They are all married here, desperately, and the grace of the poem has to exist in modulation of tone. This modulation, like the different textures of an abstract expressionist painting or like the very different modulations that create the texture of Whitman's poems—"Song of Myself" comes to mind—is the grandeur and originality of "The Quaker Graveyard." Not theme, not irony or intimacy or the consciously wrought, but absolute attention to feeling at that moment in the poem's process.

"They died / When time was open-eyed, / Wooden and childish." It takes a while—or took me a while—to see that this is the one moment in the poem that reaches back into childhood. The image has about it the helplessness of childhood. Time here must be the wooden, open-eyed figureheads on old whaling ships, probably seen in books or a maritime museum. The look of the eyes on those old sculptures, their startled and hopeful innocence, dawns on you and it creates the state of mind of the child looking up at them. *Was*, not *seemed*. The verb makes the child's seeing sovereign and irrecoverable. Lost innocence is not the subject of the poem. There is a kind of pleading between the poet and the innocence of his cousin, the ensign who went to the war and did his duty. "All you recovered . . . died with you." But the innocence of the child, of the ensign, of the figureheads is only one syntactical leap away from the stupidity and self-righteousness of the Quaker sailors— "If God himself had not been on our side"—who are swallowed up without understanding a thing. Their eyes are "cabin-windows on a stranded hulk / Heavy with sand."

Sections IV and V continue this riding out of violence but the conclusions of both take a turn that brings us to the religious issue in the poem. It didn't puzzle me much in that first excited reading because I ignored it. I was living down a Catholic childhood, and religious reference in poetry seemed to me not so much reactionary as fossilized and uninteresting. But it was surely there in a lot of what I was reading. Robert Duncan's work was thick with religious imagery, and the "Footnote to Howl" exclaimed, "Holy! Holy! Holy!" I didn't know Lowell was a convert to Catholicism or that this was a momentous rejection of his heritage. For that matter, I didn't know what a Lowell was. But I could see that the poem was not Catholic in any sense that I understood. It is true that the implicit answer to the question "Who will dance the mast-lashed master of Leviathans / Up . . ." is Christ. Orpheus, the way of art, is explicitly dismissed at the beginning of the poem. And the fifth section, the most terrible, the one in which the whale receives the sexual wound of all human violence, ends with a prayer: "Hide / Our steel, Jonas Messias, in thy side."

But the first of these passages is a question and the second is a supplication, not a statement of faith. Insofar as the poem is Christian, it seemed to me to be a very peculiar Christianity. I was prepared to grant that the killing of the whale was also an image of the crucifixion of Christ, but in the poem this act is the source and culmination of evil. "When the whale's viscera go . . . its corruption overruns this world." There is no sense here of the crucifixion as a redemption. I can imagine that three or four pages of theological explication could put it there, but it isn't in the poem. Typologically the legal torture and murder of the man-god is not the fall; in the Christian myth it was not cruelty and violence but pride and disobedience through which men fell. One can make a series of arguments, threading back through the blasphemous pride of Ahab to the dominion given man by God in the epigraph to the poem, and emerge with a case for cruelty as a form of pride, but cruelty is not pride. They're different things, and it is cruelty and death, not pride and the fall, that preoccupy the poet, no matter how much of Melville or theology we haul in to square this vision with orthodoxy.

Reading Robert Duncan has given me a way to think about this issue in Lowell:

> There was no law of Jesus then.
> > There was
> only a desire of savior. . .

Somewhere in his prose at about the same time Duncan had written that the mistake of Christianity was to think that the soul's salvation was the only human adventure. That was an enormously liberating perception. It put Christ on equal footing with the other gods. And the gods, Pound had said in a phrasing that seems now late Victorian, were "eternal moods," forms of consciousness which men through learning, art and contemplation could inhabit. They were not efficacious. We were not Mycenaean warlords, burning bulls and hoping the good scent of roast beef found its way to attentive nostrils; and the Mother of Perpetual Help did not, as my aunts seemed to believe, repair carburetors or turn up lost purses. But the gods were real, forms of imagination in which we could dwell and through which we could see. "The verb," Pound had said with the wreckage of his life around him, "is 'to see' not 'walk on.'"

I got my Catholicism from my mother's side, Foleys from Cork by way of Vermont who drank and taught school and practiced law on the frontiers of respectability until they landed in San Francisco at the turn of the century. My father's side was Protestant and every once in a while, weary probably with the catechisms of his children, he would try to teach us one of his childhood prayers. But he could never get past the first line: "In my father's house there are many mansions . . ." He would frown, squint, shake his head, but that was as far as he ever got and we children who were willing to believe Protestants capable of any stupidity including the idea that you could fit a lot of mansions into a house, would return to memorizing the four marks of the true church. (It was one, holy, catholic, and apostolic.) But that phrase came back to me as a way through the door of polytheism and into myth. If Pound could resurrect the goddesses, there was a place for a temple of Christ, god of sorrows, desire of savior, restingplace of violence. I could have the memory of incense and the flickering candles and the battered figure on the cross with the infinitely sad and gentle face and have Aphrodite as well, "the fauns chiding Proteus / in the smell of hay under olive trees" and the intoning of Latin with which we began the mass: "*Introibo ad altare Dei.*" On these terms, Lowell's prayer moved me: "Hide our steel, Jonas Messias, in thy side." And I could accept cruelty as the first fall; it was truer to my experience than pride or disobedience, which the violence of the state has made to seem, on the whole, sane and virtuous. Not the old dogma, but a piece of the unborn myth which American poetry was making. And this is the sense of things in the poem. There is no redemption promised in the prayer at the end of section V. There is only the god of sorrows and the receiving of the wound.

———◆———

Sexual wounding: it is certainly there in section V, both in the imagery and in the way the section functions, literally, as a climax to the poem. This is the fall, the moment when corruption overruns the world. And the rhetorical question, "Sailor, will your sword / Whistle and fall and sink into the fat?" wants to make us all complicit. The passage is Calvinist in feeling; every day is judgment day:

> In the great ash-pit of Jehoshaphat
> The bones cry for the blood of the white whale

In sexual imagery, not only the penetration by the death lance but the singing of stars, the dismemberment of the masthead, we are all judged:

> The fat flukes arch and whack about its ears,
> The death-lance churns into the sanctuary, tears
> The gun-blue swingle, heaving like a flail,
> And hacks the coiling life out: it works and drags
> And rips the sperm-whale's midriff into rags,
> Gobbets of blubber spill to wind and weather,
> Sailor, and gulls go round the stoven timbers
> Where the morning stars sing out together
> And thunder shakes the white surf and dismembers
> The red flag hammered in the masthead . . .

This needs to be seen straight on, so that we look at the sickening cruelty it actually describes. It's a relief and much easier to talk about myth or symbolic sexuality. This is an image of killing written by a pacifist who was willing to go to prison. It makes death horrifying; it makes the war horrifying, and the commerce of the Nantucket Quakers whom Melville reminded his readers to think of when they lit their cozy whale-oil lamps. "Light is where the landed blood of Cain . . ."

But, just as there is disgust with the mothering sea in the bilge and backwash throughout the poem, there is a deep abhorrence of sexual violence, of sexuality as violence. I'm not sure how to talk about it. There is Freud's gruesome little phrase, as gruesome in German as in English but lacking the pun: the sadistic conception of coitus. But calling it that doesn't take us very far. The fact is that there is an element of cruelty in human sexuality, though that isn't the reason for the Puritan distrust of sex. The Puritans distrusted sexuality because the sexual act dissolved human will for a moment, because—for a moment—men fell into the roots of their mammal nature. You can't have an orgasm and be a soldier of Christ. Thus *Samson Agonistes*. And the Puritan solution, hidden but real in the history of imagination whether in Rome or the Enlightenment, was to turn sex into an instrument of will, of the conscious cruelty which flowered in the writings of Sade. It is there in our history and Lowell is right to connect it with the annihilative rage of capitalism. Flesh is languor ("All of life's grandeur / is something with a girl in summer . . .") but it is also rage. It marries us to the world and the world is full of violence and cruelty. This is part of the bind of the poem which is also the Calvinist bind of determinism and free will. The way out is not-world, an identification at the end of the poem with the "unmarried" Atlantic and the Lord who survives the rainbow-covenant of evolution.

⟞◆⟝

All of which would be pretty grim if it were not for "Our Lady of Walsingham." It's a remarkable moment in the poem, the most surprising of its modulations, a little tranquil island in all the fury. I imagine that for a lot of younger writers it was the place where they learned how far you could go away from the poem and still be in it. Pound says somewhere, sounding like a surly Matthew Arnold, that a history of poetry that's worth anything ought to be able to point to specific poems and passages in poems and say here, here and here are inventions that made something new possible in poetry. This is one of those places.

Its occurrence makes emotional sense because it follows section V. It is the peace of the satisfaction of the body's rage, a landscape of streams and country lanes. The nineteenth century would have described the writing as chaste or exquisite and I'm not sure we have better words to praise it with. It's wonderfully plain and exact:

> Our Lady, too small for her canopy,
> Sits near the altar. There's no comeliness
> At all or charm in that expressionless
> Face with its heavy eyelids. As before,
> This face, for centuries a memory,
> *Non est species, neque decor*

Expressionless, expresses God: it goes
Past castled Sion. She knows what God knows,
Not Calvary's cross nor the crib at Bethlehem
Now, and the world shall come to Walsingham.

This is another temple, not the god of sorrows but the goddess of an almost incomprehensible peace. It appears to be the emphatically Catholic moment in the poem (which adds a peculiar comedy to the idea that "Lycidas" was somehow its model; I've just visited the cathedral at Ely where Milton's friend Thomas Cromwell personally beheaded all the statues in the Lady Chapel. If the set-piece digressions of Alexandrian pastoral taken over by Milton to scourge a Popish clergy have really become a hymn to the Virgin Mary, it is the kind of irony—funny, too elaborately bookish—that would please the author of *History*). But I don't think it is Catholic, or not especially Catholic, and that is its interest.

The crucial phrase is "past castled Sion." Lowell is not after sacramental mediation but a contemplative peace beyond any manifestation in the flesh, beyond thought or understanding, and—most especially—beyond desire. This isn't incompatible with Catholic theology, but it's not central to its spirit which is embodiment: the Orphean lute and the crib at Bethlehem. This apprehension of God, of a pure, calm and utterly clear consciousness, belongs equally to all mysticisms, Christian or otherwise, and it has always seemed to me that the figure of Our Lady here looks a lot like Gautama Buddha. It is the embodiment of what can't be embodied. This is a contradiction, but it is one that belongs to any intellectual pointing toward mystical apprehension. It is the contradiction that made the world-denial of Buddhists and Cathars at the same time utterly compassionate toward and alert to the world and the flesh and makes the Buddhist Gary Snyder our best poet of nature. This is not the rejection of the world which the last lines of the poem suggest; it's something else and for me it's something much more attractive as a possibility of imagination.

But how does it square with the last lines? I don't think it does. Nor does it contradict them. That's the aesthetic daring of this section. What the Lady of Walsingham represents is past contention. She's just there. The method of the poem simply includes her among its elements, past argument, as a possibility through which all the painful seeing in the poem can be transformed and granted peace. She floats; everything else in the poem rises and breaks, relentlessly, like waves.

———◆———

I finally got to hear Robert Lowell read a couple of years ago in Charlottesville, Virginia—in Jefferson country where the road signs read like a rollcall of plump Hanoverian dowagers and America comes as close as it ever will to a munching English lane. The setting made me feel truculent anyway, and when he began by murmuring an apology for the earlier poems—"rather apocalyptic," "one felt so intense"—I found myself on the poems' side. And the voice startled me, probably because I'd been hearing the work in my own for so long. I thought it sounded bizarrely like an imitation of Lionel Barrymore. It was not a voice that could say "Face of snow, / You are the flowers that country girls have caught, / A wild bee-pillaged honeysuckle brought / To the returning bridegroom—the design / Has not yet left it, and the petals shine" without sounding like a disenchanted English actor reading an Elizabethan sonnet on American television.

I had felt vaguely hostile toward Lowell's later work, though I admired it. I thought, for one thing, that the brilliant invention of "The Quaker Graveyard" had come about because he had nothing to go on but nerve and that, when the form cloyed in *The Mills of the Kavanaughs*, he had traded in those formal risks for the sculpted anecdote and the Puritan autobiography, a form about as original as John Bunyan's *Grace Abounding*. There is something new in it. Lowell found a way to accommodate realistic detail and narrative structures out of Chekhov and the short story tradition to his own resonant version of the free verse of William Carlos Williams, but out of that manner had come, not so much in Lowell himself as in the slough of poetry *Life Studies* engendered, a lot of narrative beginning "Father, you . . ." or "The corn died in the field that summer, Mother / when . . ." It struck stances toward experience, as if Williams had said "No attitudes but in things!" I wanted the clarity that "Our Lady of Walsingham" looked toward and in "Waking Early Sunday Morning" I thought he had come to something like that earlier insight and abandoned it too easily:

I watch a glass of water wet
with a fine fuzz of icy sweat,
silvery colours touched with sky,
serene in their neutrality—
yet if I shift, or change my mood,
I see some object made of wood,
background behind it of brown grain,
to darken it, but not to stain.

O that the spirit could remain
tinged but untarnished by its strain!
Better dressed and stacking birch . . .

As if you had to choose between them or tarnishing were the issue.
That glass of water interested me a lot more than the ironies about
electric bells ringing "Faith of our fathers."

Anyway, when he began to read, all this buzzing of the head stopped.
There was the sense, for one thing, of a body of work faithful to itself
through all its phases (early, middle and ceaseless revision). And there
was the reading of "Near the Ocean." Hearing it, I began to understand
the risks attendant on backing away from the drama and self-drama
of *Lord Weary's Castle*. Pain has its own grandeur. This disenchanted
seeing was not serene neutrality—it was not serene at all; it had the
clarity of a diminished sense of things not flinched at. I thought it was
a brave piece of writing and it revisits the territory of "The Quaker
Graveyard," so it seems like a place to end:

Sand built the lost Atlantis . . . sand,
Atlantic ocean, condoms, sand.
Sleep, sleep. The ocean, grinding stones,
can only speak the present tense;
nothing will age, nothing will last,
or take corruption from the past.
A hand, your hand then! I'm afraid
to touch the crisp hair on your head—

Thoughts on *The Idiot* by Dostoevsky

HERMANN HESSE

Dostoevsky's "idiot," Prince Leo Myshkin, is often compared to Jesus. This is easy enough to do. You can compare to Jesus anyone who has been touched by one of the magical truths, who no longer separates thinking from living and thereby isolates himself in the midst of his surroundings and becomes the opponent of all. Beyond that, the comparison between Myshkin and Jesus seems to me not exactly apt. Only one characteristic in Myshkin, an important one to be sure, strikes me as Jesus-like—his timid chastity. The concealed fear of sex and procreation is a characteristic that could not be wanting in the "historical" Jesus, the Jesus of the Gospels, a trait that is clearly part of his world mission and is not neglected in even so superficial a portrait of Jesus as Renan's.

But it is strange—little though I sympathize with the constant comparison between Myshkin and Christ—that I too see the two images unconsciously related to each other. It only occurred to me belatedly and in connection with a tiny matter. One day when I was thinking about the "idiot" I realized that my first thought of him always seems to be an apparently insignificant one. In the first flash of my imagination I always see him in one particular secondary scene of no importance in itself. I have exactly the same experience with the Savior. Whenever an association calls up the image of Jesus or I hear or see the word "Jesus," what leaps into my mind first is not Jesus on the cross, or Jesus in the wilderness, or Jesus the miracle worker, or Jesus risen from the dead, but Jesus in the garden of Gethsemane, tasting the last cup of loneliness, his soul torn by the woes of impending death and a higher rebirth. And as he looks about him for his disciples, in a last touching, childlike need of comfort, seeking a little warmth and human closeness, a fleeting comforting illusion in the midst of his hopeless loneliness—there are the disciples asleep! All of them together, the worthy Peter, the handsome John—all these good people about whom Jesus has again and again, intentionally and lovingly, deceived himself, with whom he has shared his thoughts, at least a part of his thoughts—as though they could understand him, as though it were possible in actual fact to communicate his ideas to these people, to awaken some related vibration in them, something like comprehension, something like a close relationship. And now in the moment of unbearable agony he turns toward these companions, the only ones he has; and he is now so openly and wholly human, so much the sufferer that he might come closer to them than ever before, find comfort and support in any silly word or halfway friendly gesture on their part—but no, they are not there, they are sleeping, they are snoring. This dreadful moment, I know not how, was impressed upon my mind in very early youth, and as I have said, if I think of Jesus, always and unfailingly the memory of this moment arises in my mind.

There is a parallel to this in Myshkin's case. If I think of him, the "idiot," likewise it is a moment of apparently lesser importance that first occurs to me and similarly it is a moment of incredible, total isolation, tragic loneliness. The scene is that evening in Pavlovsk, in Lebedev's house, when the Prince, a few days after his epileptic seizure and still recuperating from it, is being visited by the whole Yepanchin family, when suddenly into this cheerful and elegant though inwardly tense circle burst the fashionable young revolutionaries and nihilists. When the talkative Ippolit with the ostensible "son of Pavlishchev," when the "boxer" and the others rush in, this disagreeable, always repulsive and disquieting scene where these limited and misguided young people are so harshly and nakedly revealed in their helpless evil as though standing on an overlighted stage, where their every word inflicts a double pain upon the reader, first because of its impact upon the good Myshkin and then because of the cruelty with which it unmasks and lays bare the speaker—this is the strange, unforgettable, though in the novel not especially important or emphasized passage that I mean. On the one side society, the elegant worldly people, the rich, mighty, and conservative, on the other ferocious youth, inexorable, knowing nothing but rebellion and hatred for tradition, ruthless, dissolute, wild, incredibly stupid for all their theoretical intellectualism; and standing between these two groups the Prince, alone, exposed, observed by both sides critically and with the closest attention. And how does the situation end? It ends with Myshkin, despite the few small mistakes he makes during the excitement, behaving exactly according to his kind, gentle, childlike nature, accepting smilingly the unbearable, answering selflessly the most shameless speeches, willing to assume every fault and to search for every fault in himself—and his complete failure in this with the result that he is despised, not by one side or the other, not by the young against the old or the reverse, but by both, by both! All turn against him, he has stepped on everyone's toes; for an instant the most extreme social opposites in age and point of view are completely wiped out, all are united and at one in turning their backs with indignation and rage on the single one among them who is pure!

What is it that makes this "idiot" so impossible in the world of other people? Why does no one understand him, even though almost all love him in some fashion, almost everyone finds his gentleness sympathetic, indeed often exemplary? What distinguishes him, the man of magic, from the others, the ordinary people? Why are they right in rejecting him? Why must they do it, inevitably? Why must things go with him as they did with Jesus, who in the end was abandoned not only by the world but by all his disciples as well?

It is because the "idiot's" way of thinking is different from that of the others. Not that he thinks less logically or in a more childlike and associative way than they—that is not it. His way of thought is what I call "magical." This gentle "idiot" completely denies the life, the way of thought and feeling, the world and the reality of other people. His reality is something quite different from theirs. Their reality in his eyes is no more than a shadow, and it is by seeing and demanding a completely new reality that he becomes their enemy.

The difference is not that they prize power, money, family, state, and similar values and that he does not. It is not that he represents the spiritual and they the material, or however one wants to formulate it. This is not the point. For the "idiot" too the material world exists, he readily acknowledges the significance of these things even if he takes them less seriously. Nor is his demand, his ideal, a Hindu ascetic one, a dying to this world of apparent realities in favor of a spirit content in itself and confident that it alone is reality.

No, about the reciprocity of nature and spirit, about their necessary interaction, Myshkin would be quite able to reach an understanding with the others. But for them the co-existence, the equal validity of both worlds is a principle and an idea, for him they are life and reality! To make this clearer, let us try to put it somewhat differently.

Myshkin is different from others because as idiot and epileptic, and at the same time a very clever person, he has much closer and more direct relations with the unconscious than they do. For him the highest experience is that half second of supreme receptivity and insight that he has experienced a few times, that magical ability for a moment, for the flash of a moment, to be able to be everything, to empathize with everything, to sympathize with everything, to understand and accept everything in the world. There lies the essence of his being. He has not studied and accepted magic and mystical wisdom, not read and admired them, but (if only at very rare instants) actually experienced them. He has not only had strange and magnificent thoughts and inspirations but more than once he has stood on the magic threshold where everything is affirmed, where not only the most farfetched idea is true but also the opposite of every such idea.

This is the dread thing about this man, properly feared by the others. He does not stand entirely alone, not the whole world is against him. There are still a few people, very dubious, very threatened and threatening people, who at times understand him emotionally: Rogozhin,

Nastasya. He is understood by criminals and by hysterics, he, the innocent, the gentle child! But this child, by God, is not as gentle as he seems. His innocence is by no means harmless, and people quite properly fear him.

The "idiot," I have said, is at times close to that boundary line where every idea and its opposite are recognized as true. That is, he has an intuition that no idea, no law, no character or order exists that is true and right except as seen from one pole—and for every pole there is an opposite pole. Settling upon a pole, adopting a position from which the world is viewed and arranged, this is the first principle of every order, every culture, every society and morality. Whoever feels, if only for an instant, that spirit and nature, good and evil are interchangeable is the most dangerous enemy of all forms of order. For that is where the opposite of order is, and there chaos begins.

A way of thought that leads back to the unconscious, to chaos, destroys all forms of human organization. In conversation someone says to the "idiot" that he only speaks the truth, nothing more, and that this is deplorable. So it is. Everything is true, "Yes" can be said to anything. To bring order into the world, to attain goals, to make possible law, society, organization, culture, morality, "No" must be added to the "Yes," the world must be separated into opposites, into good and evil. However arbitrary the first establishment of each "No," each prohibition, may be, it becomes sacrosanct the instant it becomes law, produces results, becomes the foundation for a point of view and system of order.

The highest reality in the eyes of human culture lies in this dividing up of the world into bright and dark, good and evil, permissible and forbidden. For Myshkin the highest reality, however, is the magical experience of the reversibility of all fixed rules, of the equal justification for the existence of both poles. *The Idiot*, thought to its logical conclusion, leads to a matriarchy of the unconscious and annihilates culture. It does not break the tables of the law, it reverses them and shows their opposites written on the back.

The fact that this foe of order, this frightful destroyer, appears not as a criminal but as a shy, endearing person full of childlikeness and charm, a good-hearted, selfless, benevolent man, this is the secret of this terrifying book. Out of a profound perception, Dostoevsky has made this character a sick man, an epileptic. All representatives of the new, of the dreadful, of the uncertain future, all harbingers of an intuited chaos, are in Dostoevsky sick, dubious, overburdened. Rogozhin, Nastasya, later all four Karamazovs. All are represented as derailed, as exceptionally strange figures, but all in such a way that we feel for this derailment and mental illness something of that holy awe which Asiatics believe they owe to madmen.

What is remarkable and strange, important and fateful, is not that somewhere in Russia in the 1850's and '6o's an epileptic of genius had these fantasies and created these figures. The important thing is that these books for three decades have become increasingly important and prophetic works to the young people of Europe. The strange thing is that we look at the faces of these criminals, hysterics, and idiots of Dostoevsky quite differently than we do at the faces of other criminals or fools in other famous novels, that we understand and love them so uncannily that we must feel in ourselves something related and akin to these people.

This is not due to accident and even less to the external and literary elements in Dostoevsky's work. However disconcerting any of his traits may be—you have only to think how he anticipates a highly developed psychology of the unconscious—we do not admire his work as the expression of profound insight and skill or as the artistic representation of a world essentially known and familiar to us; rather we experience it as prophecy, as the mirroring in advance of the dissolution and chaos that we have seen openly going on in Europe for the last several years. Not that this world of fictional characters represents a picture of an ideal future—no one would consider it that. No, we do not see in Myshkin and all the other characters examples to be copied; instead we perceive an inevitability that says, "Through this we must pass, this is our destiny!"

The future is uncertain, but the road that is shown here is unambiguous. It means spiritual revaluation. It leads through Myshkin and calls for "magical" thinking, the acceptance of chaos. Return to the incoherent, to the unconscious, to the formless, to the animal and far beyond the animal to the beginning of all things. Not in order to remain there, not to become animal or primeval slime but rather so that we can reorient ourselves, hunt out, at the roots of our being, forgotten instincts and possibilities of development, to be able to undertake a new creation, valuation, and distribution of the world. No program can teach us to find this road, no revolution can thrust open the gates to it. Each one walks this way alone, each by himself. Each of us for an hour in his life will have to stand on the Myshkin boundary where truths can cease and begin anew. Each of us must once for an instant in his life experience within himself the same sort of thing that Myshkin experienced in his moments of clairvoyance, such as Dostoevsky himself experienced in those moments when he stood face to face with execution and from which he emerged with the prophet's gaze.

An Author in Search of a Subject

FRANK O'CONNOR

Katherine Mansfield is for me something unusual in the history of the short story. She was a woman of brilliance, perhaps of genius; she chose the short story as her own particular form and handled it with considerable skill, and yet for most of the time she wrote stories that I read and forget, read and forget. My experience of stories by real storytellers, even when the stories are not first-rate, is that they leave a deep impression on me. It may not be a total impression; it may not even be an accurate one, but it is usually deep and permanent. I remember it in the way in which I remember poetry. I do not remember Katherine Mansfield's stories in that way. She wrote a little group of stories about her native country, New Zealand, which are recognized as masterpieces and probably are masterpieces, but I find myself forgetting even these and rediscovering them as though they were the work of a new writer.

It may be that for me and people of my own generation her work has been obscured by her legend, as the work of Rupert Brooke has been, and the work is always considerably dimmer than the legend. The story of the dedicated doomed artist, the creature of flame married to a dull unimaginative man persists; persists so strongly, indeed, that one has to keep on reminding oneself that the story is largely the creation of the dull unimaginative man himself. Most of us who were young when the *Journal* was published took an immediate dislike to John Middleton Murry, and I suspect that some of the scornful obituaries that appeared after his death were the work of men who had taken the legend of Katherine Mansfield too seriously. Meanwhile, Murry, a man with an inordinate capacity for punishment, continued to publish letters of hers that seemed to show him in a still worse light.

Obviously there was some truth in the legend since Murry himself believed it, and since the mark left on one's imagination by the *Journal* and letters remains; and yet I get the impression that in the editing of the book he was unfair to himself and far, far too fair to his wife. There must have been another side to her which has not yet emerged from the memoirs of the time. Friends of Murry and hers have told me that they seemed less interested in each other than in the copy they supplied to each other—a likely enough weakness in two young writers who were both in love with literature, though one wouldn't gather it from what either has written. Francis Carco, after his flirtation with Katherine, portrayed her as a rapacious copyhound, while in "Je ne parle pas français" she caricatured him as a pimp. Childish, spiteful, vulgar if you like, but something that has been carefully edited out of the legend. One might even say that by creating the legend Murry did his wife's reputation more harm than good, for by failing to describe, much less emphasize, the shoddy element in her character, he suppressed the real miracle of her development as an artist.

Therefore, if I emphasize what seems to me the shoddy element it is almost by way of experiment. Most of her work seems to me that of a clever, spoiled, malicious woman. Though I know nothing that would suggest she had any homosexual experiences, the assertiveness, malice, and even destructiveness in her life and work make me wonder whether she hadn't. It would be too much to exaggerate the significance of her occasionally sordid love affairs, of which we probably still have something to learn, but the idea of "experience" by which she justified them is a typical expedient of the woman with a homosexual streak who envies men and attributes their imaginary superiority to the greater freedom with which they are supposed to be able to satisfy their sexual appetite. It is the fallacy of Virginia Woolf's *A Room of One's Own*, and one has only to think of Emily Dickinson or Jane Austen rejoicing in the freedom of a traveling salesman to realize how fallacious it is. The trouble with "experience" in the sense in which Katherine Mansfield sought it is that by being self-conscious it becomes self-defeating. The eye is always looking beyond the "experience" to the use that is to be made of it, and in the process the experience itself has changed its nature, and worldliness no longer means maturity but a sort of permanent adolescence.

> I crouched against him like a wild cat. Quite impersonally, I admired my silver stockings bound beneath the knee with spiked ribbons, my yellow suede shoes fringed with white fur. How vicious I looked! We made love to each other like two wild beasts.

If Katherine Mansfield really did write this after one of her amorous orgies—and in one way or another this was what she was always doing—the "copy" she was collecting was on a par with the "experience" and could only result in a permanent attitude of knowingness concealing a complete emotional immaturity. I sometimes wonder if Middleton Murry really knew what he was writing when he told so charmingly the story of their love affair—*her* suggestion that he should share her flat, *her* use of his surname when she said goodnight that compelled him to call her "Mansfield," *her* "Why don't you make me your mistress?" He was an innocent man: it is he who says somewhere in perfect innocence that Lawrence was as much in love with Frieda's husband as with Frieda herself, but surely it should have occurred to him that from the first moment Katherine Mansfield was adopting the position of the man in their relationship.

———◆———

There is one quality that is missing in almost everything that Katherine Mansfield wrote—even her New Zealand stories—and that is heart.

Where heart should be we usually find sentimentality, the quality that seems to go with a brassy exterior, and nowhere more than with that of an "emancipated" woman. In literature sentimentality always means falsity, for whether or not one can perceive the lie, one is always aware of being in the presence of a lie.

"Je ne parle pas français" is a good example. It is generally accepted as a free description of Katherine Mansfield's first meeting with Francis Carco, and Carco himself admits the resemblance. It describes a sensitive, dreamy girl brought on an illicit honeymoon to Paris by a Mother's Boy who, because he does not wish to hurt Momma, abandons her there to the care of his pimp friend—drawn from Carco—though the pimp friend, finding no use for her, abandons her as well.

A touching little story, and if one could read it "straight," as I am told such stories should be read, one's sympathy would go out to the heroine, every one of whose glances and tears is lovingly observed. But how can one read it straight? The first question I ask myself is how this angelic creature ever became the mistress of anybody, let alone of such a monster of egotism as her lover. Is it that she was completely innocent? But if so, why doesn't she do what any innocent girl with money in her pocket would do on discovering that she has been abandoned in a strange city by a man she had trusted and go home on the next train? Not perhaps back to her parents but at least to some old friend? Has she no home? No friend? None of the essential questions a short story should answer is answered here, and in fact, when I read the story "straight," knowing nothing of the author's life, I merely felt it was completely unconvincing.

Knowing what I do now, I do not find it much more satisfactory. Was Murry, to whom Katherine Mansfield submitted it first, supposed to read it "straight"? "But I hope you'll see (of course you will)," she wrote to him, "that I'm not writing with a sting." Apparently he did not see. Indeed, being a very sensitive man, he may even have wondered at the insensitiveness of a woman who could send such a story for his approval.

But even more than by the element of falsity in these stories I am put off by the feeling that they were all written in exile. I do not mean by this merely that they were written by a New Zealander about Germany, England, and France, three countries any one of which would be sufficient to keep a storyteller occupied for several lifetimes. I mean that there is no real indication of a submerged population, a population which is not by its very nature in need of a coherent voice. To Katherine Mansfield as to Dickens the lower classes are merely people who say "perishall" when they mean "parasol" and "certingty" when they mean "certainty." Reading the stories all through again I experienced the same shock I experienced thirty years ago when I came on "The Life of Ma Parker" and I found myself saying, "Ah, so this is what was missing! So this is what short stories are really about!"

Like much of Katherine Mansfield's work, this story is influenced directly by Chekhov, with whom she always tended to identify herself from the time when she palmed off on Orage a flagrant imitation of Chekhov's famous story about the little baby sitter who is so tired that she smothers the crying baby. "The Life of Ma Parker" is imitated from an equally famous story, "Misery," in which an old cab driver who has lost his son tries to tell his grief to his customers and finally goes down to the stable and tells it to his old nag. Ma Parker, too, having lost her little grandson, is full of her grief, but when she tries to tell her employer about it he merely says, "I hope the funeral was a—success."

And at this point I always stop reading to think, "Now *there* is a mistake that Chekhov wouldn't have made!" and I do not need to go on to the point at which Ma Parker's employer rebukes her for throwing out a teaspoon of cocoa he had left in a tin. Chekhov knew that it is not heartlessness that breaks the heart of the lonely, and it is not Ma Parker's employer who is being coarse but Katherine Mansfield. It is not the only example in her work of a story being spoiled by her assertiveness.

At the same time the story is impressive because Ma Parker is a genuine member of a submerged population, not so much because she is old and poor, which is largely irrelevant, as because, like Chekhov's teachers and priests, she has no one else to speak for her.

————◆————

It is generally agreed that the principal change in Katherine Mansfield's work occurs after the death of her brother, Chummie, in the First World War. It seems to have been her first contact with real personal grief, and her reaction was violent, even immoderate. "First, my darling, I've got things to do for both of us, and then I will come as quickly as I can," she writes in her *Journal*. What the things were she revealed when she asked herself why she did not commit suicide. "I have a duty to perform to the lovely time when we were both alive. I want to write about it, and he wanted me to. We talked it over in my little top room in London. I said: I will just put on the front page: To my brother, Leslie Heron Beauchamp. Very well: it shall be done."

Of course, it is all girlishly overdramatic in the Katherine Mansfield way, but that is no reflection on its sincerity. After all, it was done, and done splendidly.

She had always been fond of her brother, though to my mind—still speaking in the part of devil's advocate—this is scarcely sufficient to explain the violence of her grief, which sent a normally affectionate husband like Murry home from the South of France, ashamed of himself for thinking of a dead boy as a rival. Once more, I begin to wonder whether the assertive, masculine streak in her had not made her jealous of her brother. There is nothing abnormal about that: it is possible for a woman to love a brother dearly and yet be jealous of the advantages which he seems to possess; and of course, the jealousy cannot survive death, for once the superiority, real or imaginary, is removed, and the beloved brother is merely a name on a tombstone, the struggling will has no obstacles to contend with and the place of jealousy tends to be taken by guilt—by the feeling that one had grudged the brother such little advantages as he possessed, even by the fantasy that one had caused his death. All this is well within the field of ordinary human experience; it is the immoderacy of the reaction in Katherine Mansfield that puzzles me.

I feel sure that something of the sort is necessary to explain the extraordinary change that took place in her character and work—above all in her work, for here the change does not seem to be a normal development of her talent at all but a complete reversal of it. In fact, it is much more like the result of a religious crisis than of an artistic one, and, like the result of a lot of other religious crises, it leaves the critic watchful and unsatisfied. "Did he give up the drink too soon?" is a question we must all have had to ask ourselves from time to time in connection with our friends. For Katherine Mansfield, the woman, the crisis was to end in the dreary charlatanism of Fontainebleau and become the keystone of her legend, but from the point of view of Katherine Mansfield, the writer, that gesture seems immoderate, heroic, and absolutely unnecessary. No one need point out to me that this viewpoint is limited, and that it is not for a critic of literature to say what act of heroism is or is not necessary, but he must do it just the same if he is to be true to his own standards.

It seems to me that Katherine Mansfield's tragedy is, from the inside, the tragedy that Chekhov never tired of observing from the outside— the tragedy of the false personality. That clever, assertive, masculine woman was a mistake from beginning to end, and toward the close of her life she recognized it herself. Writing of herself, characteristically in the third person, she said, "She had led, ever since she can remember, a very typically false life." This is my complaint of John Murry's legend: because he loved Katherine Mansfield he gave no indication of the false personality, and so blotted the true and moving story of the brassy little shopgirl of literature who made herself into a great writer. With that sentence of hers one should compare the passage I have already quoted from Chekhov's letter to Souvorin—"Could you write a story of how this young man squeezes the slave out of himself drop by drop, and how, on waking up one morning, he feels that the blood coursing through his veins is real blood and not the blood of a slave?" That, I fancy, is how Katherine Mansfield would have wished to be described, but Murry could not bear to see how much of the slave there was in the woman he loved.

The conflict between the false personality and the ideal one is very clear in some of the stories, and nowhere more than in the second book in which the two personalities stand side by side in "Je ne parle pas français" and "Prelude." The false personality, determined largely by the will, dominates the former story; an ideal alternative personality— *not* the true one because that never emerged fully—determined by a complete surrender of the will, dominates the latter. As a result of the conflict in her, Katherine Mansfield's reply to the activity imposed on her by her own overdeveloped will is an antithesis—pure contemplation.

For obvious reasons she identified this contemplativeness with that of Chekhov, the least contemplative writer who ever lived, but her misunderstanding of the great artist with whom she identified herself was a necessary part of her development.

> How *perfect* the world is, with its worms and hooks and ova, how incredibly perfect. There is the sky and the sea and the shape of a lily, and there is all this other as well. The balance how perfect! (Salut, Tchehov!) I would not have the one without the other.

One can imagine the embarrassed cough with which Chekhov would have greeted that girlish effusiveness. His contemplativeness, the contemplativeness of a doctor who must resign himself to the death of a patient he has worked himself to death trying to save, was a very different affair from Katherine Mansfield's, and if, as a wise man he resigned himself, it was never because he had not suffered as a fool.

In one story, "The Garden Party," Katherine Mansfield tries to blend the two personalities, and her failure is even more interesting than the success of stories like "Prelude," where one personality is held in abeyance. Apparently, part of her assertiveness came from her resentment of the aimless life of the moneyed young lady in the provincial society of New Zealand, and during the religious crisis, part of her penance has to be the complete, uncritical acceptance of it. In the story the Sheridans' garden party is haunted by the accidental death of a carter who lives at their gate. Young Laura does not want the garden party to take place; she tries to talk her family out of it but is constantly frustrated and diverted, even by her beloved brother Laurie.

> "My word, Laura! You do look stunning," said Laurie.
> "What an absolutely topping hat!"
> Laura said faintly "Is it?" and smiled up at Laurie, and didn't tell him after all.

In the evening, at her mother's suggestion, Laura goes to the carter's cottage with a basket of leftovers from the party. It is true she has her doubts—"Would the poor woman really like that?"—but she manages to overcome them with no great difficulty. For one reader at least, the effect that Katherine Mansfield has been trying to achieve is totally destroyed. The moment she moves from her ideal world, "with its worms and hooks and ova," into a real world where the critical faculty wakes, she ruins everything by her own insensitiveness. It is exactly the same mistake that she makes in "The Life of Ma Parker." Any incidental poetry there may be in bands, marquees, pastries, and hats—and there is plenty—is dissipated in the sheer grossness of those who enjoy them. The Duc de Guermantes, determined not to hear of the death of an old friend in order not to spoil his party, at least knows what is expected of him. Nothing, one feels, can be expected of the Sheridans.

That is why in the best of the New Zealand stories there is no contact with the real world at all. In his excellent life of Katherine Mansfield, Mr. Antony Alpers quotes a brilliant passage by V. S. Pritchett, contrasting the absence of a real country from "At the Bay" with the flavor of old Russia in Chekhov's "The Steppe," but when Mr. Alpers replies that this quality is absent from Katherine Mansfield's story because it is absent from New Zealand he misses Mr. Pritchett's point entirely. The real reply to Mr. Pritchett—which he probably knows better than anybody—is that to introduce a real country into "At the Bay" would be to introduce history, and with history would come judgment, will, and criticism. The real world of these stories is not New Zealand but childhood, and they are written in a complete, hypnotic suspension of the critical faculties.

This is clearest in the episode in "Prelude" in which Pat, the Irish gardener, decapitates a duck to amuse the children and the headless body instantly makes a dash for the duck pond. It would be almost impossible for any other writer to describe this scene without horrifying us; clearly it horrified the critical and fastidious Katherine Mansfield since it haunted her through the years, but she permits the little girl, Kezia, only one small shudder.

> "Watch it!" shouted Pat. He put down the body and it
> began to waddle—with only a long spurt of blood where the
> head had been; it began to pad away without a sound towards
> the steep bank that led to the stream. . . . That was the crown-
> ing wonder.

"Do you see that? Do you see that?" yelled Pip. He ran among the little girls tugging at their pinafores.

"It's like a little engine. It's like a funny little railway engine," squealed Isabel.

But Kezia suddenly rushed at Pat and flung her arms round his legs and butted her head as hard as she could against his knees.

"Put head back! Put head back!" she screamed.

For me this is one of the most remarkable scenes in modern literature, for though I have often accused myself of morbid fastidiousness, of a pathological dislike of what is obscene and cruel, I can read it almost as though it were the most delightful incident in a delightful day. No naturalist has ever been able to affect me like this, and I suspect that the reason is that Katherine Mansfield is not observing the scene but contemplating it. This is the Garden of Eden before shame or guilt came into the world. It is also precisely what I mean when I say that the crisis in Katherine Mansfield was religious rather than literary.

These extraordinary stories are Katherine Mansfield's masterpieces and in their own way comparable with Proust's breakthrough into the subconscious world. But one must ask oneself why they *are* masterpieces and afterward whether they represent a literary discovery that she might have developed and exploited as Proust developed and exploited his own discovery. They are masterpieces because they are an act of atonement to her brother for whatever wrong she felt she had done him, an attempt at bringing him back to life so that he and she might live forever in the world she had created for them both. They set out to do something that had never been done before and to do it in a manner that had never been used before, a manner that has something in common with that of the fairy tale.

For instance, to have described the world of childhood through the mind of any of the children would have made this the child's own particular world, subject to time and error, and so the only observer is an angelic one for whom the ideas of good and evil, right and wrong, do not exist. Not only does the narrative switch effortlessly from one character to another, but as in a fairy tale speechless things talk like anyone else. Florrie, the cat in "At the Bay," says, "Thank goodness, it's getting late. Thank goodness, the long day is over"; the infant says, "Don't like babies? Don't like *me*?" and the bush says, "We are dumb trees, reaching up in the night, imploring we know not what"; while Beryl's imaginary voices, which describe how wonderful she looked one summer at the bay, are not more unreal—or real—than those of Linda Burnell and her husband.

These stories are conscious, deliberate acts of magic, as though a writer were to go into the room where his beloved lay dead and try to repeat the miracle of Lazarus. In this way they can be linked with the work of other writers like Joyce and Proust, who in their different, more worldly ways were also attempting a magical approach to literature by trying to make the printed page not a description of something that had happened but a substitute for what had happened, an episode as it might appear in the eyes of God—an act of pure creation.

Whether Katherine Mansfield could ever have exploited her own breakthrough into magic is another matter; and here, I think, we are getting closer to the discomfort of V. S. Pritchett before "At the Bay" and my own before that whole group of stories because they continue to fade from my mind, no matter how often I reread them.

Are they really works of art that could have given rise to other works of art and followed the law of their own being? Or are they in fact an outward representation of an act of deliberate martyrdom—the self-destruction of Fontainebleau, which was intended to destroy the false personality Katherine Mansfield had built up for herself. If they represent the former, then the old Katherine would have had to come back in however purified a form. She could never have escaped entirely into a magical version of her childhood and would have had to deal with her own sordid love affairs, her dishonesties, her cruelties. There are tantalizing hints of how this might have happened, for in "The Young Girl" and "The Daughters of the Late Colonel" I seem to see a development of her sense of humor without her coarseness.

But death came too soon, and at the end we can only fall back on the legend that her husband created for her and which has placed her forever among "the inheritors of unfulfilled renown."

Waugh's Comic Wasteland

DAVID LODGE

The early novels of Evelyn Waugh have probably given more pleasure to more readers than any comparable body of work from the
same period of English fiction (1928–1942). I discovered these books
myself in adolescence. I was, I think, fifteen when my father put into
my hands a tattered Penguin edition of *Decline and Fall*. For most of
his life he was a dance musician by profession, and at some time in the
1930s he used to play in a night club frequented by Evelyn Waugh and
his friends, whose names figured prominently in the newspaper gossip
columns of the day. This had given my father a personal interest in the
author, but it was a very tenuous link between *my* world and that of
Waugh's early fiction.

We lived in a cramped semi-detached house in a drab suburb of
southeast London, our respectable lower-middle-class life-style constrained not only by the income of a jobbing dance musician, but by the
climate of Austerity that permeated the whole country in the immediate postwar years: rationing, shortages, rules and restrictions—the
fair-minded but somewhat puritanical ethos of the early Welfare State.

I attended a local state-aided Catholic grammar school. Nothing could have been further from my experience than the world of Waugh's novels, inhabited by characters who were for the most part upper-class and in some cases aristocratic, educated at public school and Oxbridge, many of them idle, dissolute, and sexually promiscuous or deviant (though much of that went over my adolescent head), seldom seen occupied in useful work, their time mostly spent shuttling from party to party or from country house to country house, with occasional adventurous excursions Abroad. Even the fact that Evelyn Waugh was a Roman Catholic, as I was, provided little basis for identification, partly because Waugh's romantically idealised version of Catholicism (epitomised in *Brideshead Revisited*) was so remote from the religious subculture of the suburban Catholic "ghetto" which I knew, and partly because his religious beliefs were not overtly manifested in the early novels which I most enjoyed. I suppose I found these books fascinating precisely because they opened my eyes to the existence of a milieu wholly different from my own—adult glamorous, hedonistic, and quintessentially "prewar." By Christmas 1950, when I was a month short of sixteen, I was sufficiently hooked to request as a seasonal present from my mother copies of *Vile Bodies*, *Black Mischief*, and *Scoop* in the Chapman and Hall Uniform Edition—books which I still possess and frequently reread with undiminished pleasure.

***

So what sort of books are these novels, and what is the secret of their enduring and catholic (with a small "c") appeal? The first thing to be said about them is that they are funny. Very funny. Laugh-out-loud funny. Laughter, as we know (intuitively, and lately from medical science), is highly therapeutic; and the ability to provoke it, in generation after generation of readers, is a rare gift, always cherished. But to call these books "comic novels" might suggest that they belong to a sub-genre of light fiction designed merely to divert and amuse. Waugh's early novels certainly do that—but they do much more. They disturb and challenge as well as entertain the reader. P. G. Wodehouse wrote "comic novels"—with great skill and verve, which Waugh greatly admired. But they are essentially escapist and formulaic; they do not grapple with the dark side of human nature. As Waugh himself eloquently observed, late in life, "For Mr. Wodehouse there has been no Fall of Man . . . the gardens of Blandings Castle are that original garden from which we are all exiled." The world of Waugh's fiction, in contrast, is definitely a fallen one, in which people act with appalling disregard for fidelity, honesty, and all the other virtues. The fact that this behaviour is often very amusing does not make it any less shocking.

For this reason these books are sometimes described as satires. Waugh himself disclaimed this description, asserting that satire "flourishes in a stable society and presupposes homogeneous moral standards." In fact it is doubtful whether there ever was such an era—it is a historical construction or a nostalgic myth. But the idea was of the utmost importance to Waugh's imagination. His work is saturated in the idea of decline—that civilization is in a state of terminal decay. The title of his first novel, *Decline and Fall*, could stand as the title of almost all of them, and the hymn sung by Uncle Theodore in *Scoop*, "Change and decay in all around I see," could be their signature tune. Satire in any era is a kind of writing that draws its energy and fuels its imagination from an essentially critical and subversive view of the world, seizing with delight on absurdities, anomalies, and contradictions in human conduct. It is not the disposable wrapping around a set of positive moral precepts. Evelyn Waugh's early novels therefore have an essentially satirical motivation. They turn an impartial and comprehensive ironic vision upon the pretensions and follies of every class, profession, race, and even religion. They gave offence to some readers in their own day, and undoubtedly they still do in the era of Political Correctness. We all have a desire or need to protect some things from irreverent scrutiny. But in these novels nothing is immune.

In combining elements of comedy, often of a robustly farcical kind, with satirical wit and caricature, in order to explore social reality with an underlying seriousness of purpose, Evelyn Waugh belonged to a venerable and peculiarly English literary tradition which one can trace back through Dickens and Thackeray, Smollett, Sterne, and Henry Fielding. Lewis Caroll was also a perpetual source of inspiration. But Waugh's early novels were distinctively modern—indeed, they were significantly innovative in form; though it was some time before this was fully perceived or appreciated. Could novels so effortless to read, so funny and so accessible, really belong to the history of modern literature? The academic critics of the time certainly didn't think so. Reviews apart, there was virtually no serious criticism written about Evelyn Waugh until after World War II (and then, ironically, the usual complaint was that he was not as good as he had been before the War).

One reason for this neglect was that in the perspective of the dominant critical orthodoxy, that of the New Criticism, modern fiction was identified with modern*ist* fiction, that is to say the symbolist novel of subjective consciousness as represented variously by the work of Henry James, Ford Madox Ford, Joseph Conrad, James Joyce, Virginia Woolf, and D. H. Lawrence. Modernist fiction was difficult, obscure, experimental. It sacrificed story to the representation of subjective experience. It heightened and distorted language to imitate the workings of the consciousness and the unconscious. The generation of writers to which Waugh belonged (it includes Christopher Isherwood, Graham Greene, Henry Green, Ivy Compton-Burnett, and Anthony Powell) were of course well aware of this body of work, and of its poetic equivalents (Waugh's familiarity with T. S. Eliot's *The Waste Land* is particularly obvious). In many ways they shared the assumptions on which it was based—that modern life was peculiarly chaotic, disorderly, and unstable, and that the conventions of the Victorian or Edwardian realistic novel were inadequate to represent it truthfully. But like every new generation of writers, they had to free themselves from "the anxiety of influence" by their literary father-figures; they had to find a new way to "make it new." They developed a fictional technique that was antithetical to that of modernist fiction, without being a mere reversion to Victorian or Edwardian models. Instead of the over-plotted, over-moralized traditional novel, and instead of the almost plotless stream-of-consciousness novel, they wrote novels which declined either to comment or to introspect, which told interesting but often unsettling stories mainly through dialogue and objective description of external behaviour.

Of course nothing is ever entirely new in the development of literary form. There is always a precursor, a source of inspiration, for every innovation. In Waugh's case it was Ronald Firbank, that late-flowering bloom of the Decadence. Waugh's description of Firbank's eccentric but original fiction, in an essay published in 1929, is worth quoting at length:

[Firbank's] later novels are almost wholly devoid of any
attribution of cause to effect; there is the barest minimum of
direct description; his compositions are built up, intricately
and with a balanced alternation of the wildest extravagance
and the most austere economy, with conversational nuances
. . . His art is purely selective. From the fashionable chatter
of his period, vapid and interminable, he has plucked, like
tiny brilliant feathers from the breast of a bird, the particles
of his design . . . The talk goes on, delicate, chic, exquisitely
humorous, and seemingly without point or plan. Then, quite
gradually, the reader is aware that a casual reference on one
page links up with some particular inflexion of phrase on
another until there emerges a plot; usually a plot so outrageous
that he distrusts his own inferences.

This, written by Evelyn Waugh between his first and second novels,
would do very well as a characterization of his own technique. But great
writers do not merely copy other writers; they borrow and transform
the tricks they admire. Firbank's novels, amusing in short, infrequent
samplings, are fatally limited by the author's narrow interests and camp
sensibility. Waugh applied Firbank's techniques to a broader and more
recognizable social world and combined them with other methods of
fictional representation. From Firbank he derived the technique of
evoking a scene and implying a plot through a mosaic of fragmentary,
often unattributed, direct speech, but he does not entirely eschew
"direct description." Indeed, passages of carefully wrought descriptive
prose are often the source of his most effective comedy—as in, for
example, the arrival of the Welsh Silver Band at the school sports in
Decline and Fall:

Ten men of revolting appearance were approaching from
the drive. They were low of brow, crafty of eye and crooked
of limb. They advanced huddled together with the loping
tread of wolves, peering about them furtively as they came,
as though in constant terror of ambush; they slavered at their
mouths, which hung loosely over their receding chins, while

each clasped under his ape-like arm a burden of curious and
unaccountable shape.

Unfair to Welsh rustics? Of course—but the description of the upper-
class members of the Bollinger Club mustering for their Oxford reunion
on the first page of the novel is scarcely more flattering:

> . . . epileptic royalty from their villas of exile; uncouth peers
> from crumbling country seats; smooth young men of uncertain
> tastes from embassies and legations; illiterate lairds from wet
> granite hovels in the Highlands; ambitious young barristers
> and Conservative candidates torn from the London season and
> the indelicate advances of debutantes . . .

The comic surprise of that last phrase, attributing indelicacy to the
putative virgins rather than their suitors, is very typical of Waugh's
style, depending as it does on both the artful positioning of the words
and the inversion of a presumed natural order.

———————

Who was the young man who composed this droll, poised, irresistibly
readable prose? Born in London in 1903, he belonged to a very literary
family. His father, Arthur Waugh, was a publisher and man of letters;
his elder brother, Alec, wrote a novel, *The Loom of Youth*, when he was
only seventeen, and went on to become a professional writer and popular novelist. Alec had left his (and his father's) public school, Sherborne,
under something of a cloud—the source material for *The Loom of
Youth*—and in consequence Evelyn was sent to Lancing College, an
establishment which prided itself on its atmosphere of Anglican piety.
By the time Evelyn went up to Oxford in 1922, however, he had become
an agnostic.

Evelyn Waugh's adolescence was inevitably overshadowed by the
Great War and the patriotic emotions it aroused, heightened by the fact
that Alec was fighting in the trenches of Flanders. Evelyn's generation, the young men who had been just too young to fight in the War
themselves, felt an irrational guilt about this, and a certain resentment

at having been denied the opportunity to prove themselves in action. But in retrospect the War itself seemed more and more to have been a catastrophic folly, which completely discredited the older generation who had presided over it, and the values and assumptions to which they clung. In due course many of the younger generation, including Evelyn Waugh, would find ways of testing themselves by adventurous foreign travel, and would seek an alternative system of values in Communism or Catholicism. But in early youth they asserted themselves by the reckless and anarchic pursuit of pleasure. By the time Waugh went up to Oxford, the sobering presence of Great War veterans in the student body had almost disappeared, and undergraduate life was, for many at least, a continuous party. Waugh certainly did little academic work. He mixed with a fast, smart set, lived above his income, got frequently drunk, and amused himself with student journalism. He was, in his own words, "idle, dissolute and extravagant." He left Oxford with a third-class degree in History and scant prospects of employment that would enable him to keep up with his fashionable friends. He enrolled for a while in an art course (he was a skillful draughtsman, as his illustrations to his own early novels attest), taught in two private schools of the kind classified by the teaching agency in *Decline and Fall* as "School" (as distinct from Leading School, First-Rate School, and Good School), was briefly a probationary reporter on the *Daily Express*, and even contemplated an apprenticeship as a carpenter. This was a period of great frustration and depression for Waugh, and according to his volume of autobiography, *A Little Learning*, he actually tried to drown himself off a Welsh beach in 1925, but was driven back to shore, and the will to live, by the stings of jellyfish. This story, at once shocking and amusing, reminds us how much *angst* and despair lie under the urbane comic surface of his early novels.

In 1927 he obtained a commission to write a book about Dante Gabriel Rossetti, and became engaged to Evelyn Gardner, daughter of Lord Burghclere. In 1928 they married, and at first fortune seemed to smile on the union of "He-Evelyn" and "She-Evelyn" (as they were known to their friends). *Decline and Fall* was published shortly afterwards to enthusiastic reviews, and they had a belated honeymoon on a Mediterranean cruise which He-Evelyn was offered free, as part of a travel-book deal (*Labels*, 1930). Rather ominously, he took Spengler's *The Decline of the West* with him to read on this trip. On their return to England in the spring of 1929, the novelist retired to the country to write *Vile Bodies*, leaving his wife in London. A few months later she informed him that she was in love with another man; the couple separated; and civil divorce proceedings began.

This, needless to say, was a heavy blow to Waugh, a private agony and a public humiliation. It seems that he had no inkling that anything was amiss with his marriage, and the suddenness and completeness of his wife's infidelity, so early in their life together, left a permanent scar on his psyche. It also left its trace in his fiction, most powerfully in *A Handful of Dust*, where the heartless sexual betrayal of a man by a woman epitomises the general collapse of values and morals in modern society. Shortly after this experience Waugh began taking instructions from a Jesuit priest and was received into the Church in 1930, the year when *Vile Bodies* was published. The character of Father Rothschild, S.J., who pops up here and there in that novel, often in the most exalted political circles, with a false beard and heavily annotated atlas in his suitcase, parodies the Protestant stereotype of the Jesuit as devious conspirator. But he makes a serious comment on the decadence of the Young Generation which seems to reflect Waugh's own views: "Don't you think," said Father Rothschild gently, "that perhaps it is all in some way historical? I don't think people ever *want* to lose their faith in religion or anything else. I know very few young people, but it seems to me that they are all possessed with an almost fatal hunger for permanence. I think all these divorces show that."

Although *Decline and Fall* and *Vile Bodies* are obviously the work of the same writer, there are interesting differences, both formal and thematic, between them. Paul Pennyfeather, the hero of the earlier book, is, as has often been observed, a kind of latter-day Candide, an innocent *naïf*, who is both victim and observer of the folly, villainy, and corruption of modern society. Expelled, with monstrous injustice, from Oxford, he is condemned to work as the lowest form of pedagogic life, an unqualified schoolmaster at a bad private school. From this fate he is rescued by the whim of Margot Beste-Chetwynde and suddenly installed at the glittering apex of high society. But the financial basis of this luxurious life-style is a prostitution racket for which Paul chivalrously takes the rap, and he is sent to prison. He is not altogether unhappy there: "anyone who has been to an English public school will always feel comparatively at home in prison." The absence of any pity for the hero's plight is entirely typical of these novels: it is left to the reader to supply the moral outrage which events invite. But he is rescued once again by his rich friends, and given a new identity, under which he returns to Oxford to study theology. Paul thus ends up where he began—but not quite the same person. He has had enough of liberty and licence. We leave him studying early Christian heresies in a spirit of intolerant orthodoxy—perhaps a premonition of the author's later conversion to Roman Catholicism.

Adam Fenwick-Symes, the hero of *Vile Bodies*, is also the victim of duplicity and betrayal, but he is less innocent and more knowing than Paul Pennyfeather; and by the end of the story he has become a deceiver himself. The plot, such as it is, charts his constantly frustrated attempts to raise enough money to marry Nina. Promises of riches are constantly being pressed upon him—by the drunk Major, by Nina's father, by Fleet Street—only to be snatched away again, or prove worthless. Eventually Nina callously jilts Adam to marry his friend Ginger, but soon regrets her decision. While Ginger is fighting in the war which has just broken out in Europe, Adam impersonates him at the Christmas festivities in Nina's family home. This adulterous episode, framed by all the domestic sentiment that belongs to a traditional English Christmas, is richly ironic—funny, shocking, and oddly poignant, all at once.

Vile Bodies is my personal favourite among these novels, for its daring mixture of the comic and the serious, and for the brilliance of its technique. There are unforgettable comic set-pieces, like Agatha Runcible's appearance at breakfast at Number 10 Downing Street in her Hottentot fancy dress costume, or Colonel Blount's absent-minded reception of Adam at Doubting Hall. But there is also a seemingly effortless evocation and deployment of a large cast of characters on a broad social stage. The novel might be described as a kind of comic prose equivalent to *The Waste Land*. Like Eliot's poem, it had painful personal sources (Adam's relationship with Nina obviously derives in part from Waugh's courtship and the breakup of his marriage), but, like Eliot, Waugh managed to objectify this material and embed it in a panoramic picture of the decadence and confusion of English society in the aftermath of the Great War, which seems to be spinning faster and faster out of control, like Agatha Runcible in her racing car. The narrative shifts rapidly from social group to social group; Cockney accents contrast with patrician voices, the jargon of motor racing mechanics with the in-group slang of the Bright Young Things—*so bogus, so sick-making, don't you think? Or don't you?*

The technique owes a lot to cinema, in its fluid cutting from scene to scene, and in making the reader *infer* meaning from brief, telling images and fragments of conversation. Waugh belonged to the first generation of writers to grow up with the medium, and he remained a regular cinema-goer throughout his life. His early fiction does by choice what film is bound by its nature to do—it stays on the surface of things. Perhaps this explains why these novels have proved difficult to adapt successfully as films: what seems experimental on the page seems routine on the screen, and the tension between the two media is somehow lost.

Another development in technology which left its mark on Waugh's fiction was the telephone. He was perhaps the first literary novelist to exploit this instrument on a significant scale to dramatise failures of communication, either deliberate or involuntary, between characters. Much of the courtship between Adam and Nina is conducted by phone, and one short chapter (11) consists entirely of two such conversations. Behind the clipped, banal phrases—*"We aren't going to be married today?" "No." "I see." "Well?" "I said, I see." "Is that all?" "Yes, that's all, Adam." "I'm sorry." "Yes, I'm sorry too. Goodbye." "Goodbye Nina"*—there are depths of unspoken pain and betrayal. The phrases "Well" and "I see," which have a merely phatic function in the conversation, acquire an ironic and poignant resonance, for nothing is well and these interlocutors cannot see each other.

———◆———

In the 1930s, Waugh's professional life fell into a certain pattern: he would go abroad, write a travel book about his experiences, and then rework the material in a novel. In 1930 he was sent to Abyssinia by a newspaper to report on the coronation of Emperor Haile Selassie I. His nonfiction account of this trip was *Remote People* (1931), and its fictional fruit was *Black Mischief* (1932). Abyssinia is transformed into Azania, an island state off the coast of East Africa, whose young monarch, the Emperor Seth, is infatuated with western ideas of Progress and strives vainly to impose them on his still primitive subjects. He orders his commander-in-chief, General Connolly, to issue boots to the army and equip it with a tank. The tank cannot operate in jungle terrain and is useful only as a punishment cell; the soldiers assume the boots are extra rations and eat them. Seth's campaign to introduce contraception misfires when the people misinterpret his posters, with their before-and-after illustrations of the advantages of using condoms:

> See: on right hand: there is a rich man: smoke pipe like big chief: but his wife she no good; sit eating meat; and rich man no good: he only one son.
> See: on left hand: poor man: not much to eat: but his wife she very good, work hard in field: man he good too: eleven children; one very mad, very holy. And in the middle: Emperor's juju. Make you like that good man with eleven children.

It is easy to mistake this comedy for a display of racial prejudice. There is no doubt that Evelyn Waugh, like most Englishmen of his class and time, harboured a measure of such prejudice. But his imagination was more even-handed. It was the *clash* of different cultures in colonial and postcolonial Africa, all seeking to exploit each other, that fascinated Waugh, because it generated so many delicious incongruities, absurdities, and contradictions in human behaviour. In Africa, he found, the comedy of manners bordered on the surreal. Only in *Alice in Wonderland*, Waugh wrote in *Remote People*, could he find a "parallel for life in Addis Ababa . . . the peculiar flavour of galvanised and translated reality."

Seth defines his struggle as "a war of Progress against Barbarism." Waugh shows that progress is usually only another form of barbarism. Certainly its representatives in Azania are hardly to its credit: the sublimely lazy and inefficient British legation, the self-important, self-deceiving French legation, or the Englishman who becomes Seth's right-hand man, Basil Seal. As a novel, *Black Mischief* suffers perhaps from not having a really sympathetic character, unless it is the down-to-earth General Connolly. Instead of a reactive, victimized hero, we have in this book a totally amoral anti-hero, a "corker" but a cad, to whom deception and the double cross are second nature. Basil's romance with Prudence, the British Ambassador's daughter, lacks the underlying poignancy of the relationship between Adam and Nina in *Vile Bodies*, but this absence licences one of the blackest reversals in the history of comedy, when he unknowingly eats her flesh at a cannibal feast.

In the winter of 1932–33, Waugh made a trip to British Guiana and Brazil to gather material for a travel book (*92 Days*). In the course of an otherwise uneventful trek through the jungle, he encountered a lonely settler whose eccentric and slightly sinister demeanour gave him the idea for a short story about an explorer who is held captive by such a man and is made to read the entire works of Dickens aloud at gunpoint. The idea continued to fascinate him, and in due course he wrote a novel, in his own words, "to discover how the prisoner got there, and eventually the thing grew into a study of other sorts of savages at home and the civilized man's helpless plight among them." The novel was *A Handful of Dust* (1934), and the "civilized man" is Tony Last, proud owner of Hetton Abbey, a hideously ugly Victorian fake-gothic country house, happily married (or so he thinks) to Brenda. In fact Brenda, a kind of aristocratic latter-day Emma Bovary, is bored and restless, unable to share Tony's enthusiasm for Hetton and the archaic lord-of-the-manor life-style that he tries to keep up on an insufficient income. She starts an affair with the unremarkable and effete John Beaver because he offers her some escape from the crippling ennui of her domestic life, and re-entry into the shallow, sophisticated pleasures of London high society. Tony is easily deceived because he "had got into the habit of loving and trusting Brenda," but a tragic accident to their son, John Andrew, precipitates an open breach.

Of all Waugh's novels, *A Handful of Dust* draws most deeply on the traumatic breakdown of his own first marriage, which makes the poise of the book—its subtle balancing and tight control of the tragic and the comic, the emotional and the satirical—all the more remarkable. Waugh's technique of staying on the surface, giving the minimum of information about the characters' thoughts and feelings, making the reader draw the appropriate conclusions from what they say and do, prevents the novel from becoming excessively emotional or moralistic. We never, for instance, get direct access to Brenda's mind or heart. The first indication that she is attracted to Beaver comes from a conversation with her sister Marjorie in which she first denies, and then half-admits, that she "fancies" him; and when she fails to mention on returning home to Tony that she met Beaver in London, we realise that she has embarked on a course of deception. Marjorie irresponsibly encourages the affair, then tries to effect a reconciliation—too late and for the wrong reasons. "Of *course* Brenda doesn't love Beaver. How could she?" Marjorie says to Tony. "And if she thinks she does at the moment, it's your duty to prevent her making a fool of herself. You must refuse to be divorced—anyway, until she has found someone more reasonable." The callousness, snobbishness, and arrogance of that afterthought make it a devastating indictment of Marjorie and her set.

The only point at which, it seems to me, Waugh is unfair to Brenda—when, in D. H. Lawrence's phrase, he "puts his thumb in the scale, to pull down the balance to his own predilection," is the climactic moment when she is told that "John" has been killed in an accident, and presumes it is her lover. When her informant clearly implies that in fact it is her son who is dead, "She frowned, not at once taking in what he was saying. 'John . . . John Andrew . . . I . . . Oh thank God . . .' Then she burst into tears." I don't believe that any mother, however cold-hearted and selfish, would say "thank God" in these circumstances. But I have not encountered any other reader who feels the same, and indeed this scene is often cited admiringly as an example of Waugh's irony.

Our sympathies are naturally drawn to the innocent party in the triangle, Tony Last, and it is hard to suppress a cheer when, by a brilliant narrative reversal, he turns the tables on Brenda's selfish and grasping family and friends. But it is important to recognize that he is portrayed as a weak and limited man in many respects, and that his cult of Hetton is exposed as a self-indulgent illusion. "A whole Gothic world had come to grief" in the collapse of his marriage, for which he must bear some of the blame. That is why, in the novel's design, he is punished by the grotesque fate that awaits him in the depths of the South American jungle. Both Tony and Brenda are shown to be fundamentally immature, reverting to nursery rituals in times of stress, and both are shown weeping with self-pity, like children, when their fortunes reach their lowest ebb. Waugh later said of *A Handful of Dust* that "it was humanist and contained all I had to say about humanism." What he implied was that, without a transcendental religious faith, humanism was helpless in the face of human weakness, evil, and death. His title was taken from *The Waste Land*, the work of another literary convert to Christian orthodoxy: "*I will show you fear in a handful of dust.*" This work, considered by most critics to be one of Waugh's finest achievements, is certainly the most serious and complex of the early novels.

<hr>

With *Scoop* (1938) Waugh returned to a more purely comic mode. "It is light and excellent," he commented in his diary early in its composition, and he was right. For this novel he drew on the experience of two more visits which he made to Abyssinia in the 1930s, as a correspondent reporting the Italian invasion and occupation of that country for *The Daily Mail*. This campaign was, like the Spanish Civil War, part of the political preliminaries to the Second World War, and in *Scoop* there is a good deal of topical satire at the expense of both Fascist and Communist ideologies. Essentially, however, it is, as its subtitle declares, "a novel about journalists," and has achieved immortality as such. Many journalists consider it the best novel ever written about their profession. The engine of the plot—a case of mistaken identity, which sends the retiring nature columnist of the *Daily Beast*, William Boot, to the war-threatened African state of Ishmaelia instead of the fashionable novelist John Boot—is one of the oldest in comic literature, and is, in the cold light of reason, highly implausible. So are many other events in the story. That doesn't matter in the least. As the very name of the fictitious newspaper implies, the novel is not meant to be soberly realistic. Waugh's comic genius allowed him to invent fantastic incidents which seem only slightly exaggerated in the reading, because they have a *representative* truthfulness. One might cite as an example the embedded anecdote of the legendary ace reporter Wesley Jakes, who started a revolution by accidentally filing a story from the wrong country. The basic message of the book is that newspapers construct the reality they claim to report—not (as modern media studies often claim) for sinister ideological reasons, but because they are so obsessed with the mystique of their trade—the need to entertain their readers, to scoop their competitors, and so on—that they make gross errors of fact and interpretation all the time. It is precisely because he is not a professional journalist that William Boot stumbles on the truth about Ishmaelian politics; but at one exquisitely ironic point in the narrative he is unable to publish a true story about a Russian agent operating in the capital because a false story to the same effect has already been circulated and then denied. The whole novel is a tissue of mistakes, misrepresentations, lies, and evasions. Mr. Salter's formula for dealing with his employer's gross misconceptions, "Up to a point, Lord Copper," has deservedly become proverbial.

⚊◆⚊

Put Out More Flags (1942) is a kind of epilogue or *envoi* to the sequence of novels that began with *Decline and Fall*. In it, Waugh revived several characters from the previous books, like Basil Seal, Peter Pastmaster, Alastair and Sonia Trumpington, invented a lot of new ones (notably the homosexual aesthete Ambrose Silk), and exhibited this large cast reacting in various ways to the outbreak of World War II. Most of them are ill-prepared for the crisis—including the soldiers:

> Freddy was in uniform, acutely uncomfortable in ten-year-old trousers. He had been to report at the yeomanry headquarters the day before, and was home for two nights collecting his kit, which, in the two years since he was last at camp, had been misused in charades and picnics and dispersed about the house in a dozen improbable places. His pistol, in particular, had been a trouble. He had had the whole household hunting it, saying fretfully, "It's all very well, but I can get court-martialled for this," until, at length, the nurserymaid found it at the back of the toy cupboard.

The novel is diffuse and episodic in structure, and somewhat uneven in tone, combining ruthless comic satire in Waugh's old manner with a more affectionate, even at times sentimental attitude towards his characters. One might cite, as examples of the latter, Alastair's altruistic enlistment in the ranks, or Peter Pastmaster's decision to marry and beget an heir before risking his life in the armed struggle. It should be remembered, though, that Waugh himself volunteered for active service with similar idealism, and that his subsequent disillusionment with the political and military conduct of the war had not yet hardened into firm conviction when, in 1941, he wrote *Put Out More Flags* to divert himself on a long and tedious voyage by troopship. And, in spite of its flaws, this novel has many pleasures to offer. The subplot of Basil Seal's commercial exploitation of the awful evacuees, for example, the narrative thread of the lunatic bomber at large in the Ministry of Information, and the unerringly wrong prophecies of Sir Joseph Mainwaring are handled with characteristic skill. The fact is that Evelyn Waugh was incapable of writing badly, and often in this novel he writes as brilliantly as ever. But his great work of fiction about the Second World War, the *Sword of Honour* trilogy, was still to come.

Somewhere Behind

MILAN KUNDERA

Poets don't invent poems
The poem is somewhere behind
It's been there for a long long time
The poet merely discovers it.
                    —Jan Skacel

1.

In one of his books, my friend Josef Skvorecky tells this true story: An engineer from Prague is invited to a professional conference in London. So he goes, takes part in the proceedings, and returns to Prague. Some hours after his return, sitting in his office, he picks up *Rude Pravo*—the official daily paper of the Party—and reads: A Czech engineer, attending a conference in London, has made a slanderous statement about his socialist homeland to the Western press and has decided to stay in the West.

Illegal emigration combined with a statement of that kind is no trifle. It would be worth twenty years in prison. Our engineer can't believe his eyes. But there's no doubt about it, the article refers to him. His secretary, coming into his office, is shocked to see him: My God, she says, you're back! I don't understand—did you see what they wrote about you?

The engineer sees fear in his secretary's eyes. What can he do? He rushes to the *Rude Pravo* office. He finds the editor responsible for the story. The editor apologizes; yes, it really is an awkward business, but he, the editor, has nothing to do with it, he got the text of the article direct from the Ministry of the Interior.

So the engineer goes off to the Ministry. There they say yes, of course, it's all a mistake, but they, the Ministry, have nothing to do with it, they got the report on the engineer from the intelligence people at the London embassy. The engineer asks for a retraction. No, he's told, they never retract, but nothing can happen to him, he has nothing to worry about.

But the engineer does worry. He soon realizes that all of a sudden he's being closely watched, that his telephone is tapped, and that he's being followed in the street. He sleeps poorly and has nightmares until, unable to bear the pressure any longer, he takes a lot of real risks to leave the country illegally. And so he actually becomes an émigré.

2.

The story I've just told is one that we would immediately call *Kafkan*. This term, drawn from an artist's work, determined solely by a novelist's images, stands as the only common denominator in situations (literary or real) that no other word allows us to grasp and to which neither political nor social nor psychological theory gives us any key.

But what is the *Kafkan?*

Let's try to describe some of its aspects:

One:

The engineer is confronted by a power that has the character of a *boundless labyrinth*. He can never get to the end of its interminable corridors and will never succeed in finding out who issued the fateful verdict. He is therefore in the same situation as Joseph K. before the

Court, or the Land-Surveyor K. before the Castle. All three are in a world that is nothing but a single, huge labyrinthine institution they cannot escape and cannot understand.

Novelists before Kafka often exposed institutions as arenas where conflicts between different personal and public interests were played out. In Kafka the institution is a mechanism that obeys its own laws; no one knows now who programmed those laws or when; they have nothing to do with human concerns and are thus unintelligible.

Two:

In Chapter Five of *The Castle*, the village Mayor explains in detail to K. the long history of his file. Briefly: Years earlier, a proposal to engage a land-surveyor came down to the village from the Castle. The Mayor wrote a negative response (there was no need for any land-surveyor), but his reply went astray to the wrong office, and so after an intricate series of bureaucratic misunderstandings, stretching over many years, the job offer was inadvertently sent to K., at the very moment when all the offices involved were in the process of canceling the old obsolete proposal. After a long journey, K. thus arrived in the village by mistake. Still more: Given that for him there is no possible world other than the Castle and its village, his *entire* existence is a mistake.

In the Kafkan world, the file takes on the role of a Platonic idea. It represents true reality, whereas man's physical existence is only a shadow cast on the screen of illusion. Indeed, both the Land-Surveyor K. and the Prague engineer are but the shadows of their file cards; and they are even much less than that: they are the shadows of a *mistake* in the file, shadows without even the right to exist as shadows.

But if man's life is only a shadow and true reality lies elsewhere, in the inaccessible, in the inhuman or the suprahuman, then we suddenly enter the domain of theology. Indeed, Kafka's first commentators explained his novels as religious parables.

Such an interpretation seems to me wrong (because it sees allegory where Kafka grasped concrete situations of human life) but also revealing: wherever power deifies itself, it automatically produces its own theology; wherever it behaves like God, it awakens religious feelings toward itself; such a world can be described in theological terms.

Kafka did not write religious allegories, but the *Kafkan* (both in reality and in fiction) is inseparable from its theological (or rather: *pseudotheological*) dimension.

Three:

Raskolnikov cannot bear the weight of his guilt, and to find peace he consents to his punishment of his own free will. It's the well-known situation where the *offense seeks the punishment*.

In Kafka the logic is reversed. The person punished does not know the reason for the punishment. The absurdity of the punishment is so unbearable that to find peace the accused needs to find a justification for his penalty: the *punishment seeks the offense*.

The Prague engineer is punished by intensive police surveillance. This punishment demands the crime that was not committed, and the engineer accused of emigrating ends up emigrating in fact. *The punishment has finally found the offense.*

Not knowing what the charges against him are, K. decides, in Chapter Seven of *The Trial*, to examine his whole life, his entire past "down to the smallest details." The "autoculpabilization" machine goes into motion. *The accused seeks his offense.*

One day, Amalia receives an obscene letter from a Castle official. Outraged, she tears it up. The Castle doesn't even need to criticize Amalia's rash behavior. Fear (the same fear our engineer saw in his secretary's eyes) acts all by itself. With no order, no perceptible sign from the Castle, everyone avoids Amalia's family like the plague.

Amalia's father tries to defend his family. But there is a problem: Not only is the source of the verdict impossible to find, but the verdict itself does not exist! To appeal, to request a pardon, you have to be convicted first! The father begs the Castle to proclaim the crime. So it's not enough to say that the punishment seeks the offense. In this pseudotheological world, *the punished beg for recognition of their guilt!*

It often happens in Prague nowadays that someone fallen into disgrace cannot find even the most menial job. In vain he asks for certification of the fact that he has committed an offense and that his employment is forbidden. The verdict is nowhere to be found. And since in Prague work is a duty laid down by law, he ends up being charged with parasitism; that means he is guilty of avoiding work. *The punishment finds the offense.*

Four:

The tale of the Prague engineer is in the nature of a funny story, a joke: it provokes laughter.

Two gentlemen, perfectly ordinary fellows (not "inspectors," as in the French translation), surprise Joseph K. in bed one morning, tell him he is under arrest, and eat up his breakfast. K. is a well-disciplined civil servant: instead of throwing the men out of his flat, he stands in his nightshirt and gives a lengthy self-defense. When Kafka read the first chapter of *The Trial* to his friends, everyone laughed, including the author.

Philip Roth's imagined film version of *The Castle*: Groucho Marx plays the Land-Surveyor K., with Chico and Harpo as the two assistants. Yes, Roth is quite right: The comic is inseparable from the very essence of the *Kafkan.*

But it's small comfort to the engineer to know that his story is comic. He is trapped in the joke of his own life like a fish in a bowl; he doesn't find it funny. Indeed, a joke is a joke only if you're outside the bowl; by contrast, the *Kafkan* takes us inside, into the guts of a joke, into the *horror of the comic.*

In the world of the *Kafkan,* the comic is not a counterpoint to the tragic (the tragi-comic) as in Shakespeare; it's not there to make the tragic more bearable by lightening the tone; it doesn't *accompany* the tragic, not at all, it *destroys it in the egg* and thus deprives the victims of the only consolation they could hope for: the consolation to be found in the (real or supposed) grandeur of tragedy. The engineer loses his homeland, and everyone laughs.

3.

There are periods of modern history when life resembles the novels of Kafka.

When I was still living in Prague, I would frequently hear people refer to the Party headquarters (an ugly, rather modern building) as "the Castle." Just as frequently, I would hear the Party's second-in-command (a certain Comrade Hendrych) called "Klamm" (which was all the more beautiful as *klam* in Czech means "mirage" or "fraud").

The poet A., a great Communist personage, was imprisoned after a Stalinist trial in the fifties. In his cell he wrote a collection of poems in which he declared himself faithful to Communism despite all the horrors he had experienced. That was not out of cowardice. The poet saw his faithfulness (faithfulness to his persecutors) as the mark of his virtue, of his rectitude. Those in Prague who came to know of this collection gave it, with fine irony, the title "The Gratitude of Joseph K."

The images, the situations, and even the individual sentences of Kafka's novels were part of life in Prague.

That said, one might be tempted to conclude: Kafka's images are alive in Prague because they anticipate totalitarian society.

This claim, however, needs to be corrected: the *Kafkan* is not a sociological or a political notion. Attempts have been made to explain Kafka's novels as a critique of industrial society, of exploitation, alienation, bourgeois morality—of capitalism, in a word. But there is almost nothing of the constituents of capitalism in Kafka's universe: not money or its power, not commerce, not property and owners or the class struggle.

Neither does the *Kafkan* correspond to a definition of totalitarianism. In Kafka's novels, there is neither the party nor ideology and its jargon nor politics, the police, or the army.

So we should rather say that the *Kafkan* represents one fundamental possibility of man and his world, a possibility that is not historically determined and that accompanies man more or less eternally.

But this correction does not dispose of the question: How is it possible that in Prague Kafka's novels merge with real life while in Paris the same novels are read as the hermetic expression of an author's entirely subjective world? Does this mean that the possibility of man and his world known as *Kafkan* becomes concrete personal destiny more readily in Prague than in Paris?

There are tendencies in modern history that produce the *Kafkan* in the broad social dimension: the progressive concentration of power, tending to deify itself; the bureaucratization of social activity that turns all institutions into *boundless labyrinths*; and the resulting depersonalization of the individual.

Totalitarian states, as extreme concentrations of these tendencies, have brought out the close relationship between Kafka's novels and real life. But if in the West people are unable to see this relationship, it is not only because the society we call democratic is less Kafkan than that of today's Prague. It is also, it seems to me, because over here, the sense of the real is inexorably being lost.

In fact, the society we call democratic is also familiar with the process that bureaucratizes and depersonalizes; the entire planet has become a theater of this process. Kafka's novels are an imaginary, oneiric hyperbole of it; a totalitarian state is a prosaic and material hyperbole of it.

But why was Kafka the first novelist to grasp these tendencies, which appeared on History's stage so clearly and brutally only after his death?

4.

Mystifications and legends aside, there is no significant trace anywhere of Franz Kafka's political interests; in that sense, he is different from all his Prague friends, from Max Brod, Franz Werfel, Egon Erwin Kisch, and from all the avant-gardes that, claiming to know the direction of History, indulged in conjuring up the face of the future.

So how is it that not their works but those of their solitary, introverted companion, immersed in his own life and his art, are recognized today as a sociopolitical prophecy, and are for that very reason banned in a large part of the world?

I pondered this mystery one day after witnessing a little scene in the home of an old friend of mine. The woman in question had been arrested in 1951 during the Stalinist trials in Prague, and convicted of crimes she hadn't committed. Hundreds of Communists were in the same situation at the time. All their lives they had entirely identified themselves with their Party. When it suddenly became their prosecutor, they agreed, like Joseph K., "to examine their whole lives, their entire past, down to the smallest details" to find the hidden offense and, in the end, to confess to imaginary crimes. My friend managed to save her own life because she had the extraordinary courage to refuse to undertake—as her comrades did, as the poet A. did—the "search for her offense." Refusing to assist her persecutors, she became unusable for the final show trial. So instead of being hanged she got away with life imprisonment. After fourteen years, she was completely rehabilitated and released.

This woman had a one-year-old child when she was arrested. On release from prison, she thus rejoined her fifteen-year-old son and had the joy of sharing her humble solitude with him from then on. That she became passionately attached to the boy is entirely comprehensible. One day I went to see them—by then her son was twenty-five. The mother, hurt and angry, was crying. The cause was utterly trivial: the son had overslept or something like that. I asked the mother: "Why get so upset over such a trifle? Is it worth crying about? Aren't you overdoing it?"

It was the son who answered for his mother: "No, my mother's not overdoing it. My mother is a splendid, brave woman. She resisted when everyone else cracked. She wants me to become a real man. It's true, all I did was oversleep, but what my mother reproached me for is something much deeper. It's my attitude. My selfish attitude. I want to become what my mother wants me to be. And with you as witness, I promise her I will."

What the Party never managed to do to the mother, the mother had managed to do to her son. She had forced him to identify with an absurd accusation, to "seek his offense," to make a public confession. I looked on, dumbfounded, at this Stalinist mini-trial, and I understood all at once that the psychological mechanisms that function in great (apparently incredible and inhuman) historical events are the same as those that regulate private (quite ordinary and very human) situations.

5.

The famous letter Kafka wrote and never sent to his father demonstrates that it was from the family, from the relationship between the child and the deified power of the parents, that Kafka drew his knowledge of the *technique of culpabilization*, which became a major theme of his fiction. In "The Judgment," a short story intimately bound up with the author's family experience, the father accuses the son and commands him to drown himself. The son accepts his fictitious guilt and throws himself into the river as docilely as, in a later work, his successor Joseph K., indicted by a mysterious organization, goes to be slaughtered. The similarity between the two accusations, the two culpabilizations, and the two executions reveals the link, in Kafka's work, between the family's private "totalitarianism" and that in his great social visions.

Totalitarian society, especially in its more extreme versions, tends to abolish the boundary between the public and the private; power, as it grows ever more opaque, requires the lives of citizens to be entirely transparent. The ideal of *life without secrets* corresponds to the ideal of the exemplary family: a citizen does not have the right to hide anything at all from the Party or the State, just as a child has no right to keep a secret from his father or his mother. In their propaganda, totalitarian societies project an idyllic smile: they want to be seen as "one big family."

It's often said that Kafka's novels express a passionate desire for community and human contact, that the rootless being who is K. has only one goal: to overcome the curse of solitude. Now, this is not only a cliché, a reductive interpretation, it is a misinterpretation.

The Land-Surveyor K. is not in the least pursuing people and their warmth, he is not trying to become "a man among men" like Sartre's Orestes; he wants acceptance not from a community but from an institution. To have it, he must pay dearly: he must renounce his solitude. And this is his hell: he is never alone, the two assistants sent by the Castle follow him always. When he first makes love with Frieda, the two men are there, sitting on the café counter over the lovers, and from then on they are never absent from their bed.

Not the curse of solitude but the *violation of solitude* is Kafka's obsession!

Karl Rossmann is constantly being harassed by everybody: his clothes are sold; his only photo of his parents is taken away; in the dormitory, beside his bed, boys box and now and again fall on top of him; two roughnecks named Robinson and Delamarche force him to move in with them and fat Brunelda, whose moans resound through his sleep.

Joseph K.'s story also begins with the rape of privacy: two unknown men come to arrest him in bed. From that day on, he never feels alone: the Court follows him, watches him, talks to him; his private life disappears bit by bit, swallowed up by the mysterious organization on his heels.

Lyrical souls who like to preach the abolition of secrets and the transparency of private life do not realize the nature of the process they are unleashing. The starting point of totalitarianism resembles the beginning of *The Trial*: you'll be taken unawares in your bed. They'll come just as your father and mother used to.

People often wonder whether Kafka's novels are projections of the author's most personal and private conflicts, or descriptions of an objective "social machine."

The *Kafkan* is not restricted to either the private or the public domain; it encompasses both. The public is the mirror of the private, the private reflects the public.

6.

In speaking of the microsocial practices that generate the *Kafkan*, I mean not only the family but also the organization in which Kafka spent all his adult life: the office.

Kafka's heroes are often seen as allegorical projections of the intellectual, but there's nothing intellectual about Gregor Samsa. When he wakes up metamorphosed into a beetle, he has only one concern: in this new state, how to get to the office on time. In his head he has nothing but the obedience and discipline to which his profession has accustomed him: he's an employee, a *functionary*, as are all Kafka's characters; a functionary not in the sense of a sociological type (as in Zola) but as one human possibility, as one of the elementary ways of being.

In the bureaucratic world of the functionary, first, there is no initiative, no invention, no freedom of action; there are only orders and rules: *it is the world of obedience.*

Second, the functionary performs a small part of a large administrative activity whose aim and horizons he cannot see: *it is the world where actions have become mechanical* and people do not know the meaning of what they do.

Third, the functionary deals only with unknown persons and with files: *it is the world of the abstract.*

To place a novel in this world of obedience, of the mechanical, and of the abstract, where the only human adventure is to move from one office to another, seems to run counter to the very essence of epic poetry.

Thus the question: How has Kafka managed to transform such gray, antipoetical material into fascinating novels?

The answer can be found in a letter he wrote to Milena: "The office is not a stupid institution; it belongs more to the realm of the fantastic than of the stupid." The sentence contains one of Kafka's greatest secrets. He saw what no one else could see: not only the enormous importance of the bureaucratic phenomenon for man, for his condition and for his future, but also (even more surprisingly) the poetic potential contained in the phantasmic nature of offices.

But what does it mean to say the office belongs to the realm of the fantastic?

The Prague engineer would understand: a mistake in his file projected him to London; so he wandered around Prague, a veritable *phantom*, seeking his *lost body*, while the offices he visited seemed to him a *boundless labyrinth* from some unknown *mythology*.

The quality of the fantastic that he perceived in the bureaucratic world allowed Kafka to do what had seemed unimaginable before: he transformed the profoundly antipoetic material of a highly bureaucratized society into the great poetry of the novel; he transformed a very ordinary story of a man who cannot obtain a promised job (which is actually the story of *The Castle*) into myth, into epic, into a kind of beauty never before seen.

By expanding a bureaucratic setting to the gigantic dimensions of a universe, Kafka unwittingly succeeded in creating an image that fascinates us by its resemblance to a society he never knew, that of today's Prague.

A totalitarian state is in fact a single, immense administration: since all work in it is for the state, everyone of every occupation has become an *employee*. A worker is no longer a worker, a judge no longer a judge, a shopkeeper no longer a shopkeeper, a priest no longer a priest; they are all functionaries of the State. "I belong to the Court," the priest says to Joseph K. in the Cathedral. In Kafka, the lawyers, too, work for the Court. A citizen in today's Prague does not find that surprising. He would get no better legal defense than K. did. His lawyers don't work for the defendants either, but for the Court.

7.

In a cycle of one hundred quatrains that sound the gravest and most complex depths with an almost childlike simplicity, the great Czech poet writes:

> Poets don't invent poems
> The poem is somewhere behind
> It's been there for a long long time
> The poet merely discovers it.

For the poet, then, writing means breaking through a wall behind which something immutable ("the poem") lies hidden in darkness. That's why (because of this surprising and sudden unveiling) "the poem" strikes us first as a *dazzlement*.

I read *The Castle* for the first time when I was fourteen, and the book will never enchant me so thoroughly again, even though all the vast understanding it contains (all the real import of the *Kafkan*) was incomprehensible to me then: I was dazzled.

Later on my eyes adjusted to the light of "the poem" and I began to see my own lived experience in what had dazzled me; yet the light was still there.

"The poem," says Jan Skacel, has been waiting for us, immutable, "for a long long time." However, in a world of perpetual change, is the immutable not a mere illusion?

No. Every situation is of man's making and can only contain what man contains; thus one can imagine that the situation (and all its metaphysical implications) has existed as a human possibility "for a long long time."

But in that case, what does History (the nonimmutable) represent for the poet?

In the eyes of the poet, strange as it may seem, History is in a position similar to the poet's own: History does not *invent*, it *discovers*. Through new situations, History reveals what man is, what has been in him "for a long long time," what his possibilities are.

If "the poem" is already there, then it would be illogical to impute to the poet the gift of *foresight*; no, he "only discovers" a human possibility ("the poem" that has been there "a long long time") that History will in its turn discover one day.

Kafka made no prophecies. All he did was see what was "behind." He did not know that his seeing was also a fore-seeing. He did not intend to unmask a social system. He shed light on the mechanisms he knew from private and microsocial human practice, not suspecting that later developments would put those mechanisms into action on the great stage of History.

The hypnotic eye of power, the desperate search for one's own offense, exclusion and the anguish of being excluded, the condemnation to conformism, the phantasmic nature of reality and the magical reality of the file, the perpetual rape of private life, etc.—all these experiments that History has performed on man in its immense test tubes, Kafka performed (some years earlier) in his novels.

The convergence of the real world of totalitarian states with Kafka's "poem" will always be somewhat uncanny, and it will always bear witness that the poet's act, in its very essence, is incalculable; and paradoxical: the enormous social, political, and "prophetic" import of Kafka's novels lies precisely in their "nonengagement," that is to say, in their total autonomy from all political programs, ideological concepts, and futurological prognoses.

Indeed, if instead of seeking "the poem" hidden "somewhere behind" the poet "engages" himself to the service of a truth known from the outset (which comes forward on its own and is "out in front"), he has renounced the mission of poetry. And it matters little whether the preconceived truth is called revolution or dissidence, Christian faith or atheism, whether it is more justified or less justified; a poet who serves any truth other than the truth *to be discovered* (which is *dazzlement*) is a false poet.

If I hold so ardently to the legacy of Kafka, if I defend it as my personal heritage, it is not because I think it worthwhile to imitate the inimitable (and rediscover the *Kafkan*) but because it is such a tremendous example of the *radical autonomy* of the novel (of the poetry that is the novel). This autonomy allowed Franz Kafka to say things about our human condition (as it reveals itself in our century) that no social or political thought could ever tell us.

Herman Melville

ALBERT CAMUS

Back in the days when Nantucket whalers stayed at sea for several years at a stretch, Melville, at twenty-two, signed on one, and later on a man-of-war, to sail the seven seas. Home again in America, his travel tales enjoyed a certain success while the great books he published later were received with indifference and incomprehension.[1] Discouraged after the publication and failure of *The Confidence Man* (1857), Melville "accepted annihilation." Having become a customs officer and the father of a family, he began an almost complete silence (except for a few infrequent poems) which was to last some thirty years. Then one day he hurriedly wrote a masterpiece, *Billy Budd* (completed in April 1891), and died, a few months later, forgotten (with a three-line obituary in *The New York Times*). He had to wait until our own time for America and Europe to finally give him his place among the greatest geniuses of the West.

It is scarcely easier to describe in a few pages a work that has the tumultuous dimensions of the oceans where it was born than to summarize the Bible or condense Shakespeare. But in judging Melville's genius, if nothing else, it must be recognized that his works trace a spiritual experience of unequaled intensity, and that they are to some extent symbolic. Certain critics[2] have discussed this obvious fact, which now hardly seems open anymore to question. His admirable books are among those exceptional works that can be read in different ways, which are at the same time both obvious and obscure, as dark as the noonday sun and as clear as deep water. The wise man and the child can both draw sustenance from them. The story of captain Ahab, for example, flying from the southern to the northern seas in pursuit of Moby Dick, the white whale who has taken off his leg, can doubtless be read as the fatal passion of a character gone mad with grief and loneliness. But it can also be seen as one of the most overwhelming myths ever invented on the subject of the struggle of man against evil, depicting the irresistible logic that finally leads the just man to take up arms first against creation and the creator, then against his fellows and against himself.[3] Let us have no doubt about it: if it is true that talent recreates life, while genius has the additional gift of crowning it with myths, Melville is first and foremost a creator of myths.

I will add that these myths, contrary to what people say of them, are clear. They are obscure only insofar as the root of all suffering and all greatness lies buried in the darkness of the earth. They are no more obscure than Phèdre's cries, Hamlet's silences, or the triumphant songs of Don Giovanni. But it seems to me (and this would deserve detailed development) that Melville never wrote anything but the same book, which he began again and again. This single book is the story of a voyage, inspired first of all solely by the joyful curiosity of youth (*Typee*, *Omoo*, etc.), then later inhabited by an increasingly wild and burning anguish. *Mardi* is the first magnificent story in which Melville begins the quest that nothing can appease, and in which, finally, "pursuers and pursued fly across a boundless ocean." It is in this work that Melville becomes aware of the fascinating call that forever echoes in him: "I have undertaken a journey without maps." And again: "I am the restless hunter, the one who has no home." *Moby Dick* simply carries the great themes of *Mardi* to perfection. But since artistic perfection is also inadequate to quench the kind of thirst with which we are confronted here, Melville will start once again, in *Pierre: or the Ambiguities*, that unsuccessful masterpiece, to depict the quest of genius and misfortune whose sneering failure he will consecrate in the course of a long journey on the Mississippi that forms the theme of *The Confidence Man.*

This constantly rewritten book, this unwearying peregrination in the archipelago of dreams and bodies, on an ocean "whose every wave is a soul," this Odyssey beneath an empty sky, makes Melville the Homer of the Pacific. But we must add immediately that his Ulysses never returns to Ithaca. The country in which Melville approaches death, that he immortalizes in *Billy Budd,* is a desert island. In allowing the young sailor, a figure of beauty and innocence whom he dearly loves, to be condemned to death, Captain Vere submits his heart to the law. And at the same time, with this flawless story that can be ranked with certain Greek tragedies, the aging Melville tells us of his acceptance for the first time of the sacrifice of beauty and innocence so that order may be maintained and the ship of men may continue to move forward toward an unknown horizon. Has he truly found the peace and final resting place that earlier he had said could not be found in the Mardi archipelago? Or are we, on the contrary, faced with a final shipwreck that Melville in his despair asked of the gods? "One cannot blaspheme and live," he had cried out. At the height of consent, isn't *Billy Budd* the worst blasphemy? This we can never know, any more than we can know whether Melville did finally accept a terrible order, or whether, in quest of the spirit, he allowed himself to be led, as he had asked, "beyond the reefs, in sunless seas, into night and death." But no one, in any case, measuring the long anguish that runs through his life and work, will fail to acknowledge the greatness, all the more anguished in being the fruit of self-conquest, of his reply.

But this, although it had to be said, should not mislead anyone as to Melville's real genius and the sovereignty of his art. It bursts with health, strength, explosions of humor, and human laughter. It is not he who opened the storehouse of sombre allegories that today hold sad Europe spellbound. As a creator, Melville is, for example, at the furthest possible remove from Kafka, and he makes us aware of this writer's artistic limitations. However irreplaceable it may be, the spiritual experience in Kafka's work exceeds the modes of expression and invention, which remain monotonous. In Melville, spiritual experience is balanced by expression and invention, and constantly finds flesh and blood in them. Like the greatest artists, Melville constructed his symbols out of concrete things, not from the material of dreams. The creator of myths partakes of genius only insofar as he inscribes these myths in the denseness of reality and not in the fleeting clouds of the imagination. In Kafka, the reality that he describes is created by the symbol, the fact stems from the image, whereas in Melville the symbol emerges from reality, the image is born of what is seen.[4] This is why Melville never cut himself off from flesh or nature, which are barely perceptible in Kafka's work. On the contrary, Melville's lyricism, which reminds us of Shakespeare's, makes use of the four elements. He mingles the Bible with the sea, the music of the waves with that of the spheres, the poetry of the days with the grandeur of the Atlantic. He is inexhaustible, like the winds that blow for thousands of miles across empty oceans and that, when they reach the coast, still have strength enough to flatten whole villages. He rages, like Lear's madness, over the wild seas where Moby Dick and the spirit of evil crouch among the waves. When the storm and total destruction have passed, a strange calm rises from the primitive waters, the silent pity that transfigures tragedies. Above the speechless crew, the perfect body of Billy Budd turns gently at the end of its rope in the pink and grey light of the approaching day.

T. E. Lawrence ranked *Moby Dick* alongside *The Possessed* or *War and Peace*. Without hesitation, one can add to these *Billy Budd*, *Mardi*, *Benito Cereno*, and a few others. These anguished books in which man is overwhelmed, but in which life is exalted on each page, are inexhaustible sources of strength and pity. We find in them revolt and acceptance, unconquerable and endless love, the passion for beauty, language of the highest order—in short, genius. "To perpetuate one's name," Melville said, "one must carve it on a heavy stone and sink it to the bottom of the sea; depths last longer than heights." Depths do indeed have their painful virtue, as did the unjust silence in which Melville lived and died, and the ancient ocean he unceasingly ploughed. From their endless darkness he brought forth his works, those visages of foam and night, carved by the waters, whose mysterious royalty has scarcely begun to shine upon us, though already they help us to emerge effortlessly from our continent of shadows to go down at last toward the sea, the light, and its secret.

NOTES

[1] For a long time, *Moby Dick* was thought of as an adventure story suitable for school prizes.

[2] In passing, let me advise critics to read page 449 of *Mardi* in the French translation.

[3] As an indication, here are some of the obviously symbolic pages of *Moby Dick*. (French translation, Gallimard): pp. 120, 121, 123, 129, 173–7, 191–3, 203, 209, 241, 310, 313, 339, 373, 415, 421, 452, 457, 460, 472, 485, 499, 503, 517, 520, 522.

[4] In Melville, the metaphor suggests the dream, but from a concrete, physical starting point. In *Mardi*, for example, the hero comes across "huts of flame." They are built, simply, of red tropical creepers, whose leaves are momentarily lifted by the wind.

On Steinbeck's Story "Flight"

WALLACE STEGNER

There have been a few writers, such as Chekhov and Frank O'Connor, who have operated without perceptible constraint within the short story form. Their characters take on life the moment they arrive on the page, their narrative never seems to struggle for room to run in, their meanings state themselves economically as epiphanies and nuances, their humanity shines between the lines like a steady light from within. They create their worlds, and illuminate them, in miniature.

John Steinbeck was not one of those natural miniaturists. When he did write a true short story, and he wrote a few splendid ones, he did so only by exercising the strict self-discipline that some critics say he didn't possess. But quite often things that began as short stories refused to stay within bounds. Sometimes they became something longer and more complex, sometimes they developed linkages with other stories and became something less independent.

In *The Pastures of Heaven*, every story strains to include a whole lifetime, sometimes more than one lifetime, of struggle and change. As

Steinbeck himself remarked in a letter to his friend Ted Miller, "They are not short stories at all, but tiny novels." Though linked by place, by common characters, and by the pervasive, malignant influence of the Munroes, they are discrete life histories, or family histories. "You see," Steinbeck said in another letter, "each family will be a separate narrative with its own climax and end, and they will be joined by locality, by the same characters entering into each and by this nameless sense and power of evil."

In *Tortilla Flat*, many of whose episodes were begun as short stories, linkage took over more completely than in *The Pastures of Heaven*, and what resulted was not a collection of related tales but a loose novel. The stories about Danny, Pilón, and the rest of the Round Table of Monterey *paisanos* did not want to be discrete. They yearned like certain groupy biological species to operate not separately, or only separately, but in union—to become collectively a larger, more complex, and different animal. Call it a literary demonstration of the Steinbeck-Ricketts theory of the phalanx.

Something similar happened to "The Gift," "The Promise," "The Great Mountains," and "The Leader of the People," stories written separately that later demanded to be put together as *The Red Pony*, almost a short novel.

If the stories in *The Pastures of Heaven* are little novels, and those in *Tortilla Flat* are chapters, and those in *The Red Pony* are something in between, like the sonnets of a cycle, then it is only in the rest of *The Long Valley* that we may look for Steinbeck's real short stories. That is indeed where they are, all of them.

The Long Valley was not published until 1938, riding the popularity of *Tortilla Flat*, *Of Mice and Men*, and *In Dubious Battle*. But by that time Steinbeck had not written a short story for four years. After June 1934, when he wrote "The Vigilante," "The Snake," and "Breakfast," he wrote nothing more of any significance in that form, devoting himself to the longer writings that commanded a large public. That should surprise no one. It was novels, if we may count *Tortilla Flat* as one, that brought him both money and notice. Short stories had brought him little of either.

Consider the composition and publication of the sixteen stories that make up *The Long Valley* They were all written (along with *Tortilla*

Flat) between the fall of 1933 and the summer of 1934, many of them during the months when Steinbeck was living in the family house in Salinas and helping his mother die. His table was set up outside her room; he wrote in the odd half hours between pills and bedpans, and it is little wonder that he wrote short.

What is surprising is that his stories impressed practically no one, as they should have even in those deep-Depression months. Ted Miller, and later Mavis McIntosh and Elizabeth Otis, hawked them from editorial office to editorial office with a demoralizing lack of success. "You ask why you never see my stuff in *Esquire*," Steinbeck wrote Louis Paul in February 1936. "I guess they were never interested. I have a good many stories in New York but no one wants them. I wrote nine short stories in one sitting recently. I thought some of them were pretty good, too, but that's as far as it got. *The North American Review* used to print some at thirty dollars a crack."

He seems to have been wrong about the price—it was forty-five or fifty dollars, according to his biographer Jackson Benson—but it was true that for a long time only *The North American Review* showed any interest. Between November 1933 and March 1935 it published "The Gift," "The Great Mountains," "The Murder," "The Raid," and "The White Quail," to a maximum audience of a few thousand readers and at a maximum reward to the author of $250. Steinbeck gave "The Snake" to a little magazine called *The Monterey Beacon* in exchange for six months of free rides on a saddle horse. *Argosy* of London published "The Leader of the People" in August 1936, and *The Pacific Weekly* ran "Breakfast" in November of that year. Spurred by the success of *Tortilla Flat* and the advance notice of *In Dubious Battle*, *Esquire* bought "The Vigilante" for its October 1936 issue and "Johnny Bear" for the issue of September 1937. *Harper's* came aboard in 1937, publishing "The Promise" in August and "The Chrysanthemums" in October, and the *Atlantic Monthly* cleared the cupboard of "The Harness" in June 1938, more than four years after it was written. "St. Katy the Virgin" had been published as a Christmas booklet in 1936. "Flight," first called "Manhunt," remained unsold even through the building excitement of Steinbeck's early novels, and never did see publication in a magazine.

Under the circumstances, it is no wonder Steinbeck never came back to writing short stories. Sometime in 1936, when Ted Miller sent him in one batch all the rejection letters he had collected while acting as Steinbeck's agent, the bruised author had indicated how close the experience came to discouraging him utterly: "Thanks for the rejections. They still give me the shivers and always will. Each one was a little doom. Had a personal fight with each one. And it's such a short time ago and it may be again."

In 1938, suddenly famous and already deep into the writing of *The Grapes of Wrath*, he bundled together his stories, including the rejected "Flight," published them as *The Long Valley*, and put the short story behind him.

So much for publication history. But it should be noticed that there was a good practical reason why "Flight" never saw magazine publication. It was long, nearly nine thousand words, twice as long as "The Snake" and more than half again as long as "The Chrysanthemums." It approached that nebulous thing, the novelette or novella—middle-length fiction—and middle-length fiction labors under a disadvantage. At anything from eight thousand to thirty thousand words, it is too small to be a book and too large to fit comfortably into the editorial space of a general magazine. Even in flush times editors view it askance. In times like the mid-1930s they could rarely indulge themselves even with middle-length fiction that they greatly admired.

There is no way of knowing whether any editors admired "Flight," not unless those rejection letters still exist. If they do, I have not seen them. But I do know that the length of "Flight" is not simply sprawl. Neither is it a result of trying to get within the most compact space a whole life history. This is not one of those "little novels," like the stories in *The Pastures of Heaven*. It is a true short story, focused on a few critical hours during which a boy is changed into a man and bears the consequences. It is long because the material demands some length, for this story is, at least from one point of view, an ordeal, and ordeals cannot be done in shorthand. They must be excruciating, and to be excruciating they must have duration—not indefinite duration, which would make them unbearable to read, but just the right duration, which lets us participate and suffer without having to shut our eyes or our minds or the book.

It would be convenient for critics if "Flight" could be shown to have been influenced by Hemingway's "The Snows of Kilimanjaro" and "The Short Happy Life of Francis Macomber"—both published in 1936, both well beyond the usual short story length, both dealing with ordeals of a kind, and at least one of them, "Macomber," chronicling the passage of an individual from ineffective boyhood to manhood in the macho sense. One critic, perhaps yielding to temptation, has said that in "Flight" Steinbeck "grafted Hemingway onto Dreiser." I do not understand the Dreiser connection—I cannot even *smell* Dreiser in this story—and I don't know what Hemingway, unless the stylistic Hemingway, the critic had in mind. If he had "Macomber" in mind, he forgot that "Flight" was written at least two years before "Macomber" was published and could not have been influenced by it. Neither could the reverse have happened, unless Hemingway had his spies greedily reading the unsalable manuscripts in the office of McIntosh and Otis.

The fact is, no writer grafts anybody onto anybody. Steinbeck may have read both Hemingway and Dreiser, he may have liked one or both or neither, he may have been stimulated in some fashion by one or both. But I am sure that when he sat down at his table outside the door of his dying mother, with his senses alert for emergencies and his mind bent on seizing a stolen scrap of time, he was feeling his way into a situation totally *his*. His total experience was on the line, including his reading experience. A writer at that crucial point is a synthesizer, a blender, and everything he has ever heard or seen or read or known is potentially there, available for the creation of his story. It all melts and fuses. No writer as good as Steinbeck ever sat down to a story thinking about whom he would copy, or how he would appropriate what from whom.

A critic, by contrast, is not a synthesizer but an analyzer. He picks apart, he lifts a few cells onto a slide and puts a coverglass over them, he runs tests of the chemical components of spittle and sperm and heartsblood. His is a useful function and, done well, may greatly clarify the reading of a story—may even give a reader the illusion of understanding both the product and the process. But it is more reliable on the product than the process. Some Heisenberg principle frustrates critics who try to analyze how stories are written. Whatever they can analyze has to be dead before it can be dissected. As Hippolyte Taine's theory of "the race, the place, and the time" was said to explain everything but genius, so most critical analysis explains everything but the mystery of literary creation.

It is said that Gertrude Stein gave up the study of medicine because she didn't like the dissection of cadavers, and it is true that she spent her literary life trying to synthesize words—words used plastically— into some new sort of creation. But her skeptical critics always saw her poised over the marble slab with the dead body of language, oozing formaldehyde, under her scalpel. They said she was re-creating from disassembled parts, not creating. The entire problem of criticism, which is happily not the problem of this essay, is how to keep the body alive while it is being studied.

So I would not feel comfortable trying to discuss "Flight" in terms of who or what influenced it. Steinbeck's lifelong acquaintance with Californios influenced it, his reading influenced it, his discussions with Ed Ricketts and his study of marine biology influenced it. We know that he read Malory with devotion all his life, that he planned *Tortilla Flat* as the chronicle of a sort of raffish Table Round, that he went to his death struggling with a modernization of the Arthurian cycle. We know that he bossed Hispanic work gangs in the Spreckels sugar factory and had many friends among Californios and Mexican-Americans. So of course there are elements of the code of chivalry in Pepé. They would be there even if Steinbeck had never read Malory, for a variant of that code survives in the *machismo* of Spanish-American youth. Of course there is the echo of the medieval trial by ordeal. Of course there is much that Steinbeck learned from his study of biology and his friendship with Ed Ricketts—a biological view of human beings which assumes the naturalness of biological death and, like Nature, takes the species to be more important than the specimen. There is even, in the dark watchers, a hint of Steinbeck's faith in omens, a touch of the mystical fatalism so persistent in his writing, especially when he is writing about men in close relationship with the earth.

Finally, there is of course a transcendent sense of place. Steinbeck knew the Santa Lucia Mountains, from the stacks and skerries of the shore through the mist forests of the westward-draining canyons up through the high chamisal country to the baking ridges and waterless valleys of the rain shadow. The story takes Pepé from the narrow humanized belt of the coast benches, through the somber darkness of redwood and fern, and finally out of protective cover into exposure and waterlessness. In the record of that flight there is not a false note: the country is shown to us as it is. It could never have been the same story without that impeccable realization of place.

Critics have noted these and other ingredients in "Flight," including the increasing swarm of animal images as Pepé struggles deeper into the mountains, and the increasing barrenness and starkness of the mountains as his flight becomes more desperate. The ingredients are all there, and must be noticed, for they are the literal instruments of both truth and suspense. But let us not take them apart, and let us not imagine that when we have become aware of them we have "explained" the story, or laid bare the mystery of its composition.

I think very few stories are made by the conscious selection and arrangement of such touches. These had to be intrinsic to the fused experience Steinbeck was imagining, details that come up off the page and are recognized as right the moment they are written. They are as much a part of the forming conception, the discovered form and meaning, as Pepé himself. If a story "begins in delight and ends in wisdom," as Robert Frost said a poem does, then a reader is better advised to note such details in passing, as part of the flow, and understand them only afterward. They first make Pepé's ordeal compelling to us, and afterward they distance us from his private tragedy, make us one with the dark watchers on the ridges. The story is lived from within and understood from without. Steinbeck always tried to become the character he was writing about, and the change of title from "Manhunt," which suggests an exterior view, to "Flight," which expresses how it feels from within, demonstrates that tendency. Nevertheless, our final view of Pepé is from outside and above. Manhood comes to Pepé as terror, struggle, wounds, and death, and we are allowed to share his panic and his pain. But whatever *wisdom* the story suggests about manhood comes to us as spectators, almost as dispassionate as if we had assumed the terrible aloofness of the bare mountains.

Manhood is the theme of this story, and it is stated and restated early. "I am a man," Pepé keeps insisting, in his innocence and his aspiration to assume his father's place. But even armed with his father's knife, which will turn out to have a stern potential, he is still a boy playing games. His mother, though she thinks him fine and brave, knows better than he what being a man may entail, and she protects him with scorn, calling him "big lazy," and "toy-baby," and "peanut," and "foolish chicken." But she sends him to Monterey because there is no one else to send, and because she is already resigned to the knowledge that "a boy gets to be a man when a man is called for."

The irony that the ordeal leading to manhood also leads to danger and death is as true for Pepé as for Francis Macomber. A secondary irony here is that what begins with the assumption of the father's role— investiture with the father's hat, coat, horse, and weapons—ends with every scrap of that borrowed manhood stripped away. The investiture is begun with his trip to Monterey; it is completed after his return, when he is loaded down with jerky, water, his father's gun, and is mounted on a fresh horse. But even in that moment when he has most succeeded his father, he has already begun to lose. His father's knife is in the breast of a quarrelsome stranger in Monterey. "Yes, thou art a man now, my poor little Pepé," his mother says, and to the other children, "Pepé is a man now. He has a man's thing to do."

There is an interesting moment here, and I confess it delights me, for it tends to confound a too-systematic reading of something which should retain some of the contradictions of real life. At the moment when his mother admits he is a man, Pepé's mouth changes, but the change, instead of making him look like his dead father, makes him look "very much like Mama." Does this mean he is still a boy, despite what he has done and despite her words, or does it mean that the manhood toward which he has yearned is as much an attribute of his grimly competent mother as of the father he reveres? In either case, I accept it—it is the way things often are. And the moment he has kicked his horse up the trail, this woman, who remained fierce and concentrated when he looked to her for softness, turns to wailing. She has consigned him to manhood not by her words but by her knowledge that he is doomed.

The mountains at first are solitary but not forbidding. There is cover, coolness, the stream. Fear comes first with the man riding down the trail, and Pepé jacks a shell into the chamber of his father's gun and leaves the gun at half cock. Later the country gets rougher, and very dry, and without cover. Exposure brings greater fear, and along with fear a glimpse of the first of the dark watchers his mother has warned him about. Local superstition? Omen? Reflection of Pepé's emotional state? Death symbol, like the hyenas and the policemen on bicycles in "The Snows of Kilimanjaro"? If superstition, they fit Pepé's society and tradition. If reflection of his state of mind, they are grimly apt. If omen, they throw a shadow on his flight. If death symbol, they let Steinbeck suggest with great economy and force the fate that awaits Pepé. In any case they are not a mere mechanical literary device; they are something that rises from the action like smoke from a campfire.

The country grows still more desolate. Another dark watcher—or is it a pursuer? Pepé misses his knife, the most intimate reminder of his father. The wildness of the mountains is accentuated by the sight and sound of animals—doves, quail, a wildcat, later owls and a coyote—voices of wildness, unhuman but not antihuman. It is just here, in fact, that the desperate figure of Pepé, with whom we have totally identified, begins to recede from us, begins to be a speck riding through a dispassionate and impersonal wilderness, begins to be an object and not a subject. It was probably not planned that way—more likely discovered in the doing—but it is right.

Now begins the divestiture of everything that he acquired in the first stage of his manhood. He loses his father's hat. In the first rifle fire from the pursuers, he loses his horse. Wounded, he crawls on the earth like a hurt animal. As he crawls and scrambles to escape, the encounters with animals multiply—buzzards, a small brown bird, an eagle, a dove, a rattlesnake, lizards. We may read these encounters either as brute detail, the precise life-forms he would be likely to encounter in that wilderness of the Santa Lucias, or we may (the critics generally do) read them as little reiterative emphatic devices meant to show us Pepé stripped more and more completely down to his animal base, remote from family or society or human help. The mountains by now are bare stone, without a hint of softness or shelter. He has a face-to-face encounter with a mountain lion, shyest of wild creatures. Wounded, crawling through scrub and broken rocks, he goes on.

And now he loses his rifle. The pursuers have him cornered. Trying to lance his infected wound, he misses his knife again—the first, the major loss. Squeezing and scraping the wound, he whines like a dog. Eventually, as Thucydides said of the Spartans at Thermopylae, having done what man could, he endures what man must. He stands up to meet it.

But it was surely Steinbeck's intention, whether premeditated or discovered in the act of writing, that it should not be his father's son, but Pepé himself, who stands up to take his manhood and his death. Everything in the story leads to that, every detail corroborates the transformation from a boy imitating his elders to a man, helpless and without support, being nevertheless a man, doing, as Pepé's mother said, a man's thing.

Having gone this far in taking Steinbeck's story apart, we should now do him and it the justice of putting it back together again. Having played critic, we should put ourselves back into the hands of the storyteller, and open the book and read the story through once more, letting its flow carry us and its suspense grip us and its details convince us of its rightness and validity. Reading, we have to be able to accept these mountains into which Pepé flees as both the Ventana wilderness of the Santa Lucias and the mountains of repudiation and no-help, almost as allegorical as the Slough of Despond or the Valley of the Shadow of Death. It is one of the triumphs of the story that they are authentically and simultaneously both. And we should be able to recognize in Pepé not only a callow, pointy-headed Californio youth from the Big Sur coast trying to live up to the foolish and romantic ideal of manhood common to his kind, but one of the incarnations of Everyman pursuing the ideals that, foolish or not, and however harshly tested, in the end give him stature and dignity.

Contributors

SVEN BIRKERTS is the author of many books of essays, most recently *Reading Life: Books for the Ages*, a series of personal close readings. His essay on John Keats's "Ode to Autumn" was included in his second book of essays, *The Electric Life: Essays on Modern Poetry*.

ALAIN DE BOTTON is the author of seven books of nonfiction, including *How Proust Can Change Your Life* and *The Architecture of Happiness*. He lives in London and can be contacted at www.alainde-botton.com.

ALBERT CAMUS' books include *The Stranger*, *The Plague*, *The First Man*, and *The Myth of Sisyphus*. "Herman Melville" was most recently published in 1962 in *Théâtre, récits, nouvelles*.

MICHAEL CHABON's novels include *The Mysteries of Pittsburgh*, *Wonder Boys*, *The Amazing Adventures of Kavalier & Clay*, and *The Yiddish Policemen's Union*. "The Other James" introduces the 2002 edition of M. R. James's *Casting the Runes and Other Ghost Stories* and is reprinted here from *Maps and Legends*.

CHARLES D'AMBROSIO is the author of the story collections *The Point* and *The Dead Fish Museum* and a collection of essays, *Orphans*. "Salinger and Sobs" first appeared in the anthology *With Love and Squalor*, edited by Kip Kotzen and Thomas Beller.

GEOFF DYER's many books include *But Beautiful, The Ongoing Moment, Yoga for People Who Can't Be Bothered to Do It*, and, most recently, *Jeff in Venice, Death in Varanasi*. The excerpt published here is from *Out of Sheer Rage*.

"In Terms of the Toenail: Fiction and the Figures of Life" was the title piece in WILLIAM GASS's 1970 book of criticism, *Fiction and the Figures of Life*. Seven volumes of essays would follow to accompany five of fiction.

DAGOBERTO GILB is the author of a number of books, including *The Magic of Blood, Woodcuts of Women*, and *The Flowers*. "The Border Trilogy by Cormac McCarthy" first appeared in the *Nation* and was published most recently in *Gritos*.

ROBERT HASS's many books of poems include *Field Guide, Sun Under Wood*, and, most recently, *Time and Materials: Poems 1997–2005*. "Lowell's Graveyard" appears in *Twentieth Century Pleasures: Prose on Poetry*.

SEAMUS HEANEY's poetry spans four decades and is compiled in collected editions including *Selected Poems 1965–1975* and *Opened Ground: Poems 1966–1996*. "Learning from Eliot" appears in one of several collections of prose, *Finders Keepers: Selected Prose 1971–2001*.

HERMANN HESSE is the author of *Steppenwolf, Siddhartha*, and *The Glass Bead Game*. "Thoughts on *The Idiot* by Dostoevsky" appears in *My Belief: Essays on Life and Art*.

EDWARD HIRSCH has published seven books of poems, including *Special Orders* (2008). The piece included here is part of Act 5 of "Five Acts," which first appeared in *American Poetry Review* (May-June, 1998) and most recently in *How to Read a Poem and Fall in Love with Poetry* (1998), a national best-seller.

RANDALL JARRELL's *The Complete Poems* appeared in 1981, following a career that touched on fiction and returned consistently to innovative writing on poetry. "The Humble Animal" first appeared in the *Kenyon Review* and was reprinted in *Poetry and the Age*.

WALTER KIRN's books include *Up in the Air*, *Mission to America*, and, most recently, *Lost in the Meritocracy: The Undereducation of an Overachiever*. The essay on Salinger printed here first appeared in *With Love and Squalor*, edited by Kip Kotzen and Thomas Beller.

MILAN KUNDERA is the author of many books, including *The Unbearable Lightness of Being* and *The Book of Laughter and Forgetting*, as well as a number of book-length essays exploring literature and the novel form. "Somewhere Behind" is collected in *The Art of the Novel*, first published in 1986.

D. H. LAWRENCE's novels include *Lady Chatterly's Lover* and *The Rainbow*, though he is renowned for short fiction, poetry, and innovative criticism as well. "Herman Melville's *Moby Dick*" first appeared in *Studies in Classic American Literature*.

DAVID LODGE has published a wide range of fiction and criticism, including *The Picturegoers*, *Nice Work*, *Deaf Sentence*, and *The Year of Henry James: The Story of a Novel*. "Waugh's Comic Wasteland" appeared most recently in *Consciousness and the Novel*.

CZESLAW MILOSZ is the author, most notably, of *The Captive Mind*, though his poetry spans eight decades. "Robert Frost" appeared most recently in *Milosz's ABC's*.

VLADIMIR NABOKOV is the author of many books, including *Lolita*, *Pale Fire*, *Speak, Memory*, and *Bend Sinister*. "'The Metamorphosis'" first appeared in *Lectures on Literature* and was turned into a film starring Christopher Plummer in 1998.

FRANK O'CONNOR's lifetime output of short stories was compiled in *Collected Stories* in 1982. "An Author in Search of a Subject" appears in *The Lonely Voice*, a classic study of the short story form.

CYNTHIA OZICK is the author of more than a dozen books of fiction and nonfiction, including most recently *Dictation* and *The Din in the Head*. "Truman Capote Reconsidered" was published most recently in *Art & Ardor*.

PHYLLIS ROSE is the author of *Woman of Letters: The Life of Virginia Woolf* and *Parallel Lives: Five Victorian Marriages*. The excerpt printed here is from *The Year of Reading Proust: A Memoir in Real Time*.

SALMAN RUSHDIE's many novels include *Midnight's Children*, *The Satanic Verses*, and *The Moor's Last Sigh*. "Out of Kansas" first appeared in the *New Yorker* and was published most recently in a collection of nonfiction, *Step Across This Line*.

FRED SETTERBERG's essay on Hemingway first appeared in his book *The Roads Taken: Travels through America's Literary Landscapes*. He is also the coauthor of *Under the Dragon: California's New Culture*, written with Lonny Shavelson, and the forthcoming *Lunch Bucket Paradise: Tales from a Blue-Collar Suburb*.

SUSAN SONTAG's many books of essays and fiction include *On Photography*, *Against Interpretation*, and *In America: A Novel*. "Loving Dostoyevsky" introduces the 2001 reprint of Leonid Tsypkin's *Summer in Baden-Baden* and appeared most recently in the posthumous *At the Same Time: Essays and Speeches*.

WALLACE STEGNER published a wide variety of fiction, nonfiction, and books about writing, including *The Big Rock Candy Mountain*, *The Spectator Bird*, and *Beyond the Hundredth Meridian*. "On Steinbeck's Story 'Flight'" first appeared as an introduction to the story in a limited edition book from Yolla Bolly Press and was later reprinted in *Where the Bluebird Sings to the Lemonade Springs*.

E. B. WHITE is equally regarded for his many essays in the *New Yorker*, his children's literature, and his partial authorship of *The Elements of Style*. "A Slight Sound at Evening" appeared on the one-hundred-year anniversary of the publication of Thoreau's *Walden*.

OSCAR WILDE's vast output includes *The Importance of Being Earnest* and *The Picture of Dorian Gray*, as well as a broad range of stories, poetry, and essays. "Mr. Pater's Last Volume" first appeared in *Speaker* in 1890.

JAMES WOOD is a staff writer at the *New Yorker* and a visiting lecturer in English and American literature at Harvard. He is the author of *The Irresponsible Self* and *How Fiction Works*, as well as a novel, *The Book Against God*. "What Chekhov Meant by Life" first appeared in *The Broken Estate*.

VIRGINIA WOOLF is the author of *A Room of One's Own, Mrs. Dalloway, The Waves*, and a variety of short fiction and criticism. "An Essay in Criticism" was first published in the *Times Literary Supplement* and most recently appeared in *Granite & Rainbows*.

Copyright Notes and Permissions

J. C. Hallman is the author of two books of nonfiction, *The Chess Artist* and *The Devil Is a Gentleman*, and a collection of short fiction, *The Hospital for Bad Poets*. A third book of nonfiction, *In Eutopia*, will appear from St. Martin's Press in 2010.